THE JEWISH-
CHRISTIAN
DEBATE IN
THE HIGH
MIDDLE AGES

THE JEWISH-CHRISTIAN DEBATE IN THE HIGH MIDDLE AGES

A Critical Edition of the
Nizzahon Vetus

introduction, translation
and commentary by –

David Berger

JASON ARONSON INC.
Northvale, New Jersey
London

First Jason Aronson Inc. edition—1996

10 9 8 7 6 5 4 3 2 1

Library of Congress Cataloging-in-Publication Data

Sefer nitsahon yashan. English & Hebrew.
   The Jewish-Christian debate in the high Middle Ages : a critical
edition of the Nizzahon vetus / introduction, translation, and
commentary by David Berger.
     p. cm.
   Previously published: 1st ed. Philadelphia : Jewish Publication
Society of America, 1979.
   Includes bibliographical references and index.
   ISBN 1-56821-919-9 (alk. paper)
   1. Christianity—Controversial literature—Early works to 1800.
2. Judaism—Apologetic works—Early works to 1800. 3. Bible. O.T.—
Criticism, interpretation, etc.   I. Berger, David, 1943-   .
II. Title.
BM590.S4313   1996
296.3—dc20

                                          95-48485

Manufactured in the United States of America. Jason Aronson Inc. offers books and cassettes. For information and catalog write to Jason Aronson Inc., 230 Livingston Street, Northvale, New Jersey 07647.

In memory of my parents, Isaiah and Shirley Berger ז״ל

ACKNOWLEDGMENTS

My introduction to polemical literature—and to Jewish scholarship in general—came through my father's library. Growing up in a home where Jewish learning was the supreme value made my own interest almost inevitable, although I shall never reach the point, as my father did, where Jewish books are vocation and avocation, work and play, professional concern and consuming passion. My mother's confidence and encouragement were a central element in the atmosphere of that home, and the dedication of this book to the memory of my parents is a minimal acknowledgment of the role they played in making it possible.

With respect to formal training, there are two professors who made indispensable contributions to my academic development. Dr. Louis H. Feldman of Yeshiva College not only taught me Greek and Latin, which anyone studying Jewish-Christian polemic must know, but he also made college a rewarding and exciting intellectual experience. The first version of this book was completed in 1970 at Columbia University under the guidance of Dr. Gerson D. Cohen, whose vast erudition, exacting scholarship, and stimulating teaching made a fundamental and enduring impact on my approach to historical research.

I should like to thank the following libraries for various forms of assistance: the Jewish division of the New York Public Library, the Columbia University library, the Brooklyn College library, the manuscript division and the Institute of Microfilms of the National and University Library in Jerusalem, the library of the Jewish Theological Seminary in New York, the Staatsbibliothek in Munich, the Vittorio Emanuele Library in Rome, the Universiteitsbibliothek of Amsterdam, the library of the Alliance Israélite Universelle, the

Bibliothèque Nationale in Paris, and the Bibliothèque Nationale et Universitaire in Strasbourg. I should also like to express my appreciation to the American Academy for Jewish Research for providing a grant that aided my work.

Finally, to my wife Pearl and to Miriam, Yitzhak, and Gedalyah, I must express the most deeply felt thanks of all—for inspiring me to complete the book and for so much more.

CONTENTS

Hebrew Text

ANALYTICAL TABLE OF CONTENTS FOR THE TRANSLATION

THE PENTATEUCH

xii

JOSHUA

JEREMIAH

EZEKIEL

ISAIAH

xiv

THE TWELVE MINOR PROPHETS

PROVERBS

ECCLESIASTES

JOB

SELECTIONS FROM DANIEL, PSALMS, AND THE TWELVE MINOR PROPHETS

PSALMS

SONG OF SONGS

A CRITIQUE OF THE GOSPELS AND CHRISTIANITY

xviii

INTRODUCTION

Abbreviations

Auteurs	B. Blumenkranz, *Les Auteurs Chrétiens Latins du Moyen Age sur les Juifs et le Judaisme,* Paris, La Haye, 1963
B.	*Bavli* (Babylonian Talmud)
CC, Ser. Lat.	*Corpus Christianorum, Series Latina*
CSEL	*Corpus Scriptorum Ecclesiasticorum Latinorum*
De Fide Cath.	Isidore of Seville, *De Fide Catholica ex Veteri et Novo Testamento Contra Judaeos,* PL 83.449–538
Eggers	*Der Althochdeutsche Isidor,* edited by Hans Eggers, Tübingen, 1964 (*Altdeutsche Textbibliothek,* no. 63)—includes an edition of the early chapters of *De Fide Catholica*
Gloss	*Glossa Ordinaria*
HTR	*Harvard Theological Review*
HUCA	*Hebrew Union College Annual*
JJS	*Journal of Jewish Studies*
JQR	*Jewish Quarterly Review*
Judenpredigt	B. Blumenkranz, *Die Judenpredigt Augustins,* Basel, 1946
Juifs et Chrét.	B. Blumenkranz, *Juifs et Chrétiens dans le Monde Occidental 430-1096,* Paris, 1960
M.E.	Mordecai of Avignon, *Maḥaziq* (or *Meḥazzeq*) *Emunah,* Vatican ms. 271, pp. 1a–17b
MGH	*Monumenta Germaniae Historica*
MGWJ	*Monatsschrift für Geschichte und Wissenschaft des Judentums*
Mil. HaShem	Jacob ben Reuben, *Milḥamot HaShem,* ed. by J. Rosenthal, Jerusalem, 1963
Mil. Ḥovah	*Milḥemet Ḥovah,* Constantinople, 1710
Mil. Miẓvah	Meir of Narbonne, *Milḥemet Miẓvah*
N.V.	*Niẓẓaḥon Vetus*
PG	*Patrologia Graeca*
PL	*Patrologia Latina (1844-65)*
Pos. ms.	Posnanski manuscript (Posnanski alone refers to A. Posnanski's manuscript notes on N.V.)
REJ	*Revue des Études Juives*
Tela	J. Wagenseil, *Tela Ignea Satanae,* Altdorf, 1681
TNA	E. Martène and U. Durand, *Thesaurus Novus Anecdotorum,* vol. 5, Paris, 1717
Tränkle	H. Tränkle, *Q.S.F. Tertulliani Adversus Judaeos mit Einleitung und Kritischen Kommentar,* Wiesbaden, 1964
Trypho	Justin Martyr, *Dialogue with Trypho*
Ver. Israel	M. Simon, *Verus Israel,* Paris, 1948
Yer.	*Yerushalmi* (Palestinian Talmud)

INTRODUCTION

I. On Jewish-Christian Polemic

Polemical literature is one of the liveliest manifestations of Jewish-Christian relations in the Middle Ages. At times calm and almost dispassionate, at other times angry and bitter, religious polemic is a reflection of the mood and character not only of the disputants themselves but of the age in which they wrote and spoke. While the tone of the Jewish-Christian debate ranges from somber to sarcastic to playfully humorous, the underlying issues were as serious to the participants as life itself. Failure on the part of the Christian polemicist could encourage Jews in their mockery of all that was sacred and might engender doubts in Christian minds; failure by the Jew could lead to apostasy and, on some occasions, severe persecution and even martyrdom. Religious arguments could be stimulating and enjoyable, but the stakes involved were monumental.

The *Nizzahon Vetus,* or *Old Book of Polemic,* is a striking example of Jewish disputation in its most aggressive mode. The anonymous author collected an encyclopedic array of anti-Christian arguments current among late thirteenth-century Franco-German Jews. Refutations of christological exegesis, attacks on the rationality of Christian doctrine, a critique of the Gospels and Church ritual, denunciations of Christian morality—all these and more are presented in an exceptionally vigorous style that is not especially scrupulous about overstepping the bounds of civility. Although both the style and comprehensiveness of the book are not altogether typical of Jewish polemic, they make the *Nizzahon Vetus* an excellent and unusually interesting vehicle for the study of this crucial and intriguing dimension of medieval Jewish-Christian relations.

3

Jewish-Christian polemic begins at the very dawn of Christianity. The reasons for this are built into the essence of the Christian faith, for a religion that was born out of Judaism had to justify the rejection of its parent. Indeed, theological and exegetical approaches which can be labeled polemic can also be seen as the elementary building blocks of the developing faith, since certain early doctrines grew naturally out of a reading of the Hebrew Bible. Isaiah 53, which could easily be read as a reference to the vicarious atonement of a "servant of the Lord," served as an almost inevitable explanation of the paradox of the Messiah's crucifixion. Whether or not Jesus applied such an understanding of this passage to his own career (and he probably did not),[1] this is a case in which a crux of later polemic was read christologically for fundamental, internal reasons.

Some doctrines, of course, did not develop out of the Hebrew Scriptures. Nevertheless, Christian acceptance of the divine origin of those Scriptures, together with an espousal of central beliefs that did not seem to be there, generated a need to explain this omission. Thus, even if Jews had not pressed their opposition to statements concerning the divinity of the Messiah, the virgin birth, or the abrogation of the Law, almost any serious Christian would have tried to find biblical justification for these doctrines. It is, in fact, often difficult to tell when a given Christian argument is directed against Jews and when it is an attempt to deal with a problem raised by the writer's own study of the Bible. This uncertainty applies even to some works ostensibly aimed against the Jews, because the number of such works through the ages seems disproportionate to the threat that Judaism could have posed.[2]

Were Jewish questions, then, the primary factor behind the search for biblical testimonies to Christian truth? Was it, as one

---

1. See M. D. Hooker, *Jesus and the Servant* (London, 1959); Y. Kaufmann, *Golah VeNekhar* (Tel Aviv, 1929/30), 1: 381–89.

2. The major anti-Jewish polemics through the twelfth century were summarized by A. L. Williams, *Adversus Judaeos* (Cambridge, 1935). See also B. Blumenkranz, *Les Auteurs Chrétiens Latins du Moyen Age sur les Juifs et le Judaisme* (Paris, La Haye, 1963). J. Pelikan has remarked that as Judaism became less of a threat to Christianity, Christian writers tended "to take their opponents less and less seriously" (*The Christian Tradition, vol. 1, The Emergence of the Catholic Tradition [100-600]*, [Chicago and London, 1971], p. 21). There is some validity to this observation, but precisely this fact leads one to ask why Christians continue to write books refuting people that they do not take seriously.

scholar has suggested, because of Jewish arguments that Christians became concerned with the conflict between the genealogies of Jesus in Matthew and Luke?[3] Did the incredulous inquiries of Jews inspire the various rationales concerning the need for the incarnation, up to and including Anselm's *Cur Deus Homo?*[4] The extent of Jewish influence is difficult to determine, but it is clear that such issues would not have been ignored in the absence of Jewish disputants. It is surely evident that when Isidore of Seville, in a work on Leviticus, has a Jew ask why Christians fail to bring sacrifices or observe the sabbatical year, he is raising problems suggested by his own reading of the Bible, and yet Peter Damian transferred these passages without change into a polemical work against the Jews.[5] Christians undoubtedly wrote books against Judaism in response to a challenge actually raised by Jews, but they were also motivated by the internal need to deal with issues that were both crucial and profoundly disturbing.

One approach to the puzzling conflict between the Hebrew Bible and Christian beliefs was a frontal attack. Marcion and other Christian heretics rejected the Jewish Scriptures and subjected them to a wide-ranging critique. In one respect this was a simple and straightforward solution since the problem vanishes entirely; there was no longer any need to engage in point by point exegesis of individual passages. On the other hand, this radical solution of one problem created another even more intractable difficulty. The Gospels, after all, clearly recognized the divine origin of the Hebrew Bible; indeed, many of the biblical testimonies central to later polemic are found in the New Testament. The suggestion that offending New Testament passages be emended was hardly palatable to most Christians, and mainstream Christianity rejected the one approach that would have sharply limited the scope of the Jewish-Christian debate.

3. See A. B. Hulen, "The Dialogue with the Jews as Source for the Early Jewish Argument against Christianity," *Journal of Biblical Literature* 51 (1932): 61.
4. On the polemical implications of *Cur Deus Homo?* see A. Funkenstein, "HaTemurot Be-Vikkuaḥ HaDat Shebein Yehudim LeNoẓerim BaMe'ah HaYod-Bet," *Zion* 33 (1968): 129-32.
5. See my "St. Peter Damian: His Attitude toward the Jews and the Old Testament," *Yavneh Review* 4 (1965): 102-4. The issue of Christian sacrifices in the Middle Ages is raised in N.V. (pp. 207-09), but only in response to a Christian argument.

It seems a bit strange to assert that the vigorous anti-Jewish position of the heretics would have minimized polemical activity, but this is indeed the case. Absolute rejection of the Hebrew Bible by Christians would have eliminated much of the wrangling over the meaning of verses which plays such a prominent role in medieval polemic. Moreover, the heretics' reading of the Bible was, in an ironic way, closer to that of the Jews than to that of orthodox Christians, because, like the Jews, they understood it literally. Total rejection eliminated the need for allegory entirely.[6]

In one area, however, such heretics enriched the Jewish-Christian argument. One of the central heretical methods of defending their pejorative evaluation of the Hebrew Bible was to show that it is replete with absurdities and contradictions. In discussions with heretics, orthodox Christians tended to shrink from such arguments, but in debates with Jews they changed their tune. Of course, the arguments were rechanneled; they were no longer proof of the absurdity of the Hebrew Bible, only of the absurdity of literal interpretation. In effect, therefore, Jews found themselves defending their Bible against both heretical barbs and orthodox allegory.[7]

One of the sharpest points of contention in the early confrontation between Jews and Christians—one in which the Christian position was formed by both internal and external factors—was the famous assertion that Christians are the true (*verus*) Israel. Here again, acceptance of the Hebrew Bible led naturally to the need to transform it into a Christian document, and the process through which Israel came to refer to Christians was almost inevitable. In this case, however, powerful forces from the outside combined to make this an argument of extraordinary significance. The pagan accusation that Christianity was an innovation had to be answered because it could affect the very legitimacy of the new faith, and the only effective response was to don the mantle of antiquity through the identification of Christendom with Israel.

6. For a summary of Marcion's attitude toward the Hebrew Bible and his manipulation of the New Testament text, see E. C. Blackman, *Marcion and His Influence* (London, 1948), pp. 42–60, 113–24. Cf. also Pelikan, p. 77.

7. See appendix 3.

Jews could hardly have been expected to suffer such a claim with equanimity. The most succinct summary of the instinctive Jewish reaction to this assertion is the Greek quotation from the *Dialogue with Trypho* which Marcel Simon placed on the cover of his *Verus Israel.* "What?!" said Trypho. "You are Israel?!"[8] After the initial shock wore off, Jews realized that this was a direct assault against the fundamental underpinnings of Judaism, an effort to abscond with the Bible. They pointed with outrage to the arbitrariness of applying all favorable biblical statements about Israel to the church and all pejorative ones to the Jews, and by the high Middle Ages they had assembled passages from the Bible in which favorable and unfavorable references were inextricably intertwined. The same Israel would be exiled and redeemed, and since the church would not suffer the former fate it could hardly lay claim to the latter reward.[9] Whatever the Jewish response, the issue was critical, because it appeared that Christianity could lay claim to legitimacy only by denying it to Judaism. There was no room (at least according to the dominant view) for two spiritual Israels.

The corpus of early Christian works directed against Judaism is, as we have already noted, rather extensive. Anti-Christian works by Jews, on the other hand, are virtually nonexistent before the twelfth century. One reason for this disparity is that Jews had no internal motivation for writing polemics against Christians; in times or places where Christianity was not a threat, we cannot expect Jews to be concerned with a refutation of its claims. Moreover, during much of the so-called Dark Ages, Jews in Christian lands produced no literature that has survived. Consequently, aside from some largely philosophical material in Arabic, our sources for the Jewish side of the discussion consist of scattered references in rabbinic literature,[10] the collections of folk polemic that go by the name *Toledot*

8. Tί οὖν; φησὶν ὁ Τρύφων. Ὑμεῖς Ἰσραὴλ ἐστε; *Dialogue with Trypho,* ch. 123.

9. On the subject of *verus Israel,* see pp. 169-71, and the notes to p. 126. On the typology of Jacob and Esau, see G. D. Cohen, "Esau as Symbol in Early Medieval Thought," in *Jewish Medieval and Renaissance Studies,* ed. A. Altmann, pp. 19-48, and cf. the notes to p. 55.

10. A list of such references appears in H. H. Ben Sasson's "Disputations and Polemics," *Encyclopaedia Judaica* (Jerusalem, 1971), 6: cols. 81-82.

Yeshu,[11] and quotations in Christian works.[12] The last group of sources is by far the richest, but determining the authenticity of Jewish arguments cited in some of the purely literary Christian dialogues is a risky procedure. The genuineness of such arguments can usually be tested by their appearance in later Jewish polemic or by their inherent plausibility, and despite the usefulness of these criteria it hardly needs to be said that they are far from foolproof. It is therefore not until the second half of the twelfth century that we can begin to speak with confidence about the details of the Jewish argument against Christianity.

An examination of Jewish-Christian polemic in the high Middle Ages reveals an arena in which most of the battles take place along well-charted lines but where certain new approaches are beginning to make themselves heard. The Christian side is usually on the offensive with respect to biblical verses, although, as I have indicated, there is a fundamentally defensive element in the entire enterprise of searching for biblical testimonies. Indeed, we find Jews arguing that Christianity is so inherently implausible that only the clearest biblical evidence could suffice to establish its validity.[13] Nevertheless, the structure of the Jewish-Christian debate was such that the initiative was taken by Christians in the area of scriptural evidence. On the other hand, Jews usually initiated the discussion of doctrinal questions, because they felt that the irrationality of Christianity could be established through such an approach. In each area, however, the initiative could shift; Jews did not refrain from citing specific verses to refute Christian beliefs and Christians did not hesitate to attack Jewish doctrines on philosophical or moral grounds.

11. See S. Krauss, *Das Leben Jesu nach Jüdischen Quellen* (Berlin, 1902).

12. See B. Blumenkranz's "Die Jüdischen Beweisgründe im Religionsgespräch mit den Christen," *Theologische Zeitschrift* 4 (1948): 119–47, and his *Juifs et Chrétiens dans le Monde Occidental, 430–1096* (Paris, 1960), pp. 213–89. It is likely that the brief *Sefer Nestor HaKomer* (Altona, 1875) also predates the high Middle Ages. For a short summary of some sporadic references to other early Jewish polemics, see J. Rosenthal, "Haganah VeHatqafah BeSifrut HaVikkuaḥ shel Yemei HaBeinayim," *Proceedings of the Fifth World Congress of Jewish Studies* (Jerusalem, 1969) 2: 354–55. On the degree to which early disputations reflect real encounters, see the summary in A. P. Hayman, *The Disputation of Sergius the Stylite against a Jew,* vol. 2 (Louvain, 1973), introd., pp. 64*–70*.

13. See J. Rosenthal's introduction to his edition of *Sefer Yosef HaMeqanne* (Jerusalem, 1970), p. 27.

The bulk of polemical discussions continued to center around the time-honored issue of christological verses in the Hebrew Bible. Before such discussions could take place, ground rules had to be set up. What is the scope of the Hebrew Bible, and what text can legitimately be cited? Particularly in the early centuries, Christians would have liked very much to include the apocrypha in their arsenal, and they were even more anxious to quote certain Septuagint readings. The very nature of this issue, however, forced a resolution in favor of the Jews. It can be very frustrating and unprofitable to argue with someone who simply denies the legitimacy of your quotations, and it was nearly impossible to prove that the apocrypha should be canonical or that Septuagint variants are superior to the Masoretic text (especially when some of those variants were a result of the corruption of the Septuagint text itself). Jerome's respect for the Hebrew text accelerated the resolution of this matter in favor of the Jewish position, and despite the persistence of a handful of apocryphal quotations and a few Septuagint variants, Christians settled down to the task of demonstrating the christological nature of the biblical text accepted by Jews.[14]

This task was pursued on two levels, and it would be useful to draw a distinction between genuine polemic and what could be called exegetical polemic. Genuine polemic involved those verses whose christological interpretation provided a genuine challenge to a Jew. If *'almah* meant virgin, then Isaiah 7:14 really seemed to speak of a virgin birth. Jeremiah 31:31 really spoke of a new covenant that God would make with the house of Israel. What did that mean? Isaiah 53 really did refer to a servant of the Lord who would suffer, despite his innocence, as a result of the sins of others. Who was that servant, and how was such suffering to be explained? If *shiloh* somehow meant Messiah (and many Jews conceded that it did), then Genesis 49:10 could reasonably be taken to mean that Jewish kingship would last until the messianic age and then cease. If the Messiah had not yet come, why was there no Jewish king? Specific rejoinders were necessary to blunt the force of such arguments, and it is no accident that

14. See the notes to p. 132.

the verses which fall into this category constitute the *loci classici* of polemical literature.

Nevertheless, a great deal of that literature is devoted to a discussion of passages of such weak polemical force that specific refutation was hardly even necessary. Such passages multiplied as a result of Christian exegesis of the Bible, and their christological interpretation was probably not even intended to persuade the non-believer. As time passed, however, this type of material began to make its way into polemical works, and the refutation of such "exegetical polemic" became a major concern of some Jewish writers. Although they used many of the same techniques that were applied to more serious arguments, Jewish polemicists confronted a situation in which the most straightforward response was the obser-vation that there was simply no evidence for the christological asser-tion. Why should Cyrus in Isaiah 45 be Jesus? On what basis are the heavens in Psalm 19 identified with the apostles? Who says that David in Psalm 17 is Jesus, and why should we assume that the speaker in Psalm 13 is the church?[15] The inclusion of such material blurred the already fuzzy line between polemic and exegesis, and bib-lical commentaries become a particularly important source of polem-ical material.

This is true not only of Christian commentaries, which are obviously a major source of exegetical polemic, but of Jewish com-mentaries as well. When a Jewish exegete reached a passage that was a crux of Christian polemic, he would frequently make an effort, whether implicitly or explicitly, to undermine the christological interpretation.[16] One exegetical tendency that was greatly encour-aged by such polemical goals was the denial of the messianic nature of certain biblical passages and the assertion that they referred instead to historical figures. Such a tendency appears in nonpolemical

15. Naturally, there are many scriptural arguments that resist neat classification, and not every weak argument should be labeled "exegetical." Nevertheless, these examples are illustrative of christological interpretations that hardly made any pretense of being demonstrably true. (Isaiah 45 was in a different category during the early stages of its polemical history; see the notes to p. 111.)

16. Some examples can be found in E.I.J. Rosenthal, "Anti-Christian Polemic in Medieval Bible Commentaries," *JJS* 11 (1960): 115-35. Jewish commentaries, of course, deal primarily with what I have called genuine polemic.

contexts as well, and some scholars have argued that the polemical motivation has been overstated; it is, nevertheless, beyond question that the desire to refute Christian interpretation played some role in the development of this type of exegesis. This is especially clear when surprising historical interpretations appear in overtly polemical works. In the *Niẓẓaḥon Vetus,* the most striking use of such exegesis appears in the discussion of Isaiah 11. While the author himself apparently understood that chapter messianically, he made use of a long-standing but clearly radical Jewish interpretation by maintaining that it could be referred to Hezekiah and Sennacherib. This view eliminates any christological reference, but it also does away with one of the central messianic passages in the Bible. Polemic, then, was at least a factor in stimulating and legitimizing an important development in medieval Jewish exegesis.[17]

Christians were genuinely puzzled at the Jewish failure to accept the overwhelming array of scriptural arguments which they had marshaled. Every major Christian doctrine could be supported by several verses in the Hebrew Bible, and some of these appeared utterly irrefutable. Indeed, a few verses seemed so impressive that the persuasive force of any one of them should in itself have caused Jews to abandon their faith.[18] Only preternatural blindness or a conscious refusal to accept the truth could account for Jewish resistance, and both of these explanations played a major role in the medieval conception of the Jew.[19]

Jewish refutations of Christian interpretations of the Bible had to proceed on a verse-by-verse basis. There are, nevertheless, certain general principles that were applied time and again, and the most important of these was the argument from context. Jews argued that christological explanations of individual verses could rarely withstand scrutiny from the wider perspective of the passage as a

17. On Isaiah 11, see the notes to p. 108. Cf. also p. 125 and the notes there. For a general treatment of medieval Ashkenazic exegesis, see S. Poznanski, *Mavo lePerush 'al Yeḥezqel u-Terei 'Asar leRabbi Eliezer miBalgenẓi* (Warsaw, 1913; reprinted Jerusalem, 1965).

18. So Peter the Venerable with respect to Proverbs 30:4; see his *Tractatus adversus Judaeorum Inveteratam Duritiem,* PL 189.519.

19. On blindness, see p. 68 and the notes there. For a possible Jewish reversal of the argument that Jews reject what they know to be the truth, see the notes to pp. 216 and 219.

whole, and they constantly cited adjoining verses to demonstrate this point. Perhaps the most important use of this argument was its application to the virgin birth explanation of Isaiah 7:14. This verse was by far the most significant evidence for the virgin birth in the Hebrew Bible, and its importance was enhanced by the fact that it was cited for this purpose in Matthew. Nevertheless, it was only with the greatest difficulty that Christians could respond to the Jewish argument that the birth was clearly expected to take place very shortly after Isaiah's announcement.[20] While the argument from context was not always as effective as it was here, it was the stock-in-trade of any medieval Jewish polemicist.

The Jewish posture with respect to the citation of biblical verses was not always defensive. Indeed, the very essence of the Jewish position rested upon certain monumental assertions built upon the straightforward reading of the Hebrew Bible as a whole; it is precisely because of this that Jews were less concerned with the citation of specific controversial verses. A reading of the Bible as a whole leaves the unmistakable impression that the Messiah would bring peace, that he would be a human being, that God is one, and that the ritual law means what it says. The burden of proof that any of these impressions should be modified, elaborated, or rejected was upon the Christians; this was recognized to some degree by the Christian side, and it was one of the fundamental assumptions of Jewish writers. Nevertheless, some Jewish polemicists did compile lists of verses to demonstrate the validity of certain basic Jewish beliefs.[21]

There was another Jewish approach that involved the citation of specific verses, but it is difficult to decide how seriously to take it. *The Niẓẓaḥon Vetus,* the earlier *Sefer Yosef HaMeqanne,* and some other Jewish polemics cite a series of verses which, they say, are aimed directly at Christianity. Several of these constitute clever responses to Christian assertions and are surely not to be taken seriously (e.g.,

---

20. See the notes to p. 101.

21. The clearest instance of such an approach in pre-fourteenth-century Jewish polemic is Solomon de' Rossi's *'Edut HaShem Ne'emanah,* ed. J. Rosenthal, *Meḥqarim u-Meqorot* (Jerusalem, 1967), 1:373-430. Jewish arguments based on the nonfulfillment of messianic prophecies of peace were very common; see the notes to p. 107.

the copper serpent does indeed represent Jesus and that is why Moses was commanded to hang it). I am inclined to think, however, that Jews were entirely serious about some of these quotations. One polemicist, in fact, cited such a verse immediately after a Christian question asking how the Torah could have omitted all reference to Jesus. Thus, the Bible explicitly warned against trusting in a man (Jer. 17:5; Ps. 146:3); it told Jews to punish a man who would claim to have a mother but not a father (Deut. 13:7); and it spoke of the humbling of anyone who pretended to be divine (Isa. 2:11). Such citations were hardly central to Jewish polemic, but they represent an effort by Jews to turn the tables on their opponents by finding "christological" verses of their own.[22]

With respect to doctrinal issues, it was the Jewish side that usually took the offensive. Jews were convinced that some of the central articles of faith professed by Christians were not only devoid of scriptural foundation but were without logical justification as well; to use Christian terminology, they lacked both *ratio* and *auctoritas*.

The trinity, which was an obvious target for logical questions, posed a peculiar problem for Jewish polemicists; they considered it so irrational that they had trouble in coming to grips with it. Although no Jewish writer formulates his difficulties in precisely this fashion, it seems clear that Jews, in effect, asked themselves the following questions: "What do they mean when they talk about a triune God? They say that there are three, and then they say that the three are one. But this is patent nonsense. What, then, do they really believe? Which of these contradictory assertions am I to take seriously and which shall I dismiss as meaningless double-talk? Since they talk about the separate incarnation of one of the three persons, it

---

22. See pp. 46 and 147 and the notes there. The problem of determining how serious Jews were in their citations of such verses was pointed out briefly by Judah Rosenthal in connection with a sixteenth-century polemic; see his introduction to Ya'ir ben Shabbetai da Correggio's *Ḥerev Pifiyyot* (Jerusalem, 1958), p. 9. Cf. also his citation of several relevant verses in his "Haganah VeHatqafah . . . ," pp. 348-49. There is a non-polemical source which may contribute to the impression that there was some degree of seriousness in this enterprise. R. Jacob Tam, we are told, requested divine guidance in a dream to determine whether or not Jesus and Mary are alluded to in Scripture; see A. J. Heschel, " 'Al Ruaḥ HaQodesh Bimei HaBeinayim," *Alexander Marx Jubilee Volume,* New York, 1950, Heb. vol., p. 182, n27. See also Talmage's note in "HaPulmus HaAnti-Noẓri BaḤibbur Leqet Qaẓar," *Michael* 4 (1976): 71.

is apparently the assertion of multiplicity that they really mean. In that case, I shall have to demonstrate to them that there is only one God."

It is only some such line of reasoning that can explain the persistent Jewish efforts to persuade Christians to accept monotheism on both logical and scriptural grounds. Jacob ben Reuben cites philosophical evidence that the world was created by no more than one God. The author of the *Niẓẓaḥon Vetus* wants to know what will happen if one person of the trinity makes a decision and another person reverses it. Solomon de' Rossi compiles a list of biblical verses which say that there is one God. Writer after writer reminds Christians that God proclaimed, "I, I am he, and there is no God beside me" (Deut. 32:39). To the Christian polemicist, of course, such arguments were virtually inexplicable and missed the point entirely. Christians, he would reply, believe in monotheism as much as Jews; the question is only the nature of that one God. On this issue, Jews and Christians were operating on different wavelengths, and the essence of the problem was the rationality of the Christian belief.[23]

Christians attempted to defend the plausibility of the trinitarian faith by analogies with physical phenomena or by the identification of the three persons of the trinity with major attributes of God. Such arguments raised complex philosophical questions about divine attributes which transcended the boundaries of the Jewish-Christian debate but did play a role in some of the more sophisticated polemical works. Some Jews tried to undermine this type of explanation by arguing that it could not coexist comfortably with the doctrine of the incarnation which implied the sort of separability among the persons of the trinity that could not be attributed to divine power, wisdom, and will.[24]

---

23. See the notes to pp. 42 (l. 12) and 75. The most sophisticated Jewish discussion of the trinity during our period is in Moses of Salerno's *Ta'anot,* and not all Jewish polemicists based their arguments on the undefended assumption that trinitarianism is simply a polytheism of three. There was, nevertheless, a pervasive Jewish feeling that this is the case. On this topic in general, see D. Lasker, *Jewish Philosophical Polemics against Christianity in the Middle Ages* (New York, 1977), pp. 48-104. (Lasker's important study appeared too late to be utilized systematically in this book; for an assessment, see my review in the *Association for Jewish Studies Newsletter* 22 [March 1978]: 16-17, 19.)

24. See appendix 5 for a detailed discussion.

The incarnation itself was subjected to a Jewish critique that ranged from the questioning of its necessity to the contention that it is impossible even for an omnipotent God.[25] Christian works quote several Jewish polemicists who became so carried away with the tendency to maintain the impossibility of Christian dogmas that they made such an assertion even with respect to the virgin birth. Here they were on very shaky ground; Christians presented effective rebuttals, and the extant Jewish polemics which discuss the matter concede that God could theoretically have caused a virgin to conceive.[26]

One Christian doctrine that Jews attacked on moral rather than philosophical grounds was the belief in the universal damnation which came in the wake of original sin. They argued that such treatment is clearly unfair and inconsistent with the mercy of God, and at least one Jewish writer made the same argument with respect to the damnation of the unbaptized, especially unbaptized infants.[27] The terrible consequences of a failure to accept Christianity seemed particularly unjust in light of what Jews considered the unimpressive nature of the miracles associated with Jesus' career.[28] Moreover, some of the central assertions of the Christian faith appeared not only implausible but demeaning to God, and it did not seem right that someone who refused to believe such doctrines should be punished so severely.[29]

For their part, Christians were more than willing to engage in arguments appealing to reason, morality, or fairness. The ritual law, they said, was demonstrably unreasonable. Even where it did not contradict itself, no plausible reasons could be discovered for many of its precepts, and the contention that no reasons need to be given for the divine will is the refuge of desperate, unintelligent men.[30] The very fate of the Jewish people constitutes a rational argument against the validity of Judaism.[31] As for moral arguments, Jews believed that

25. See appendix 2.
26. See p. 103 and the notes there.
27. See the notes to p. 218.
28. See especially the notes to p. 146.
29. See the notes to p. 222.
30. See appendix 3.
31. See the notes to p. 89.

God revealed himself only to them,[32] they apparently thought that only they would be saved,[33] and they possessed a harsh and carnal Law.[34]

Each side, then, was well fortified with arguments from both Scripture and reason, and polemical activity in the twelfth and thirteenth centuries reached new heights. Among Christians, the outpouring of anti-Jewish polemic began in the late eleventh century and reached a crescendo in the twelfth. Peter Damian, Gilbert Crispin, Petrus Alfonsi, Rupert of Deutz, Peter the Venerable, "William of Champeaux," Peter of Blois, Walter of Châtillon, Alan of Lille—these and others made their contributions to the refutation of Judaism. Among Jews, the writing of polemic began in the late twelfth century and reached a peak (at least in France and Germany) in the thirteenth. Joseph Kimhi, Jacob ben Reuben, the author of the *Vikkuah LehaRadaq,* Meir of Narbonne, Joseph Official (Yosef HaMeqanne) and his father Nathan, Moses of Salerno, Mordecai of Avignon, Naḥmanides, Jacob of Venice, Solomon de' Rossi and, finally, the anonymous author of the *Nizzahon Vetus* were the representatives of a concerted Jewish effort to present the case against Christianity. The renaissance of Christian polemic was as much a result of a general intellectual revival as of a new concern with Jews; the Jewish response, though somewhat delayed, was inevitable, and in two important instances, it was imposed in the form of forced disputations. Confrontations between Jews and Christians were on the increase, and their frequency, their tone, and even their content were being deeply influenced by the political, social, and economic changes of the twelfth and thirteenth centuries.

32. See Tertullian, *Adversus Judaeos,* PL 2.599 = Tränkle, p. 4. On Jewish selfishness, cf. also the citations from Bernard in my study, "The Attitude of St. Bernard of Clairvaux toward the Jews," *Proceedings of the American Academy for Jewish Research* 40 (1972): 100.

33. So a priest of Étampes quoted by Joseph Official; see the notes to p. 89 for the full quotation and reference. There is, of course, a well-known talmudic view that righteous Gentiles are admitted into the world to come (*Tosefta Sanhedrin,* ch. 13; *B. Sanhedrin* 105a), but the definition of righteousness was subject to several ambiguities. Moreover, this priest can hardly be faulted in light of comments made by Joseph Official's own father; see below, p. 68.

34. On the carnality of the Law, see p. 80 and the notes there.

II. *Polemic and Historical Reality*

The *Niẓẓaḥon Vetus,* as we shall see, is a virtual anthology of Ashkenazic polemic in the twelfth and thirteenth centuries, and these centuries constitute a pivotal period in the history of the Jews of France and Germany. In France a major factor in the inexorable decline of the status of the Jews was the growing centralization of power in the hands of an unfriendly monarchy. The growing national unification, together with the increase in mass piety that had been stimulated as early as the eleventh century by the Gregorian reform and the Crusades, sharpened the awareness of the alien character of the Jew both nationally and religiously. The Christian piety of some of the French monarchs, particularly Louis IX, resulted in a major effort to bring about large-scale Jewish conversion, and considerable sums were expended for this purpose.[35] An investigation of the Talmud was pursued in 1240 by means of a Jewish-Christian debate that was really a trial, and the eventual burning of the Talmud shortly thereafter was a devastating psychological and cultural blow to French Jewry.[36] One Jewish source reports that the king of France encouraged the arrangement of public disputations in 1272-73 by a Jewish convert to Christianity who promised to show the Jews that they were without faith and that, like heretics, they deserved to be burned.[37] Thus, for at least some Jews in thirteenth-century France, religious polemic was simply unavoidable.

Religious motives, however, were not the only factors which undermined the position of the Jews. The French monarchy saw its Jewish subjects as a convenient target for fiscal exploitation, and the

35. See S. W. Baron, *A Social and Religious History of the Jews* (New York, 1965), 10: 60.

36. See Ch. Merchavia, *HaTalmud BiRe'i HaNaẓrut* (Jerusalem, 1970), pp. 227-48.

37. See A. Neubauer, "Literary Gleanings, IX," *JQR,* o.s. 5 (1893): 713-14; cf. Baron, op. cit., 10: 63-64. See also R. Chazan, *Medieval Jewry in Northern France* (Baltimore and London, 1973), pp. 149-153, for indications that this convert was Pablo C(h)ristia(ni) and that the events may have taken place in 1269.

economic security of the Jews grew more and more precarious.[38] A feeling of economic insecurity had, in fact, been developing for some time and had even made its way into legal discussions by the twelfth century. The Talmud had recorded a view limiting the amount of interest that a Jew might collect from a Gentile to whatever the Jew needed for bare sustenance. In discussing this passage, some French Jewish commentators argued that such a ruling was of no practical effect under prevailing conditions; since "we do not know how much tax the king will demand," any sum must be regarded as bare sustenance.[39]

Similar evidence of such insecurity can be found in the application of another talmudic law. A Jew who was owed money by a Gentile was not supposed to collect the debt on a pagan holiday unless it was an oral debt; in the latter case, he could collect at any time because he had no assurance that he would be able to collect later. Here again Ashkenazic jurists maintained that under the conditions prevailing in medieval Europe, a debt for which the Jew had written proof (or even a pledge) could be collected on a Christian holiday because there was never any real assurance that even such a debt could be collected at a later date.[40]

It would, of course, be easy to argue that these rulings were rationalizations to justify widespread violations of the relevant talmudic regulations and that they do not therefore reflect genuine insecurity. The tosafists, however, did not manipulate talmudic law in quite so facile a manner. Whatever their motivations, they were convinced that they were describing their status accurately. It is clear, then, that considerable economic uncertainty was a genuine element in the Jewish psyche as early as the twelfth century, and in the thirteenth such uncertainty must have become more disturbing than ever. Legal attacks against Jewish moneylending were made by

38. See Baron, op. cit., 10: 57 ff. On the economic and political decline of French Jewry in the twelfth and thirteenth centuries, see esp. Chazan, op. cit., pp. 39–40, 63–96, 100–24, 133–41, 148, 154–86.

39. See S. Albeck, "Rabbenu Tam's Attitude to the Problems of His Time," (Hebrew), *Zion* 19 (1954): 107–08; cf. *Tosafot Bava Meẓi'a,* 70b, s. v. *tashshikh.*

40. *Tosafot Avodah Zarah,* 2a, s. v. *velifroa' mehen.* On Christian efforts to minimize the effectiveness of documents held by Jews which proved Christian indebtedness, see S. Grayzel, *The Church and the Jews in the Thirteenth Century* (Philadelphia, 1933), p. 57, note 78, and pp. 106–07, note 3. The Jewish feeling of economic insecurity is also reflected in the texts in B. Dinur, *Yisrael BaGolah* II. 1 (Tel Aviv and Jerusalem, 1965), pp. 157–68.

both Louis IX and Philip the Bold, while Philip the Fair resorted to outright extortion and eventual banishment in 1306. Even during those periods in the fourteenth century when the Jews were invited back, their security was tenuous. They were subjected to the indirect pressure of the Inquisition, they were vulnerable to the depredations of mobs like the Pastoureaux in 1320, and they were constantly aware of the possibility of another sudden expulsion.[41]

The status of German Jewry in the late thirteenth and early fourteenth centuries was also undergoing a precipitous decline. The most important change involved a new application of the old conception of Jewish servitude. As a theological concept, this doctrine goes back to the early Christian centuries, and it even gave rise to certain practical conclusions. Jews, for example, were not supposed to hold positions that would give them control over Christians, since that would constitute a violation of the biblical injunction (Gen. 25:23) that the older (i.e., the synagogue) must serve the younger (i.e., the church);[42] although honored more in the breach than the observance, this rule was not entirely without practical effect. Even the contention that Jews somehow belong to the royal treasury appears much earlier than the thirteenth century. Nevertheless, it was in that century that the fateful phrase *servi camerae* (serfs of the chamber) first appeared, and it was then that the potentially disastrous consequences of that phrase came to be applied in earnest.

Ironically, the immediate origins of this expression probably lie in a conflict that had no direct connection with the Jews and affected them at first in the form of an offer of protection. The Jewish question was a peripheral element in the struggle between pope and emperor concerning papal "fullness of power," and the assertion by Frederick II that the Jews were the serfs of his chamber meant, at least initially, that he was their legitimate protector.[43] It did not take long, however, for this doctrine to be transformed into an instrument

---

41. On the early fourteenth century, see Y. Yerushalmi, "The Inquisition and the Jews of France in the Time of Bernard Gui," *HTR* 63 (1970): 317-77. See also R. Anchel, *Les Juifs de France* (1946), pp. 79-91, and Chazan, op. cit., pp. 191-205.

42. See the notes to p. 55.

43. See Baron, op. cit., 9: 141-47. For a recent discussion of the doctrine of fullness of power, see W. D. McCready, "Papal *Plenitudo Potestatis* and the Source of Temporal Authority in Late Medieval Papal Hierocratic Theory," *Speculum* 48 (1973): 654-74.

of severe economic exploitation that reflected an effort to deny to Jews the status of free men.[44] This development was aggravated by recurring blood libels, anti-Jewish riots, local expulsions, and "feudal anarchy";[45] consequently, although German Jews were spared the agony of a nationwide banishment, their legal and social status had sunk to an almost intolerable level.

Polemical works in general and the *Nizzaḥon Vetus* in particular both reflect and illuminate the historical epoch in which they appear. It is true that many aspects of polemic remained relatively static throughout the Middle Ages, particularly the various arguments and counterarguments regarding the exegesis of specific biblical verses. Nevertheless, the *realia* of any historical period quickly found expression in polemic, and the impact of various political, philosophical, and religious developments can be measured in part by the degree to which they are reflected in this literature. Examples of this can be cited from virtually every period in the development of polemic. The failure of the Bar-Kokheba revolt was reflected almost immediately in Justin's *Dialogue with Trypho;* the problems of "Judaizers" in the church were discussed in the diatribes of John Chrysostom; Agobard's works reflected the challenge of Jewish economic development and political influence; the relatively calm tone of the polemics of Peter Damian and Gilbert Crispin as compared with the vituperation in works of the later Middle Ages mirrored basic differences in Jewish-Christian relations; various philosophical developments had a major impact on the discussions of the trinity, incarnation, and virgin birth.[46]

In light of the deteriorating status of Ashkenazic Jewry described above, it is particularly interesting that one of the most striking characteristics of the *Nizzaḥon Vetus* and other Ashkenazic

44. See especially G. Kisch, *The Jews in Medieval Germany* (Chicago, 1949), pp. 159–68, and cf. Baron, op. cit., pp. 152 ff.

45. Baron, op. cit., pp. 193 ff.

46. There is no really good survey of Jewish-Chistian polemic as a whole until the fourteenth century. A few studies, however, do give a picture of some of the areas of interaction between polemic and historical *realia*. See *Ver. Israel; Auteurs; Juifs et Chrét.;* J. Parkes, *The Conflict of the Church and the Synagogue* (London, 1934); I. Loeb, "La Controverse Religieuse entre les Chrétiens et les Juifs au Moyen Age," *Revue d'histoire des Religions* 17 (1888): 311–37; 18 (1888): 133–56 (also printed as a separate monograph); Baron, op. cit. 9:55–134, 266–307; Funkenstein, op. cit., pp. 125–44.

polemics of this period is their aggressiveness, vigor, and vituperation. The Jewish reader is instructed to press his arguments vigorously and not to permit the Christian to change the subject.[47] Christians are told that they will be condemned ·to hellfire.[48] A rabbi is said
to have informed the king of Germany that "if one were to load a
donkey with vomit and filth and lead him through the church, he
would remain unharmed."[49] Sarcastic stories are told of conversa-
tions between Jesus and God,[50] while Jesus, Peter, Mary, and the
holy spirit are all referred to in an insulting manner.[51] Some of these
comments and witticisms are a reflection of what might be called folk
polemic, since such arguments and anecdotes must have enjoyed
wide circulation among Jews who were incapable of appreciating
more complex and abstract discussions.[52]

Aggressiveness and vituperation were by no means universal
among Jewish polemicists of this period and are characteristic primarily of *Sefer Yosef HaMeqanne* and the *Nizzahon Vetus,* which were
written in northern France and Germany. Other writers were far
more cautious and restrained. Jacob ben Reuben, for example, pre-
fixed his pioneering critique of Matthew with a diffident, even fearful, introduction. He wrote that Jews should really keep silent on
such matters, that he recorded only a few of the errors in Matthew,
and that he did even this much only at the insistence of his friends.
Moreover, he asked that his name not be mentioned in connection
with the critique for fear that Christians would find out.[53] Solomon
de' Rossi also counseled restraint at the beginning of his *'Edut
HaShem Ne'emanah.* Indeed, he suggested that the Jewish polemicist
avoid entirely such subjects as the trinity, incarnation, host, saints,

---

47. N.V., p. 169.
48. Ibid., p. 68.
49. Ibid., p. 69.
50. See pp. 43, 77.
51. See the notes to p. 152.
52. Nevertheless, Rosenthal (*Jewish Social Studies* 27 [1965]: 121) justly rejects H. J. Schoeps's contention that N.V. stems from "the completely uneducated circles of German Jewry."
53. *Mil. HaShem,* p. 141. While Rosenthal is no doubt correct in suggesting that such factors as the higher philosophical level of *Mil. HaShem* were largely responsible for its less vituperative tone (introduction to *Sefer Yosef HaMeqanne,* p. 28), this passage shows that fear was also a factor. These ob-servations by Rosenthal revise his earlier judgment that *Mil. HaShem* was the sharpest polemic written by a medieval Jew (introduction to *Mil. HaShem,* p. 19).

priesthood—in short, anything that might be offensive. Discussion should be limited to "the coming of the Messiah, the signs of his time, the commandments of the Torah, and the words of the prophets." Moreover, Solomon's advice on the tactics of the Jewish polemicist provides a striking contrast with the above-mentioned instructions given by the author of the *Nizzaḥon Vetus*. "One who argues with them," says our author, "should be strong willed by asking questions and giving responses that deal with the specific issue at hand and not permitting his antagonist to extricate himself from that issue until it has been completed."[54] Solomon, on the other hand, suggests that if the Jew sees that he is winning the argument, he should not try to appear like the victor but should instead change the subject.[55]

Our author's practical advice to the Jewish polemicist is not the only evidence indicating that the aggressiveness reflected in the *Nizzaḥon Vetus* was at least partly expressed in actual debate. Agobard accused Jews of blaspheming Jesus in the presence of Christians.[56] In the twelfth century, Jews were said to have challenged Christians to battle in the manner of Goliath.[57] Walter of Châtillon asserted that Jews not only fail to accept the truth of Christianity but actively pose objections to it.[58] The oft-quoted remark of Louis IX that a Christian layman who is confronted by a Jewish polemicist should refute his adversary by stabbing him assumes that Jews were in the habit of initiating religious discussions.[59] Recent research has revealed that the unflattering explanation of Christian confession proposed in the *Nizzaḥon Vetus* was actually suggested to a Christian by a thirteenth-century French Jew; the priest, it was said, uses confession to obtain a list of adulterous women whom he can then

54. N.V., p. 169.

55. See Solomon de' Rossi, *'Edut HaShem Ne'emanah*, Rosenthal's *Meḥqarim*, 1:378–79. Cf. also the citations in Rosenthal's introduction to *Yosef HaMeqanne*, p. 17. The contrast between Solomon and N.V. was noted briefly by E. Urbach, "Études sur la littérature polémique au moyen âge," *REJ* 100 (1935): 61.

56. PL 104.71, quoted in Williams, p. 355.

57. The *Tractatus* in TNA 5.1509 =PL 213.749; cf. M. Guedemann, *HaTorah VehaḤayyim Bimei HaBeinayim* . . . (Tel Aviv, 1968; first printing, Warsaw, 1897), pp. 11–12.

58. Walter of Châtillon, *Tractatus* . . ., PL 209.424.

59. See Anchel, op. cit., pp. 106–7. On "the Jewish mission" through the eleventh century, see also *Juifs et Chrét.*, pp. 159–211.

seduce.[60] In light of this evidence, it appears that the assertiveness and self-confidence of Ashkenazic Jews were remarkable, and the view that most of the sarcastic comments in Jewish polemic were intended for internal consumption should probably be modified though not entirely discarded.[61]

Whether or not vituperative polemical remarks were intended for a Christian audience, such expressions of contempt toward the *sancta* of Christianity became known to the Inquisition. Bernard Gui, who directed the Inquisition in France in the early fourteenth century, referred to a *cematha* (= *shamta,* or curse) proclaimed by the Jews on the Day of Atonement which indicated through circumlocution that Jesus was the illegitimate son of a prostitute and Mary a woman of voluptuousness. In his study of Gui and the Jews of France, Y. Yerushalmi points to a liturgical poem quoted in *Endecktes Judenthum* that reads: "The nations link your holiness to the yoke of promiscuity, [but] your bethrothed revile the relation to the promiscuous woman (יחוס אשת הזימה).''[62]

60. See J. Shatzmiller, *Recherches sur la communauté juive de Manosque au moyen age* (Paris, La Haye, 1973), pp. 123-27; cf. below, p. 223. Although I find Shatzmiller's analysis quite persuasive, several cautionary remarks should be added. First of all, the text is fragmentary, and Shatzmiller's reconstruction is based in part on the existence of the parallel in N.V. Secondly, the Jew was subjected to a formal accusation as a result of his remarks, and this must obviously temper any conclusions to be drawn from this incident concerning Jewish aggressiveness and freedom of speech. Finally, the Jew denied the charges by presenting a significantly different version of what he had said, and this denial, as Shatzmiller indicates, cannot be dismissed with absolute certainty.

61. See Urbach, op. cit., pp. 60 ff., for a discussion of this problem. I. Levi had pointed to several sources which reflected Jewish initiation of vigorous religious debate, but he considered this a pre-thirteenth-century phenomenon; see his "Controverse entre un Juif et un Chrétien au XIe Siècle," *REJ* 5 (1882): 238. The view that Provençal Jews "took advantage of their freedom of speech" to a greater extent than other Jews was expressed by Grayzel, *The Church and the Jews in the Thirteenth Century,* p. 29. Baron has even suggested that outspoken polemical remarks may have been inspired by the Official family, and they themselves may have spoken as they did because of their roots in Narbonne, where Jews enjoyed exceptional privileges (op. cit., 9:277). Many remarks of this type, however, cannot be traced to the Officials, and quite a few are attributed to earlier Ashkenazic figures. The truth probably lies in the most straightforward reading of the evidence, which indicates that the Jews of northern France and Germany did not shrink from outspoken polemic, at least in private conversation, even in the dark days of the late thirteenth century. On the assertiveness that marked Ashkenazic Jewry in the pre-Crusade period, see I. Agus, *The Heroic Age of Franco-German Jewry* (New York, 1969), especially pp. 11-20; despite certain exaggerations, the main thrust of Agus's portrayal of this characteristic is valid. For an even earlier period, see Anchel, op. cit., pp. 31-32.

62. Yerushalmi, op. cit., pp. 362-63. The phrase אשת הזימה is taken from Ezekiel 23:44. See also Merchavia, "HaShamta BeSifrut HaPulmus HaNoẓerit Bimei HaBeinayim," *Tarbiz* 41 (1971): 95-115; cf. especially pp. 97, 100, where he cites the reading יחום rather than יחוס

This sort of expression appears in the *Nizzahon Vetus* several times, and Gui's attack points up the danger inherent in the use of such rhetoric even to a Jewish audience. Indeed, Gui was aware of a substantial number of Jewish works and expressions that he felt were directed against Christians or contained blasphemies. Among these were the *Alenu* prayer, Rashi's commentaries, Maimonides' *Mishneh Torah,* R. David Kimhi's commentary on Psalms, and the Talmud itself. Moreover, he was particularly sensitive to the Jewish practice of calling Christians "heretics" (*minim*), a practice that goes back to the Talmud and is reflected frequently in the *Nizzahon Vetus.*[63] Finally, it might be pointed out that a religious disputation actually became part of an inquisitorial proceeding in 1320; not surprisingly, the inquisitor emerged victorious in a debate whose ground rules left something to be desired.[64]

The increasing economic exploitation of Jews was reflected all too clearly in the polemical work of Meir of Narbonne. Here the satirical veneer that often concealed Jewish bitterness was dropped, and Meir allowed himself an undisguised outburst which reveals how deeply Jews were hurt by their growing insecurity. The unfair expropriation of property on such a scale "is worse for a man than being murdered. When a person is subjected to shame and disgrace, he would rather be dead; moreover, when he loses his money and he and his family remain 'in hunger, in nakedness, and in want of all things' (Deut. 28:48), then he will in fact die before his time." The culmination of this cry of anguish is Meir's anticipation of the day when the Gentiles will have to repay what they stole from the Jews.[65]

Many other aspects of the changing historical situation were also reflected in Jewish polemic. The growing importance of money-lending, for example, led to considerable discussion of its ethics and its biblical justification. Christians not only cited various time-

---

63. See Yerushalmi, op. cit., pp. 350 ff. In the Talmud, *minim* probably referred primarily to Jewish Christians. For the charge that Jews curse Christians in prayer, cf. also Jerome and Agobard cited in Merchavia, *HaTalmud BiRe'i HaNazrut,* pp. 82–83. Cf. also the list of pejorative Jewish expressions about Christianity compiled by Christians in 1239 and summarized by Merchavia, p. 278.

64. See S. Grayzel, "The Confessions of a Medieval Jewish Convert," *Historia Judaica* 17 (1955): 89–120, and cf. Yerushalmi, op. cit., pp. 328–33.

65. *Mil. Mizvah,* p. 23b. See also the quotation from Meir in Chazan, op. cit., p. 123.

honored verses to prove that usury is a moral offense of universal relevance, but were apparently willing to use Jewish typology to buttress their argument. Several Jewish works of this period cite the Christian contention that even if Christians are Edom (a Jewish stereotype), Jews should be forbidden to take interest from them in light of the verses which refer to Edom and Israel as brothers. Moreover, the Jewish response did not restrict itself solely to legalistic refutations; Christian polemicists were charged with hypocrisy on the grounds that Christians themselves were involved in extensive usurious activities.[66]

The truth is that this last accusation is but one expression of the more general contention that Christians behave immorally. Whatever the historical validity of such remarks may be, they are significant for what they reveal about the self-image of the Jews and the use of polemic to strengthen that image. One of the beliefs which sustained medieval Jewry through centuries of adversity was the firm conviction that Jews were clearly superior to their Gentile persecutors. No medieval Jew felt that he was subjected to other nations because they were morally, let alone religiously, superior to him. On the contrary, Ashkenazic Jewry in particular developed the theory that one reason for its suffering was that it was chosen because of its unique qualities to sanctify the divine name through martyrdom.[67] Consequently, martyrdom itself became evidence of the outstanding qualities of the Jews of France and Germany.

Indeed, Ashkenazic Jews were hardly able to discuss the issue of martyrdom, even in a halakhic context, without a passionate, emotional response. A remarkable *tosafot,* for example, points out that a certain talmudic passage seems to require a normative legal decision that a Jew is not obligated to resist to the death when forced to engage in a private idolatrous act. But, say the tosafists, "this is difficult," and one expects that this standard formula will be followed by the ordinary kind of legal or exegetical argumentation.

---

66. See pp. 133-34 and the notes there. For a discussion of the Christian accusations that Jews engage in extensive usury, see Kisch, op. cit., pp. 327-9.

67. See H. H. Ben-Sasson, *Peraqim beToledot HaYehudim Bimei HaBeinayim* (Tel Aviv, 1958), pp. 174-84. Cf. N.V., p. 70, and the notes there.

Instead, we are confronted, at least initially, by an emotional outburst. "This is difficult, for God forbid that we should rule in a case
of idolatry that one should transgress rather than die."[68] A similar
reaction appears in a responsum of R. Meir of Rothenburg, who was
asked whether atonement is necessary for a man who had killed his
wife and children (with their consent) to prevent their capture by a
mob demanding conversion to Christianity. Although he concedes
the difficulty of finding justification for such an act in rabbinic
sources, R. Meir will not even consider seriously the possibility that
such behavior is illegal. "This is a matter," he says, "whose permissibility has been widely accepted, for we have heard of many great
rabbis who slaughtered their sons and daughters. . . . And anyone
who requires atonement for this is besmirching the name of the pious
men of old."[69]

The *Niẓẓaḥon Vetus* supplies additional evidence of the cen-
trality of martyrdom in the thought of Franco-German Jewry in this
period. It contains a fascinating passage which illustrates how an
Ashkenazic Jew transformed a story that contained no reference to
martyrdom into one in which it emerges as the central theme; indeed,
it becomes virtually a criterion of religious truth. In Judah Halevi's
Kuzari, a pagan king calls in a philosopher, a Jew, a Muslim, and a
Christian so that each can argue the merits of his position. The king
is eventually persuaded of the truth of Judaism, partly because both
the Muslim and the Christian grant it a certain degree of authenticity.
The *Niẓẓaḥon Vetus,* on the other hand, tells an elaborate story in
which a king threatens a Jew, a Christian, and a Muslim with death
unless each one will convert to one of the other faiths. The Jew
remains steadfast even at the very edge of the grave, while the other
two ultimately lose their resolve and succumb to the king's threats.
Both, however, choose Judaism, and "when the emperor heard that
the Jew was willing to die for his Torah and would not move from his

---

68. *Tosafot Avodah Zarah,* 54a s. v. *ha beẓin'a.* See J. Katz, *Bein Yehudim LeGoyim* (Jerusalem,
1960). p. 90. (The equivalent passage in the English version [*Exclusiveness and Tolerance* (New York, 1961),
pp. 83–84] presents such a bland paraphrase of the *Tosafot* that the emotional force of the argument is
virtually lost.)

69. R. Meir of Rothenburg, *Teshuvot, Pesaqim, U-Minhagim,* ed. Y.Z. Kahane (Jerusalem,
1960), 2:54.

faith one bit, while the priest and the Muslim both denied their vain beliefs and accepted our faith, he himself chose our religion; he, the priest, and the Muslim were all converted and became true and genuine proselytes." The modification of the *Kuzari* story to make the willingness to die a proof of the truth of Judaism is a truly striking indication of the role martyrdom had come to play in the psyche of the medieval Ashkenazic Jew.[70]

The one aspect of medieval Christian life that challenged the Jewish image of moral superiority was the monastic ideal. At least some Christians, it appeared, were leading pure and ethical lives which could be compared favorably with those of ordinary Jews and perhaps even of rabbinic leaders. It is possible that it was the implicit challenge of monasticism that provoked the vigorous attacks against both the monastic ideal and its practical implementation which are found in Jewish polemic. The author of the *Niẓẓaḥon Vetus* argues that at best monks and nuns are overcome with lustful desires that cannot be consummated, and at worst, "they wallow in licentiousness in secret." Only marriage can assure that a person will remain pious and God-fearing. Moreover, monastic orders, some of which were expanding vigorously in the twelfth and thirteenth centuries, were accused of unfair appropriation of land and portrayed as depraved and unethical. Thus, the threat to the Jewish self-image was negated, and Jews were even able to strengthen their conviction of ethical superiority by a partisan examination of monasticism.[71]

It is significant that the relatively recent charge of ritual murder appears in Ashkenazic polemic of the thirteenth century. Whatever the roots of this accusation may be, official church doctrine never sanctioned it. Indeed, at least the charge of ritual consumption of Christian blood was vigorously condemned by the

---

70. For further references, see the notes to pp. 216–18.

71. See pp. 69–70, 98–99, 223, and cf. the notes there. On the alleged immorality of priests, see also Guedemann, op. cit., pp. 42–43, 67–68. My feeling that monasticism posed a psychological threat to the Jewish self-image is almost impossible to substantiate definitively because no medieval Jew would say this openly. There is, however, interesting evidence that some Ashkenazic Jews in the early modern period felt insecure in the presence of genuine priestly celibacy; see the curious legend in *Shivḥei HaBesht* about the Baal Shem Tov's conversation with a priest (D. Ben-Amos and J. Mintz, *In Praise of the Baal Shem Tov* [Bloomington, 1970], p. 248).

papacy, and it may even be appropriate to speak of a thirteenth-century rivalry between pope and emperor over the right to protect the Jews against this libel.[72] It is consequently a matter of particular interest to find Christians searching the Scriptures to discover evidence, and rather complicated evidence at that, to prove that Jews eat human beings and drink their blood.[73] This is one of the earliest concrete indications of an attempt at a reasoned defense of the blood libel.

The spread of heresy was one of the most important social and religious developments in this period and had particularly sensitive implications with regard to Jewish-Christian relations. Christians had traditionally labeled members of any schismatic group "Jews," and had occasionally attacked the latter as a means of getting at the former.[74] Moreover, Jews were occasionally accused of harboring heretics, encouraging them, and even of leading orthodox Christians into heresy.[75] Nevertheless, despite considerable scholarly efforts, virtually no hard evidence concerning significant contacts between Jews and medieval heretics has been unearthed.[76]

Precisely such evidence, however, may be found in Jewish polemic. I have argued elsewhere that the *Niẓẓaḥon Vetus* contains a refutation of a heretical Christian doctrine, that a thirteenth-century French polemicist makes explicit reference to Albigensians and Bogomils in order to attack orthodox Christianity, and that Jacob ben Reuben's *Milḥamot HaShem* may preserve evidence of an even more intriguing nature. Jacob's Christian disputant may have unwittingly quoted the arguments of a friend which were ostensibly aimed at Judaism but were really designed to undermine orthodox Christian-

---

72. Baron, op. cit., 9:144–45.

73. See pp. 54, 229 and the notes there.

74. So Cassiodorus, PL 70.74D ("Judaei vel Donatistae"); Hadrian I, PL 98.1255–56. Cf. *Juifs et Chrét.*, pp. xvi–xvii and note 11 there. See also Damian's *De Sacramentis per Improbos Administratis,* PL 145.529, and his *Liber Qui Dicitur Gratissimus,* ch. 37, PL 145.153, discussed in my "St. Peter Damian," pp. 86–87, 89–90. Cf. Humbert, PL 143.1093 C. On this practice in the Byzantine Empire, see Parkes, op. cit., pp. 300–03. Cf. also Baron, op. cit., 9:58–60.

75. Cf. Baron, op. cit., 59, 267–68.

76. See L. I. Newman, *Jewish Influence on Christian Reform Movements* (New York, 1925); G. Scholem, *Ursprung und Anfänge der Kabbala* (Berlin, 1962), pp. 206–210; F. Talmage, "An Hebrew Polemical Treatise: Anti-Cathar and Anti-Orthodox," *HTR* 60 (1967): 335–37.

ity. Thus, Christian heretics may have used anti-Jewish polemic as a cover for attacks against the orthodox Christian faith.[77]

The twelfth and thirteenth centuries were also characterized by the broadening of the horizons of Europe that took place in the wake of the Crusades; indeed, the rise of heresy in Western Europe may have been stimulated by the new contacts between East and West.[78] These contacts with the Muslim world aided Jewish apologists in a very old and critical area of polemic, namely, the Christian argument that the success and wide diffusion of Christianity proved its superiority over a religion with a small number of adherents who were growing progressively weaker. Jews could now argue with genuine conviction and greater effectiveness that even by the numerical test alone, Christianity would not prevail; Muslims, they said, rule "half the world," and God's promise to Abraham that all nations of the world would be blessed in him and his seed was certainly not fulfilled through Christianity. Jews even attempted to make Christians feel isolated by arguing that the disgust at eating pork is really a *consensus omnium* with the sole exception of Christians. In fact, even the existence of Christian heresy could be cited as proof of the limited extent of orthodox Christianity. Finally, the failure of the Crusades was cited to show that the alleged success of Christianity was illusory; consequently, Christians would have to admit that temporal success is unrelated to religious truth. Once this admission was made, the old argument against Judaism would have to be abandoned.[79]

One of the most striking characteristics of the polemic reflected in the *Niẓẓaḥon Vetus* is the extensive use of the New Testament. The first extant critique of the New Testament by a European Jew is in the eleventh chapter of Jacob ben Reuben's *Milḥamot HaShem* (1170);[80] this work, however, deals only with Matthew.

77. See my "Christian Heresy and Jewish Polemic in the Twelfth and Thirteenth Centuries," *HTR* 68 (1975):287-303. See also p. 153 below and the notes there.

78. On the causes of the rise of heresy, see J. Russell's "Interpretations of the Origins of Medieval Heresy," *Medieval Studies* 25 (1963): 26-53, and his *Dissent and Reform in the Early Middle Ages* (Berkeley, 1965).

79. See p. 89 and the notes there for specific references and a fuller discussion.

80. For a discussion of this date, see J. Rosenthal's edition of *Mil. HaShem,* introduction, p. viii.

On the other hand, *Sefer Yosef HaMeqanne, Milḥemet Miẓvah* of Meir b. Simon of Narbonne, and the *Niẓẓahon Vetus* reflect an intimate knowledge of all the Gospels and some awareness of the other books of the New Testament.[81]

There are certain instructive similarities between Jewish use of the New Testament in polemic and the Christian approach to the Talmud, which became important in the thirteenth century. Both religions had one sacred text—the Hebrew Scriptures—which they held in common, and another sacred body of teaching about whose authority they differed. Traditionally, polemical writings had largely restricted themselves to different interpretations of the text whose authority and divine origin both groups accepted. In our period, however, the usefulness of the New Testament for Jewish polemicists and of the Talmud for Christians began to become evident. There is, in fact, a clear parallelism between the approaches developed by each group to the sacred literature of its adversaries. On the one hand, that literature was subjected to a vigorous critique; on the other, it was exploited to disprove the beliefs of its own adherents.

Thus, beginning in the twelfth century a series of Christian authors attacked the Talmud as a work replete with absurdities, and in the 1230s, Nicholas Donin asserted that it contained blasphemies against Jesus which made it a candidate for destruction. The Jewish defense presented at the so-called disputation in Paris in 1240 did not succeed in thwarting Donin's wishes, and within a relatively short time a public burning of the Talmud took place. A few decades later in Spain the Talmud was again the focus of a disputation, but the approach was entirely different. Here, Pablo C(h)ristia(ni) maintained that the dogmas of Christianity could be demonstrated from the Talmud; the rabbis, for example, were said to have indicated that

81. Cf. the reference to 1 Corinthians on p. 70. The impression of close familiarity with the New Testament is marred by the frequent attribution of a quotation to the wrong book of the Gospels. See, e.g., pp. 180, 183, 188. These inaccurate ascriptions may offer a partial explanation for the lack of a systematic order in the section of N.V. that contains a critique of the Gospels. N.V. also contains some non-authentic quotations from Christian literature (e.g., pp. 160, 201) which J. Wakius complained about in a late seventeenth-century refutation. See his *Teshuvat HaDin 'al HaYehudim sive Recriminatio Actionis in nuperos Christi Accusatores cujus pars prima agit contra. . . librum Nizzachon Vetus* (Jenae, 1699), pp. 20–21, 28–29.

the Messiah had already come and that he is a preexistent being. Significant, though less spectacular, consequences resulted from this disputation as well, and the use of the Talmud to support Christianity became a central element of the Jewish-Christian debate in the centuries to come. Some later Christians even combined the two approaches, arguing that the Talmud contains both blasphemies and evidence of Christian truths.[82]

The Jewish critique of the Gospels had a similar twofold nature. Jews attacked the Christian Scriptures for their alleged absurdities and contradictions, and at the same time they tried to prove that later Christian dogmas are inconsistent with the Gospels themselves. It was, of course, much easier to maintain both Jewish attitudes at the same time than it was to do the same for both Christian arguments, and the dual approach is used without hesitation throughout the latter section of the *Nizzahon Vetus*.[83]

The knowledge of the New Testament displayed in *Yosef HaMeqanne* and the *Nizzahon Vetus* was at least partly firsthand since there are a substantial number of Latin quotations in both works.[84] Nevertheless, various citations of the opinions of proselytes leave no room for doubt that some of the familiarity with Christian texts

82. Both views were expressed in the Tortosa disputation in the early fifteenth century; cf. the citations in Baron, op. cit., 9: 90, 91. Baron, however, does not note that two originally disparate approaches are represented here. On medieval Christian use of the Talmud through the Donin episode, see Merchavia, *HaTalmud BiRe'i HaNazrut*, passim. Pablo's approach was adopted by Raymund Martini in his classic *Pugio Fidei* (Leipzig, 1687), which became a manual for Christian polemicists in late medieval Spain. For Donin's approach in thirteenth-century Italy, cf. C. Roth, *History of the Jews of Italy* (Philadelphia, 1946), pp. 99–100.

83. On the search for contradictions, see, for example, N.V., pp. 167–68, regarding the contradictory genealogies in Matthew and Luke. The argument against Christian dogma through Gospel citations is very common; see especially the notes to p. 183.

84. There is some discussion of Jacob ben Reuben's Hebrew translations of Matthew in Rosenthal's "Targum shel HaBesorah 'al pi Matti leYa'aqov ben Reuven," *Tarbiz* 32 (1962): 48–66. On Jacob's translation of selections from Gilbert Crispin's *Disputatio*, see my "Gilbert Crispin, Alan of Lille, and Jacob ben Reuben: A Study in the Transmission of Medieval Polemic," *Speculum* 49 (1974): 34–47. On Jewish knowledge of Latin see also the references in Merchavia, op. cit., p. 245. The author of the *Dialogus* attributed to William of Champeaux refers to his supposed Jewish disputant as a man expert in Jewish law and "not ignorant" of Christian literature (PL 163.1045). Gilbert Crispin, after whose work "William" modelled this passage, had used an even stronger expression; the Jew "was well-versed (*bene sciens*) in our law and literature" (*Disputatio*, ed. Blumenkranz, p. 27). Solomon de' Rossi lists such knowledge as one of the requirements for a Jewish polemicist (*'Edut HaShem Ne'emanah*, in Rosenthal's *Mehqarim*, 1: 378).

and especially with Christian prayers, festivals, and rituals resulted from contact with these converts; indeed, the Rome manuscript passages that served as a source of the *Nizzahon Vetus* may well have been written by a student of a proselyte's son. Similarly, the Christian awareness of the Talmud stemmed largely from information supplied by Jewish converts. Petrus Alfonsi, for example, had proposed arguments against certain talmudic passages as early as the beginning of the twelfth century,[85] and both Nicholas Donin and Pablo C(h)ristia(ni) were recent converts to Christianity when they began their polemical activities.[86]

Jewish polemic, then, reflects some of the most important social, economic, and intellectual changes that were taking place in the twelfth and thirteenth centuries. Embittered relations, economic exploitation, usury, the expansion of monasticism, martyrdom, the blood libel, Christian heresy, the failure of the Crusades, wider familiarity with the New Testament and the Talmud—all these played a role in the Jewish-Christian debate, and polemical works can frequently supply insights into the impact of some of these momentous developments. Relations between Christians and Jews were indeed deteriorating, but the very symptoms of that deterioration lent greater variety and renewed interest to the vigorous religious discussions that persisted throughout this tragic age in the history of medieval Jewry.

III. The Book and Its Author

Finally, we come to the *Nizzahon Vetus* itself. Some of the basic information concerning the work is either unknown or uncertain, and even the very title has been subjected to varying translations. In this context, the word *nizzahon* probably means polemic rather than victory;[87] the reason that this is the "old *Nizzahon*" is that

---

85. See Merchavia, op. cit., pp. 93–127.
86. See below, note 91. On the role of converts, see Blumenkranz, "Jüdische und Christliche Konvertiten im Jüdisch-Christlichen Religionsgespräch des Mittelalters," in Paul Wilpert's *Judentum im Mittelalter* (Berlin, 1966), pp. 264–82, and cf. Guedemann, op. cit., p. 11.
87. See the notes to p. 41.

a more famous polemic of the same name was written by Rabbi Yom Tov Lipmann Mühlhausen at the beginning of the fifteenth century, and the later work came to be the *Sefer HaNizzahon* par excellence. Our *Nizzahon* was published in the seventeenth century by a Christian scholar who hesitantly dated it in the twelfth century, because, he said, no one who lived after that time is mentioned in the book.[88]

We now know that at least one or two later figures are named and that the book is probably dependent upon the thirteenth-century *Sefer Yosef HaMeqanne;*[89] consequently, the most plausible date for the *Nizzahon Vetus* is the latter part of the thirteenth century, and this is the date that has been accepted by most modern scholars.[90] Urbach dates the work in the fourteenth century, apparently because its two major sources are from the second half of the thirteenth; this reasoning, however, does not preclude a late thirteenth-century date.[91] In the absence of clearer evidence, therefore, a cautious approach is advisable, and the book must be dated either in the late thirteenth or early

88. *Tela,* 2: 1.

89. This work was probably written in the mid-thirteenth century. See the discussion and references in Rosenthal, *Sefer Yosef HaMeqanne,* pp. 15 ff.

90. See L. Zunz, *Zur Geschichte und Literatur* (Berlin 1845), p. 85 (cited also in M. Steinschneider, *Catalog der Hebräischen Handschriften in der Stadtbibliothek zu Hamburg und der sich anschliessenden in anderen Sprachen* [Hamburg, 1878], p. 72); A. Posnanski, *Schiloh. . .* (Leipzig, 1904), p. 148; J. Rosenthal, "Sifrut HaVikkuah HaAnti-Nozerit," *Areshet* 2 (1960): 173; Baron, op. cit., 9: 294. Zunz dates the work a bit earlier than the others. See especially Rosenthal's introduction to *Yosef HaMeqanne,* p. 15.

91. Urbach, op. cit., pp. 60, 76–77. The sources are *Sefer Yosef HaMeqanne* and the third part of Hebrew manuscript no. 53 in the Vittorio Emanuele library in Rome.

In an unpublished dissertation written after this book was substantially completed (*The Sefer Nitzahon: A Thirteenth Century Defense of Judaism,* New York University, October, 1974), A. Ehrman has argued for a date between 1220 and 1229 (pp. 4–5) or 1220 and 1235 (p. 163), and in a forthcoming article he has extended the final terminus to 1242. His most important arguments are the author's failure to mention the disputation at Paris in the short final paragraph on the Talmud and the fact that none of the few names that we can identify with certainty belongs to anyone who flourished in the second half of the century. Neither of these arguments strikes me as especially persuasive. That final passage on the Talmud in itself suggests a *terminus a quo* of 1240 or even a bit later, and since the events of 1240 were in France while N.V. is largely an anthology written in Germany, prudence would appear to dictate our allowing a decent interval after that date for its composition. Moreover, there is no internal evidence that *Yosef HaMeqanne* is an anthology as there is with respect to N.V. (see just below), but if we date N.V. before *Yosef HaMeqanne,* we would have to assume that much of the Gospel critique in the Rome manuscript version of the latter work was copied from N.V. or its source while the source of N.V. is lost. Finally, our anthology would have to be credited with a whole series of polemical firsts probably originating in lost sources. None of this is impossible, but it hardly seems like the course to choose in the absence of compelling evidence.

fourteenth century. As we shall see, however, the bulk of its material stems from an earlier period.

Several writers have assumed that the seventeenth-century scholar Wilhelm Schickard reported that the author of the *Nizzahon Vetus* was named R. Mattityahu; moreover, this assertion by Schickard is supposed to have been repeated by Wagenseil in the introduction to his edition of the book. The very brief introduction to the Jerusalem reprint of the Hebrew section of *Tela Ignea Satanae* attributes this view to Wagenseil, and this attribution has been repeated by at least two other scholars.[92] Judah Rosenthal also pointed to a book by Schickard that refers to a *Triumphator R. Matthias* (which Rosenthal evidently identified with the *Nizzahon Vetus*),[93] and he went on to note Schickard's unfinished *Nizzahon Beli Nezah sive Triumphator Vapulans* (Tübingen, 1623), which he described as a refutation of the *Nizzahon Vetus* that he was unable to consult. Finally, he suggested that the attribution of the *Nizzahon Vetus* to a R. Mattityahu may have resulted from a confusion with the fifteenth-century author of *Sefer Ahituv VeZalmon*, which was also called *Nizzahon*.[94]

It can now be asserted with full confidence that Rosenthal's conjecture is correct, but neither Schickard nor Wagenseil were guilty of confusing the two books. The *Nizzahon Beli Nezah*, which is available from the Bibliothèque Nationale in Paris, does not deal with the *Nizzahon Vetus* at all; the book Schickard had in fact was the later *Sefer Ahituv VeZalmon*, and his only error was in dating it somewhat too early. It was to this *Triumphator* that he referred in *Jus Regium Hebraeorum*, where he even cited a poetic passage from *Sefer Ahituv VeZalmon* that is nowhere in the *Nizzahon Vetus*. Moreover, a careful reading of Wagenseil's introduction shows that he never meant to say that Schickard had begun editing the same *Nizzahon* that he was now publishing. Wagenseil was merely reviewing the history of the publication of Jewish polemics called *Nizzahon*, and he therefore mentioned both Schickard's work and T. Hackspanius's edition of Mühlhausen's polemic.

92. J. Rosenthal, introduction to *Sefer Yosef HaMeqanne*, p. 15, note 15; J. Shatzmiller, op. cit., p. 126.

93. See Schickard's *Jus Regium Hebraeorum* (Leipzig, 1764), p. 449.

94. Rosenthal, loc. cit.

All references by seventeenth- and eighteenth-century scholars to a *Niẓẓaḥon* of R. Matthaeus are to the work utilized by
Schickard. Although there was some confusion about the various
books called *Niẓẓaḥon,* these writers generally knew that Schickard's
text was not the same as the book edited by Wagenseil. Nevertheless, neither they nor any subsequent scholar that I know recognized
the fact that Schickard's *Triumphator* was the same as *Sefer Aḥituv
VeẒalmon,* which some of them list separately.[95] In any event, there is
no tradition at all concerning the author of the *Niẓẓaḥon Vetus,* and any
search for the appropriate "R. Mattityahu" would be futile.

Although the identity of the author himself is unknown, it is
very likely that he was a German Jew. The book contains a substantial number of German words as well as a passage that says that
"the main body of the Gentiles is called Ashkenazim."[96] There is no
evidence for the assumption made by Loeb that the German words are
later interpolations;[97] consequently, although there is a great deal
(perhaps even a preponderance) of French material in the work, the
author himself almost certainly lived in Germany.[98]

The *Niẓẓaḥon Vetus* is largely an anthology whose two major
identifiable sources were *Sefer Yosef HaMeqanne* (at least in the section
on the Gospels)[99] and the third part of Hebrew manuscript number
53 in the Vittorio Emanuele library in Rome.[100] Its character as an anthology is clear not only from the fact that we have some of its
sources but from the occasional repetition of similar material in the
same section of the work[101] and from the scattered references to
issues that are not found in the book as matters discussed by the

95. See T. Hackspanius, *Liber Nizachon Rabbi Lipmanni* (Nuremberg, 1644), pp. 218–219; J.
Buxtorf, *Bibliotheca Rabbinica* (Herborn, 1708), pp. 145–47; J. C. Wolf, *Bibliotheca Hebraeae,* vol. 1 (Hamburg
and Leipzig), 1715, pp. 738–41, and cf. vol. 2 (Hamburg, 1721), pp. 1051, 1052, 1259; G. B. de Rossi,
Bibliotheca Judaica Antichristiana (Parma, 1800), pp. 63–64.

96. P. 156. Ashkenazim in this passage probably means specifically Germans; cf. the notes
there. See also Steinschneider, loc. cit.

97. Loeb, op. cit., p. 329.

98. So Zunz and Urbach, loc. cit. Posnanski, loc. cit., places the book in either northern
France or Germany.

99. Cf. below in the discussion of "The Text of the *Niẓẓaḥon Vetus.*"

100. Cf. note 91 and see the section on the text. Urbach (op. cit., p. 77) refers to N.V. as "an
anthology of all the [Ashkenazic] polemical literature of the twelfth and thirteenth centuries."

101. See especially pp. 48–51; 100–104.

author.[102] Nevertheless, the *Niẓẓaḥon Vetus* contains a great deal of material for which we cannot identify precise parallels, let alone word-for-word sources, and there is every reason to believe that the author added his own material and revised that of others. Consequently, although he followed the widespread medieval practice of making extensive, often verbatim, use of his predecessors' works, he deserves the title of author and not merely compiler.[103]

The array of arguments in the *Niẓẓaḥon Vetus* is almost encyclopedic, and the book is therefore an excellent vehicle for an analysis of virtually all the central issues in the Jewish-Christian debate during the twelfth and thirteenth centuries. In the Commentary I have tried to indicate many of the parallels with earlier works,[104] and these

102. See, e.g., p. 65, and cf. the notes to p. 122.

103. On the order of the book, see p. 388.

104. Both Jewish and Christian parallels have been cited only through the thirteenth century and have usually been arranged chronologically. I have tried to consult all Jewish polemics and what I hope is a representative selection of Christian works. (In some respects, Raymund Martini's *Pugio Fidei* can be regarded as the inauguration of a new era of Spanish polemic, and I have not cited it here even though its appearance toward the end of the thirteenth century makes it technically eligible for inclusion.) Needless to say, the citation of a parallel in the notes is not always intended to show that the author of N.V. was influenced by that particular source.

There is one recurring reference which requires some clarification at this point. The passage in Rome ms. 53, pp. 21a–21b, begins with a report that Pablo C(h)ristia(ni) arrived in Montpellier in 1269 and continues with a summary of Naḥmanides' earlier disputation with him; this summary is followed by an unrelated collection of miscellaneous arguments (pp. 22a–25b), some of which are in the standard form of a debate between a "believer" and a "heretic." (A lengthy section of this collection [pp. 22b–23a] is a reworking of a passage from Joseph Kimḥi's *Sefer HaBerit* [Talmage's edition, pp. 26–29].) Most of the material from p. 21a through p. 25a, line 16, was transcribed (though never published) by Adolph Posnanski and attributed by him to Mordecai b. Yehosafah of Avignon, apparently because Mordecai is known to have had a dispute with Pablo. Recently, Judah Rosenthal published this section of the manuscript (through p. 25b) as "Vikkuaḥ Dati Bein Ḥakham BeShem Menaḥem U-vein HaMumar VehaNazir HaDominiqani Pablo Christiani," *Hagut 'Ivrit BaAmeriqah*, ed. by M. Zohori, A. Tartakover, and H. Ormian (Tel Aviv, 1974), pp. 61–74. Rosenthal's ascription of the work to a "Menaḥem" is based on the remark that "these are the words of Menaḥem," which appears twice in the final passage (on "true Israel"); that passage, which begins on p. 25a, line 17, was omitted by Posnanski and placed instead on p. 25b in his edition of N.V. (It is clear that Rosenthal was unaware of Posnanski's edition, which is generally superior to his.) There is really no firm basis for any decision about the authorship of this collection (which also contains a note in a different hand that "these are the words of Asher" [p. 22a]), and I have cited it by giving the page number of the Rome ms. followed by references to both Posnanski's "Mordecai of Avignon" ms. and Rosenthal's "Menaḥem."

Finally—an apology. For a variety of not particularly good reasons, translations of biblical verses are not consistently based on a single translation of the Bible (although I have avoided inconsistent translations of any one verse). The enormous effort that would have been necessary to correct this defect did not seem worth the trouble, and the rabbinic observation that no two prophets prophesy in the same style no longer needs to be restricted to the original Hebrew text. (When the author of N.V. misquotes a verse or understands it in a peculiar fashion, I have, of course, deliberately "mistranslated" it in order to reflect his text or interpretation.)

similarities leave no doubt about the existence of a Jewish polemical tradition. Whether or not the author of the *Niẓẓaḥon Vetus* read such works as Kimḥi's *Sefer HaBerit* or Jacob ben Reuben's *Milḥamot HaShem,* their influence, or the influence of the tradition upon which they drew, certainly reached him. The argument that the christological interpretation of Isaiah 53:2-3 is inconsistent with the christological interpretation of Psalms 45:2-3 is not likely to have been made independently in *Milḥamot HaShem* and the *Niẓẓaḥon Vetus.*[105] Our author's discussion of signs in connection with the Immanuel prophecy is clearly indebted to a tradition represented in *Sefer HaBerit,* in Meir of Narbonne's *Milḥemet Miẓvah,* and in Moses of Salerno.[106] The fact that at least five Jewish polemicists cite the argument from the limited diffusion of Christianity specifically in connection with Psalms 72:11 is no coincidence.[107] These examples can easily be multiplied, and it is clear that both Christians and Jews had polemical traditions that drew upon the past but which remained flexible enough to accommodate, and sometimes even influence, new social, political, religious, and philosophical realities.

105. See the notes to p. 115.

106. See the notes to p. 101. Note immediately that parallels between *Mil. Miẓvah* and Moses of Salerno's *Ta'anot* result from the fact that much of the nonphilosophical section of the *Ta'anot* consists of verbatim copying from Meir's work. See page correlations in Joel Rembaum, "The Influence of *Sefer Nestor Hakomer* on Medieval Jewish Polemics," *Proceedings of the American Academy for Jewish Research* 45 (1978):167, note 54. (Those correlations require two corrections: "41-55" should be "40-55," and the material on Isa. 7:14 in *Mil. Miẓvah,* pp. 111a-12a, should be listed as appearing on pp. 33-34 of the Posnanski ms. Although I had noted almost all the relevant parallels between these two works, I had not realized the full extent of the copying before reading Rembaum's article.) Most of the remaining material in this section of the *Ta'anot* is found in the Rome ms. version of *Yosef HaMeqanne* and in N.V.; see the notes to pp. 180, 192, 193 and 198.

107. See the notes to p. 159.

THE
NIẒẒAḤON VETUS

TRANSLATION

[THE PENTATEUCH]

[1]

With good fortune I shall begin to write *The Book of Polemic*.

My help comes from the Lord, Creator of heaven and earth [Ps. 121:2].

5   Blessed is he who gives power to the weak and increases strength to them that have no might [Isa. 40:29].

[2]

Bereshit

A Gentile defiantly asked a Jew: Why did the Holy One, blessed be he, begin his Torah with the word *Bereshit* [in the begin-
10 ning]? The reason is that by doing so he referred to the son, the holy spirit, and the father. The Jew answered him: You have expounded the *bet, resh,* and *aleph* as you wished. Now finish the word and you will find *shin, yod, tav*; these too constitute an acrostic. Thus I knew how to uphold the truth. Furthermore, I might add that if you know a
15 man who persists in his error by expounding Scripture in a manner contradictory to our Torah, then with God's help I have many ways of silencing his error, upholding truth by means of acrostics as well.

[3]

The Gentile continued his defiant questioning and asked: Why did the Holy One, blessed be he, begin the Torah with a *bet* and
20 not with a different letter? Surely, he did so in order to make reference to the existence of two persons who are father and son, and it is also in reference to them that David said, "My God, my God, why have you forsaken me?" [Ps. 22:2]. Moreover, it is for this reason that you will find "the Lord God" as one name in a number of passages. And if
25 you will ask, "Where is the trinity?" the answer is that the spirit was not included because it is intertwined in the two of them—in the

father and son—and is a substance that is between them. Similarly you say of the two attributes law and mercy that the attribute of grace mediates between them.

5   One may respond to this: The reason he began the ten commandments with the word *anokhi,* which begins with the letter *aleph,* was to inform everyone that he is one and there is no second, that he cannot be separated into different bodies, that his attributes are not unequal in age as a father is older than a son, and that there is no separability in him as would be implied by the belief that the father

10 dwelt in heaven and the son went down to earth. Moreover, according to your belief that there are two persons equal in age, greatness, and wisdom, one could make a decree which the other might annul, and one could send abundant food to the world while the other sent famine.

[4]

15   "In the beginning God created" [Gen. 1:1]. The apostates may say: Why is the word "God" written in the plural form *Elohim* when it should have been written in the singular form *Eloah*? Surely it is because there are two—father and son.

     One may answer: *Elohim* is sometimes singular, as one can

20 determine by the context; for example, "Behold I have made you an *Elohim* to Pharaoh" [Exod. 7:1]. One may also answer that it is an expression of respect, for noblemen, who are flesh and blood, write of a single individual in the plural to this day; e.g., "We, so and so." How much more is it proper to refer to the Holy One, blessed be he, him-

25 self in the plural as a sign of respect. However, God is one and his name is one as is proven further on where it says, "He created" [Gen. 1:21, 27], and not, "They created." Moreover, it is written, "[I] stretch forth the heavens alone and spread out the earth by myself" [Isa. 44:24].

[5]

30   "Let us make man" [Gen. 1:26]. Answer the apostates: The Holy One, blessed be he, told the earth, "Let us make man between the two of us; you contribute your share—dust, and I my share—spirit." Indeed, Scripture [Gen. 2:7] goes on to explain, "And the

Lord God formed man of the dust of the ground"—this came from the
earth—"and he breathed into his nostrils the breath of life"—this is
the spirit from the Holy One, blessed be he. This, then, is the meaning of "in our image, after our likeness" [Gen. 1:26]: dust in your
5   image after your likeness, and spirit in my image after my likeness.
This too is the meaning of the verse, "By the sweat of your brow
shall you eat bread till you return to the ground, for out of it were you
taken" [Gen. 3:19], and of Solomon's words, "The dust shall return
to the earth as it was, and the spirit shall return unto God who gave
10 it" [Eccles. 12:7].

"Let us make man." The heretics say that "Let us make" implies two, and they are the father and son. You can put off such a heretic by answering: Indeed, the matter is as you say. The father told the
son, "My son, help me, and let you and I make man." However, the
15 son rebelled and did not wish to help his father, and so the father
made man alone without the son's help, as it is written, "And God
created man," with a singular rather than a plural verb. Consequently, the father became angry with his son and said, "If the time
should come when you need my assistance, I shall not help you just
20 as you have not helped me." So when the day came for the son to be
stoned and hanged, he cried out in a bitter voice, "My Lord, my Lord,
why have you forsaken me? Why are you so far from saving me . . .?"
and he begged for his help [Matt. 27:46]. Then the father told him,
"When I asked you to help me make man, you rebelled against me and
25 did not come to the aid of the Lord, and so my own power availed me
and I made him without you. Now you too help yourself, for I shall
not come to your aid."

[6]

Moreover, if he [i.e., the son] is God, why did he cover himself with flesh and why did he not appear publicly to renew his Torah
30 and give it openly so that the people of that generation would not err
and the people of the world not be misled? He should, on the contrary,
have done his deeds openly and in a clearly recognizable fashion so
that all would believe in him. Indeed, the loss that resulted from this
disguise outweighed the salvation; people refrained from believing in
35 him, since the disguise involved separation from holiness and purity

and association with what the Torah regards as stringent impurities.
See what is written of the time when the Torah was given: "Be ready
for the third day, do not approach a woman, for on the third day the
Lord will come down in the sight of all the people" [Exod. 20:15, 11].
5 Because of the imminent revelation of the Lord the people were sanctified in this manner. Consequently, how could this man be God, for
he entered a woman with a stomach full of feces who frequently sat
him down in the privy during the nine months, and when he was born
he came out dirty and filthy, wrapped in a placenta and defiled by the
10 blood of childbirth and impure issue. The Torah, on the other hand,
warns against approaching a menstruant woman, a woman who has
had an impure issue, and one who has just given birth, as it is written,
"And she shall continue in the blood of purification three and thirty
days; she shall touch no hallowed thing . . . until the days of her puri-
15 fication be fulfilled" [Lev. 12:4]. Hence he was not worthy of association with anything sacred.

You may argue that he was not defiled in her womb since
Mary had ceased to menstruate and it was the spirit that entered her;
subsequently, he came out unaccompanied by pain or the defilement
20 of blood. The answer is that you yourselves admit that she brought
the sacrifice of a childbearing woman. Now, it is clear that this sacrifice is brought as a consequence of impurity from the fact that the
same sacrifice of two turtle-doves or two pigeons is brought by a
leper, a woman who has had an impure issue, and one who has just
25 given birth. Indeed, to this day they call the day that she came to the
Temple and brought her sacrifice "Light" ["Lichtmess"], and they
fast for forty days in commemoration of the forty days that she remained impure from Christmas till "Light," as it is written, "If a
woman be delivered and bear a manchild, then she shall be unclean
30 seven days" [Lev. 12:2]. The additional "three and thirty days" [Lev.
12:4] make forty.

[7]

"And the Lord God formed man" [Gen. 2:7]. The heretics
speak irreverently of the two names "the Lord God" by saying that
they are father and son. The answer is: It is for this very reason that

it is written, "And God created man" [Gen. 1:27] without the second name, for in this way the Torah shows that God is one and not two.

[8]

Ask the Christians why they do not observe the Sabbath. It was, after all, on the seventh day that the Lord rested from all his
5   work, and it is written, "Remember the sabbath day to keep it holy. Six days shall you labor and do all your work, but the seventh day is a sabbath unto the Lord your God . . . for in six days the Lord made heaven and earth, the sea, and all that is in them, and rested on the seventh day; wherefore the Lord blessed the seventh day, and hal-
10 lowed it" [Exod. 20:8-11]. Moreover, you must admit that the Sabbath which we observe is the seventh day on which the Lord rested, for this is proven by the fact that the stones of the Sambation River rest, as you know, on our Sabbath. Furthermore, your own words force you to make this admission since you call it *septem die*. Now,
15 *septem* means seventh and *die* means day; thus, you call it the seventh day.

You might then argue that the one who was hanged changed the Sabbath to Sunday, which you call *Dominica*; nevertheless, by the fact that you do work on the Sabbath, when God commanded you not
20 to work, you violate and contradict the words of Moses. Further-more, even according to your view that the Sabbath has been trans-ferred to Sunday, why don't you stone those who violate it as the Israelites, commanded by God, did in the desert to the man found gathering sticks on the Sabbath?

25 The Christians continue their irreverent exegesis of the pas-sage dealing with the Sabbath by saying that the phrase "And on the seventh day God finished" [Gen. 2:2] implies that the work was com-pleted during the seventh day. The answer to this is in the adjoining passage: "And he rested on the seventh day from all his work which
30 he had made . . . and he hallowed it, for on it he rested from all his work . . ." [Gen. 2:2-3]. The interpretation of this passage is as fol-lows: "For on it he rested" since he had completed his work on the sixth day. Consequently, there was nothing left for him to do, for he had finished and concluded his work on the sixth day, and so he
35 rested on the seventh.

[9]

Ask the heretics: It is written in the portion of *Bereshit* that God said, "Behold, the man has become like one of us, [to know good and evil; and now lest he put forth his hand and take also of the tree of life, and eat,] and live for ever" [Gen. 3:22]. Now, why should the
5 Holy One, blessed be he, have been concerned and why should it have bothered him if man would live forever? It is, after all, a natural inclination for a man not to want his works to perish; if he plants a vineyard or tree he does not want it to dry up, and if he builds a house he does not want it to fall. However, the reason for God's concern
10 was that he foresaw that Jesus would attempt to mislead the world by saying he is God, and so the Holy One, blessed be he, decided that it would be better that men should die so that Jesus could be hanged without having eaten from the tree of life and all the world would know that he is not God.

[10]

Lekh Lekha
15

"Melchisedek king of Salem brought forth bread and wine, and he was priest of God the Most High" [Gen. 14:18]. The heretics say that this refers to Jesus; the bread refers to his body and the wine to his spilled blood. His body, moreover, was, as it were, eaten up
20 and tormented. Therefore, they ask what Melchisedek hinted to Abraham by giving him bread and wine. The answer is that he hinted to him that his children would eventually sacrifice libations and meal-offerings.

If the heretic will then ask why God should have commanded
25 such sacrifices, one may answer by asking why he chose an ox, sheep, goat, or birds as sacrifices. Why, too, did he command that blue, purple, or scarlet material as well as gold and silver be brought for the sanctuary, and why did he command us to bring the firstfruits of the earth? The intention in all this is only to have us obey his com-
30 mandments, as it is written, "Has the Lord as great delight in burnt-offerings and sacrifices as in hearkening to the voice of the Lord? Behold, to obey is better than sacrifice . . ." [1 Sam. 15:22]. One may

also answer that it is for the following reason that God requires
sacrifice: When a man sacrifices an animal, he thinks to himself, "I
am a greater animal than it, for I sinned, and because of this sin I am
bringing it; indeed, it would be more fitting to sacrifice the sinner
5   than the animal." Thus, as a result of this sacrifice, he will become
penitent.

[11]

"Whereby shall I know that I shall inherit it?" [Gen. 15:8]. He
may ask: This verse implies that Abraham did not believe in God
while an adjoining verse says, "And he believed in the Lord, and he
10   counted it to him for righteousness" [Gen. 15:6]. The answer is that
one can see Abraham's belief in God from the fact that God promised
him, "This man"—Ishmael—"shall not be your heir, but he that
shall come forth out of your own loins shall be your heir. And he
brought him forth outside and said . . . If you will be able to count the
15   stars, so shall your seed be" [Gen. 15:4-5]. This caused him to understand and to believe in God. Abraham, however, was a prophet, as it
is written, "Restore the man's wife, for he is a prophet" [Gen. 20:7],
and God showed him the four exiles of his children. He then saw that
they would have to remain in the fourth exile very long, and he feared
20   that they would give up hope of redemption; consequently, he asked
for a sign so that they would all know that they would ultimately
inherit the land. The heifer in this vision is Egypt, as it is written,
"Egypt is a very fair heifer" [Jer. 46:20]; the three she-goats are the
kingdom of Greece, as it is written, "The goat is king of Greece"
25   [Dan. 8:21]; the three rams are the kingdom of Media and Persia, as it
is written, "The ram which you saw with the horns represents the
kings of Media and Persia" [Dan. 8:20]; the turtledove (*tor*) is the
Ishmaelites who thresh the Jews like an ox which in Aramaic is
called *tora*; and the pigeon is Israel, who are forced to labor, as it is
30   written, "My dove in the clefts of the rock" [Song of Songs 2:14].

[12]

"And Abraham was ninety-nine years old when he was circumcised" [Gen. 17:24]. One may ask why God did not command him

to be circumcised at an earlier age. The answer is that he waited so
that the people of the world would see and learn from Abraham who,
although an old man, did not balk at circumcision.

[13]

Vayera Elav

5   "And behold, three men stood over against him" [Gen. 18:2].
The heretics say: "He saw three and prayed to one," and they are the
father, the son, and the impure spirit; he saw that the three are one
and prayed to him. In answering this question you can trip him up and
refute him with his own words by telling him: Of course Abraham
10   saw three, but he did not pay attention to them and prayed instead to
one, for God is one and his name is one. And this is precisely what we
do. This refutation is valid because according to their words, it
should have said, "He saw three and prayed to him," for only then
would it mean that the three were one and Abraham prayed to that
15   one. As it is, when it says that he prayed to one, the implication is
that this one is not one of the three.

       One may respond further: "And he lifted up his eyes and saw,
and behold, three men . . . and he saw them and ran to meet them"
[Gen. 18:2]. Why was it necessary to say "and he saw" twice? The
20   answer must be that the first time the phrase conveys its straightforward meaning while the second time it refers to the perception of
the heart; i.e., he understood in his heart that they were human
beings. This phrase has the same meaning in the verse, "And Jacob
saw that there was corn in Egypt" [Gen. 42:1]; he obviously did not
25   literally see this but rather perceived it in his heart.

       There is, moreover, no reason to wonder why Abraham did
not recognize that they were angels. In the story of Manoah, for example, it says, "Then the woman came and told her husband, saying,
A man of God came to me, and his countenance was like the counte-
30   nance of an angel of God, very terrible; but I asked him not whence he
was" [Judges 13:6]. Thus, although he appeared to her in the form of
an angel and although he later said, "Though you detain me, I will not
eat of your bread" [Judges 13:16] and ascended to heaven in a flame,
Manoah and his wife nevertheless believed that he was a human

being. Abraham, then, could certainly be expected to make this error
since they appeared to him in human form.

     Furthermore, if he considered them the father, the son, and the
impure spirit, why did he give them food? Does God eat and drink?
5 After all, in the story of Manoah it is written, "Though you detain me,
I will not eat of your bread" [Judges 13:16], while here it is written, "So
do, as you have said." And it is written, "And he stood by them under
the tree, and they did eat" [Gen. 18:5-8]. And if the heretic will say
that he gave them to eat in order to prefigure the son's future incarna-
10 tion when he will eat and drink, the answer is that in that case he
should have told one of them, "My lord, you eat and drink, for you are
the son." Furthermore, according to their view, all three should have
been one body, while these were three bodies and did not cleave
together.

15   Moreover, we must say that they were three separate beings
who performed three missions. One informed Sarah, saying, "At the
set time I will return unto you . . ." [Gen. 18:14]. Now, one angel does
not perform two missions so that we may know that the legions of
the Lord are numberless. Proof of this is furnished by the verse,
20 "And the two angels came to Sodom at evening" [Gen. 19:1], for the
third was no longer with them, having left after completing his
mission of informing Sarah. One of the remaining two rose up early
and overthrew Sodom, while the second rescued Lot, as it is written,
"And *he* said, Escape for your life" [Gen. 19:17]; the verse does not
25 say, "*They* said."

     If the heretic will ask you the meaning of the verse, "My lord
. . . pass not away, I pray you, from your servant" [Gen. 18:3], you
may answer that he said this to their leader, and the others were
included. And if he will then ask how Abraham knew who the leader
30 was, the answer is that he assumed that the one who passed before
them was the leader, as it is written, "And their king shall pass before them" [Mic. 2:13]. One may respond further: Abraham was
addressing God and asked him, "Do not, I pray you, pass from me,
for I must go and welcome guests," as it is written, "And the men
35 turned from thence and went to Sodom, but Abraham stood yet before
the Lord" [Gen. 18:22] who is one God.

"And behold, three men . . ." [Gen. 18:2]. They say in the Gospels, "He saw three and prayed to one." They thus refer the matter to the trinity saying that the three are the father, the son, and the holy spirit, who are one, as it is written, "And behold, three men,"
5   and it is written "My Lord, pass not, I pray you" [Gen. 18:3] in the singular. The answer is: According to you, they are four. Now tell me to which one he prayed, to the one who appeared to him alone, i.e., the Creator, or to his angel who was one of these three?

Moreover, what prayer did he say? And when he prayed, did
10 he do so with proper intent or as a blind man, understanding nothing? If you will say that he knowingly prayed to his Creator, then why did he prepare a meal for him, as it is written, "Make ready quickly three measures of fine meal . . . and he took curd and milk . . ." [Gen. 18:6-8]? Was Abraham ignorant of the fact that the Creator has no
15 need of food and drink? Furthermore, why did he not build him an altar as was his custom? And why did he say, "Satisfy your heart" [Gen. 18:5], for what sort of satiety can be attributed to God, of whom it is written, "And Lebanon is not sufficient to burn, [nor the beasts thereof sufficient for a burnt offering"] [Isa. 40:16]? There is, more-
20 over, an a fortiori argument from Moses and Elijah. Moses ascended on high and remained there forty days and forty nights without eating bread or drinking water, and had he remained there longer he would still not have grown hungry or thirsty since he was sustained by the divine glow, as it is written, "And they beheld God, and did eat and
25 drink" [Exod. 24:11], i.e., they took as much pleasure and delight as they would have from food and drink. Consequently, God himself would surely not require food.

Moreover, where do we find that bowing means prayer? Must you say that because he bowed to one, he also prayed to him? And if
30 you will argue that his prayer consisted of the verse, "My Lord, if I have found favor in your sight, pass not away, I pray you, from your servant," then the question of how he prepared him a meal must again be confronted.

Furthermore, where do we find a man addressing God in the
35 plural? He should have said, "Wash your feet and satisfy you heart" in the singular, just as he said, "Pass not away, I pray you, from your servant."

Indeed, the true explanation is clear. When Abraham spoke in the singular he was addressing his Creator and trying to persuade him to remain until he would receive the guests that he saw after God revealed himself. Then, Abraham went to welcome them, bowed to
5   them, and prepared them a meal.

The context further proves that one of them was sent to inform Sarah, as it is written, "I will return unto you" [Gen. 18:14], in the singular. This, then, was one of the three, and after he performed his mission he departed, as it is written, "And the two angels came to
10 Sodom at evening" [Gen. 19:1]. At that time, then, there were two and not three or one, as it is written, "And the men laid hold upon his hand, and upon the hand of his wife" [Gen. 19:16], as it is written, "For we will destroy this place" [Gen. 19:13]. Thus you have clear proof that they were three separate bodies, and each one peformed his
15 own mission.

[14]

"Then the Lord caused to rain upon Sodom and upon Gomorrah [brimstone and fire from the Lord out of heaven"] [Gen. 19:24]. Here the heretics irreverently say that "the Lord caused to rain" refers to the son and "from the Lord" refers to the father. The
20 answer is: If so, you admit that the son is only a messenger who can do nothing without the father's permission and command. Then according to you, rather than beseeching the son, it would be better for you to pray to the father who rules all and commands without being commanded.

25 If he will tell you that the father and son are inseparably one, answer him: Have you ever heard of someone commanding himself to do something? Moreover, since according to you "and the Lord caused to rain" refers to the son and "from the Lord" means from his father who empowered him to do this, then there must be two—the
30 one who gave the power and the one who received it—and so how can you say that the two are inseparably one? Furthermore, according to your view what could both the son and father do without the third, i.e., the spirit, whose absence means that there was no true divinity? And if the heretic will say that the spirit was with them, why was it
35 not mentioned separately as were the son and father? The verse, then,

means the following: "Then the Lord caused to rain" by means of the
clouds which are normally in charge of rain "brimstone and fire,"
even though this is not their natural custom; this thing occurred and
was decreed "from the Lord."

[15]

5   "And God tested Abraham" [Gen. 22:1]. The heretics ask
why God tested Abraham and Job; did he not know beforehand that
they would withstand these tests in the end? The answer is to be
found in what is said regarding Abraham, "Now I know that you are a
God-fearing man" [Gen. 22:12]. Did he not know this beforehand?
10   The meaning of the verse, then, must be as follows: Now I know how
to answer the stern principle and make this answer known to the
world.

[16]

         The heretics also say that this passage refers to the hanged
one who gave his life to atone for them, as it is written, "And he
15   offered it up for a burnt offering in the stead of his son" [Gen. 22:13].
Similarly, they say of the paschal lamb, concerning which it is written, "They shall take to them every man a lamb according to their
fathers' houses" [Exod. 12:3], that it prefigures the execution of the
hanged one. There are, indeed, many verses which they interpret as
20   references to the hanged one, and they tell us: Fools, we know that the
Torah was given to you and not to us; why, then, do you not perceive
its nature? Why do you not consider the apparently peculiar nature of
the laws which God commanded you, such as, "Eat not of it raw, nor
cooked at all with water . . . nor shall you break a bone of it"
25   [Exod. 12:9, 46]? What difference does it make whether or not it is
cooked with water? Indeed, there are many peculiarities in that passage, and what could be the reason for them? Are you truly animals
that you do not perceive what these things symbolize? [Indeed, it is
concerning this that Jeremiah said, "And I am like a sheep led to
30   slaughter; I did not know that they were hatching plots against me,
saying, 'Let us cut down the tree while the sap is in it; let us destroy
him out of the land of the living, so that his very name shall be forgotten' " (Jer. 11:19).]

The answer is: If your view is correct, then how could it be possible to maintain that Jeremiah said this of himself, compared himself to his Creator and claimed such glory for himself? Yet we must say that this was said of him, for the Jews did beat and chastise
5   him, as it is written, "Now it came to pass, when Jeremiah had made an end of speaking all that the Lord had commanded him to speak unto all the people, that the priests and the prophets and all the people took him, saying, You shall surely die" [Jer. 26:8], and it was only with difficulty that he was saved many times.
10   Now I shall explain the reason why they were commanded to observe all these laws. "They shall take to them every man a lamb according to their fathers' houses, a lamb for a household" [Exod. 12:3]: The requirement that each household have only one refers to the fact that Abraham's household had only one, i.e., Isaac, who was
15   especially set aside. "A yearling" [Exod. 12:5]: Why a yearling? The purpose is to show that through these sacrifices Israel will be free of all sin and iniquity like a one-year-old, as it is written with regard to Saul, "Saul was one year old when he became king" [1 Sam. 13:1]. Now, was Saul one year old when he became king? It is written, after
20   all, that "he was taller than any of the people from his shoulders and upward" [1 Sam. 10:23]. Furthermore, does one enthrone an infant of one year? Rather, the verse means that he was as free of sin as an infant of one year.
        Moreover, if you were right and this passage prefigured the
25   hanged one, then it would imply that many Jesuses would be destined to be born and hanged, inasmuch as God commanded the Jews to take not one lamb but many.
        "And they shall take of the blood" [Exod. 12:7] refers to three drops: "Put it on the lintel" refers to one, "and on the two side-
30   posts" refers to two more. Thus the passage refers to three types of blood—[the blood of the paschal lamb], of circumcision, and of the menstruant woman.
        "Nor cooked at all with water" [Exod. 12:9] refers to the exile where they take us and "cook" us, as it is written, "We have gone
35   through fire and water" [Ps. 66:12].
        "The head with its legs and with the inwards thereof" [Exod. 12:9] indicates that the exile oppresses us from head to foot, as it is

written, "From the sole of the foot even unto the head there is no soundness in it, but wounds, and bruises, and putrifying sores" [Isa. 1:6].

"They shall eat it with unleavened bread and bitter herbs"
5 [Num. 9:11; cf. Exod. 12:8] refers to the fact that the nations subject us to hard work, embitter our lives, and revile us by saying that we eat human beings and the blood of Christian children. Indeed, the heretic may attempt to bolster this last assertion by arguing that Ezekiel refers to such a practice when he says to the land of Israel,
10 "Thus said the Lord, Because they say unto you, You devour up men, and have bereaved your nations . . ." [Ezek. 36:13]. The people of Israel are also called "land," as it is written, "You shall be a delightful land" [Mal. 3:12]; thus, the verse in Ezekiel must refer to the people of Israel. The answer to this argument is that Scripture can be
15 cited to prove that they too eat human beings, as it is written, "For they have eaten up Jacob" [Jer. 10:25].

"But that which remains of it until the morning you shall burn with fire" [Exod. 12:10]. This means that one should not remain without the sufferings of the exile, for one who does "remain" with-
20 out suffering "until the morning," i.e., the morning of the redemption, shall "burn with fire," i.e., he will fall into hell.

"And thus shall you eat it: with your loins girded etc." [Exod. 12:11]. The purpose of this commandment was that they be prepared to leave quickly, but they were not commanded to eat it this way in
25 future years.

"Nor shall you break a bone of it" [Exod. 12:46] signifies that although the Jews will be in exile, the Holy One, blessed be he, will preserve and save them, as it is written, "Many are the afflictions of the righteous man, but the Lord delivers him out of them all. He keeps
30 all his bones, etc." [Ps. 34:20-21]. Even the bone, then, will be guarded.

[17]

They also ask: Did Abraham do such a great thing when he was willing to slaughter his son pursuant to a divine command? Why, there is not an evil man in the world who would refrain from doing so if the Holy One, blessed be he, appeared to him in all his glory and told him to slaughter his son. The answer is that it was nevertheless a great thing, for he was an only son in their old age, and yet they did not hesitate or hold him back. This lack of hesitation is

5   confirmed when we ask why Abraham did not realize that he was only being tested. After all, God had already promised him, "For in Isaac shall seed be called to you" [Gen. 21:12], and how could he contradict his earlier promise? It must be, then, that Abraham did not stop to think the matter through at all. This last question, however, might

10   also be answered by assuming that Abraham thought that God, who quickens the dead, would resurrect Isaac.

[18]

Toledot Yitzḥak

    "And the first one came out ruddy" [Gen. 25:25]. The heretic might point out that the Holy One, blessed be he, is also called ruddy,

15   as it is written, "My beloved is bright and ruddy" [Song of Songs 5:10]. This verse, then, means that he who is first of all ancient things and is called ruddy came out of a stomach but was not born in the strict sense. Silence this heretic by reminding him that both God and Nebuchadnezzar are called "lion" in Scripture, the former in the

20   verse, "The lion has roared, who will not fear?" [Amos 3:8] and the latter in the verse, "The lion is come up from his thicket" [Jer. 4:7]. Does the fact that Nebuchadnezzar is called a lion mean that he is particularly beloved by God? The truth of the matter is that Esau was called Edom, i.e., ruddy, because of the evil that would befall him, as

25   it is written, "Who is this that comes from Edom with dyed garments?" [Isa. 63:1]. This implies that God will kill Edom.

[19]

    "The voice is the voice of Jacob, but the hands are the hands of Esau" [Gen. 27:22]. Consequently, when it thunders they make the sign of the cross with their hands as a sign that Esau's hands were

30   always committing murder. We, however, say only prayers and blessings as a sign that the voice is Jacob's.

[20]

"I am Esau your firstborn" [Gen. 27:19]. One can say that
Jacob did not lie. In fact, this can be said without distorting the simple
meaning of the verse, but by explaining it as follows: I am Esau your
firstborn, for Esau sold him the birthright in a manner as clear as day.
5 It is, indeed, clear that Jacob was careful not to state an outright lie
from the fact that when Isaac asked him, "Are you my son Esau?" he
responded, "I am," [Gen. 27:24] and not, "I am Esau."

They go on to say that because Jacob obtained the blessings
through trickery, they were fulfilled for the Gentiles and not the
10 Jews. The answer is that even the prophet Amos prayed for Jacob, for
he is in possession of the truth, as it is written, "You will grant truth
to Jacob and mercy to Abraham, which you have sworn unto our
fathers" [Mic. 7:20]. That is, had not the truth been with Jacob, then
you would not have sworn to our fathers.

[21]

15 ### *Vayeẓe Ya'aqov*

On most of the Gentile holidays, they read this chapter and
bark it. Ask them the following: It is written, "And he took of the
stones of the place" [Gen. 28:11], which implies that there were many
stones, and later it is written, "And he took the stone that he had put
20 under his head" [Gen. 28:18], which implies that there was only one.
Moreover, it is written that "He called the name of that place Bethel"
[Gen. 28:19], and of that very place it is written, "And he was afraid
and said, How full of awe is this place! This is none other than the
house of God, and this is the gate of heaven" [Gen. 28:17]. Thus, he
25 prophesied that Bethel would be the house of God and the gate of
heaven from which prayer would be received. If so, however, then
why did Abraham say, "In the mount where the Lord is seen" [Gen.
22:14] of Mount Moriah in Jerusalem, thereby indicating that the
Temple would be built there? In fact, R. Judah said that it was on this
30 basis that Jeroboam argued that the Temple should really be in
Bethel, and thus he caused the Jews to sin, putting one calf in Bethel
and the other in Dan.

[22]

Vayeshev Ya'aqov

The heretics say: "And they dipped the coat in the blood" [Gen. 37:31]; this story of Joseph prefigures the hanged one. For example, the fact that Joseph's mother was barren prefigures Mary, 5 who was a virgin. The answer is: How can one draw such an analogy between the living and the dead? Joseph was not killed; they merely desired to kill him. Jesus, on the other hand, was actually hanged. If the heretic will reply that only the human part of Jesus was killed, the answer is that if this is so, how did he differ from other men? In other 10 men, too, the flesh dies while the soul goes either to paradise or to hell.

[23]

"No, I will go down mourning to my son in *sheol*" [Gen. 37:35]. On the basis of this verse the heretics say that Jacob descended to hell, for because of Adam's sin it was decreed that all men, good or 15 evil, must descend there. The answer is: If so, they contradict their own books, for it says in their book of errors that Jesus told his students, "I have come for sinners and not for the righteous since they do not need me" [Matt. 9:11]. Thus we see that even according to their own words written in their own books Jacob and other righ- 20 teous men did not descend to hell nor did they need Jesus' advent and salvation. Moreover, the view that all were damned is untenable in light of the verse, "I will praise you, O Lord my God, with all my heart, and I will glorify your name for evermore; for great is your mercy toward me, and you have delivered my soul from the lowest 25 hell" [Ps. 86:12-13].

One can also answer as follows: Does every *sheol* in Scripture mean hell? After all, it is written, "What man lives, and shall not see death? Shall he deliver his soul from the hand of *sheol*?" [Ps. 89:49]. Similarly, it is written, "For the living know that they shall die" 30 [Eccles. 9:5], for they shall all become dust, as it is written, "For dust you are, and to dust you shall return" [Gen. 3:19]. Now, according to their view, is it possible that everyone is worthy of going to hell with

no possibility of escaping? Is there no righteous man on earth who is
not worthy of escaping? Moreover, can it be that Job, who said, "O
that you would hide me in *sheol*" [Job 14:13], was desirous of descending into hell? Job, rather, wished that he would be buried and hidden in
5   the earth until the Lord's wrath would pass. Similarly, we must say
that the word *sheol* used by Jacob also means grave.

Indeed, *sheol* sometimes means hell, but this is only when the
context proves that this is the meaning. For example, it is written in
Ezekiel concerning the punishment of Egypt, "Thus said the Lord
10   God: In the day when he went down to *sheol* I caused a mourning; I
covered the deep for him" [Ezek. 31:15]. "I covered the deep for him"
proves that *sheol* in the beginning of the verse means hell. Similarly, in
the verse, "You should be brought down to *sheol,* to the sides of the
pit" [Isa. 14:15], the words "the sides of the pit" prove that *sheol*
15   means hell. Thus, every *sheol* in Scripture means grave except in
cases like these where the context proves that it means hell.

[24]

"While she was in labor, one of them put out his hand" [Gen.
38:28]. On the basis of this verse, the heretics say that although the
Jews came before the children of Esau and took the blessings from
20   them, it appears that the birthright nevertheless remained with Esau.
The answer is that the Holy One, blessed be he, himself testifies that
"Israel is my firstborn son" [Exod. 4:22], and the proof is that David,
Solomon, and the Messiah come from the seed of Perez.

[25]

"On the vine were three branches" [Gen. 40:10]. The heretics
25   distort this passage and refer it to the hanged one, arguing that just as
the chief baker was hanged, so Jesus was hanged. Furthermore, they
say, the three openwork baskets represent the three days that he was
buried. You may answer that just as the bread of the chief baker was
not seemly, so the Torah that Jesus wanted to give was not proper
30   and seemly. Moreover, just as the chief baker was hanged and passed
away from the world, so Jesus was hanged and passed away from the
world. Furthermore, one may respond: Fools, why should you compare him with the chief baker? Compare him instead to Absalom, who

was a king's son. And just as the latter was a deceiver, as it is written, "So Absalom stole the hearts of the men of Israel" [2 Sam. 15:6], so was Jesus. And just as Absalom rebelled against his father, so Jesus rebelled against his father in heaven.

5   Now, the explanation of this passage is as follows: The vine is Jerusalem, as it is written, "He tethers his ass to a vine" [Gen. 49:11]. The three branches are the Temple, king, and high priest. "It had barely budded" [Gen. 40:10] refers to the young priests, as it is written of Aaron's staff, "It had brought forth sprouts and produced
10   blossoms" [Num. 17:23]. "Its clusters ripened into grapes" [Gen. 40:10] refers to the libations.

[26]

Vayeḥi Ya'aqov

The apostates say: If "there is a mother to tradition," then one should consider the fact that in the verse, "Then Israel bowed at
15   the head of the bed" [Gen. 47:31], the Hebrew word for bed (*mittah*) is written without a *yod* and can therefore be read *matteh*, which means staff. Consequently, it is probable that it was customary to place a cross at the head of dying men, and it was to the cross that Jacob bowed. One may answer them according to their own foolishness
20   and say that Jacob was distraught as a result of his illness, and he therefore bowed to the cross. But when he came to his senses, he changed his mind and regretted what he had done, as it is written, "And he sat up on the bed (or staff)" [Gen. 48:2]. Thus, Jacob put it under his anus.

[27]

25   "He crossed his hands, for Manasseh was the firstborn" [Gen. 48:14]. The heretics say that he made a kind of cross with his two arms by placing one on the other, and thus he blessed him. Answer them: Therefore, "Joseph thought it wrong and said, Not so, father" [Gen. 48:17-18], it is wrong to do this. And Jacob answered
30   him, "I know, my son, I know" [Gen. 48:19] that it is wrong to do this, but I was forced to cross my hands because the younger brother will be the greater and I must therefore put my right hand on his head

even though he is standing to my left. I did not, therefore, do it with
the intention of making a cross.

[28]

A certain apostate argued that the Hebrew verse, "Until Shilo
comes and to him . . ." (*ad ki Yavo Shiloh velo* [Gen. 49:10]) constitutes
5   an acrostic for Jesus (*Yeshu*). The answer to this is in the very same
verse, for the Hebrew verse, "The scepter shall not depart from
Judah, nor the ruler's staff from between his feet, until Shilo comes
and to him . . ." is an acrostic of the Hebrew phrase, "There is no
blemish as evil as Jesus." Furthermore, the phrase "Shilo comes and
10 the homage of peoples shall be his" yields the acrostic, "Jesus will
lead them astray."

"The scepter (*shevet*) shall not depart from Judah nor the
ruler's staff (*meḥoqeq*) from between his feet." This means that exile
will not cease from the tribe (*shevet*) of Judah nor the error of Jesus,
15 who was fastened (*meḥuqqaq*) with nails between his feet, until Shiloh,
i.e., the Messiah, comes, and the homage of the peoples will be his, as
it is written, "And many people will go and say, Come ye and let us go
up to the . . . house of the God of Jacob" [Isa. 2:3].

The heretics, however, say that the verse means "until the
20 messenger," i.e., Jesus, "comes"; then the kingdom of Judah will
cease. And so, indeed, it came to pass that when Jesus came the kingdom of Judah ceased. Moreover, it is written, "And the homage of
peoples shall be his"; i.e., the nations shall congregate before him
and turn to him. Furthermore, "he tethers his ass to a vine" [Gen.
25 49:11] refers to Jesus, who entered Jerusalem on a donkey.

The answer is that they are refuted by their own words, for
how can one maintain that the kingdom of Judah did not cease until
Jesus? There was, after all, no king in Israel from the time of
Zedekiah, for even in the days of the second Temple there was no
30 king in Israel but only governors subordinate to the kings of Media,
Persia, or Rome. Now, a long time passed between Zedekiah and the
birth of Jesus, and so how can the verse say that the kingdom would
not depart from Judah until Jesus comes? Furthermore, what relationship is there between "Shiloh" and Jesus' name?

35   Moreover, the inference that there would be a king in Israel

until the advent of Shiloh, i.e., Jesus, but afterwards the kingdom would cease and no king would arise again is refuted by the following prophecy of Jeremiah: "And I will gather the remnant of my flock [out of all countries whither I have driven them, and will bring them again
5 to their folds; and they shall be fruitful and increase. And I will set up shepherds over them who shall feed them: and they shall fear no more, nor be dismayed, neither] shall they be lacking, says the Lord. Behold, the days come, says the Lord, that I will raise [unto David a righteous branch, and a king shall reign and prosper, and shall exe-
10 cute judgment and justice in the earth. In his days Judah shall be saved, and Israel] shall dwell safely" [Jer. 23:3-6].

If he will then tell you that all of these verses refer to Jesus, who stemmed from the tribe of Judah and the house of David, ask him how he knows this genealogy. After all, in all the genealogies of
15 Matthew and Luke one does not find that of Jesus and Mary, for it is written in the Gospel of Matthew, "So-and-so begat so-and-so, and so-and-so begat so-and-so" until "Jacob begat Joseph *virum Mariae*," i.e., the husband of Mary [Mat. 1:2-16]. Now, if, as you say, Jesus was not Joseph's son, then he has no relationship to this genealogy.
20 If, however, you trace his lineage through Joseph, then you must admit that he had a father. But unless you trace his lineage through Joseph, how can you prove that he stemmed from Judah and David?

Moreover, it is written, "In his days Judah shall be saved, and Israel shall dwell safely" [Jer. 23:6], yet from the time of this Jesus
25 we, Judah and Israel, have wandered about and been killed more than we were before. He may then tell you that the Judah and Israel mentioned in this verse are the believers in Jesus, who indeed dwell safely; the verse, however, says, "And I will gather the remnant of my flock out of all countries whither I have driven them" [Jer. 23:3].
30 Now, to what countries has the nation believing in his divinity, namely Christendom, been driven? There is no doubt, therefore, that the verse refers to the dispersed Jews whom the Holy One, blessed be he, will ultimately gather together.

The final section of this verse can also be explained satis-
35 factorily even if one grants their basic interpretation. This then is the exegesis of the verse: "The scepter shall not depart from Judah"

means that sometimes there will be kings in Judah and sometimes
only *meḥoqeqim*, i.e., rulers (cf. the verse, "By the lawgiver [*meḥoqeq*]
with their staffs" [Num. 21:18]) such as princes, communal leaders,
and rabbis. All of these, however, will be within Israel and not exer-
5   cise hegemony over the nations. Sometimes, indeed, the kings will
rule over the nations as well, but the *meḥoqeq* will not rule over the
nations at all. However, when the messenger, i.e., Elijah, will come,
as it is written, "Behold, I will send you Elijah the prophet before the
coming of the [great and dreadful] day of the Lord" [Mal. 3:23], then
10   "the homage of the peoples shall be his," as it is written, "And many
people shall go and say, Come and let us go up to . . . the house of the
God of Jacob" [Isa. 2:3]. At that time, the kings shall indeed rule over
all.

R. Isaac the proselyte said: According to your interpretation
15   of this verse, the advent of Jesus marks the end of the Davidic kingdom, yet you refer the verse "of the increase of his government and
peace there shall be no end" [Isa. 9:6] to Jesus. This would imply that
his advent would mark the establishment of the Davidic kingdom, as
it is written in that verse, "Upon the throne of David and upon his
20   kingdom, to order it and to establish it with judgment and with justice
from henceforth even forever."

Moreover, R. Samuel interprets "Shiloh" to mean peace and
quiet, as in the verse "her enemies are at peace" [Lam. 1:5]; i.e.,
when the Messiah comes there will be peace and quiet.

[29]

25   "He crouches, lies down like a lion" [Gen. 49:9]. The heretics
say: Just as a lioness crouches over her cubs after giving birth, and
the young are dead for three days until they come to life as a result of
their mother's warmth, so Jesus remained in his grave for three days
until his father revived him on the third day. The answer is: Fools! Do
30   you really think that all these prophecies were restricted to the kingdom of Judah alone? They were intended for all Israel as well, for
Balaam, clearly referring to all Israel, said, "God who freed them
from Egypt is for them like the horns of the wild ox. . . .They crouch,
they lie down like a lion. . . ." [Num. 24:8-9]. And if you ask how we
35   explain this parable, the answer is that we too are like the dead in our

exile, as it is written, "He has set me in dark places like the dead of old" [Lam. 3:6], and it is written, "On the third day he will raise us up and we shall live" [Hos. 6:2].

[30]

Ve'elleh Shemot

5   "And behold there was a bush all aflame, yet the bush was not consumed" [Exod. 3:2]. They say that this refers to the one who was hanged. The answer is that it refers to the exile, as it is written, "In all their affliction he was afflicted, and the angel of his presence saved them" [Isa. 63:9]. That is why he revealed himself at the bush,

10   as it is written, "I am with him in trouble" [Ps. 91:15]. And in the blessing of Joseph it says, ". . . and the favor of the Dweller in the bush, may these rest on the head of Joseph [Deut. 33:16]." Now why did he bless Joseph and not the others in his capacity as Dweller in the bush? Surely because Joseph suffered affliction and was sold as a

15   slave to the Egyptians.

[31]

       "Make someone else your messenger" [Exod. 4:13]. They say that this was said about the son. The answer is: Note that the passage continues, "The Lord became angry [with Moses, and he said, There is your brother Aaron the Levite.] He, I know, speaks readily"

20   [Exod. 4:14]; i.e. he is worthy of performing my mission and not Jesus. So you see that you should refrain from making any further shameful remarks. Moreover, one may refute the argument that this verse refers to Jesus because he is called a messenger, as it is written, "Until Shiloh comes" [Gen. 49:10], by arguing that it refers to

25   Elijah, of whom it is said, "Behold, I send you Elijah the prophet" [Mal. 3:23].

[32]

       "The magicians did the like with their spells" [Exod. 8:3, 14]. R. Abraham the proselyte proved from here that Jesus did not know the secret name of God, for it was not known even in the generation of

30   Moses, which was a holy one, and certainly not thereafter. Thus, all

he did must have been done by magic. Indeed, it is written in the Gospels that he was in Egypt for two years, and there he must have learned magic, as the Rabbis say, "Ten measures of magic came down into the world; Egypt took nine and the rest of the world—
5   one."

[33]

Bo El Par'oh

"And apply [the blood] to the lintel and to the two doorposts" [Gen. 12:22]. They say that the blood in these three places formed a cross and that is why they were saved. The answer is that this is not
10   the meaning. What God meant, rather, was that he would judge the Jews innocent when he would see the three dabs of blood on the entrance, for they symbolize the blood of Abraham's circumcision, of the binding of Isaac when Abraham was willing to slaughter his son, and of the paschal lamb. Indeed, it is these three types of blood that
15   are also referred to in the verse, "And I saw you polluted in your blood"—one—"and I said to you, In your blood, live!"—two—"and I said to you, In your blood, live!"—three [Ezek. 16:6].
     "And apply. . . ." It was because God knew that people would err by following the cross that he did not command that blood be
20   placed on the threshold (*Dorschwell* in German). Thus, he omitted the fourth corner so that there would be no cross here and no crucifixion.

[34]

"Your lamb shall be without blemish, a yearling male. . . . You shall keep watch over it until the fourteenth day [of this month]" [Exod. 12:5-6]. The heretics say that this refers to Jesus, who was
25   crucified the day before Passover. The answer is: What reference is there here to Jesus, who was thirty-three years old when he was hanged? Moreover, it says here, "And they shall slaughter it" [Exod. 12:6], which means at the neck, while he was crucified with nails. Furthermore, according to their opinion that the crucifixion was the
30   result of the divine will, why were those who killed him punished for their deed as it is written in their Scriptures that the Jews received retribution for having harmed him? Is one who carries out the com-

mand of the King and his will worthy of punishment? Moreover, it is written here, "And all the aggregate community of the Israelites shall slaughter it in the afternoon" [Exod. 12:6], while Jesus was hanged in the morning, for all executions took place in the morning before the
5 time of eating, as it is written, "House of Israel, execute judgment in the morning" [Jer. 21:12]. And to their argument that the verse "nor shall you break a bone of it" [Exod. 12:46] refers to Jesus who was crucified without the breaking of a bone, you may respond by asking why the verse should find it necessary to mention this. That, after all,
10 is the case of all people executed by a court; their bones are never broken. The correct interpretation of this verse and passage is quite different.

[35]

Vayehi Beshallaḥ

Here the heretics say that all Israel was baptized in the sea in
15 accordance with their impure practice, but we have already explained why God commanded immersion.

[36]

"They came to Marah. . . . So he cried out to the Lord, and the Lord showed him a piece of wood; he threw it into the water and the water became sweet" [Exod. 15:23–25]. They say that the wood was a
20 cross, and that is why the water became sweet. The answer is: On the contrary, it was because of the cross that the water was bitter and dirty, and so "the Lord showed him a piece of wood" and told him, "See, this wood is the cause." So Moses took it and threw it into the depths of the sea so that they might all be able to drink, as it is writ-
25 ten, "And the water became sweet." This is how you should answer them in accordance with their error.

[37]

Vayishma' Yitro

"Remember the Sabbath day . . ." [Exod. 20:8]. The heretics say that the proper interpretation is not that work is prohibited but that one must not sin. This would mean that it is prohibited to sin only on the Sabbath but the rest of the week it is permitted.

[38]

Ve'elleh HaMishpatim

"I am sending an angel before you to guard you [on the way
5   and to bring you to the place which I have made ready.] Pay heed to him and obey him. Do not defy him, for he will not pardon your offenses, since my name is in him; but if you obey him [and do all that I say, I will be an enemy to your enemies and a foe to your foes]" [Exod. 23:20-22]. The heretics say that this refers to Jesus. The
10   answer is: We see that Moses and all Israel were not satisfied with him and were unwilling to accept him or follow him, for the angel mentioned here is the same as the one referred to in a subsequent passage that reads, "I will send an angel before you, and I will drive out [the Canaanites] . . ." [Exod. 33:2]. And there it is written, "And
15   he (Moses) said to him (God), Unless you go in the lead, do not make us leave this place. For how shall it be known [that your people have gained your favor unless you go with us] . . ." [Exod. 33:15-16]. And it is written, "Pray, let the Lord go in our midst" [Exod. 34:9]. We see, then, that they did not accept him, and so how can we do so? More-
20   over, you see with your own eyes that they did not accept the messenger or agree to go in his ways, but they chose the one who sent him instead; how, then, can you say that the sender and the messenger are one? Furthermore, it is written, "If you do all that I say, I will be an enemy to your enemies and a foe to your foes." Was
25   he, then, unable to love or hate or be an enemy independently of his sender? If so, what sort of divinity did he possess? Finally, here it is written, "He will not pardon your offenses," while of the God of heaven it is written, "Preserving kindness for the thousandth generation, forgiving iniquity and transgression" [Exod. 34:7]. It is clear,
30   then, that Scripture speaks of an ordinary angel, and that is why it says, "If you do all that I say, I will be an enemy to your enemies and a foe to your foes," for an angel can perform only his mission, and he was sent "to bring you to the place which I have made ready." "For he

will not pardon your offenses, since my name is in him"; i.e., this is part of his mission. Therefore, I warn you, "Pay heed to him. . . ."

[39]

Ki Tissa [*until the end of the Torah*]

"And the people saw that Moses delayed [in coming down
5 from the mountain]" [Exod. 32:1]. The heretics say that Moses was a sinner and a liar for not coming punctually. Why did he delay? The answer may be found in a rabbinic midrash: "For this man Moses" [Exod. 32:1]: it should merely have said, "Moses—we do not know what has happened to him," since he was not there. The use of the
10 demonstrative indicates that Satan showed them something that looked like Moses. Moreover, the "mixed multitude" led them astray, and so the transgression was not basically the fault of the Israelites; this multitude, rather, was the cause of all the evil, as it is written elsewhere, "The rifraff in their midst felt a gluttonous
15 craving" [Num. 11:4].
      "Come, make us a god" [Exod. 32:1]; i.e., cherubim.
      R. Nathan Official answered the priests who asked him, "Why did you make the golden calf?" He told them, "I too ask this question. After all, Moses called them a 'wise and understanding
20 people' [Deut. 4:6], for they saw the miracles and wondrous deeds of the Lord when he took them out of Egypt and gave them manna and quail, and they obeyed him when he gave them the Torah and when they saw his glory upon the sea and said, 'This is my God and I will glorify him' [Exod. 15:2]. Yet afterwards they erred in following the
25 golden calf and saying, 'This is your god, O Israel!' [Exod. 32:4]. Why, the worst fool would not be guilty of such idiocy." They were silent and gave no answer.
      He went on, "Now I shall tell you what explanation I would suggest in this matter. When they saw the calf walking by itself
30 and grazing in the pasture, as it is written, 'They exchanged my glory for the similitude of an ox that eats grass' [Ps. 106:20], they said to themselves, 'There is nothing in the world so pure and clean as gold. Perhaps the spirit of God has entered it and it possesses the holy spirit.' "

The priests told him, "You have spoken well; this was undoubtedly their error."

He replied, "Accursed are you blind men who have eyes but
5 do not see how you will be judged and entrapped in hell. Why, an a
fortiori argument applies here: They erred in worshiping a clean thing
like gold, and yet their iniquity was marked before God who said,
"When I make an accounting, I will bring them to account for their
sins" [Exod. 32:34] and refused to grant them complete forgiveness.
10 Certainly, then, you who err in saying that something holy entered
into a woman in that stinking place—for there is nothing in the world
as disgusting as a woman's stomach, which is full of feces and urine,
which emits discharge and menstrual blood and serves as the recep-
tacle for man's semen—you will certainly be consumed by "a fire not
15 blown" [Job 20:26] and descend to deepest hell.

[40]

"He put a veil over his face" [Exod. 34:3]. The heretics say
that this alludes to the curtain hung over our face, i.e., to the fact that
we do not understand the commandments of God. They are mistaken,
however, because its real purpose is to serve as an indication that one
20 should not believe in the hanged one. For if as a result of a face-to-
face conversation with God the face of Moses, who was flesh and
blood, shone to the point where people were afraid to approach him,
then the divine presence itself would certainly do so. Jesus' face,
then, should have shone from one end of the earth to the other. In fact,
25 however, no light radiated from his face any more than it does from
anyone else, so that one ought not to believe in him, for it was all
sorcery.

[41]

"Moses could not enter the Tent of Meeting . . . and the
presence of the Lord filled the Tabernacle" [Exod. 40:35]. The evil
30 King Henry once called Rabbi Kalonymus of Spires after the former
had completed the building of the ugly church in Spires. The king
asked him, "In what way was the building of the Temple greater than
this so that several books should have been written about it?"

He answered, "My lord, if you will permit me to speak and

swear that you will not harm me, then I shall explain it to you."

The king replied, "I swear. You may rely on my royal faithfulness that no evil will befall you."

Rabbi Kalonymus then told him, "If you would combine the
5 money that you have already spent with all the gold and silver remaining in your treasury you would still be unable to hire sufficient
workers and craftsmen to supervise and perform the work, for it is
written, 'And Solomon had seventy thousand that bore burdens and
eighty thousand hewers in the mountains' [1 Kings 5:29], and the
10 Chronicler adds, 'And three thousand six hundred to oversee them'
[2 Chron. 2:1]. Moreover, they labored eight years to build the
Temple, something that you did not do for this church. And regarding
the time when Solomon completed the building, see what is written:
'And the priests were unable to stand and minister because of the
15 cloud, for the glory of the Lord had filled the house of the Lord' [1
Kings 8:11]. In this case, however, if one were to load a donkey with
vomit and filth and lead him through the church, he would remain
unharmed."

The king replied, "If not for my oath, I would have you
20 decapitated."

[42]

"You shall not offer to the Lord anything with its testes
bruised or crushed or torn or cut" [Lev. 22:24]. This is how I confute
the heretics and priests who assert that they refrain from being fruitful and multiplying: They say, " 'For thus said the Lord to the
25 eunuchs (*sarisim*). . .: Even unto them will I give in my house and within my walls a place and a name better than of sons and daughters; I
will give them an everlasting name that shall not be cut off' [Isa.
56:4–5]. But it is forbidden to practice castration, as it is written,
'You shall have no such practices in your own land' [Lev. 22:24].
30 Where, then, do these eunuchs come from? There is no alternative to
the view that these are people who become priests and refrain from
begetting children." Tell them, "Foolish and weakminded men, what
do eunuchs have to do with priests? The latter have testicles, and
even if they do not engage in reproduction legally and publicly, they
35 wallow in licentiousness in secret. Moreover, *saris* here refers to

nobility as it does when used of Haman, and the reason for its use in this context is that Scripture is fond of playing on words. Furthermore, it is written, 'Your wife shall be as a fruitful vine . . .' [Ps. 128:3], and before that it is written, 'Blessed is everyone that fears the Lord'
5   [Ps. 128:1]. Thus we see that having children is a characteristic of the God-fearing man."

"You shalt not act thus toward the Lord your God, for they perform for their gods every abhorrent act that the Lord detests; they even offer up their sons and daughters in fire to their gods" [Deut.
10   12:31]. Ask the heretics: Did they actually burn their sons and daughters in fire? If they say yes, silence them by saying: See how you do not know the proper interpretation of the Torah. Does God really consider it an abhorrent act for them to burn their children because of their love of God? Why, it might even be regarded as a meri-
15   torious act, as we see in the case of Abraham who was prepared to slaughter his son. This, then, is the proper explanation: Burning refers to the priests and nuns who burn up in their lustful desire but are unable to consummate it; this is the sort of burning which is an abhorrent act that the Lord detests. Indeed, licentious behaviour is
20   called burning, as it is written, "They are all adulterers . . .; like an oven, flaming fire is within them" [Hos. 7:4-6], and it is written, "Its coals are coals of fire that has a most vehement flame" [Song of Songs 8:6]. Moreover, it is written in their own book of errors that Paul said, "It is better to marry than to burn" [1 Cor. 7:9], and so you
25   can see that adultery is called burning.

[43]

"You shall eat old grain long stored, and you shall have to clear out the old to make room for the new" [Lev. 26:10]. The heretics distort this verse by saying that it refers to their invalid Scripture which is new, and they say that the old must therefore be cleared out
30   to make room for it. The answer is: If so, the verses would contradict each other, for immediately before it is written, "And I will maintain my covenant with them" [Lev. 26:9], i.e., to uphold the Torah. (There are, in fact, many other things that the Torah said which they are unable to interpret correctly as I have written in the discussion of their
35   changes in the law.) If they will argue: Just as a man divorces a

woman after she commits adultery, so God divorced you and gave a
new Torah, the answer is: Divorce is legal because there was never
an oath to the contrary, but God swore to us several times, and so
how could he divorce us? It is, after all, written, "Where is the bill of
5   your mother's divorcement" [Isa. 50:1], and Hosea said, "[They
say,] If a man should put away [his wife and she goes from him and
becomes another man's shall he return unto her again? Shall not that
land be greatly polluted? But you have played the harlot with many
lovers;] yet return again to me, said the Lord" [Jer. 3:1]. And it is
10   written, "He shall not break his pledge; he must carry out all that has
crossed his lips" [Num. 30:3]. How, then, can he give a new Torah?

[44]

Ask the heretic: It is written in the Torah of Moses, "For man
may not see me and live" [Exod. 33:20]; how, then, did all the members of Jesus' generation see him and live? After all, anyone who saw
15   the son saw the father and spirit as well, for the three of them are
bound together; one cannot be separated from the other since they are
one and inseparable. He may attempt to point out a contradiction by
citing Isaiah who said, "I saw the Lord sitting upon a throne, high and
lifted up" [Isa. 6:1], and Micaiah who said, "I saw the Lord sitting
20   upon his throne, and all the host of heaven standing on his right hand
and on his left" [2 Chron. 18:18], and Ezekiel who saw the vision and
said, "This is the appearance of the likeness of the glory of the Lord"
[Ezek. 1:28], and Moses himself of whom it is said, "And he beholds
the likeness of the Lord" [Num. 12:8]—and they all lived. We say,
25   however, that these prophets beheld God in a "nonluminous mirror"
except for Moses who was the only one able to behold him in a luminous one. One may also respond on the basis of the rabbinic statement
that at the time of a person's death he sees the divine presence and
immediately expires. This, then, is the meaning of the verse, "For
30   man may not see me and live," that as a man sees him he immediately
dies, as it is written, "All they that go down to the dust shall bow before him, and none can keep alive his own soul" [Ps. 22:30]. However,
at the time when God speaks to the prophet for the purpose of his
mission, the prophet sees him and lives.

[45]

"And he struck the rock twice" [Num. 20:11]; twice to symbolize the cross, and if not for this the water would not have come out. The answer is: This is indeed so, and therefore God became angry and said, "Because you did not believe in me . . ." [Num. 20:12].

[46]

5   "You cannot see my face" [Exod. 33:20]. The heretics ask: It is, however, written of Jacob, "I have seen God (*Elohim*) face to face, yet my life has been preserved" [Gen. 32:31]. Answer them: "Elohim" in this verse refer to angels, who are called *Elohim*, as it says regarding Manoah, "And Manoah said unto his wife, We shall
10   surely die, because we have seen an angel (*Elohim*)" [Judg. 13:22], and it says, "I have said, You are angels (*Elohim*)" [Ps. 82:6].

[47]

"And the staff of Aaron of the house of Levi had sprouted" [Num. 17:23]. The heretics say that this was said of Mary who was a virgin when she gave birth to Jesus. May their breath fail, for their
15   eyes are shut so that they cannot see and their hearts closed so that they cannot understand that Mary was not from the tribe of Levi; according to them, the staff of Judah should have sprouted, for they trace Jesus' genealogy to him. Moreover, does it say "will sprout"? "Had sprouted" is what it says—in the past. It must be, therefore,
20   that it sprouted because of the dispute regarding Korah in order to eliminate the disagreement. One may reply further: If the staff prefigured Jesus, then Mary should have given birth to him on the same day she conceived. Moreover, just as the almonds were complete in their growth, so Jesus should have been an adult on the day of his
25   birth rather than waiting twenty or thirty years. Furthermore, why does it say "and borne almonds" in the plural? If it refers to Jesus, there should have been one almond; as it is, it would imply that there were many Jesuses.

[48]

If he will ask you: Who permitted Moses to make the copper

serpent that he fashioned in the desert? Does it not say, "You shall not make for yourself a sculptured image or any likeness . . ." [Exod. 20:4]? Answer him: The mouth which prohibited is the same mouth that permitted. Similarly, with regard to the prohibitions on the
5   Sabbath, it is written, "You shall kindle no fire . . ." [Exod. 35:3], yet it is also written, "On the sabbath day: two lambs" [Num. 28:9]. Thus, one should not scrutinize the commandments of the Creator, blessed be he, on the basis of human reason; rather, what he prohibited is prohibited and what he permitted is permitted. Indeed, it is
10   for this reason that Moses warned, "All that I enjoin upon you: neither add to it nor take away from it" [Deut. 13:1]. This is also what you should say regarding the cherubim, for that is what Scripture intended in saying, "You shall not make for yourself" [Exod. 20:4], i.e., on your own authority, but on my authority you may. Moreover,
15   when Moses made the serpent he did not make it in order to bow to it or err in worshiping it but rather to show the people the power of God's wonders, to wit, that he cured them with the very thing with which they had been smitten.

[49]

"What I see for them is not yet, what I behold will not be
20   soon: A star rises from Jacob, a meteor comes forth from Israel . . ." [Num. 24:17]. The heretics say that Balaam said this about Jesus. The answer is in the same verse, as it is written, "It smashes the brow of Moab, the foundation of all children of Seth" [Num. 24:17]; now when did this happen? Moreover, it is written, "Edom becomes a posses-
25   sion, yea, Seir a possession of its enemies; but Israel is triumphant" [Num. 24:18]. Now, the main adherents of their god are Edomites; why, then, does he call them his enemies? Moreover, what mention or hint of Jesus is found here? Scripture, then, must be referring to that redeemer who will redeem Israel and gather them together from the
30   place of their dispersion, a redeemer who will come from the seed of David who came from Jacob. Indeed, see what is written in Jeremiah: "And I will gather the remnant of my flock out of all the countries . . . and I will raise unto David a righteous branch and a king shall reign and prosper. . . . In his days Judah shall be saved and Israel shall

dwell safely" [Jer. 23:3–6], and this is the meaning of "but Israel is triumphant."

    "The foundation of all children of Seth" [Num. 24:17]. This is what Obadiah prophesied concerning those days: "For the day of the
5 Lord is near upon all the heathen: as you have done it shall be done unto you. . . . For as you have drunk upon my holy mountain, so shall all the heathen drink [continually]. . . . And the house of Jacob shall be a fire and the house of Joseph a flame, and the house of Esau for stubble. . . . And they of the south shall possess the mount of Esau. . . .
10 And saviors shall come up on Mount Zion to judge the mount of Esau" [Obad. 1:15–21]. And it is written at the end of the prophecy of Amos, "In that day will I raise up the tabernacle of David that is fallen . . . that they may possess the remnant of Edom" [Amos 9:11–12]. Finally, if he argues that the above passage from Jeremiah
15 refers to Jesus, you will find the answer in our discussion of Jeremiah.

[50]

    "The Lord your God will raise up for you a prophet from your midst, from your brothers, like myself; him you shall heed" [Deut. 18:15]. The heretics have said that this is Jesus. The answer is: See
20 what is written at the end of the verse: "[This is just what you asked of the Lord your God at Horeb, on the day of the Assembly, saying,] Let me not hear the voice of the Lord my God any longer" [Deut. 18:16]. How, then, do you say that he came to live among them and spoke with them all the time? Moreover, according to their own view
25 they must admit that it is written in the same passage, "I will raise up a prophet for them from among their own people, like yourself: I will put my words in his mouth" [Deut. 18:18]. We see, then, that this prophet has the power to speak only what his Creator commands him and puts in his mouth; he himself cannot speak or command anything
30 on his own authority. And it is written, "And if anybody fails to heed the words he speaks in my name" [Deut. 18:19], but not the words he speaks on his own. This clearly describes a prophet and not a god. Moreover, it is written "like yourself": Just as you are a prophet and not a god, so he will be a prophet and not a god; just as you were born
35 of a father and mother, so he will be born of a father and mother.

Furthermore, can it be that Moses said "him you shall heed" about this man who came to abrogate his entire Torah?

"I will raise up a prophet for them from among their own people, like yourself" [Deut. 18:18]. The heretics say that this refers to Jesus. The answer is: If Moses said this of Jesus, then he said that he would be a prophet and not a god. But since he made himself a god, urged disloyalty and betrayed God, see what Moses said about him: "If there appears among you a prophet or a dream-diviner and he gives you a sign or a portent, [saying, Let us follow and worship another god—whom you have not experienced—] even if the sign or portent that he named to you comes true, [do not heed the words of that prophet or that dream-diviner.] For the Lord your God is testing you" [Deut. 13:2-4]. Now, an a fortiori argument applies here: If Moses said, "That prophet shall die" [cf. Deut. 13:6; 18:20] about one who urged the worship of other gods, this would certainly apply to one who claimed to be a god. Indeed, it is concerning him that Moses said, "If your brother, the son of your mother entices you" [Deut. 13:7]; this refers to Jesus, who denied his father and said that he had a mother but no father or that he was son of God and God himself. Moses then continued, "Do not assent [or give heed to him. Show him no pity or compassion, and do not shield him; but take his life. Let your hand be] the first against him to put him to death" [Deut. 13:9-10]. This, then, is what they did to him. Indeed, they hanged him in order to point out the relevance of the verse, "You must not let his corpse remain on the stake overnight, but must bury him the same day. For he that is hanged is accursed of God" [Deut. 21:23]. Yet you have the temerity to say that he flew up to heaven.

Indeed, it was with you in mind that Moses berated us and said, "They incensed me with no-gods" [Deut. 32:21], and therefore he placed us under your control, as the verse concludes, "I shall incense them with a no-folk, vex them with a nation of fools." You see, then, that he called you a no-folk and a nation of fools, for you have no shame in saying of him who spoke and the world came to be, of him who lives forever, that he accepted death and suffering for you. Why, Moses said in the name of God, "Lo, I raise my hand to heaven and say: As I live forever . . ." [Deut. 32:40], and David, Elijah, and Daniel all swore by the life of God. Moreover, it is written, "See then, that I,

I am he; there is no god beside me" [Deut. 32:39]; yet you say that
he has a partner, that there are two, nay, three gods. Know clearly
that God will exact revenge from you, as it is written, "For the Lord
will vindicate his people and take revenge for his servants. . . . O na-
5 tions, acclaim his people! For he will avenge the blood of his servants" [Deut. 32:36, 43]. And Jeremiah said, "But fear not, O my servant Jacob, and be not dismayed, O Israel . . . for I am with you; for I will
make a full end of all the nations whither I have driven you, but I will
not make a full end of you" [Jer. 46:27–28; 30:10–11]. Furthermore, he
10 promised us, "But fear not, O my servant Jacob, and be not dismayed,
O Israel, for, behold, I will save you from afar off and your seed from
the land of their captivity; and Jacob shall return and be in rest and at
ease, and none shall make him afraid" [Jer. 46:27; 30:10], but none of
the house of Esau shall remain or escape [cf. Obadiah 1:18].

15   "A prophet from your midst . . ." [Deut. 18:15]. The heretics
refer this to Jesus, but this is impossible, for Asaf testified that there
were no longer any prophets after the destruction of the first Temple,
as it is written, "We see not our signs; there is no longer any
prophet: neither is there among us anyone that knows how long" [Ps.
20 74:9]. And if you will argue that Daniel and Ezra were prophets after
the destruction, the answer is that they saw only visions of the night
or that they were merely interpreters of dreams. One may also respond by referring to the words "like myself": Just as I have a father
and mother, so will the prophets have fathers and mothers; just as I
25 shall not die as a result of execution by the government, so the
prophets will not die that way. But Jesus was crucified. Rabbi
Abraham the proselyte added: Once it said "from your midst" why
was it necessary to add "from your brothers"? It must be to indicate
that he will be exactly similar to a brother, and only such a prophet
30 must be heeded.

[51]

           "Let the mother go, and take only the young" [Deut. 22:7]. The
heretics say: Let the "mother" of the Torah go; i.e., you should not
understand the Torah literally but rather in accordance with cryptic
symbols (*Zeichnisse*). "And take only the young" refers to the saints.
35 The answer is: Isaiah was referring to this dispatch of the "mother"

when he said, "Where is the bill of your mother's divorcement, whom I have put away? . . . For your transgressions was your mother put away. Wherefore when I came was there no man? . . . I clothed the heavens with blackness" [Isa. 50:1-3]. Furthermore, even according
5 to their interpretation, how is one to know when to send away the mother? Moreover, I say that "Let the mother go" refers to their law. Indeed, their own requirement of baptism is proof that this was written for them; i.e., let them wash off their iniquities, as Isaiah said, "Wash yourself, make yourself clean; put away the evil of your
10 doings" [Isa. 1:16]. For it was certainly never required to throw a man into water arbitrarily. Why should Jesus have commanded such an immersion; what was it and why was it?

[52]

"If a man has a wayward and defiant son . . ." [Deut. 21:18]. Rabbi Solomon son of Abun used to answer the heretics' argument
15 from the verse, "The Lord said unto my lord, Sit at my right hand" [Ps. 110:1] as follows: The father told his son, "Sit at my right hand in heaven and don't descend among your enemies the Jews until I destroy them, subdue them, and make them a footstool for you." But the son, i.e., the hanged one, was a wayward and defiant son who did
20 not obey his father and descended in defiance of his will. The father, then, in his anger, caused the Jews to judge him as a wayward and defiant son should be judged; indeed, the Jews are sons of prophets and knew that this is what he actually was, and so they killed him for violating his father's command. When, however, they were unable to
25 carry out the precise sentence of a wayward and defiant son because of his sorcery, they carried out the sentence mentioned in an adjoining verse: "If a man is guilty of a capital offense and is put to death, and you hang him . . ." [Deut. 21:22].

[53]

Ask a heretic: It is written, "No Ammonite or Moabite shall
30 be admitted into the congregation of the Lord" [Deut. 23:4]. Now, the hanged one came from the Moabite Ruth; thus, he is disqualified and ineligible to be admitted into the congregation. If he should then ask how it is that David, Solomon, and all the kings of Israel were also

descended from Ruth, answer him: We explain the verse to refer to
Ammonite and Moabite men and not to women.

[54]

One heretic taunted us from a verse in *Ha'azinu* and asked:
Why is the *he* of the word "Haladonai" ("Is it to the Lord") in the
5   phrase, "Is it to the Lord that you requite this" [Deut. 32:6] written
large? It must refer to the five (*he*) wounds that you inflicted upon the
hanged one. And will you not be requited for this, O you "dull and
witless people" [Deut. 32:6]? The Jew who was asked responded:
Just as you explained the *he* using hermeneutical principles, so you
10 should explain the *lamed*. This, then, is the explanation: He who was
wounded five times is not (*lo*) the Lord; i.e., he is no god but only
flesh and blood born of a woman.

[55]

"'Hear, O Israel! The Lord is our God, the Lord is one"[Deut.
6:4]. The heretics say in their arrogance: These three divine names
15 refer to the trinity. One may respond that the answer is to be found in
an adjoining verse: "You shall love the Lord your God with all your
heart" [Deut. 6:5]. Here he omitted one of the names, reducing the
number to two so that people should not err in saying there are three.

[56]

"With your gear you shall have a spike, [and when you have
20 squatted you shall dig a hole with it and cover up your excrement]"
[Deut. 23:14]. There are priests who ask: Why don't you observe this
now? The answer is: First of all, this proves that even men of flesh
and blood are commanded to be clean. This would certainly be true of
God; so how can you say that Jesus was both flesh and blood and
25 God? Moreover, you don't know the proper explanation, for this
spike was a requirement only in time of war. Alternately: "You shall
have a spike" for the time when one of your brethren goes outside the
camp, separating himself from the the camp and adhering to another
faith, and then decides to immerse himself in order to remove this
30 impurity, i.e., their baptism, and return to the camp of Israel; you
shall have this spike in order to cover this up and conceal it. Another

interpretation: "You shall have a spike" ready to hang him, i.e., to hang Jesus, "and then cover up your excrement," because he was a filthy sinner who wanted to cause you to sin. Indeed, they admit that the cross originally had but three corners, like this: ⊤ . It was on
5 such a cross, which resembles a spike, that they hanged him, until a passerby took pity on him when he saw that his head had no support and added a fourth corner behind the head.

[57]

"Cursed be he who will not uphold the terms of this Torah" [Deut. 27:26]. The heretics say: If you will not observe the entire
10 Torah, then you will be subjected to this curse. The answer is: This is true only if a person sins and fails to repent.

[58]

A certain apostate said: It is written, "For it is your life and longevity" [Deut. 30:20]; thus, the Torah is called life. It is also written, "And your life shall be hung before you" [Deut. 28:66]; this,
15 then, refers to the fact that the hanged one is life. Rabbi Abraham of Spires answered: The answer is in the same verse: "And you shall not believe in your life," i.e., in this "life" of yours that was hanged. Believe only in the true life, i.e., the living God and eternal king; believe in him.

[59]

20 "Honor your father and your mother, that your days may be long" [Deut. 5:16; Exod. 20:12]. It is also written, ". . . in order that you may fare well and have a long life" [Deut. 22:7]. To what does Scripture refer? If it refers to longevity in this world, what sort of promise or hope of consolation can one find here? Why, evil men also
25 live long, as Solomon said, "There is a wicked man that prolongs his life in his wickedness" [Eccles. 7:15], and even one who observes the commandment of honoring his father and mother will eventually be brought to his grave. Concerning this Solomon said, "Though he live a thousand years twice, [yet has he seen no good;] do not all go to one
30 place?" [Eccles. 6:6]. The true interpretation must therefore be: "In

order that you may fare well" in this world, "and have a long life" in the world to come.

He may then say: But it is written, "To the end that your days may be numerous . . ." [Deut. 11:21]. It also says, "Now if you obey
5 the Lord your God, [to observe faithfully all his commandments which I enjoin upon you this day,] the Lord your God will set you high above all the nations of the earth. All these blessings shall come upon you . . ." [Deut. 28:1–2]. Now, all the blessings listed deal with the rewards of this world, but the soul is not mentioned at all. The answer
10 is: Moses told Israel: "The Lord your God commands you this day to observe [these laws and rules: observe them faithfully] with all your heart and soul. . . . And the Lord has affirmed this day that you are his treasured people" [Deut. 26:16, 18]. Now, God will naturally take to himself the soul and spirit of anyone who is treasured and beloved in
15 the eyes of his Creator. Moses thus told them: It is unnecessary to tell you anything further about the soul, because it is obvious to all that anyone who observes the commandments of his Creator is embraced and desired by him and God will not permit his soul to descend to the netherworld, as David said, "You will not allow your faithful
20 one to see hell" [Ps. 16:10]. But in case you wonder how anyone can assure you of what will happen after death, I am informing you that you will see the reward of your good deeds even in this world. Then, at the end of the passage, he refers to the soul when he says, "And you shall be a holy people to the Lord your God" [Deut. 26:19], and
25 there is nothing greater than one who is holy, as it is written, "To the holy ones that are in the earth and to the excellent in whom is all my desire" [Ps. 16:3].

JOSHUA

[60]

The heretics ask: What is symbolized by the fact that Joshua led the
Jews across the Jordan while Moses was unable to do so? They
answer that this indicates that the Torah which Moses gave was
ineffectual in bringing them into paradise. This goal was accomplished only when Jesus, whose name was actually Joshua, came and
passed through the Jordan, i.e., when the evil John baptized him in it.
But it says, "And the Lord said to Joshua, This day will I begin to
magnify you in the sight of all Israel that they may know that as I was
with Moses so I will be with you" [Josh. 3:7]; i.e., he was my agent to
split the sea and you will be my agent to split the Jordan, but not for
the purpose of baptism as the heretics say. Indeed, in connection with
the pronouncements on Mount Ebal and Mount Gerizim which were
to take place after the crossing of the Jordan it says, "Cursed be he
who will not uphold the terms of this Torah" [Deut. 27:26], and
Joshua himself wrote a copy of the Torah of Moses on the stones.

[61]

"Then the children of Reuben and the children of Gad and half
the tribe of Manasseh answered, and said to the heads of the thousands of Israel. The Mighty One, God, the Lord! The Mighty One,
God, the Lord! He knows . . . if it be in rebellion or if in transgression
against the Lord . . . that we have done this" [Josh. 22:21-24]. Here the
priests say that these three names refer to the father, the son, and the
impure spirit. The answer is: According to their own interpretation,
this verse would imply that all three are a unified God and that he who
was born from a clod of earth—from Mary—was not the son.

THE BOOK OF JEREMIAH

[62]

"Before I formed you in the belly I knew you, and before you came forth out of the womb I sanctified you. . . . See, I have this day set you over the nations and over the kingdoms to root out and to pull down,
5   to destroy and to throw down, to build and to plant" [Jer. 1:5–10]. The heretics say that this was said of Jesus. The answer is in an adjoining verse at the beginning of the passage: "And the word of the Lord came to me, saying" [Jer. 1:4]. Who said this? Jeremiah must have said it, for if Jesus had said it, the passage would not have been
10   ascribed to that period; it must be, then, that Jeremiah said it, and that is why it says immediately afterwards, "The word of the Lord came to me again, saying, What do you see, Jeremiah?" [Jer. 1:11].

Moreover, even according to their view that Jeremiah was standing and speaking in place of the Lord, it should have said, "Be-
15   fore he was formed in the belly, I knew him, and before he came forth out of the womb I sanctified him," but to whom did he say "I formed you in the belly" and "I sanctified you"? After all, Jesus was not standing before him. Furthermore: "And I said, Ah, Lord God! I cannot speak" [Jer. 1:6]; now, is this the way a god speaks? Also: "Then
20   the Lord put forth his hand and touched my mouth. And he said, Behold, I have put my words in your mouth" [Jer. 1:9]. This implies that up to that time he possessed no such power of speech and certainly not divinity. In their book of errors it is written that Gabriel announced to Mary that she would give birth to a god; notice, then,
25   their shame, for he was supposed to have been divine from birth yet Jeremiah says that the divine word was granted him only now. If the heretic will respond by arguing that Jesus spoke this way because of his humility, refute him by asking why humility should be necessary in a conversation between himself and his father. Moreover, it is

written, "I ordained you a prophet unto the nations" [Jer. 1:5]. Now, if he is a prophet he is not God, and if he is God he is no prophet, for a prophet is defined as one who transmits a message from the Creator to his creatures. Furthermore, they say in another place that "before I

5 formed you in the belly" refers to John the Baptist. In this case too he should have said, "Before he was formed I knew him." It also says, "I have set you this day" [Jer. 1:10], referring to the days of Jeremiah. Finally, even if you concede everything, you can embarrass them by saying: According to you, his father betrayed him, for here it says,

10 "Be not afraid of them. . . . And they shall fight against you, but they shall not prevail against you, for I am with you, says the Lord, to deliver you" [Jer. 1:8, 19], while in actuality they did prevail against him and hanged him, and the father did not deliver him from their hands. It is clear, then, that the passage refers to Jeremiah.

[63]

15 "Return, O backsliding children, says the Lord, for I have married you and shall take you . . . and give you pastors according to my heart. . . . If you will return, O Israel, says the Lord, return unto me and you will put away your abominations out of my sight . . . and swear, The Lord lives, in truth. . . . Circumcise yourselves to the

20 Lord, and take away the foreskins of your heart, you men of Judah and inhabitants of Jerusalem, lest my fury come forth like fire" [Jer. 3:14—4:4]. The heretics say that the entire passage was said by Jeremiah to chastise the Jews and cause them to return to belief in Jesus. Now, you can see with your own eyes that there is no substance in

25 their words. First of all, Jesus is neither mentioned nor hinted at here. Moreover, is it conceivable that Jeremiah would chastise the Jews and exhort them to follow the Torah of Jesus, who would not be born for another thousand years? His Torah, after all, was not yet known. Why, then, should Jeremiah chastise them concerning it and threaten

30 them by saying, "Lest my fury come forth like fire" [Jer. 4:4]?

Moreover, according to their interpretation, before Jeremiah chastised Israel concerning Jesus' Torah, why did he not chastise himself about it? Why did he not observe it by baptizing himself in the abominable water and observing their holidays? If he will respond by

35 arguing that Jeremiah believed in the divinity of Jesus but was not

baptized because the latter's Torah was not yet given and its time
would not come until Jesus' advent, tell him: Let your ears hear what
your mouth emits. If this is so, then why should Jeremiah warn the
Jews concerning the observance of this Torah, as it is written, "Lest
5   my fury come forth like fire"[Jer. 4:4]? He may then tell you that Jeremiah was prophesying concerning the end of days when Elijah will
come and Israel will return and follow the error of Jesus. The passage, however, contradicts him and proves him wrong, for Jeremiah
undoubtedly said this only to chastise his contemporaries so that
10 they would follow the ways of the Lord, as it is written at the beginning of this passage, "The Lord said also unto me in the days of
Josiah the king, Have you seen that which backsliding Israel has
done? She goes up upon every high mountain. . . . And I said after she
had done all these things that she should return unto me. . . ." [Jer.
15 3:6-7]. Moreover, it is written in a different passage, "Who is the
wise man that may understand this, and who is he to whom the Lord
has spoken that he may declare it, for what the land perishes. . . ? And
the Lord said, Because they have forsaken my Law. . . ." [Jer.
9:11-12]. You see, then, that Jeremiah chastised and warned them
20 concerning the past and not the future. Similarly, Elijah said, "I have
been very jealous for the Lord of Hosts, for the children of Israel have
forsaken your covenant" [1 Kings 19:10]. Indeed, in the Torah of
Moses, it is also written, "All nations will ask, Why did the Lord do
thus to this land . . . ? They will be told, Because they forsook the
25 covenant of the Lord, God of their fathers . . ."[Deut. 29:23-24]. It follows, therefore, that Jeremiah warned and chastised them concerning
the covenant of the Torah of Moses and not concerning anything else.
If the heretic will then ask, "What is the meaning of 'The ark of the
covenant of the Lord' [Jer. 3:16]?" the answer is: The Jews customar-
30 ily took the ark with them when they went out to war. But now the
prophet tells them, "I will give you pastors" [Jer. 3:15] in the future
so that you will have no need to do this, "and they shall say no more,
"The ark of the covenant of the Lord" will go to battle with us,
"neither shall it come to mind" to do so, for they shall no longer go to
35 war, as it is written, "In his days Judah shall be saved, and Israel
shall dwell safely" [Jer. 23:6].

[64]

"Lord, the hope of Israel" [Jer. 17:13]; i.e., the hope of Israel is the Lord. "All that forsake you [shall be ashamed]" [ibid]; i.e., those who turn away from him to follow other gods will be ashamed when they see the salvation of Israel. "And they that depart from me
5 shall be written in the earth, because they have forsaken the Lord, the fountain of living waters" [ibid], and they choose instead to seek standing, stinking water, i.e., the abomination of their baptism which they call *Taufe*.

[65]

"O Lord, my strength, and my fortress, and my refuge in the
10 day of affliction, the nations shall come unto you from the ends of the earth and shall say, Surely our fathers have inherited lies, vanity, and things wherein there is no profit" [Jer. 16:19]. The heretics say that this is what Jesus said when the Jews seized him: "O Lord, my strength and my fortress . . . the nations shall come unto me from the
15 ends of the earth and shall believe in me." The answer is in the following verse: "Shall a man make a god unto himself" [Jer. 16:20]; i.e., can a man make a god of himself and say I am God? Why, if he is God he is not a man, and if he is a man he is not God; for divinity does not rest in a man, as it is written and explained in the portion of *Bereshit*,
20 "My spirit shall nevermore abide in man, since he too is flesh" [Gen. 6:3], and this is the meaning of "Shall a man make a god unto himself, when such gods are no gods" [Jer. 16:20]. And this is the Latin of the first verse: "Non permanebit spiritus meus in homine quia caro est." Similarly, it says in Daniel, "Divine beings whose dwelling is not
25 with flesh" [Dan. 2:11], and it was concerning this belief that Jeremiah said at the end of the passage, "Cursed be the man who trusts in man" [Jer. 17:5]. Moreover, according to their view he lied when he said, "And my refuge in the day of affliction" [Jer. 16:19], for what refuge did he have? He was hanged! Furthermore, it is written,
30 "In the day of affliction." Now, what sort of affliction did he experience because of what they did to him? If, so they say, it was all done in accordance with his will, why should he have been unhappy about it?

And if they acted against his will, why did he not object so that he would be without affliction? Consequently, there can be no doubt that the correct interpretation of the passage is different.

[66]

["For you have kindled a fire in my anger] which shall burn
5   forever" [Jer. 17:4]. If an adversary should answer you, "No! 'Which shall burn forever' implies that God's anger against the Jews will never abate," silence him by saying: Even you admit that all the Jews who will live when Elijah comes will be saved; thus, even according to your own view this "forever" is not to be taken literally.

[67]

10   "Thus said the Lord: Cursed be the man that trusts in man and makes flesh his arm, and whose heart departs from the Lord" [Jer. 17:5]. Inasmuch as the prophet said above, "Shall a man make a god unto himself" [Jer. 16:20], he again warned them against such a god and cursed all those who strayed after him. "That trusts in
15   man"—in that man who made himself a god. Similarly, Balaam prophesied concerning him, saying, "Alas, who shall live when making him God" [Num. 24:23], i.e., when a man makes himself God. David too said, "It is better to trust in the Lord than to put confidence in man" [Ps. 118:8]. Now, one cannot argue that Scripture here refers
20   to one who trusts in a king or a prince, for there is no one who does not trust in a nobler and richer man than himself to help him; surely, Jeremiah would not pronounce a curse against such a practice. Scripture must then be referring to one who trusts in the divinity of a man in matters relating to his soul, as it is written, "And whose heart de-
25   parts from the Lord." Moreover, an adjoining verse shows that Scripture is referring to divinity, as it is written, "Blessed is the man that trusts in the Lord" [Jer. 17:7].

"The heart is deceitful [above all things], and afflicted (*anush*); who can know it?" [Jer. 17:9]. This refers to the deceit in
30   their words, for they say, "We fear the God of heaven." There is, however, no truth in their words since they say after all that their god was born from Mary. He is thus a human being (*enosh*); consequently, they are believers in a human being (*enoshiyyim*) according to

their words. "But I the Lord search the heart . . ." [Jer. 17:10], for the
Lord knows that they really believe in the son of Mary. "As a partridge sits on eggs it did not bring forth, so he that accumulates
wealth, and not by right, shall leave it in the midst of his days, and at
5 his end shall be a fool" [Jer. 17:11]. The prophet is thus comparing
Jesus, son of Mary, to a partridge, a bird that is called a partridge
whose practice is to collect eggs of other birds and sit on them as if
they were his. However, when chicks come out the partridge sees
that they do not resemble him and therefore flies away from them
10 and leaves them to their destruction. Indeed, this is the meaning of
"And at his end shall be a fool"; i.e., then he will realize that he did a
foolish thing. Similarly, Jesus incited people to err, gathering many of
them to him, and he accumulated this wealth "not by right" or in
accordance with the law. "Shall leave it in the midst of his days"
15 refers to the fact that he lived only thirty-two years, for men usually
live seventy years, as it is written, "The days of our years are
seventy" [Ps. 90:10], while he did not live even half of seventy. "And
at his end shall be a fool": When they will abominate him, they will
say, "Surely our fathers have inherited lies, vanity, and things
20 wherein there is no profit" [Jer. 16:19]. This, too, is the meaning of
"Shall a man make a god unto himself, when such gods are no gods"
[Jer. 16:20]. Not so, however, is the God of Israel, for Israel's faith is
only in him whose dwelling place is in "a glorious high throne" [Jer.
17:12].

[68]

25   "Thus said the Lord, the God of Israel: Like these good figs,
so will I acknowledge the captivity of Judah that I have sent out . . .
and I will set my eyes upon them for good . . . and I will give them a
heart to know me, that I am the Lord. And they shall be my people, and
I will be their God, for they shall return unto me with their whole
30 heart" [Jer. 24:5-7]. The heretics say that this was said of the future
when the Jews will turn to their god. The answer is: What, indeed,
will happen to them on that day? It is written in another passage, in
Ezekiel, "Thus said the Lord God: I will gather you from the people
and assemble you out of the countries where you have been scattered,
35 and I will give you the land of Israel. And they shall come thither, and

they shall take away all the detestable things thereof and all the abominable things thereof from thence" [Ezek. 11:17-18]. You see then that on that day, when God will return and gather Israel into Jerusalem, he will clear away all forms of worship that are now there
5 from before them. Now, let your ears hear what is coming out of your mouth. Ezekiel testifies that God said that he would remove and clear away this god of theirs that is now in the land of Israel from before the people of Israel, and you say that on that day the Jews will turn to that god? Moreover, before Jeremiah prophesied concerning those
10 who would ultimately turn to the divinity of Jesus, why did he not prophesy concerning those who believed in him earlier? Furthermore, according to their view why does he mention only Judah here and not the rest of Israel? If he will respond by arguing that all Israel is called Judah in a number of places, answer him: The verse itself testifies
15 and proves that it does not refer to the ten tribes but only to Judah and to Benjamin who was exiled alongside Judah, as it is written, "The captivity of Judah that I have sent out of this place into the land of the Chaldaeans" [Jer. 24:5], for the ten tribes were not sent to the land of the Chaldaeans but to the area beyond the river Sambation where they
20 remain to this day. The true interpretation is that the verse refers to the return to the Second Temple where the captivity of Judah was to be found but not the captivity of the ten tribes.

[69]

"For thus said the Lord, Your bruise is incurable, and your wound is grievous" [Jer. 30:12]. And it says, "And their powerful one
25 shall be of themselves, and their ruler shall proceed from the midst of them; and I will cause him to draw near, and he shall approach unto me" [Jer. 30:21]. The heretics say that this was said of Jesus who was born from the midst of Israel, from Mary. Furthermore, they say of the verse, "Therefore all they that devour you shall be devoured,
30 and all your adversaries shall go into captivity; and they that spoil you shall be spoil, and all that prey upon you will I give for a prey" [Jer. 30:16] that it refers to the Jews who were exiled because they hanged him. The answer is in the adjoining verse: "Your bruise is incurable, and your wound is grievous. . . . All your lovers have for-
35 gotten you, they seek you not; for I have wounded you with the

wound of an enemy, with the chastisement of a cruel one, for the multitude of your iniquity, because your sins are increased. Why cry you
for your affliction? Your sorrow is incurable for the multitude of your
iniquity; because your sins were increased I have done these things
5   unto you" [Jer. 30:12-15]. Now, according to your view that the passage refers to Jesus, note and understand who the verse says
wounded him, as it is written, "For I have wounded you with the
wound of an enemy." You see, then, that the true meaning must be
that God did this to the Jews because of their iniquity. Moreover, it is
10 written, "For the multitude of your iniquity, because your sins were
increased I have done these things unto you"; according to you we
would have to conclude that what was done to him was just because
he sinned before the Lord. Furthermore, could one concerning whom
the verse testifies that he is guilty of sin and iniquity be a god?

[70]

15   "Is Ephraim my dear son?" [Jer. 31:20]. The heretics say that
they are called Ephraim because they were fruitful and multiplied.
The answer is: It is as you say; "Ephraim has surrounded me with
lies" [Hos. 12:1]. Moreover, do not all nations such as Qedar and
Philistines and Ishmaelites and other nations also multiply?

[71]

20   "And I will make a new covenant with Israel and with the
house of Judah" [Jer. 31:31]. Here the heretics defiantly say that he
prophesied concerning Jesus who, from the time of his birth, gave .
them a new Torah, the abomination of their baptism instead of circumcision, and Sunday instead of Sabbath. The answer is: With these
25 words they contradict their own Torah, for it is written in the book of
their error that Jesus himself said, "I have not come to destroy the
law of Moses or the words of the prophets, but to fulfill them.
Heaven and earth shall pass, but not a thing shall pass from the
words of Moses. Whosoever therefore shall destroy one thing of the
30 words of Moses shall be called the least in the kingdom of heaven"
[Matt. 5:17-19]. Yet according to their words, he himself caused the
Torah of Moses to be truncated by abolishing circumcision, observance of the Sabbath, and many commandments. For they say,

"'And I will make a new covenant with them' [Jer. 31:31]; this is the
new Torah. 'And not according to the covenant that I made when I
took them out of the land of Egypt' [Jer. 31:32]—and not according to
the Torah that I already gave them when I took them out of the land of
5   Egypt." In this way they say that Jesus abolished the entire Torah of
Moses. We find, however, that David praised the first Torah, as it is
written, "Your word is true from the beginning, and every one of
your judgments is eternally righteous" [Ps. 119:160]. Moreover,
when he said, "But this shall be the covenant that I will make with the
10   house of Israel" [Jer. 31:33], that is where he should have publicly
written that new Torah of Jesus. All he does say, however, is, "I will
put my law in their inward parts" [ibid]; it is therefore clear that this
was said about the Torah that he had already given which they had
forgotten and that he was promising that he would write it on their
15   hearts so that it would no longer be forgotten. Moreover, why should
he mention the house of Israel and Judah more than other nations?

[72]

"Behold, the days come, says the Lord, that I will fulfill the
good covenant which I have made with the people of Israel and the
house of Judah. In those days and at that time will I cause the branch
20   of righteousness to grow up unto David, and a king shall reign and
prosper, and shall execute judgment and righteousness in the land"
[Jer. 33:14-15; 23:5]. The heretics explain this as a reference to Jesus,
who was descended from David. The answer is: From where do they
learn that Jesus is descended from the house of David? In the book of
25   their error it does not say so, for both Matthew and Luke, who wrote
the genealogy, wrote only the lineage of Joseph the husband of Mary
which they begin with Abraham: "Abraham begat Isaac and Isaac
begat Jacob" until "and Eleazar begat Matthan, and Matthan begat
Jacob, and Jacob begat Joseph, to whom Mary was betrothed" [Matt.
30   1:2-16; cf. Luke 3:23-34]. The lineage of Mary, however, is not in any
of their books. Understand, then, that they are refuted by their own
words, for if Jesus was born without a father, as they say, then there
is no evidence that Jesus comes from the house of David. If, however,
Jesus' lineage should be traced through Joseph and that is the basis
35   for tracing him to the house of David, that would indicate that Joseph

was his father, and so why do you say that he was born without intercourse with a male?

      Moreover, there is an answer in these verses themselves, as
it is written, "And shall execute judgment and righteousness in the
5 land" [Jer. 33:15; 23:5]. Now, is there any more judgment and righteousness in the world since the days of Jesus than there was before?
It is also written, "For thus said the Lord: David shall never lack a
man to sit upon the throne of the house of Israel" [Jer. 33:17]; how,
then, can you say he is a god when the verse calls him a man? You may
10 say that he is called a man because he took on flesh and dwelled in the
lower regions, but even so you must admit that while he was a man he
did not rule or exercise kingship nor did he sit on the throne of Israel.
Moreover, according to their interpretation, if he is divine it should
have said "upon the throne of God." Furthermore, it is written,
15 "Neither shall the priests the Levites lack a man before me to offer
burnt offerings. . . and sacrifice always" [Jer. 33:18], and when was
this fulfilled? Note too the adjoining verse, "And shall execute judgment and righteousness in the land" [Jer. 33:15]. It is also written,
"In his days shall Judah be saved, and Jerusalem shall dwell safely"
20 [Jer. 33:16], and, owing to our sins, it is perfectly clear to all that from
that day on Judah and Israel have not been saved and Jerusalem has
not dwelled safely; for the Ishmaelites came, conquering and destroying it, so that it has not dwelled safely to this day. Indeed, armies
wage war in it every day. How, then, can you say that this passage is
25 a prophecy of Jesus?

EZEKIEL

[73]

"Then I washed you with water and washed away your blood from
you and anointed you with oil" [Ezek. 16:9]. The heretics say that this
refers to their filthy water and to the oil with which they anoint their
5 foreheads in the ceremony they call *firmen.* The answer is in an adjoining verse, as it is written, "And when I passed by you, and saw you
wallowing in your blood, I said to you, Live in your blood; yea, I said
to you, Live in your blood" [Ezek. 16:6]. So you see that blood is better than water, as it is written, "Live in your blood." Now, what is
10 the blood of a man in which he lives? It must be the blood of circumcision. This is also what Zechariah meant when he said, "As for you
also, by the blood of your covenant I have sent forth your prisoners
out of the pit" [Zech. 9:11]; here, too, there is no mention of water as
an agent of salvation. Indeed, I have already explained the passage
15 which says that "they must be circumcised" [Gen. 17:13]. Moreover,
is it written, "And you shall wash with water"? "I washed you" is
what it says; he is speaking of the past, for the prophet was chastising Israel in the name of God for having strayed from the path of God
despite all the good things that he had done for them.
20   Furthermore, he will tell you that "I washed you with water"
refers to the defilement of their baptism and that "And your renown
went forth among the nations . . . and you were exceedingly beautiful,
and you did prosper into a kingdom" [Ezek. 16:14, 13] refers to Jesus,
for this is what the father told his son Jesus. Tell him: You have
25 spoken correctly. Now read on: "And you did trust in your beauty,
and played the harlot because of your renown, and poured out your
fornications on every passerby. . . . You have taken your fair jewels
of my gold and of my silver which I had given you, and made for yourself images of men. . . . Wherefore, O harlot, hear the word of the
30 Lord. . . . And I will judge you as adulteresses and murderesses are
judged, and I will give you blood in fury and jealousy." And it is writ-

ten, "And your younger sister that dwells at your right hand is Sodom and her daughters . . ." [Ezek. 16:15-46]. After this reply the heretic will be embarrassed and ashamed of his question.

[74]

Moreover, it might enter the minds of heretics to tell you that the following verses refer to their god: "Son of man, put forth a riddle. . . . A great eagle with great wings, long winged, full of feathers, which had diverse colors . . . took the highest branch off the cedar. . . . It was planted in a good soil by great waters that it might bring forth branches and that it might bear fruit, that it might be a goodly vine" [Ezek. 17:2-8]. Answer him: You have spoken correctly. Now read on: "Shall it prosper? Shall it not utterly wither when the east wind touches it? It shall wither in the furrows where it grew" [Ezek. 17:10]. You see, then, that all the great things done by that eagle shall wither and disappear.

[75]

The following verses are written at the end of the visions of Ezekiel: "Then he brought me back the way of the gate of the outward sanctuary which faces the east; and it was shut. Then said the Lord unto me: This gate shall be shut, it shall not be opened, and no man shall enter in by it, because the Lord the God of Israel has entered in by it; therefore it shall be shut" [Ezek. 44:1-2]. Here one heretic defiantly said that this refers to Jesus who was born of a virgin who had no intercourse with a man; indeed, her womb was closed and not opened, and "no man shall enter in by it, because the Lord . . . has entered in by it." And from then on it was closed; i.e., no man ever entered the mother of Jesus either before his birth or after it. The Jew answered him: Read on and see the following verse: "It is for the prince; the prince, he shall sit in it to eat bread before the Lord" [Ezek. 44:3]; thus, the prince sat in that gate to eat bread. Now, if it were speaking of the approach to a woman's womb, does the prince eat his bread there? And I might add that one could understand why it is called the outer gate according to your view that it refers to that place, but the "east" gate?! Why should the gate of the womb be called the east gate (*sha'ar haqadim*)? It should rather be called the gate of male organs (*sha'ar hagidin*).

[76]

"The hand of the Lord was upon me, and carried me out in the spirit of the Lord to the midst of the valley" [Ezek. 37:1], and then he
5 prophesies concerning the dead, saying "And it was full of bones" [ibid]. It is then written, "He said unto me: Son of man, prophesy upon these bones . . ." [Ezek. 37:4], and it says, "These bones are the whole house of Israel. . . . Therefore prophesy and say unto them: Thus said the Lord God, Behold O my people, I will open your graves
10 and cause you to come out of your graves, and bring you into the land of Israel" [Ezek. 37:11-12]. If he will tell you that these are the ones whom Jesus raised from hell and that Ezekiel prophesied concerning them, the answer is in this very passage, for it is written, "I will lay sinews upon you and will bring up flesh upon you and cover you with
15 skin and put breath in you, and you shall live" [Ezek. 37:6]. Now, if Jesus did this, then you are right, but if he did not, then it is clear that your words are nothing but "false and misleading oracles" [Lam. 2:14].

[77]

"Wherefore I gave them also statutes that were not good and
20 judgments whereby they should not live" [Ezek. 20:25]. Now, it is written above, "Because they had not fulfilled my laws and had despised my statutes" [Ezek. 20:24]. This, then, is what the prophet was telling them in the name of God: Because they did not fulfill my laws, I shall give them different ones; i.e., I shall do the following to
25 them: because they did not properly observe the laws and statutes which I gave them for good and for life, as it is written, "So that you may live and that it may go well with you" [Deut. 5:33], it shall instead not go well for them and they shall not live by them.

[78]

"And I will purge out from among you the rebels and trans-
30 gressors" [Ezek. 20:38]. These are the apostates who accept their defiling baptism, rebelling against God and denying him. "For in my

holy mountain, in the mountain of the height of the God of Israel, says the Lord God, there shall all the house of Israel serve me" [Ezek. 20:40], i.e., those who believe in me with all their heart and soul, and "there will I accept them" [ibid.].

ISAIAH

[79]

"Your new moons and your appointed feasts my soul hates . . . ." [Isa.
1:14]. The heretics say that he told them this because Jesus has come
and given a new Torah; i.e., you have had enough of the Torah that
has existed until this point, and let it be abolished as of now. The
5 answer is: But it is written, "Forever, O Lord, your word stands"
[Ps. 119:89], and David added, "Your word is true from the beginning, and every one of your judgments is eternally righteous" [Ps.
119:160]. Moreover, the heretics defiantly say that God hates us, our
10 sabbaths, and our feasts, and so we should not continue to observe
the Sabbath and other festivals, for Isaiah said, "Your new moons
and your appointed feasts my soul hates . . ." [Isa. 1:14]; i.e., you
should no longer adhere to that Torah. "Cleave to us," they say,
"observe Sunday like us, and follow our new religion." We may
15 answer them by showing that God has no desire for their new religion, for Jesus himself did not come to destroy the old but to uphold it
as truth; indeed, he said, "Even if heaven and earth shall pass, the
words of Moses and the other prophets shall not pass" [Luke 16:17;
cf. Matt. 5:17–18]. Now, Moses and all the prophets commanded and
20 warned us concerning the observance of the Sabbath; consequently,
you are violating the religion of the hanged one by not observing the
Sabbath. Moreover, this prophecy, i.e., "Your moons and your
appointed feasts . . . ," was said in the days of Isaiah, and the hanged
one was born many years thereafter. Furthermore, if he hated the
25 sabbaths, festivals, and new moons, why did Jesus accept the Jewish
religion—circumcision, the Sabbath, indeed, the entire religion—all
the days of his life? As if this were not enough, you don't even observe Sunday properly by resting in an acceptable fashion; on the
contrary, you and your animals do work on that day and do not rest.
30 The following, then, is the interpretation of the passage, as the context makes clear: He is referring to the new moons and festivals

which they "devised of their own heart" [cf. 1 Kings 12:23] and which
God did not command; it is concerning this that he says, "Your new
moons and your appointed feasts my soul hates."

[80]

"The word that Isaiah son of Amoz saw concerning Judah and
5   Jerusalem: And it shall come to pass in the last days that the mountain of the Lord's house shall be established in the top of the mountains and shall be exalted above the hills, and all nations shall flow
unto it. And many people shall go and say, Come and let us go up to
the mountain of the Lord, to the house of the Lord of Jacob . . . for out
10   of Zion shall go forth the law, and the word of the Lord from Jerusalem" [Isa. 2:1–3]. The heretics say that this prophecy was said of
the return of the nations to the Torah of Jesus. The answer is: You
are quite right that this passage refers to Jesus. Now read further:
"The lofty looks of man shall be humbled, and the haughtiness of men
15   shall be bowed down; and the Lord alone shall be exalted in that day"
[Isa. 2:11]. And it says, "Cease ye from man, whose breath is in his
nostrils, for wherein is he to be accounted of?" [Isa. 2:22]. You see,
then, that the prophet is warning people not to sin by erring in following Jesus, for his claims are of no substance. Indeed, the verse, "The
20   lofty looks of man shall be humbled" must refer to Jesus, for if you
will say that it refers to other people such as kings and princes,
would it then be necessary to say, "And the Lord alone shall be exalted on that day"? Was God not exalted alone even before the day of
the humbling of such men? The verse, then, undoubtedly refers to
25   Jesus, and this is what the prophet said: In the last days the mountain
of the Lord's house shall be established, and then the lofty looks of
man shall be humbled; i.e., Jesus, who exalted and raised himself
above all men by claiming to be a god, will then be humbled, bowed
down, and forgotten by all men together with the other gods of the
30   nations. In that day, the Lord alone shall be exalted, as it is written,
"In that day, the Lord shall be one and his name one" [Zech. 14:9];
i.e., no name of a foreign god shall be mentioned, not that of Jesus nor
that of Muhammad but only that of the Lord, blessed be he.

"Cease ye from the man" who claimed to be a god, for he
35   lives, hears and speaks only when "breath is in his nostrils," but

after it leaves him, "wherein is he to be accounted of?" Indeed, it was
concerning their claim that he ascended to heaven afterwards that
King Solomon said, " 'Who knows if the spirit of man goes upward'
[Eccles. 3:21] or descends to the earth?" Thus you see with your own
5 eyes that the prophet contradicts the belief in Jesus at the end of the
passage. Similarly, it is written in Psalm 143 [*sic!*], "What is man that
you take knowledge of him or the son of man that you make account of
him?" [Ps. 144:3], and Jesus is called son of man—*fili homo*—
throughout the Gospels. Moreover, what hint of Jesus is there in the
10 entire passage? The real meaning of the passage, then, is quite
different.

The priests explain "And the loftiness of man shall be bowed
down" [Isa. 2:17] as a reference to haughty men. The truth is that this
passage refers to their god, as it is written, "And the loftiness of man
15 shall be bowed down . . . and the idols he shall utterly abolish" [Isa.
2:17-18]. Moreover, why should he have said, "And the Lord alone
shall be exalted" [Isa. 2:17] with regard to haughty men? There is no
doubt, then, that he said this concerning foreign gods.

"In that day a man shall cast his idols of silver and his idols of
20 gold which they have made of him (*lo*) to worship, to the moles and to
the bats" [Isa. 2:20]. It does not say "which they have made for themselves" (*lahem*) but "which they have made of him." This means that
the idol, or image, which they made "of him," i.e., as an image of their
god, as the worshipers of Jesus do, will be cast by these worshipers
25 to group of moles and bats.

[81]

"Woe unto them that join house to house" [Isa. 5:8]. You can
explain this passage too as a reference to the worshipers of Jesus:
These are the priests who have taken all the land for themselves, who
join house to house and lay field to field until they have no place re-
30 maining. "That you may be placed alone in the midst of the earth"
[ibid.]: This refers to their sitting in monasteries.

"Woe unto them that rise up early in the morning that they
may follow strong drink; that continue until night till wine pursues
them" (*yadliqem*) [Isa. 5:11]. The word *yadliqem* is used in the same
35 sense as it is in the phrase "that you have pursued me" (*dalaqta aḥaray*)

[Gen. 31:36]. This verse refers to the priests who rise early and stay up late in their houses of abomination for their portion which they call *praebenda.*

5   "Therefore my people are gone into captivity"[Isa. 5:13]. This refers to those who say that they are his people although they are "without knowledge" [ibid.] of him, for when "a man shall cast his idols of silver and his idols of gold which they have made of him to worship, to the moles and to the bats" [Isa. 2:20], then they will all go, exiled and travel-weary, without food or clothing.

10   "Woe unto them that draw iniquity with cords of vanity" [Isa. 5:18]. This refers to the ropes with which they pull the bells in their house of abomination as part of the worship of their god.

"Woe unto them who call evil good, and good evil"[Isa. 5:20], for they exchange the God of heaven for the god of their abomination.
15   "That put darkness for light" [ibid.]; i.e., they consider Jesus, who descended to hell, to be light.

"Woe unto them that are wise in their own eyes . . ." [Isa. 5:21]. This was said of the rest of the people of Jesus that they call *Laien.*

20   "Woe unto them that are mighty to drink wine . . . who justify the wicked for reward . . ." [Isa. 5:22–23]. All these things are characteristic of them.

[82]

Some say that the reason why the Gentiles cannot pronounce either *ḥet* or *'ayin* is that they do not believe in the Sustainer of the
25   universe (*ḥe 'olamim*). It may also be a result of the fact that David cursed them for their worship of idols, as it is written, "They give no sound through their throat. They that make them shall be like them. . . ." [Ps. 115:7–8].

[83]

This is the Latin of the verse, "Israel shall be saved by the
30   Lord. . ." [Isa. 45:17]: "Israel salvatus in Domino saluti aeterna, non confundemini et non erubescetis usque in saecula saeculorum."

[84]

"Behold, a young woman (*'almah*) shall conceive and bear a son, and shall call his name Immanuel" [Isa. 7:14]. The heretics say that this was said of Jesus, and they argue: What sort of novelty is it that a young woman should conceive in the natural way through inter-

5   course with a man? You must say, therefore, that Scripture refers to a virgin who had no such intercourse. The answer is: King Solomon said, "There are threescore queens and fourscore concubines, and young women (*'alamot*) without number" [Song of Songs 6:8], and in Proverbs too it is written, "The way of a man with a maid (*'almah*)"

10 [Prov. 30:19]; thus, even one who is not a virgin is called *'almah*. Indeed, such a woman can even be called *betulah*, as it is written, "Lament like a *betulah* girded with sackcloth for the husband of her youth" [Joel 1:8]. Moreover, since they interpret this prophecy as a reference to Jesus, why did they not call him Immanuel? The fact is

15 that in their entire Torah he is called only Jesus.

There can be no doubt, therefore, that Isaiah had recently married a young virgin, and this is what he said thereafter: "The Lord shall give you a sign" [Isa. 7:14], and when the sign will come you will know that my words are true and that God will protect you from

20 these two kings, Pekah and Rezin. And what is the sign? This maiden who is young and of whom it is not known whether she is sterile or not shall conceive as soon as I have intercourse with her and shall give birth to a boy. And this is what is referred to in the verse, "And I came unto the prophetess and she conceived" [Isa. 8:3]; you see,

25 then, that she conceived as a result of intercourse. Then she, the prophetess, called his name Immanuel through the influence of the holy spirit; i.e., God will help us in the face of these two kings, "for before the child shall know to refuse the evil and choose the good the land that you abhor shall be forsaken of both her kings" [Isa. 7:16].

30 The land will then become rich with everything good, and butter and honey will not be lacking in the land, as it is written, "Butter and honey shall he eat in accordance with his knowledge" [Isa. 7:15]; for when he is born these two kings will go on their way and leave the land in peace.

35   Moreover, it is written, "And he said to me, call his name

Maher Shalal Hash Baz, for before the child shall have knowledge to cry: My father, and My mother"—this shows that he had a father and mother—"the riches of Damascus and the spoil of Samaria shall be taken away before the king of Assyria" [Isa. 8:3-4], and all this took
5   place more than three hundred years before Jesus was born. Moreover, on what basis should Isaiah's wife have been called a prophetess, as it is written, "And I came unto the prophetess" [Isa. 8:3], if not because the holy spirit rested on her when she had her first child and called him Immanuel? This too is the reference in the verse, "Be-
10   hold, I and the children whom the Lord has given me are for signs and wonders in Israel from the Lord of hosts who dwells in Mount Zion" [Isa. 8:18]. Now, where did he get two children? It must be that Immanuel was also his son and they were both signs, one for the saving of the land and the other for the downfall of Rezin and Pekah.
15   Furthermore, if you were right in maintaining that this maiden is the mother who was involved in that defiling union, then what sort of sign would this have been for Ahaz? After all, the events concerning Jesus took place more than three hundred years after the death of Ahaz. Indeed, when Hezekiah asked for a sign, saying, "What shall
20   be the sign . . . that I shall go up into the house of the Lord?" he was immediately given a sign which he saw with his own eyes: "Behold, I will bring back the shadow of the degrees . . ." [2 Kings 20:8-9; Isa. 38:8]. A similar thing was done for Gideon—"And it was dry upon the fleece" [Judg. 6:40]—and Moses too transformed the staff into a
25   serpent and his hand became leprous as snow; this, then, is the manner of all who give signs.

[85]

"For unto us a child is born, unto us a son is given, and the government shall be upon his shoulder" [Isa. 9:5]. The heretics say that this refers to the cross which was nailed to him. "And his name
30   shall be called wonderful counselor, mighty God, everlasting father, prince of peace" [ibid.]. Answer him as follows: If this understanding of the verse were correct, then it should have said, "and his names shall be called," for there are four or five names according to you. Moreover, how could Jesus be called wonderful counselor when

Judas frustrated his counsel? One can also reply: He was not mighty
for he was killed; he was not an everlasting father, for he died in his
prime; and he was not a prince of peace, for there was strife throughout his lifetime, and from then on the world has not rested from wars.
5 Moreover, it is written immediately afterwards, "Of the increase of
his government and peace there shall be no end, upon the throne of
David and upon his kingdom, to order it and to establish it with judgment . . . from henceforth even for ever" [Isa. 9:6]. This shows that
you cannot refer the passage to Jesus, for Jesus was born three
10 hundred years and more after this prophecy, and the prophet said,
"From henceforth even for ever." Furthermore, it is written in their
Gospels that Jesus said, "I came not to send peace on earth, but a
sword" [Matt. 10:34]; thus, their words contradict each other. If he
will then ask, "Concerning whom was this verse said?" answer him:
15 He is prophesying concerning the downfall of Sennacherib which was
accomplished by this child, i.e., by Hezekiah. Thus he says, "And he
called his name"; i.e., God, who is a "wonderful counselor, mighty,
and an everlasting father," called him "prince of peace," as it is written, "And he said, Good . . . for there shall be peace and truth in my
20 days" [Isa. 39:8].

"For unto us a child is born" [Isa. 9:5]. The heretics say that
this is the one descended from that defiling union. Answer them: It
says of this son that he will establish the throne of David and his
kingdom. If so, then their words contradict each other, for they say
25 that the verse, "The scepter shall not depart from Judah . . . until
Shiloh comes" [Gen. 49:10] means that power and kingdom shall not
pass from Judah until Shiloh, i.e., the messenger, or Jesus, shall
come, and then the kingdom and power shall pass from the house of
Judah. Furthermore, they interpret the verse, "With the coming of the
30 Most High . . . the Messiah shall be cut off" [Dan. 9:24, 26] in a similar way. Thus, he does not establish the kingdom of Judah but rather
destroys it.

[86]

The heretics also say that "Behold, a young woman shall conceive and bear a son" [Isa. 7:14] was said about Mary, who was a vir-
35 gin and bore a son, for otherwise this would not constitute a novelty
or a sign. "And shall call his name Immanuel" [ibid.], for when he is

born God will be with us; i.e., he will be God. "And I came unto the prophetess" [Isa. 8:3]—that is Mary. "Come together, O people, and you shall be broken in pieces. . . .Take counsel together, and it shall come to nought . . ." [Isa. 8:9-10]—these are the Jews who took coun-
5   sel together to kill him.

      Now listen, men of understanding, and see how confused their words are and how they contradict the words of the living God. The book of Isaiah is, after all, in our possession, and it testifies that these verses are not written together but are found in two or three
10 different places; moreover, it testifies further that Isaiah prophesied concerning two sons, one named Immanuel and another named Maher Shalal Hash Baz.

      Now, if you would prefer to answer briefly, then tell him: Granted that the prophet said that a virgin would give birth to a son.
15 So what? There is, after all, no doubt that the Lord's hand is not incapable of fulfilling his will and desire, and that he is a ruler who can do whatever he wishes, but still how do you know that this virgin is Mary? Where do you find her name or that of her son so that you may know? I could say, rather, that this refers to another virgin or that it
20 will happen in the future. And if your view is based on the name Immanuel, i.e., God is with us, this is no proof, for you could make the same claim of divinity regarding Ishmael the son of Hagar if you use this sort of reasoning. There too the angel told her, "Behold you are with child and shall bear a son, and you shall call his name
25 Ishmael" [Gen. 16:11], and you can interpret that name as follows: Everyone will listen to him because he is God. Similarly, it says of Hannah, "And she called his name Samuel" [1 Sam. 1:20], a name that can be explained as "His name is God." If he will then say that Hagar and Hannah were not virgins while Mary was, this would contradict
30 Solomon, who said, "There is no new thing under the sun . . . that which has been is that which shall be" [Eccles. 1:9]. Moreover, where do we find that the prophets warned us concerning his Torah and the belief in his divinity as we were warned at Sinai by Moses, as it is written, "I am the Lord your God . . . you shall have no other gods
35 beside me" [Exod. 20:2-3]? Thus, one can understand that your words have no substance and that these prophecies do not deal with divinity.

      Moreover, you can defeat him and respond with true and

proper words by telling him: According to you that Isaiah said, "Behold, a young woman conceives" and the entire passage concerning
Mary and her son, come and examine the language of the verse and let
your ears hear what comes out of your mouth. With regard to the
5   verse, "Behold, a young woman conceives (*harah*)," you cannot explain *harah* except as a reference to the past, i.e., that she has already
conceived, while Mary had not yet conceived and would not do so for
another thousand years. According to you, then, why does it say
harah? It should have said *tahar* which would have been a reference to
10   the future. Moreover, see what it says soon after: "For before the
child shall know to refuse the evil and choose the good, the land that
you abhor shall be forsaken of both her kings" [Isa. 7:16]. Now, if he
was God, what is the meaning of "before the child shall know etc."?
Why, he should have known and understood the difference between
15   good and evil from the day of his birth if God was within him. Indeed,
with regard to your statement that he eventually performed wonders
so that people would believe that he was God, what could have been a
greater sign than distinguishing between good and evil as soon as he
came out of his mother's womb and remaining without food and
20   drink? Then, people would have believed in him. As it is, however,
the fact that we saw nothing in him during his youth to distinguish
him from other infants leads us to disbelieve those wonders performed in his adulthood and to conclude that he performed them
through magic in the manner of charmers, diviners, and observers of
25   times. Moreover, where do these verses indicate that Mary was a
virgin when she gave birth to her son? After all, *'almah* is nothing but
the word for a young woman, as I shall explain, for *'almah* in Hebrew
does not necessarily denote a virgin. Indeed, even in Latin it is not
virgo but *puella* that means virgin; *virgo* means young woman.
30   "Take counsel together and it shall come to nought, speak the
word [and it shall not stand]" [Isa. 8:10]. Now, according to them,
who nullified the counsel taken against him? Indeed, that counsel was
fully carried out. And with regard to the verse, "And I came unto the
prophetess" [Isa. 8:3], which you say refers to Mary, on the basis of
35   what prophecy is she called a prophetess? Moreover, "And I came
unto" (*va'eqrav*) refers to intercourse, as it is written, "[If a woman]
approach (*tiqrav*) any beast and lie down with it" [Lev. 20:16], and

"You shall not approach (*tiqrav*) unto a woman during her menstrual impurity" [Lev. 16:19]. Indeed, you find many adjoining words which prove that *tiqrav* refers to intercourse, as it is written, "And lie down" [Lev. 20:16] and "To uncover her nakedness" [Lev. 18:19]. In
5 fact, the same sort of thing is found here, where it is written, "And I came unto the prophetess and she conceived and bore a son" [Isa. 8:3], just as it is written elsewhere, "And he came unto Hagar and she conceived" [Gen. 16:4].

Furthermore, you may answer as follows in light of the order
10 of the verses: At the beginning of this passage it says, "Ask a sign of the Lord" [Isa. 7:11], and Ahaz answered, "I will not ask, neither will I test the Lord" [Isa. 7:12]. The prophet then responded, "Therefore, the Lord himself shall give you a sign: Behold, a young woman conceives etc." [Isa. 7:14]. Thus, your eyes see and your ears hear that
15 this sign ("Behold, a young woman etc.") was given to Ahaz of the house of David so that people should believe the prophet's statement that the Lord intends to save Jerusalem from Rezin and Pekah. Now, then, if the verse refers to Mary, what sort of sign was this for Ahaz and the house of David? After all, Mary did not live in the time of
20 Ahaz and would not be born for another thousand years. Moreover, whenever a prophet gives a sign to establish faith in the word of God, he performs that sign immediately so that people will believe that his words will be fulfilled because he is a messenger of God. This is what Moses did, as it is written, "And he did the signs in the sight of
25 the people" [Exod. 4:30], and in Gideon's case it is written, "And it was dry upon the fleece" [Judg. 6:30]. Furthermore, it is written in our passage, "In that day a man shall nourish a young cow and two sheep . . . for the entire land shall eat butter and honey" [Isa. 7:21-2]. Now, where do we find that this took place in the days of Jesus,
30 namely, that the world changed because of him?

[87]

"And the Lord said unto me, Take a great roll and write in it with a man's pen Maher Shalal Hash Baz. And I took unto me faithful witnesses to testify, Uriah the priest and Zechariah the son of Jeberechiah. And I came unto the prophetess . . ." [Isa. 8:1-3]. Now,
35 according to your view that this passage refers to Mary, how could

Uriah and Zechariah testify concerning this matter? Did they live in
the time of Mary? Indeed, they never even saw each other, for Uriah
lived in the period of the First Temple and Zechariah in that of the
Second. "And I came unto the prophetess and she conceived and bore
5   a son" [Isa. 8:3]. Now, when did Isaiah come unto the prophetess
who bore that son? He certainly never saw Mary in his life since she
did not live in his time. And with regard to the verse "For unto us a
child is born" [Isa. 9:5] which is written in this passage, if it refers to
God why does it say, "Of the increase of his government and peace
10 there shall be no end upon the throne of David and upon his kingdom"
[Isa. 9:6]? Does the greatness of God consist of his ruling upon the
throne of David and upon his kingdom? That much was done by King
Solomon, as it is written, "Then Solomon sat upon the throne of his
father David" [1 Kings 2:12], but with regard to God it is written, "I
15 saw the Lord sitting upon a throne, high and exalted" [Isa. 6:1].
Moreover, the phrase "upon his kingdom" indicates that this child
ruled over David's kingdom alone and nothing more; is it, then,
proper to say of one whose rule did not exceed that of flesh and blood
that he is God?
20   Therefore, men of understanding, hearken and understand,
observe and know that their words have no substance. Indeed, it was
concerning them that Isaiah said, "Woe unto them that seek deep to
contradict counsel from the Lord, and their works are in the dark"
[Isa. 29:15], for they contradict and overturn the words and counsel of
25 the living God and attribute to the prophets things which God did not
say. Anyone who reads the passage from beginning to end will understand that their words contain nothing but vain emptiness, for there
isn't a single heretical statement of theirs the refutation of which is
not to be found in an adjoining verse. The correct interpretation of the
30 passage is that it refers to Hezekiah.

[88]

"And there shall come forth a rod out of the stem of Jesse. . . .
And the spirit of the Lord shall rest upon him, the spirit of wisdom
and understanding, the spirit of counsel and might, the spirit of
knowledge and of the fear of the Lord. And he shall be of quick under-
35 standing in the fear of the Lord . . ." [Isa. 11:1–3]. They explain this

entire passage as a reference to Jesus and say that he was the root of
Jesse. The answer is: How do they know that Jesus the son of Mary
came from Jesse and David? If this belief is based on the genealogy
written in the Gospels, the fact is that this genealogy traces the
5   lineage back through Joseph, as it is written in their book of errors
that so-and-so begat so-and-so until it says at the end, "And Jacob
begat Joseph *virum Mariae*" [Matt. 1:16], i.e., the husband of Mary.
Now, once you say that Joseph was not his father, where do we find
that Jesus comes from David? With regard to his mother, Mary, we
10 find no genealogy at all, and we do not know from which family she
came.

He might then tell you: We have a tradition that the Jews
always married their relatives; thus Mary was a relative of Joseph
and his genealogy is hers as well, both of them having been de-
15 scended from David. You should then respond by telling him: Are
you coming to put together a puzzle and make a god through fabrication and indirection? It is undoubtedly the custom of our Torah that
everyone marries the woman whom he deems proper, whether she be
related or not, provided that she is in a legally permitted category, for
20 even though the Torah permitted certain relatives it certainly did not
prohibit other people. Moreover, members of one tribe married
women of another tribe, as we see in the story of the concubine from
Gibeah that the tribes made an enactment which said, "Accursed is
the man who gives his daughter to Benjamin" [Judg. 21:1]; this
25 shows that their previous custom was to marry into that tribe. Now,
since this is so, on what basis do you maintain that Mary and Joseph
were from the same family? Furthermore, if you were right that Mary
was of the same descent, why should they have traced Jesus' lineage
through Joseph? They should have done it through Mary instead.
30 Thus we see that they have no plausible basis for determining Mary's
family.

"And the spirit of the Lord shall rest upon him." Thus, he
himself was not the Lord. "The spirit of knowledge and of the fear of
the Lord." Now, does it make sense to say such a thing about God?
35 Moreover, were the prophecies written in this passage fulfilled during the time of Jesus, as it is written, "The wolf also shall dwell with
the lamb, and the leopard shall lie down with the kid" [Isa. 11:6]? If he

will then assert that this is to be understood allegorically, i.e., that at
that time evil and righteous men will live together, such a situation
would be nothing new. Has this not been the case from time immemorial? It is also written, "They shall not do evil nor destroy in all my
5   holy mountain" [Isa. 11:9]; now, was there no evil done in Jerusalem
from then on, and was the land not destroyed? Why, several wars
were waged there after that time both while Israel dwelt there, as it is
written in the book of Joseph son of Gorion, and afterwards, for the
Ishmaelites came after that time and desecrated the grave. Further-
10   more, even granting all his arguments, you can finally tell him: How
do you know that the passage refers to the son of Mary? I can say that
it refers to the son of a different woman inasmuch as not a single one
of the signs of prophecy were found in Jesus. The proper interpretation of the passage is that it refers to Hezekiah and Sennacherib.
15   "And there shall come forth a rod out of the stem of Jesse,
etc." [Isa. 11:1]. Answer them as follows: "The spirit of counsel"
[Isa. 11:2] was not in him, for Judas confounded his counsel, nor was
the spirit of might within him, for he was killed. "The spirit of
knowledge and of the fear of the Lord" [ibid.]: Let others fear him. He
20   himself, however, should not fear, for there is no one whom he
should fear. Thus, the fact that it says that he feared the Lord indicates that he was not divine. Moreover, it is written in the same passage, "The wolf also shall dwell with the lamb . . ." [Isa. 11:6], and
peace has not yet come to the world. If you will then argue that this
25   prophecy is an allegory referring to Jesus, who lived on earth among
evil men—i.e., he is the lamb, the kid, and the calf, while the wolf,
leopard, and young lion are the evil men—the answer is: In that case
what is the meaning of "And the cow and the bear shall feed; their
young ones shall lie down together" [Isa. 11:7]? Did Jesus have chil-
30   dren? This would indicate that he was not God. Moreover, it is written, "And it shall come to pass in that day that the Lord shall set his
hand again the second time to recover the remnant of his people that
shall be left from Assyria and from Egypt, and from Pathros, and
from Cush, and from Elam, and from Shinar, and from Hamath, and
35   from the islands of the sea. And he shall set up an ensign for the
nations and shall assemble the outcasts of Israel, and gather together
the dispersed of Judah from the four corners of the earth. The envy

also of Ephraim shall depart, and the adversaries of Judah shall be cut
off. . . . They shall spoil the children of the east together; they shall
lay their hand upon Edom and Moab. . . ." [Isa. 11:11–14]. From this it
follows that the Jews will rule over the nations; now, when was this
5   entire prophecy fulfilled?

[89]

"And the government shall be upon his shoulder" [Isa. 9:5].
The shoulder normally suffers and carries burdens; thus, he too
carried on his shoulder the rope on which he was hanged, which they
call *Reepe*. Indeed, the bishop himself explained it this way during
10   prayer, saying that Saul, whom they call Paul, and Isaiah said the
same thing—thus the Christian assertion that they were brothers in
word and deed. Isaiah said, "And the government shall be upon his
shoulder" and not, "The crown shall be on his head." Similarly, Saul
said that when Jesus was brought to be hanged he had no one to carry
15   his cross and rope, and so he himself carried it on his shoulder. However, when it says, "Of the increase of government" [Isa. 9:6]—i.e.,
when the Messiah will reign with great sovereignty and there will be
no end to both sovereignty and peace—then it does not say "on his
shoulder."

[90]

20   "And in mercy shall the throne be established, and he shall sit
upon it in truth in the tent of David, judging and seeking judgment"
[Isa. 16:5]. The heretics refer this to Jesus. The answer is: How do
you know this? What hint of Jesus can be found here? Furthermore, if
this verse refers to Jesus, then you must conclude that he did not pos-
25   sess all this honor until now; consequently, he must be a god "who
came but lately" [Deut. 32:17] and not the primeval Creator.
Moreover, where do we see that Jesus ever sat in the tent of David
and sought judgment? If he will then ask, "To whom, then, does the
verse refer?" you can answer: You see, then, that your position is un-
30   tenable. If you really want to know to whom the verse refers look at
the beginning of the passage and you will see that it refers to
Hezekiah.

[91]

"And it shall be said in that day, Lo, this God of ours in whom
we placed our hope has saved us" [Isa. 25:9]. The heretics say: In that
day when Jesus comes to Jerusalem, then it will be said, "Lo, this
God of ours etc." The answer may be found in the adjoining verses,
5 for what is written immediately after this? "When the hand of the
Lord shall rest on this mountain, Moab shall be trodden down under
him, even as straw is trodden down for the dunghill. And he shall
spread forth his hands in the midst of them as a swimmer spreads
forth his hands to swim. . . . And the fortresses of your walls [shall
10 he bring down] . . ." [Isa. 25:10–12]. Now, where was this fulfilled on
the day Jesus entered Jerusalem? Moreover, it is written a little later,
"In that day shall this song be sung in the land of Judah: We have a
strong city; salvation [will God appoint for walls and bulwarks].
Open the gates, that the righteous nation which keeps faith may enter
15 in" [Isa. 26: 1–2]. If he will then say that this is what Jesus said to the
gates of Jerusalem when he entered, then you will be able to see how
all their words are words of falsehood and fabrication, for what hint
of Mary or her son can be found here? Moreover, if this passage
refers to Jesus, we may ask what strength or salvation was ap-
20 pointed for the walls of Jerusalem as a result of his coming. Why, it
suffered exile twice thereafter: once in the days of the wicked Titus
and again when the Ishmaelites destroyed it and desecrated the
grave.

[92]

"With my soul have I desired you in the night; yea, with my
25 spirit within me will I seek you early" [Isa. 26:9]. They say that the
prophet prophesied concerning the advent of Jesus. The answer is:
On what grounds do you say that this refers to Jesus? What hint of
Jesus is there here? On the basis of your methods, the Ishmaelites
can say that the prophet said this concerning the divinity of their god
30 Muhammad. Moreover, if they were right in saying that the Torah of
Jesus and his advent were known to the prophets, then why did the
prophets not observe his Torah and baptize themselves in accordance
with it? And if the heretic will say that their baptism consisted in
their faith in him, then why did they go down to hell (for they say that

all people went to hell until Jesus came and saved them)? Moreover,
why is it that neither his name nor that of his mother is mentioned in
all the prophetic writings? It must be, then, that it was concerning
Jesus, his "divinity" and the like that Isaiah prophesied, "They are
5   dead who shall not live, deceased who shall not rise; therefore have
you visited and destroyed them and made all their memory perish"
[Isa. 26:14]. The true interpretation of the passage is that it deals with
the future which they call *Römisch Reich* in the end of days.

[93]

"Behold, a king shall reign in righteousness, and princes shall
10 rule in judgment" [Isa. 32:1]. The heretics refer this to Jesus. The
answer is: According to them, one must conclude that Jesus was not
God from earliest times, for "shall rule" implies "from now on";
this shows that he did not rule until now, and it was of him that it
says, "New ones, who came but lately" [Deut. 32:17]. Moreover, the
15 Ishmaelites can also say that the passage refers to their god, for there
is no evidence for one more than the other. Indeed, there is no reference to any divinity here, for the verse refers to Hezekiah.

[94]

"And the redeemed of the Lord shall return and come to Zion
with song" [Isa. 35:10]. This refers to Israel, whom God will redeem
20 from the nations. The heretics, however, say that the verse refers to
the souls which Jesus took out of hell. The answer is: It is written,
"And come to Zion with song"; now, will these souls return to Zion?
And if he will tell you that Zion represents heaven, i.e., that they will
return to the Zion in heaven, the answer is in the verse, "Zion shall be
25 ploughed as a field" [Mic. 3:12] which would also have to be explained as referring to a heavenly Zion. This clearly shows that there
is no Zion in heaven.

[95]

"Thus said the Lord to his anointed, to Cyrus" [Isa. 45:1].
The heretics refer this entire passage to Jesus by saying that Cyrus
30 is Jesus. The answer is in this very verse, as it is written, "I will
loose the loins of kings." Hence, the power is in God's hands and not
in those of Jesus, for it does not say, "He will loose."

It is written, "I will go before you and make the crooked places straight; I will break in pieces the gates of brass and cut in sunder the bars of iron" [Isa. 45:2]. They say that these are the doors of hell, and they go on to say that "I will give you the treasures of darkness, the hidden riches of secret places" [Isa. 45:3] refers to the souls in hell. Now, according to them, when did Jesus go to hell to take the souls out? After his death, no doubt. Now, after his death, who went before whom, as it is written, "I will go before you" [Isa. 45:2]? If you will say that the father went before the son, then there are two, and you deny your own Torah which says that father and son are one. It is, of course, true that in other places you say that although father and son are one, Scripture nevertheless separates them and discusses them as two, as in the verse, "The Lord said to me, You are my son" [Ps. 2:7], and, "The Lord said unto my lord" [Ps. 110:1]. All this, however, is possible only with regard to things which were said or took place before his death since you can argue that the son was flesh while his father was in heaven. But with regard to events that took place after his death, you must recognize that the flesh had already returned to the earth as it was. Thus, if you say that the spirit which was within him was divine, then you must say that after he died and entered hell to take the souls he was actually God. Now, since there is no other god, to whom could he have said, "I will go before you"?

Moreover, it is written, "That you may know that I, the Lord, who call you by your name, am the God of Israel" [Isa. 45:3]. Thus, you say that this Cyrus whom you identify with Jesus did not know God until the point when all these things were done to him. In light of this, how can you say that the spirit of God entered Mary and took on flesh? If that were true, he certainly should have known God even before his birth. According to your interpretation it should have said, "That *they* may know God," i.e., that from then on they will know that God redeemed them. However, once it says, "That you may know that I am God," that indicates that beforehand he did not know God. Similarly, it says a bit later, "I have named you though you have not known me" [Isa. 45:4].

Moreover, it is written, "Who call you by your name, the God of Israel" [Isa. 45:3], and Jesus is not the God of Israel but the God of

Christendom to this day. The nonbeliever may say, "We are called Israel," but the answer is: If so, then any people can make that claim, for we were called by that name because of our father Israel, but why should you be named Israel? Indeed, we had that name even before the
5 birth of Jesus—since the time of our father Jacob.

Furthermore, it is written, "For the sake of my servant Jacob and Israel my elect" [Isa. 45:4]. Now, this verse contradicts their books, which say that Jesus redeemed these souls because until that time everyone went to hell—good and evil, sons of Jacob and sons of
10 Esau and Ishmael, Philistines, Kedarites, Moabites, Lydians, Hagarenes, Ethiopians, and all other nations. From this belief it would follow that he came for all of them, and yet the verse testifies that he came for Jacob alone.

It also says, "I have named you though you have not known
15 me" [Isa. 45:4]. Thus, the verse testifies that this Cyrus whom you identify with Jesus did not know God. It is also written, "That they may know from east to west that there is none beside me; I am the Lord and there is none else" [Isa. 45:6]. According to them, however, the opposite is true, for now they will say that there are two
20 powers—father and son.

[96]

"For the Lord shall comfort Zion" [Isa. 51:3]. The heretics say that Zion is Christendom, which he took out of hell. The answer is: Were all those who died before Jesus' birth part of Christendom? It also says, "He will comfort all her ruins" [ibid]; now what ruins
25 did Christendom have? Furthermore, what does Zion have to do with Christendom? Israel, on the other hand, was called Zion, as it is written, "And the daughter of Zion is left as a cottage in a vineyard" [Isa. 1:8]. And here is another answer when he tells you that they are called Zion. Tell him: You are quite right. Now see what Micah the Mor-
30 ashtite prophesied concerning Zion: "They build upon Zion with blood. . . . Therefore shall Zion be ploughed as a field" [Mic. 3:10-12]. Thus, they shall be destroyed.

Furthermore, it is written, "He who justifies me is near" [Isa. 50:8]. All of his justifiers, however, were far away, while his
35 accusers were near, for they say that even his father in heaven was

too far away to save him in his time of trouble, as it is written in a
chapter which they refer to Jesus, "My God, my God, why have you
forsaken me? Why are you so far from helping me?" [Ps. 22:1; cf.
Matt. 27:46]. It goes on to say, "But be not far from me, O Lord; O my
5   strength, hasten to help me" [Ps. 22:20]; you see, then, that salvation
was far from him. Know, then, that this passage was written to teach
Israel how to answer the heretics.

[97]

"For they shall see eye to eye when the Lord returns to Zion"
[Isa. 52:8]. The heretics refer all these visions to Jesus. The answer
10   is to be found in an adjoining verse, for Scripture testifies that the
divine presence has not rested in Zion from the time Israel was exiled, as it is written, "Now, therefore, what have I here, says the
Lord, for my people is taken away for nought . . ." [Isa. 52:5].
Moreover, it says, "When the Lord returns to Zion"; now, when did
15   Jesus rule in Zion and then leave it that the verse can speak of him as
returning to it? It is also written, "And all the ends of the earth shall
see the salvation of our God" [Isa. 52:10]. They say that this refers to
the salvation he wrought when he took the souls out of hell, but what
evidence can they cite for this view?

[98]

20   "Behold, my servant shall succeed; he shall be exalted and
extolled, and be very high" [Isa. 52:13]. The heretics refer this entire
passage to Jesus because he experienced torture, death, and suffering
for them. The answer is in the very same passage: "He shall be exalted and extolled"; thus, this was not the case until now. It is also
25   written, "His visage was marred more than any man, and his form
more than the sons of men" [Isa. 52:14]; now, if he was God, why
was his face marred? Even if you will say that this was because
people hit him and caused him pain, this should not have marred him
if he was God. "So shall he sprinkle many nations; kings shall shut
30   their mouths in his presence" [Isa. 52:15]. It should have said, "So
shall he bring many nations near to him," i.e., that he would gather
many nations to his faith. "That which had not been told them shall
they see" [ibid.]—but they say that all the prophets prophesied con-

cerning him. "And to whom is the arm of the Lord revealed?" [Isa. 53:1]. This would prove that the deeds of Jesus were never revealed either to sages or to prophets. "He had no form nor comeliness. . . . He is despised and rejected of men" [Isa. 53:2–3]. But they say that
5 the verse in Psalms, "My heart is inditing a good thing. . . . You are fairer than the children of men" [Ps. 45:2–3] refers to Jesus, and yet here it says, "He is despised and rejected of men." If he will reply that in his life he was handsome but in his death he had no form, the answer is: If he is God, what sort of death did he suffer and what
10 change should have taken place in his appearance? "And when he hid his face from us, he was despised and we esteemed him not" [Isa. 53:3]. Now, these are very confusing words, because everyone knows that it was before he died and became hidden from people that he was not esteemed, while after his death people erred by following
15 him and thinking that he ascended to heaven.

"Surely he has borne our griefs" [Isa. 53:4]. To what does the verse refer? If you will say that it refers to his forgiving of their sins, was there no forgiving of sin before Jesus was born? Does it not say, "Forgiving iniquity and transgression . . ." [Exod. 34:7; Num. 14:18]?
20 Moreover, it says with regard to sacrifices, "He shall make expiation on his behalf for his sin, and he shall be forgiven" [Lev. 4:26], and it says, "And the Lord said, I forgive, as you have asked" [Num. 14:20]. You may argue that this forgiveness did not save them from hell but only from punishment and suffering, but we find that he did
25 punish them during their lifetime, as it is written, "And Moses said, Each of you put sword on thigh" [Exod. 32:27], and it says, "And some three thousand of the people fell that day" [Exod. 32:28]. You see then that this forgiveness did not save them from punishment; consequently, its function must have been to save them from hell.
30 "But he was wounded for our transgressions, bruised for our iniquities" [Isa. 53:5]. They say that he suffered all his tortures for their sins, i.e., to redeem them from hell. However, according to them this fate was not a result of transgressions and iniquities, for they say that even those without sins went down to hell. Thus, it was
35 not because of our transgressions that he had to suffer death but in order to nullify his decree that all men, good or evil, must descend to hell. If you will then say that it was for the sake of his believers and

because of their sins that he suffered all this—for his death expiates all the sins of those who believe in him—then all his believers are free of any commandments and needn't hesistate to rob, steal, murder, or commit adultery since all is expiated by his death. Thus, the
5   good he did is really an evil which brings a curse to the world.

[99]

"Seek the Lord while he may be found . . ." [Isa. 55:6]. The heretics say that the verse, "Hearken diligently unto me" [Isa. 55:2] was spoken by Jesus. The answer is: Where is Jesus' name mentioned or even hinted at in this verse? Furthermore, the entire passage
10 refers to Israel's exile, and why, according to them, should Israel have been exiled because of disbelief in Jesus any more than other nations? "Behold, you shall call a nation that you know not . . . because of the Lord your God" [Isa. 55:5]; thus, there is a God above Jesus. It also says, "And for the Holy One of Israel" [ibid.]; according to
15 them, it should have said, "Of Christians." If he will then tell you that they are Israel, answer him by saying: Before the birth of Jesus who did not call us Israel? Moreover, of whom was it said, "But fear not, O my servant Jacob and be not dismayed, O Israel, for behold I will save you from afar off and your seed from the land of their captiv-
-20 ity" [Jer. 46:27]? It was obviously said about us, because where were they exiled?

[100]

"And a redeemer shall come to Zion" [Isa. 59:20]. The heretics refer this to Jesus. The answer is: Where is Jesus even hinted at in this verse? It also says, "*Veyir'u* from the west" [Isa. 59:19], which
25 they derive from the word meaning to see, i.e., that people will see Jesus with their eyes. However, the object of the verb is "the name of the Lord" [ibid.], and a name cannot be seen. "And to them that turn from transgression in Jacob" [Isa. 59:20]. Now, why should he mention Jacob in connection with Jesus? Moreover, according to their
30 view that Zion is Christendom, you may point to the verse, "Zion shall be ploughed as a field" [Mic. 3:12], which indicates that it will be destroyed. Undoubtedly, then, the prophet said this concerning our redemption, and the following chapter, which begins, "Arise, shine, for your light has come" [Isa. 60:1], supports this view.

[101]

"The spirit of the Lord God is upon me, because the Lord has anointed me to preach good tidings unto the meek; he has sent me to bind up the brokenhearted, to proclaim liberty to the captives, and the opening of the prison to them that are bound" [Isa. 61:1]. The heretics
5   refer this to Jesus. The answer is: Read on: "To proclaim the acceptable year of the Lord, and the day of vengeance of our God" [Isa. 61:2]. Against whom did he either take vengeance or come to do so? Moreover, it says, "The spirit of the Lord is upon me," and, "Because the Lord has anointed me"; thus, he admits that he is not an equal. And
10 here too one can ask what hint of Jesus there is here; Ishmaelites and other nations can also say that this was said of their god.

[102]

"And the nations shall see your righteousness, and all kings your glory" [Isa. 62:2]. The heretics refer this to Jesus. Read on: "And a royal diadem in the hand of your God" [Isa. 62:3]; this shows
15 that Jesus was no different from other men. It also says, "You shall no more be termed forsaken" [Isa. 62:4], which indicates that until now he was forsaken; but if he was God, who forsook him? "The Lord has sworn by his right hand and by his strong arm, Surely I will no longer give your corn to be food for your enemies . . ." [Isa. 62:8].
20 Now, if the verse refers to Jesus, what sort of corn did he have? Furthermore, if he were God what would be the meaning of "Surely I will no longer give your corn to be food for your enemies"? Doesn't God give food to those who rebel against him as well as to those who believe in him? And it says, "For which you have labored" [ibid.],
25 while of God it says, "He grows not faint, neither is he weary" [Isa. 40:28].

[103]

"I am sought by them that asked not for me; I am found by them that sought me not. . . . I have spread out my hands all day unto a rebellious people" [Isa. 65:1–2]. The heretics say that this is what
30 Jesus told the Jews, who do not listen to him. The answer, again, is in the adjoining verse, as it is written, "A people that provokes me to anger continuously to my face" [Isa. 65:3]; it is probable that all this

was said of the Jews who followed Jesus. "Those who sacrifice in gardens" [ibid.] refers to their monasteries, and "those who burn incense on bricks" [ibid.] is a reference to the high place which they call *altar*. "Those who sit among the graves" [Isa. 65:4] refers to their
5   custom of surrounding the graves of the "saints." "Who eat swine's flesh and broth of abominable things" [ibid.] in which the swine was cooked: they put this in "their vessels" to go with bread as a relish because of its fat. "Who prepare a table for Gad" [Isa. 65:11], and set up tables in groups like kings, and fill numberless glasses of wine;
10 this is what they eat in another house, namely, the monastery.

[104]

"And I will bring forth a seed out of Jacob" [Isa. 65:9]. The heretics maintain that this is Jesus. The answer is in the very same verse: "My elect shall inherit it and my servants shall dwell there" [ibid.]; in that case there were many Jesuses, for he did not say this
15 of Jesus alone. Moreover, does it say, "I will bring forth a seed out of Jacob, and he shall be God"? Or, "Believe in him and his commandments"? What then can be proved from this reference? Indeed, all the verses till the end of the passage constitute an answer to their arguments. Similarly, it says in Ezekiel, "And I will bring you out from
20 the peoples and gather you out of the countries. . . . And I will bring you . . . and plead with you. . . . And I will bring you into the bond of the covenant. And I will purge out from among you the rebels and transgressors" [Ezek. 20:34-38]. Similarly, too, it says in the prophecy of Hosea, "As for Ephraim, their glory shall fly away like a bird,
25 from birth, from the womb, and from conception" [Hos. 9:11], i.e., from the time they believed in Jesus' birth—that it began in the womb in the manner of conception and that he was there month by month and week by week.

[THE TWELVE MINOR PROPHETS]

[105]

"I will ransom them from the power of the grave; I will redeem them from death" [Hos. 13:14]. The heretics refer this to Jesus, who took the souls out of hell. The answer is in the same verse: "I shall decree
5 your death; I shall cut you off to sheol" [ibid.]; thus, he returned them to their place. Moreover, it is written, "Samaria is guilty, for she has rebelled against her God" [Hos. 14:1]; now, did Samaria alone rebel against Jesus that he should mention only Samaria which includes only the people of the kingdom of Israel and not those of the
10 kingdom of Judah? It also says, "O Israel, return unto the Lord your God, for you have fallen by your iniquity. . . . Assyria shall not save us; we will not ride upon horses, neither will we say any more to the work of our hands, you are our gods" [Hos. 14:2–4]. Thus, the prophet warned and chastised them only concerning idols that they
15 made with their hands and not concerning another God. Furthermore, it does not say, "For she has rebelled against Jesus" or "against God," but "against her God," i.e., against the God that she already had, and that was not Jesus. It also says earlier, "I am the Lord your God who brought you out of the land of Egypt, and you shall know no
20 god but me, for there is no savior beside me" [Hos. 13:4], and Jesus did not bring us out of Egypt.

[106]

"The breaker has come up before them; they have broken up and passed through the gate and have gone out by it, and their king shall pass before them and the Lord at the head of them" [Mic. 2:13].
25 The heretics refer this to Jesus who broke through the gates of hell and removed the souls from it and then passed before them. The answer is in this very passage: See what is written earlier and later. Earlier it says, "I will surely assemble all of you, O Jacob; I will surely gather the remnant of Israel. I will put them together as the

119

sheep of Bozrah, as the flock in the midst of their fold. . . . The
breaker has come up etc." [Mic. 2:12-13]. The context, then, testifies
that this "breaker" refers to the gathering together of Jacob and
Israel, while from the time of Jesus they were dispersed and not gath-
5   ered together. Moreover, it says, "And their king shall pass before
them, and the Lord at the head of them"; thus, the verse refers to
two—the king and the Lord—and according to them, who was the
king and who the Lord?

Later on, it says, "Hear, I pray you, O heads of Jacob and
10   princes of the house of Israel. Is it not for you to know judgment?"
[Mic. 3:1]. Now, if the verses are referring to Jesus, why do Israel
and Jacob have any more to do with the matter of Jesus than any other
nations? The heretic might tell you that the reason Jacob and Israel
are mentioned in connection with Jesus' Torah rather than other na-
15   tions is that the former were originally loved by God, for we find that
in all the Torah of Moses only Israel is mentioned in connection with
the commandments, as it is written, "Speak to the people of Israel."
The answer is: What was the reason for this love of God for Israel?
When God approached all the nations to offer them the Torah, the
20   only nation he found that was willing to accept it was Israel, as it is
written, "All that the Lord has spoken we will do and obey" [Exod.
24:7]; this was the basis of God's love, as it is written, "Thus shall
you say to the house of Jacob and declare to the children of Israel"
[Exod. 19:3]. But now that you say that Jesus came to make it known
25   that anyone who believes in his birth will be saved from the punishment of hell and merit life in the world to come, this announcement
and warning should have been made to every nation, since all men are
the handiwork of God. Thus, he should have had mercy on all of them
and exhorted them to follow the right path. Nevertheless, in all the
30   prophets we find that he exhorts Israel alone, which is most difficult
to explain. Moreover, it is written, "Who hate the good and love the
evil, who pluck their skin off them and their flesh from off their
bones" [Mic. 3:2]. We see, then, that the prophet was chastising
them for robbery and not concerning belief in God, as it is written
35   above, "Woe to them that devise iniquity and do evil upon their beds:
when the morning is light, they practice it, because it is in their
power. And they covet fields and take them by violence, and houses,

and take them away; so they oppress a man and his house, even a man and his inheritance" [Mic. 2:1-2].

[107]

"And you, Bethlehem Ephratah, though you be little among the thousands of Judah, yet out of you shall come forth unto me one
5 who is to be ruler in Israel, whose goings forth . . . have been from days of old" [Mic. 5:1]. The heretics say that this refers to Jesus who came out of Bethlehem to be a ruler. The answer is: Let us assume that you are right. If so, however, would you also say that the prophecy at the beginning of Nahum, "There is one come out of you
10 that imagines evil against the Lord" [Nah. 1:11], refers to Jesus? And here is another answer: It says, "To be a ruler in Israel"; now, what sort of divinity is there in one who rules only in Israel? Also, read on: "Then the remnant of his brethren shall return unto the children of Israel" [Mic. 5:2]; now, does God have brothers? Moreover, it says,
15 "And he shall stand and feed in the strength of the Lord, in the majesty of the name of the Lord his God" [Mic. 5:3]; we see, then, that this ruler has a God, as it is written, "In the majesty of the name of the Lord his God." But if he is God, who is his God? It also says, "With this there shall be peace when Assyria shall come into our
20 land" [Mic. 5:4]; now, was making peace with their enemies the purpose of Jesus' advent and birth from Mary? The proper explanation of this passage is that it deals with the house of David.

[108]

"There is one come out of you that imagines evil against the Lord, a wicked counselor" [Nah. 1:11]. The heretics say that this was
25 said of Judah, whom they call Judas Iscariot, because he betrayed Jesus, as it says in their book of errors. The answer is: It makes sense to say that one man betrayed another, because a man does not know what another is thinking, but what sort of thought or counsel can one prepare against God? After all, it is written, "There is no
30 wisdom nor understanding nor counsel against the Lord" [Prov. 21:30]. Thus, if Jesus were God, who could have betrayed him? And if he did not know what was in the heart of the man who betrayed him, then he was not God. On the contrary, it is probable that this verse

refers to Jesus himself because he plotted against God by pretending
to be God himself. This interpretation would follow the pattern set
by your own explanation of the above-mentioned verse, "And you,
Bethlehem Ephratah . . . out of you shall come forth unto me one who
5   is to be ruler in Israel" [Mic. 5:1], which you take as a reference to
Jesus. Moreover, according to you what evil did Judas Iscariot imagine and what betrayal did he perpetrate? After all, Jesus came to earth
for the very purpose of handing himself over to man in order to be
killed; consequently, what evil did Judas do? Furthermore, how do
10 you know that "out of you" refers to Israel? After all, Israel is not
even mentioned in this entire passage. The true interpretation is entirely different.

[109]

"Sing, O barren woman who did not give birth" [Isa. 54:1].
Here the heretics speak defiantly and say that this refers to the
15 mother of the crucified one. The answer is: It does not say, "Sing, O
virgin," and a woman is not called barren unless she lives with a man
and does not give birth. Moreover, all the preceding passages—"For
you shall not go out with haste. . . . Behold my servant shall succeed"
[Isa. 52:12-13]—refer to Israel when it leaves its exile. In addition, it
20 says of this man, "For he was cut off from the land of the living" and,
"He made his grave with the wicked and with the rich in his death"
[Isa. 53:8-9], while Jeremiah testifies that God is "the living God and
an everlasting king" [Jer. 10:10]. And Habakkuk too says, "Are you
not from everlasting, O Lord my God, my holy one? We shall not die"
25 [Hab. 1:12]. Now, the last phrase is a scribal correction since he did
not want to say, "You will not die," inasmuch as death cannot be attributed to God.

[110]

Now to the earlier verse, "Give me my price; and if not, forbear. So they weighed for my price thirty pieces of silver" [Zech.
30 11:12]. The heretics speak defiantly and say that this was said about
the hanged one who was sold for thirty coins. The answer is that this
verse is to be understood in light of the earlier verse, "I cut off the
three shepherds in one month" [Zech. 11:8], and the explanation is

that the shepherd spoke the following parable: I tended the sheep for seven days, but because of their rebelliousness and evil ways I was unable to bear the trouble they caused. Consequently, I handed them over to another shepherd instead. However, he too was unable to

5 bear them for more than seven days, and so he returned them to me. I then gave them to another shepherd who was also unable to tend them for more than seven days, and he too gave them back to me. Finally, I gave them to a third shepherd who also tended them seven days. Thus, I cut off the three shepherds in one month since all of us com-

10 bined were unable to tend the sheep more than one month, i.e., thirty days. I then asked for my price and said, "If it is all right with you, give me my price, and if not, forbear." So they weighed for my price thirty pieces of silver, one piece per day, making thirty pieces for the thirty days that I and my friends tended the sheep.

[111]

15   "Thus said the Lord, For three transgressions of Israel, and for four I will not return him" [Amos 2:6]. The heretics interpret this to mean, "I will not return you to your land again from the fourth exile." Rabbi David answered that the opposite interpretation is more reasonable: For three transgressions I returned you to your place of

20 exile, but once they have been exiled for the fourth transgression, I shall not return them to exile again after they have been gathered together, as the prophets said, "And they shall no more be pulled up out of their land" [Amos 9:15]. In order to prove this, ask him whether Gog and Magog have come yet. If he says no, answer him by pointing

25 out that it is written in connection with the coming of Gog and Magog, "Then shall they know that I am the Lord their God who caused them to be led into captivity among the heathen, but I have gathered them unto their own land and have left none of them there anymore. Neither will I hide my face anymore from them. . ." [Ezek.

30 39:28-29]. The truth is that this is the correct interpretation: For three transgressions of Israel I forgave them, and for four will I not forgive them?! Of course I shall as I have in the past. The verse thus constitutes a rhetorical question. Another interpretation might be as follows: Until now I left you alone until you yourself repented, and then

I accepted you; now, however, on the fourth occasion, I shall not give you time to repent on your own, for before you repent I shall accept you and redeem you since I have already tested you many times.

[112]

"A prayer of Habakkuk the prophet. . . . O Lord, I have heard
5   your speech and was afraid. O Lord, give life to your work in the midst of the years (*shanim*)" [Hab. 3:1-2]. The heretics say that this refers to Jesus who was born in a manger in a place where two (*shenei*) animals, an ox and a donkey, stand. The answer is: Why should Habakkuk have been afraid of this, as it is written, "O Lord, I have
10 heard your speech and was afraid"? Furthermore, why should he have prayed concerning this? Does a man pray for the life of God, as it says, "Give it life"? Moreover, it says, "God came from Teman" [Hab. 3:3], but according to them it should have said, "God came from Bethlehem." There is also a different answer that you can give: It is
15 true; the passage refers to Jesus. Indeed, that is why Habakkuk was fearful and taken aback; it was because of Jesus' advent and what the prophet heard of it. He was dumbfounded when he heard of the advent of a god who is born of a woman and is killed, and he said, "How is such a thing possible? Why, in the past when God revealed himself at
20 Sinai he did not come in such a way. Rather, 'God came from Teman, and the holy one from Mount Paran . . . His glory covered the heavens' [Hab. 3:3]; he came in glory and in a manner worthy of God." And the prophet went on, "When I heard, my stomach trembled" [Hab. 3:16]—when I heard of Jesus. "And I trembled in myself, that I might
25 rest in the day of trouble" [ibid.], for how could I find a haven from such a day of trouble in which Jesus will pretend to be God and gather many legions to his banner, when all his deeds are like "a fig tree" that "shall not blossom, neither shall fruit be in the vines, the labor of the olive shall fail (*kiḥesh*) and the fields shall yield no food" [Hab.
30 3:17]? So do those who draw people after him lie (*yekhaḥashu*) in all their deeds. "The flock shall be cut off from the fold and there shall be no herd in the stalls" [ibid.], for in the end of days that god who was born in the stall will be killed and will be no more. "And I will rejoice in the Lord" [Hab. 3:18] and not in such a god.

[113]

"Therefore, wait for me, says the Lord, until the day that I rise up to the prey" [Zeph. 3:8]. The heretics say that Jesus said this. The answer is: According to you why was the adjoining prophecy not fulfilled, namely, "For then will I turn to the people a pure language,
5 that they may all call upon the . . . one . . . Lord" [Zech. 3:9]? This, of course, has not yet been fulfilled, for every nation calls upon the name of its own god. You may also reply: You are quite right; Jesus said, "Wait for me until the day that I rise up to the prey." In this manner you can see that he did not remain true to his word and did not fulfill
10 his promise, for it says, "Then will I turn to the people a pure language," "then" implying "when I come"; yet quite a few years have passed since his advent and this promise remains unfulfilled.

[114]

"Sing and rejoice, O daughter of Zion, for, lo, I come. . . . And many nations shall be joined to the Lord . . ." [Zech. 2:14-15]. The
15 heretics explain this as a reference to Jesus. The answer is in this very passage, as it is written, "And I will dwell in the midst of you, says the Lord" [Zech. 2:14], while Jesus was killed and passed away from there. You may then argue that his spirit rests in the midst of Zion, but the divine presence has not been found in Jerusalem from
20 the time of the exile, as it is written, "Now, therefore, what have I to do here, says the Lord, for my people has been taken away for naught" [Isa. 52:5]. The true interpretation of the passage, then, is that it refers to the Second Temple.

[115]

"Thus says the Lord of hosts, It shall yet come to pass that
25 there shall come nations and the inhabitants of many cities. And the inhabitants of one city shall go to another, saying, Let us go speedily to pray before the Lord and to seek the Lord of hosts . . . in Jerusalem and to pray before the Lord" [Zech. 8:20-22]. The heretics explain this as a reference to Jesus, who sat in Jerusalem and whom the
30 nations sought so that they could follow him in their error. The answer is in the adjoining verse, as it is written, "Thus says the Lord

of hosts: In those days ten men from all the languages of the nations
shall take hold of the edge of a Jew's garment, saying, We will go
with you, for we have heard that God is with you" [Zech. 8:23]. The
verse thus testifies that they will come to the God of the Jews and not
5   of the Christians, that it is referring to our God in heaven, and it em-
bodies a prophecy concerning the end of days. Similarly, it says in
Isaiah, "The mountain of the Lord's house shall be established in the
top of the mountains . . . and all nations shall flow into it. And many
people shall go and say, Come, and let us go up to the mountain of the
10   Lord, to the house of the God of Jacob; and he will teach us of his
ways, and we will walk in his paths" [Isa. 2:2–3].

   If he tells you that they are called Jews (*yehudim*) because they
believe (*modim*) in Jesus and confess (*mitvadim*) the *Beichte* to the
priest, point out the verse in Jeremiah which says, "The word that
15   came to Jeremiah the prophet concerning all the Jews who dwell in the
land of Egypt" [Jer. 44:1]; here is proof that we were called Jews before the birth of Jesus. Moreover, throughout their book of errors
they are called not Jews or Israel or Jacob but Christians. Furthermore, if they are called Israel and Judah and their faith is true, then
20   why did the prophet Hosea son of Beeri say, "And the pride of Israel
testifies to his face. Therefore shall Israel and Ephraim fall in their
iniquity; Judah also shall fall with them" [Hos. 5:5]? In addition, it
says, "The sin of Judah is written with a pen of iron" [Jer. 17:1]. One
must therefore conclude that they cannot be saved. He may then tell
25   you: Similarly, we can say of you that there is no way you can be
saved, for you admit that these things were said about you. The
answer is: There is no doubt that this and many other punishments in
Scripture were said concerning us, but this was because we forsook
the Torah and our fathers worshiped other gods. God's anger was
30   therefore directed against us and our fathers, and he exiled us in
order to purge us of our sins. At the end of days, however, God will
console us and gather us together in accordance with all that is written in the Torah, the Prophets, and the Hagiographa, as it is written,
"When I have removed them into the land of their enemies, then at
35   last shall their obdurate heart humble itself, and they shall atone for
their iniquity. Then will I remember my covenant with Jacob . . ."
[Lev. 26:41–42]. They, however, were not called Judah and Israel until

they came to their present faith, and yet the prophet says that they will fall in their iniquity after they attained this name; at what time, then, can they expect to rise?

5   Moreover, it is written just above, "Thus says the Lord of hosts: The fast of the fourth month, and the fast of the fifth, and the fast of the seventh, and the fast of the tenth shall be to the house of Judah joy and gladness and cheerful feasts" [Zech. 8:19]. Now, concerning whom was this said? If you say that it refers to you, then why don't you fast on these four days until the end of days? And if you say
10 that this verse speaks of Jesus, then these fast days were made dependent upon his advent; yet despite the fact that he has come, you have not declared them holidays. There is consequently no doubt that this was said of us who are called Judah and that we must fast until the end of days when God's wrath is reversed and he has mercy upon
15 us. He may then tell you: This promise will be fulfilled for you at the end of days when you recognize the truth and turn to the belief in Jesus' divinity, as it is written at the end of the verse, ". . . and for cheerful feasts; therefore love the truth and peace" [ibid.]. Answer him: You are wrong, for "truth" here means truthful dealing between
20 man and man. Indeed, the adjoining verses testify to this, as it is written, "These are the things that you shall do: Let every man speak the truth to his neighbor . . . and love no false oath, for all these are things that I hate, says the Lord" [Zech. 8:16-17]. Know, moreover, that any repentance mentioned in connection with Israel refers to a
25 return to the God whom we accepted at Sinai and to his Torah, as it is written, "And return to the Lord your God" [Deut. 30:2], and not to a Torah given at a later time. If you then say that this means that we will return to you and be one nation, see what it says a little bit later: "The Lord your God will inflict all those curses upon the enemies and
30 foes who persecuted you" [Deut. 30:7]; now you are surely in this category. Consequently, we cannot become one nation, for we are written down for life and you for death since you are our enemies and persecutors.

[116]

"My covenant of life and peace was with him, and I gave them
35 to him for the fear with which he feared me and was afraid before my name. The law of truth was in his mouth and iniquity was not found in

his lips; he walked with me in peace and equity and turned many away
from iniquity. For the priest's lips should keep knowledge and they
should seek the law at his mouth, for he is the messenger of the Lord
of hosts. But you have departed from the way, have caused many to
5　stumble at the law, and have corrupted the covenant of Levi, says the
Lord of hosts. Therefore, have I also made you contemptible and base
before all the people, according as you have not kept my ways, but
have been partial in the law" [Mal. 2:5-9]. The heretics refer this
entire passage to Jesus. The answer is: Quite true; the passage does
10　refer to Jesus. Consequently, because he would mislead people, the
verse points out, "For he is the messenger of the Lord of hosts," a
messenger and not God. Moreover, it is written, "That my covenant
might be with Levi" [Mal. 2:4], and what does Jesus have to do with
Levi? "Of life and peace" [Mal. 2:5]. Now, in Jesus there was neither
15　life nor peace. Moreover, it says, "And I gave them to him for the fear
with which he feared me" [ibid.]; we see, then, that Jesus was a
worshiper of God and was not worshiped. The proper interpretation
is that Scripture is referring to ordinary priests.

[PROVERBS]

[117]

"Who has ascended up into heaven, or descended. . . ?" [Prov. 30:4].
The heretics say that this is Jesus. The answer is: Why does he say,
"What is his name" [ibid.]? Is it not known that his name is Jesus?
5 "And what is his son's name?" [ibid.]. Did Jesus have a son? "Who
has ascended up into heaven or descended?" Now, when did it ever
happen in the world that God descended to live with people? Yet the
author would say that it will happen again only if it had already
occurred, for Solomon has said, "What has been is what will be . . .,
10 and there is no new thing under the sun" [Eccles. 1:9]; therefore,
since it had not occurred it would never occur. "Who has gathered
the wind in his fists?" [Prov. 30:4]; i.e., what man has ever gathered
the blowing wind in his hands and caught it? Now, if this wind cannot
be caught and gathered together, is the Lord, who is the holy spirit,
15 capable of being gathered together in a woman? "Who has bound the
waters in a garment?" [ibid.]; it is an impossibility. "Who has set up
all the ends of the earth?" [ibid.]; i.e., what man ever picked up the
earth and carried it? This has never happened. How then could she
carry the holy spirit about which it is said, "Behold, the heaven and
20 heaven of heavens cannot contain you" [1 Kings 8:27]? Thus, it is undoubtedly a lie, and I would be a child to believe it. And if you say that
there is indeed nothing new under the sun and that it did occur in the
past that God descended to live with men, then "What is his name
and what is his son's name" [Prov. 30:4] that I may know something
25 of this matter? But since no one knows, it must be that such a thing
never happened and never will. "Every word of God is pure" [Prov.
30:5], specifically his statement that "The heavens are the heavens of
the Lord" [Ps. 115:16], and he would thus not live on earth with
human beings. "He is a shield" [Prov. 30:5] to those who believe this.
30 "Do not add to his words" [Prov. 30:6] by saying that God descended
to live on earth, "lest he reprove you" [ibid.] in the future for speaking lies concerning him.

[ECCLESIASTES]

[118]

"That which has been is named already, and it is known that it is
man" [Eccles. 6:10]. The heretics defiantly maintain that this was
said of the hanged one. However, look at the end of the verse:

5   "Neither may he contend with him that is mightier than he" [ibid.].
Thus, there is someone mightier and stronger than he.

[JOB]

[119]

Job said, "Man that is born of woman is of a few days and full of
trouble. He comes forth like a flower, and is cut down; he flees as a
shadow and does not abide. You open your eyes upon this as well"
5   [Job 14:1–3]. Consequently, since you say that the hanged one was
born of a woman though he was not the son of a man, Job has already
prophesied that he is of no use. And God "opened his eyes upon
this," knowing that the world will err with regard to this man and
prepared to bring to judgment all those who follow him.
10   Moreover, Eliphaz the Temanite said, "What is man that he
should be pure, and he who is born of woman, that he should be righteous?" [Job 15:14]. All this was said of Jesus, who maintained that
he was the son of a woman and not of a man. Thus, Eliphaz said that
he would not be righteous because of this assertion that he was born
15   only of a woman.

[SELECTIONS FROM DANIEL, PSALMS, AND THE TWELVE MINOR PROPHETS]

[120]

"When the most holy one comes, an anointed one will cease to exist among you." Here they compose a nonexistent verse, for you will not
5 find this verse anywhere in the book of Daniel. What you do find is that in one verse it says, "And to anoint the most holy" [Dan. 9:24], and in the third verse after that it says, "And after sixty-two weeks, an anointed one shall be cut off and be no more" [Dan. 9:26]. They combine the two verses into one and say that when the one of impure
10 descent comes, the kingdom of the house of David and Judah will cease. Answer them according to their own folly: If so, you contradict yourself, for you often cite the verse, "Of the increase of his sovereignty and peace there shall be no end upon the throne of David and upon his kingdom to order it and to establish it with judgment and
15 with justice from henceforth even for ever" [Isa. 9:6], and yet here you say that that kingdom will cease. If so, he would not establish it but destroy it. In addition, how can a person destroy something that does not exist? Before Jesus' advent, after all, the kingdom had left Judah for more than two hundred years, and they were subjugated to
20 the kingdom of Greece; indeed, Jesus himself was judged by the kingdom of Greece. Moreover, put them off by asking, "Who was Daniel, a Jew, Muslim, or Christian?" They will say, "He was a Jew." Answer then: The reason that Daniel said this prophecy about other nations and not about Israel is that even before the prophecy there
25 was no king in Israel. This, then, is what he said: When the most holy, i.e., God, comes to judge the earth, then your kingdom will cease and there will be no king or anointed ruler in the world, for God will be king over all the earth and he alone will be exalted on that day. Now since you say that Daniel was a Jew, why does he say that "your
30 kingdom will cease"? He should have said "our kingdom."

[121]

"Who will abide in your tabernacle?" [Ps. 15:1]. This chapter was said to warn and encourage people and to guide them on the right path.

[122]

"Preserve me, O God, for in you do I put my trust" [Ps. 16:1]. The heretics say that the *ecclesia* is speaking. The answer is: "Their
5 sorrows shall be multiplied who hasten after another" [Ps. 16:4], and they hasten after another god. The correct interpretation of the chapter is that David said it about himself.

[123]

"Who shall abide in your tabernacle and who shall dwell in your holy hill? He who walks uprightly and works righteousness,
10 and speaks the truth in his heart. He who does not gossip with his tongue. . . . [He who does these things] shall never stumble" [Ps. 15]. On the basis of this psalm, the heretics curse us and ask why we take interest from Gentiles. After all, it says in this psalm, "He who does not lend his money at interest" [Ps. 15:5] without any qualifications;
15 neither the uncircumcised nor the circumcised are excluded. The answer is: Who gave the Torah to Israel? God. Through whom? Through Moses. Now, Moses said, "You may take interest on loans to a Gentile, but do not take any on loans to your brother" [Deut. 23:21]. If you then say that the descendants of Esau are also called
20 brethren, as it is written, "You shall not abhor an Edomite, for he is your brother" [Deut. 23:8], the answer is: It is true that they were once brethren and it was forbidden to take interest from them; now, however, they have disqualified themselves and are considered strangers, for when the Temple was destroyed they did not come to
25 help, as it is written, "In the day that you stood aside . . . even you were as one of them" [Obad. 1:11]. Indeed, they themselves actually helped destroy it, as it is written, "Remember, O Lord, the children of Edom in the day of Jerusalem . . ." [Ps. 137:7]. Moreover, they consider themselves foreigners, for they are not circumcised; and it is
30 written, "Every foreigner who fails to circumcise the flesh of his foreskin" [cf. Exodus 12:43-48]. You may then ask: Even if the fathers sinned, what is the sin of the children? The answer is that this

applies indefinitely, as long as they remain rebellious. Indeed, even if
they repent and become proselytes, they cannot enter the congregation of the Lord until the third generation. Moreover, one can respond
concerning interest that it represents legitimate gain, for Solomon
5   said, "He who increases his wealth through usury and unjust gain
will gather it for one who pities the poor" [Prov. 28:8]; i.e., his sin
can be expiated through charity. Now if this were regarded as robbery, how could charity help? Why, it is written, "The sacrifice of the
wicked is an abomination" [Prov. 15:8]. Moreover, it is written,
10 "You may not take interest from loans to your brethren, but you may
do so on loans to a Gentile," i.e., to one who is uncircumcised.

[124]

"Because they sold the righteous for silver and the poor for a
pair of shoes" (Amos 2:6). The heretics say that this refers to Jesus
whom the Jews sold for thirty pieces of silver which was sufficient
15 for each of them to buy a pair of shoes. The answer is: Is it proper to
call God poor so that the verse could say, "And the poor for a pair of
shoes"? Moreover, if he considered the sale sinful, why, if he was
God, did he not protest and prevent them from carrying out their plan?
And if you will say that this sale was in accordance with his will, then
20 this would show that Jesus wants the death of one who dies, while
Ezekiel said, "For I do not desire the death of one who dies" [Ezek.
18:32]. And in Psalms it says, "For you are not a God who desires
evil" [Ps. 5:5]. Now, if he was God, why did he set up a situation in
which they would be likely to sin? You can say that he was content to
25 die because his death would enable him to bring souls out of hell, but
how did this sale help the souls so much that he was willing to cause
punishment to Israel because of it? The proper interpretation of this
passage would undoubtedly refer it to a different matter.

[125]

"While I live will I praise the Lord" [Ps. 146:2]. While I live;
30 but after my death there is neither speech nor words. So Jesus turned
to worms and became worthless after his death. "Do not put your
trust in princes, in a human being in whom there is no salvation" [Ps.

146:3]. This refers to the "saints" who gave their lives for their faith
in Jesus; do not trust them to pray for you, for there is no prayer after
death. "In a human being in whom there is no salvation." Do not trust
in Jesus, who was a human being and was hanged, because he will not
5   save; he was unable to save himself, and so how could he save
others? "His breath goes out, he returns to his earth" [Ps. 116:4].
This refers to the breath of that man in whom you trust and who you
say is the son of God. "On that day his thoughts perish" [ibid.] as
well as all his opinions, and all who trust in him will be ashamed.
10   However, "Happy is he who has the Lord of Jacob for his help, whose
hope is in the Lord his God" [Ps. 146:5], for he is the true God, our
God who lives forever, the eternal king who created heaven and earth.

[126]

"In that day the Lord shall be one and his name one" [Zech.
14:9]. Now, however, although he is certainly one, his name is not
15   one, for not all people call him God. The accursed heretics, for example, call him Jesus. Similarly, every nation and every idolatrous
religion calls the Deity by the name of its idolatry.

[PSALMS]

[127]

"Happy is the man who does not walk in the counsel of the wicked . . ."
[Ps. 1:1]. The heretics say that David said this of those who sinned
and made themselves wicked by hanging Jesus, and he said that that
5   man is happy who did not participate in their counsel. The answer is:
According to you, Jesus could not be God, because it says of God,
"For you are not a God who desires evil" [Ps. 5:5]. Similarly, it says
in Ezekiel, "As I live, says the Lord, I do not desire the death of the
wicked" [Ezek. 33:11], but he did want the death of the wicked, for
10 you say that he came to die at the hands of man. If so, those who killed
him fulfilled his will, and it was through them that his counsel and
decree to redeem the souls from hell were carried out, while nothing
at all was accomplished through those who did not touch him. Indeed,
if the former had also refrained from harming him like the latter, then
15 his entire advent would have been useless and in vain. Consequently,
you should reverse your words and say that those who fulfilled his
will and through whom his counsel was carried out are the righteous
men, while those who did not touch him are wicked because they did
not hasten to carry out his counsel so that he might redeem people
20 from hell. Indeed, it is amazing that you call those who hanged him
evil men and sinners; why, they fulfilled the will of both father and
son, as it is written in a verse that they refer to Jesus (as I shall explain in the proper place among the prophecies of Zechariah),
"Awake, O sword, against my shepherd and against the man that is
25 my fellow . . .; smite the shepherd, and the sheep shall be scattered . . ."
[Zech. 13:7]. Moreover, where is the story of Jesus or even a hint of
his life to be found in this chapter? Consequently, wise men will understand that all their words are falsehood and lies and have no substance. The truth is that David said this chapter concerning all men in
30 order to teach them and guide them in the straight and true path so
that they might go far away from the ways of evil men who are no
good.

[128]

"The Lord has said unto me, You are my son; this day have I begotten you" [Ps. 2:7]. They defiantly say that this verse refers to the hanged one. The answer is: In the account of creation it says, "Let us make man" [Gen. 1:26], and they interpret it as meaning that the
5 father told the son, "Let the two of us make man." Now, if he existed then and was born today, it follows that he was born twice. In addition, tell him: If they are merely three names, but all is really one, then when the son was born, so was the father; they were both born at the same time, since they are inseparable. If so, which of them calls the
10 other my son and which one is called father? After all, one did not precede the other by so much as a hairbreadth. You are therefore forced to the conclusion that the father preceded the son by many days during which the father was childless and alone with no son. Moreover, as I have shown above, according to your own words, one
15 must assume that the son was born twice.

I shall now ask a further question to which I should appreciate an answer: You say that the son was formed in Mary's womb. Inform me as to whether the father and the impure spirit were in the stomach with the son or whether the son was there alone. If you will say the
20 son alone, then your words are self-contradictory, for you say that they are never separated from each other. On the other hand, if you will say that the three of them were in the stomach and grew there, then all three were also on earth among people and all three were hanged. Who, then, was in heaven all that time, inasmuch as they are
25 inseparable? Furthermore, who ran the world during the three days when they were buried and none of them was either in heaven or on earth? Consequently, any wise man can understand that their words have no substance.

[129]

"But you, O Lord, are a shield for me . . ." [Ps. 3:4]. The here-
30 tics say that Jesus said this psalm when he was seized and tried. The

answer is in this very verse. How did he shield him? He was hanged! "I cried unto the Lord with my voice and he answered me" [Ps. 3:5]. But it says, "My God, why have you forsaken me? Why are you so far from helping me, and from the words of my roaring? O my God, I cry

5   in the daytime, but you answer not" [Ps. 22:2], and they say that Jesus said this chapter when he was seized. Thus, their words are contradictory; here he said, "And he answered me," and there he said, "But you answer not." "I lay down and slept" [Ps. 3:6]. Elijah mocked a sleeping god, saying, "Perhaps he is sleeping and must be

10 awakened" [1 Kings 18:27]. "Salvation belongs to the Lord" [Ps. 3:9]. About what did Jesus say this? What salvation was wrought for him? It must be, then, that David recited this chapter because God saved him from his son Absalom, who had pursued him, and the beginning of the chapter supports this view.

[130]

15   "But know that the Lord has set apart him that is pious for himself" [Ps. 4:4]. In their book of errors it says, "Him that is holy for himself," and they explain it as a reference to Jesus. The answer is in the very same verse: "The Lord will hear when I will call unto him" [ibid.]. Now, here you have verses that contradict each other,

20 for it is written, "O my God, I cry in the daytime, but you answer not" [Ps. 22:3], as I explained above. Moreover, it says, "I shall lie down and sleep at the same moment in peace" [Ps. 4:9], and that is what Elijah said, "Perhaps he is sleeping and must be awakened" [1 Kings 18:27]. And it says, "You have put gladness in my heart" [Ps.

25 4:8]; if he is God, who put gladness in his heart? It should have said, "I rejoiced in my heart and I gave wine and oil." "Offer sacrifices of righteousness" [Ps. 4:6]. If he said this about himself, why did he call those who killed him wicked and sinful men at the beginning of Psalms? After all, he himself commanded that this be done. The fact

30 is that David himself said this when he fled from Saul to Keilah.

[131]

"Give ear to my words, O Lord, consider my meditation" [Ps. 5:2]. The heretics refer this to Jesus. The answer is: You see, then,

that Jesus was not even on the level of a pious man, for of a righteous man it says, "You shall decree a thing and it shall be established for you" [Job 22:28]. Jesus' prayer, on the other hand, was not heard, as it says, "Destroy them, O God, let them fall by their own counsels"
5 [Ps. 5:11], and yet we see that their entire counsel against him was fulfilled. Moreover, it says, "The foolish shall not stand in your sight" [Ps. 5:6]; he calls all those who rebelled against him fools, and yet they did stand up against him. It also says, "My king and my God" [Ps. 5:3]; we see then that there was a king, a God, and a ruler
10 over Jesus. There is therefore no doubt that the chapter really refers to the event involving Saul, and the psalm beginning, "O Lord, rebuke me not in your anger" [Ps. 6] was also said of Saul's pursuits. Similarly, David also recited "A Shiggayon of David" [Ps. 7] concerning Saul, as it says, "Concerning the words of Kush the
15 Benjamite" [Ps. 7:1].

[132]

"O Lord, rebuke me not in your anger" [Ps. 6:2]. It is written in the *glossa* that this is the voice of the son speaking to the father. Ask him: According to your view that he is God, what sort of rebuke did he require? A rebuke, after all, results only from improper be-
20 havior. Similar arguments apply to the rest of the chapter. It also says, "For your name is not found in death" [Ps. 6:6], and so Jesus admits that anyone who dies can no longer be called by the name of God. What, then, can be said of the saints and even of Jesus himself in the light of the fact that they say this of him?

[133]

25 The heretics interpret the chapter beginning "A Shiggayon of David" [Ps. 7:1] as a reference to Jesus. This is the answer: We must conclude, then, that his prayer did not ascend to heaven, for it is written, "Save me . . . lest he tear my soul like a lion" [Ps. 7:2-3], and we see that he was indeed torn apart. Moreover, we learn from here that
30 Jesus was a sinner, for it is written, "O Lord my God, if I have done this, if there be iniquity in my hands. . . . let the enemy persecute my soul" [Ps. 7:4-6]. Thus, we may say that his soul was indeed perse-

cuted because there was iniquity in his hands. Furthermore, it says, "He has also prepared for him the instruments of death; he ordains his arrows against the persecutors" [Ps. 7:14]. We know, however, that none of his persecutors was hurt; we conclude, then, that there
5　is no substance to any of his words. If you will then argue that what he said had reference to his father and that the punishment would be meted out not in his lifetime but thereafter, then Jesus' words would contradict each other; for it is written in the Gospels that Jesus, at the time of his hanging, said, "Father, forgive them, for they know
10　not what they do" [Luke 23:24].

[134]

"O Lord our Lord, how great is your name in all the earth" [Ps. 8:2]. In the book of the heretics this chapter is referred to Jesus. "What is man that you are mindful of him and the son of man that you remember him?" [Ps. 8:5]. This constitutes an answer to the here-
15　tics, for they say that Jesus was a man; indeed, throughout the Gospels he is called son of man, *fili homini*. Consequently, there is reason to think that this verse was said of him. It also says, "How great is your name in all the earth" [Ps. 8:2]; i.e., there is none like him in all the earth. How, then, do you say that Jesus was on earth and
20　there were many like him? We, on the other hand, will not forget that David is thanking and praising God concerning the matter of Kush the Benjamite, for this chapter is connected with the one before it.

[135]

"I will praise you, O Lord, with all my heart" [Ps. 9:2]. The heretics say that Jesus is speaking. "When my enemies are turned
25　back" [Ps. 9:4] is regarded as a reference to the Jews. The answer is: "I will show forth all your marvelous works" [Ps. 9:2]; "All *my* marvelous works" is what he should have said. Moreover, it says here, "You have blotted out their name for ever and ever" [Ps. 9:6], and yet they admit that in the future we shall all live; their words thus
30　contradict each other. It is written, "He who seeks after blood remembers them; he forgets not the cry of humble men" [Ps. 9:13]. "He forgets not the cry of a humble man" is what he should have said.

Moreover, you can shorten your argument by telling him: Of course
the passage is speaking of Jesus, and that is why he says at the end,
"Arise O Lord, let not man prevail; let the nations be judged before
you. Put them in fear, O Lord, that the nations may know that they"
5 worshiped "a man" [Ps. 9:20-21]; this was indeed said of Jesus. In
their books it does not say *Selah* here. The correct interpretation of
the chapter would explain that he said "*Selah*" [Ps. 9:21] of the
messianic age; i.e., all the nations will ponder this judgment forever.
"Arise, O Lord, let not man prevail" [Ps. 9:20]; i.e., let no man grow
10 strong again. This is a reference to Jesus, whom they claim to be both
man and God, and also to Muhammad. "Let the nations be judged"
who worshiped them "beside you" (*'al panekha*) [ibid.]. In the book of
the priests it says, "In your sight" (*be-panekha*). It is also written,
"Put them in fear" (*morah*) [Ps. 9:21]. One should interpret this phrase
15 as referring to one who points out (*moreh*) something with his
fingers; i.e., show them things so that they may see and understand
that you alone are God, and let them realize that what they worshiped
until now was a man and not God.

[136]

"Why, O Lord, do you stand afar off?" [Ps. 10:1]. They refer
20 this chapter to Jesus, as I explained above, but the true explanation is
that it refers to the end of our exile.

[137]

"I put my trust in the Lord" [Ps. 11:1]. In the book of priests
they explain that this chapter too was said of those who did not believe in Jesus, and the Gentiles, whom they call *ecclesia*, are speaking.
25 They also maintain that the phrase, "What did the righteous man
do?" [Ps. 11:3] refers to Jesus. The answer is: According to you, it
should have said, "What did Jesus do?" Furthermore, what hint of
Jesus can be found here? Indeed, any man can similarly say that
"What did the righteous man do?" refers to himself and to his own
30 activity on this earth. "The Lord is in his holy temple; the Lord is in
heaven" [Ps. 11:4]; Jesus' temple, however, was on earth. If you then
argue that this refers to the time after his death, then how does he

differ from other people? Why, their souls are also in heaven after
they die. The true interpretation is that the chapter was said concerning Israel's exile, and the people of Israel are giving this answer to
the nations of the world.

[138]

5   "Help, Lord, for the godly man has ceased" [Ps. 12:2]. The
heretics maintain that their *ecclesia* is the speaker in this chapter. The
answer is: When did the *ecclesia* say this? If it was after Jesus was
killed, then what is the meaning of, "Now I will arise, says the Lord"
[Ps. 12:6]? He had, after all, already gone away. If, on the other hand,
10   the passage is referring to the end of days, the problem is the verse,
"The wicked walk on every side, when the vilest men are exalted"
[Ps. 12:9], which they explain as a reference to the day of his hanging,
when he was being led and the Jews walked before him and mocked
him. Moreover, according to them, this *ecclesia* also spoke improperly
15   of Jesus, for it says, "Faithfulness fails from among the sons of
man" [Ps. 12:2]; now, Jesus is also in the category of sons of man
since throughout the Gospels he is called son of man, *fili homini*. You
see, then, that they do not maintain a consistent position. The truth is
that this chapter too was said concerning the exile, and David prayed
20   for them, "Help, Lord, for the godly man has ceased" [Ps. 12:2].

[139]

"How long will you forget me, O Lord? For ever?" [Ps. 13:2].
The heretics say that these were the words of the *ecclesia* before Jesus
came, because it desired him, "Lest I sleep the sleep of death" [Ps.
13:4] in hell. The answer is: Any wise man will understand how con-
25   fused their words are. If the Gentiles had been one nation before he
came and had desired him, then they could say this, just as Israel was
one nation in Egypt and wanted their redeemer to come. But how can
the verses, "How long will you forgive me, O Lord? For ever? . . . .
How long shall I take counsel in my soul, having sorrow in my
30   heart?" [Ps. 13:2-3] be applied to Christendom which was gathered
together one by one from all the nations only after he came? What
group could have been taking counsel concerning him, and who was in

sorrow because of him? You may then maintain that the reference is to those in hell, but it says, "The dead know nothing" [Eccles. 9:5]; how, then, can you say that they pray and worry? Moreover, according to you it should have said, "*For* I sleep the sleep of death." "*Lest* I
5 sleep the sleep of death" is the statement of one who does not want to die. The correct interpretation of the chapter is that David participated in the sorrow of Israel; the chapter is thus about the exile.

[140]

"The fool has said in his heart, There is no God" [Ps. 14:1]. They maintain that David said this chapter about the Jews who said
10 that Jesus was not God. The answer is: It says, "They are all gone aside, they have all together become filthy; [there is none that does good,] no not one" [Ps. 14:3]; did not even one Jew follow Jesus? It also says, "Those who eat up my people eat bread" [Ps. 14:4]; "Those who eat *him* up" is what David should have said. Moreover, it
15 says, "For God is in the generation of the righteous" [Ps. 14:5], and they refer this to Jesus; but above it says, "The fool has said in his heart, There is no God" [Ps. 14:1]. The true interpretation of the chapter is that it was said of the destruction of the Temple and the exile.

[141]

20 "A prayer of David. Hear righteousness, O Lord . . ." [Ps. 17:1]. The heretics say that Jesus said this prayer to his father concerning the Jews who judged him. Thus, they say that David here is *Christus,* and so also in many other passages. The answer is: Can you say that every time it says David in Samuel and Kings the meaning is
25 Jesus? Moreover, it says, "Let my sentence come forth from before you" [Ps. 17:2]; now, if Jesus were God and the verse referred to him, it would have said, "From before me." You have tested my heart" [Ps. 17:3]; is this a proper thing to say of God? "I have called upon you, for you will hear me, O God" [Ps. 17:6]; this shows that he
30 himself was not God. "Save my life from the wicked with your sword" [Ps. 17:13]. Jesus, however, neither escaped nor was saved, for he was killed. Moreover, why did he pray for his life? (It must be

pointed out that although their books say, "My soul," *anima mea,* their commentary, which they call *glossa,* nevertheless explains it as his life.) "From the wicked with your sword." They say that this refers to Satan. The answer is: Why should he fear Satan either in life or

5   death if he is God? "I will behold your countenance in righteousness; I shall be satisfied, when I awake, with your likeness" [Ps. 17:15]. In their books it says, "With your glory," and they say that this is what Jesus told his father. The answer is: According to them, it should have said, "With my glory." Moreover, how can you apply the verse,

10   "I will behold your countenance in righteousness" to fewer than two, one who sees and the other who is seen? How then do they say that the father and son are one? The truth is that David recited this prayer for himself, and even the priests admit that it has a dual meaning— one concerning David and the other concerning Jesus. Indeed, this is

15   their method with regard to all the chapters of Psalms; one meaning refers to us and another to Jesus and those who believe in him.

[142]

"To the chief musician, a psalm of David, the servant of the Lord" [Ps. 18:1]. The heretics refer this entire psalm to Jesus. In their book it says *puero,* the son, rather than the servant, and they say

20   that David is *Christus.* "On the day that the Lord delivered him from the hand of all his enemies" [ibid.]. They say that God raised Jesus from the grave and saved him from his enemies, the Jews, who were guarding his grave to make sure that he would not escape from them. "And from the hand of Saul" [ibid.]; that is Satan. "My God, my

25   strength, in whom I will trust" [Ps. 18:3]; that is his father. "In my distress I called upon the Lord" [Ps. 18:7]; Jesus said all this to his father. "Then the earth shook and trembled; all those who dwell on earth were shaken up" [Ps. 18:8] with the coming of Jesus. "Then the channels of the sea were seen, and the foundations of the world were

30   revealed" [Ps. 18:16]; these are the apostles who were revealed in the world to tell the story of Jesus' deeds and his religion. And so they explain the entire chapter partly concerning Jesus and partly concerning the *ecclesia.* The answer is: With regard to the phrase "of David" which they say refers to Jesus, this might be at least superficially

plausible if they could say that every "David" in Scripture refers to
Jesus; however, since they cannot say this, what proof can they cite
that this David is Jesus? The truth is that it refers to David himself
and not to Jesus. Moreover, if the chapters referred to Jesus and he
5   himself were God, the verse should have read as follows: "Who
spoke the words of this song on the day that he delivered him from
the hand of all his enemies and from the hand of Saul." This could
have been taken to mean that he was speaking of himself, i.e., that the
poet saved himself. But the fact that he says, "Who spoke unto the
10   Lord . . . on the day that the Lord delivered him" [Ps. 18:1] shows us
that this poet thanked God with his song for saving him, because he
could not have saved himself alone.

In the language of the priests it is written, "I love you, O God,
my strength" [Ps. 18:2]. Thus, there must be two—the one who
15   strengthens and the one strengthened; yet you say that Jesus and his
father are one. You may argue that the human aspect of Jesus said
this because God strengthened him and raised him from the grave,
but if Jesus' body were God, then he should have strengthened himself and arisen. If, on the contrary, his body is not God and is like that
20   of other men except that his father's spirit entered it so that he could
come to the earth in order to redeem the souls from hell, then this
body of Jesus was no more worthy of being raised up than those of
other men whom the holy spirit also entered, like Moses, Ezekiel, and
other prophets. Once the holy spirit left these prophets, their bodies
25   returned to the earth as they were and the spirit returned to God;
now, the same thing should have happened to Jesus if his divinity
took on flesh in order to go to the trouble of taking the souls out of
hell. Indeed, after having done all that there was no need to do any
more; rather, when the divine spirit returned to its original place the
30   body should have returned to the earth when the time came for the ful-
fillment of the curse against Adam, as it is written of him and his
descendants, "For you are dust, and unto dust will you return" [Gen.
3:20], for the body that was born of Mary came from the seed of
Adam. Now, since this was the case, the body should have become
35   dust as soon as the spirit departed from it just like the bodies of other
prophets and holy men. If you will point out that the bodies of Elijah

and Enoch did not return to dust, the distinction is that they did not
experience death. However, in the case of Jesus, who did experience
death, the body would not escape or be excused from the requirement
of returning to the dust like those of other men. You may then argue
5   that he was more important than other men who had the holy spirit.
The answer is that once he intended to rise in the flesh, he should
have done so openly in the sight of the guards and the entire people,
so that they would believe in him and tell the tale to the last generation. However, he did not do this, as it is written in their books that
10   no one but Mary Magdalene saw his ascent. If you will argue that this
was in order to reward his believers for believing on the basis of the
prophecies about him even though they saw nothing, then the question is why he performed wonders during his lifetime. Thus, according to your own statements, Jesus himself was responsible for the
15   disbelief in him since no one saw him ascend from earth to heaven.
Consequently, men of understanding, you can see that there is no
substance to their words. Indeed, all of these verses would have to be
explained with reference to two powers, since the body certainly did
not escape the curse of Adam.
20   The psalm allegedly goes on to explain his descent: "He made
darkness his secret place, his pavilion around him" [Ps. 18:12]. Now,
who saw this? The fact is that all people looked at him the way they
look at everyone else. With regard to the verse, "Then the channels of
water were seen" [Ps. 18:16], which they refer to the apostles, the
25   answer is: You are quite right. That is why it says, "As a result of
your anger, O God" [ibid.], because their appearance was an expression of God's wrath. You may then say that this is indeed so since the
apostles taught the nations Jesus' word and expressed his anger, but
if so it should have said, "The anger of God." Why does it say,
30   "Your anger"? The only reasonable explanation, therefore, is the one
mentioned above. Moreover, if the apostles had said, "Then the
channels of water were seen . . . as a result of your anger, O God. . . .
He sent from above, he took me" [Ps. 18:16-17], then it should have
said, "He took us." If, on the other hand, Jesus himself is the
35   speaker, then you are saying that he was unable to save himself, as it
is written, "He took me, he drew me out" [Ps. 18:17].

[143]

They interpret the following psalm as a reference to the apostles: "The heavens declare" [Ps. 19:2]; these are the apostles who told men the story of Jesus. "Day unto day it utters speech" [Ps. 19:3]; every day the prophets prophesied concerning Jesus and his
5 advent, and no one listened to them. "And for the sun he made a tent within them" [Ps. 19:5]. In their books it says, "He made him a tent among them in the sun," and they say that this refers to Jesus for whom Mary was a tent when he was a fetus inside her. Moreover, this Jesus was "as a bridegroom coming out . . ." [Ps. 18:6]. Now,
10 any wise man can understand that their words have no substance but are lies and falsehood which overturn the words of the Torah, and it was of them that Isaiah said, "Woe unto them that seek deep to hide their counsel . . ." [Isa. 29:15]. Where, after all, is there any reference to Jesus in this entire chapter? Why, any nation could explain the
15 same words as a reference to its god. Furthermore, with regard to their statement here that the prophets prophesied about him every day, I say that the reverse is true, that all the prophets said not to listen to him. Moses said, "If your brother, the son of your mother, entices you" [Deut. 13:7]. Now, does the son of a mother entice but
20 not the son of a father? This must therefore be a reference to Jesus who would come and say that he is the son of a mother and not of a father. Balaam said, "Alas, who shall live when God does this (*missumo*)" [Num. 24:23]; i.e., woe unto them who live when that man comes who will make (*yasim*) himself into a god and deceive people
25 into following him. That man, of course, was Jesus. Jeremiah said, "Accursed is the man who puts his trust in a man" [Jer. 17:5]. This is a reference to Jesus, for throughout the Gospels he is called son of man. Isaiah said, "The lofty looks of man shall be humbled . . . and the Lord alone shall be exalted in that day" [Isa. 2:11], and the verse un-
30 doubtedly refers to Jesus, who exalted himself above all men and pretended to be God. David said, "Put not your trust in princes" [Ps. 116:3]—these are the apostles—"in the son of man, in whom there is no salvation" [ibid.]—this is Jesus, who is called son of man. We see, then, that all the prophets contradict the story of Jesus.

Moreover, you can see that the meaning of the verses does not support the heretical interpretation, for according to their view that the apostles are the subject of this chapter, the verb "proclaims" should have been in the plural just like the verb "declare." Now, as
5 for the reading, "He made him a tent among them in the sun," Jerome objected to this practice in the Vulgate and said, "I and my friends make every effort to translate the Hebrew text into Latin without changing a thing"; yet those who came after him wrote their own text and overturned everything. The heretic may then argue that the later
10 scholars wrote according to the intent of the verse and not according to its literal meaning, but the fact remains that in any event what they have is worthless mockery, since they have distorted the words in accordance with their error and written things which God did not say.
Furthermore, how can they say that he came out of his
15 mother's womb, where he had placed his "tent," like "a bridegroom coming out of his chamber" and like "a strong man who rejoices to run a race" [Ps. 19:6]? The fact is that he came out dirty and filthy, and he was laid down in a crib like all other children. According to their view, what he should have done was come out of his mother's womb
20 and immediately run in the street, grow into manhood within the hour, and no longer have any need of his mother; then all who saw him would have recognized him and believed in him. We know, however, that he did not come forth like a bridegroom. Moreover, how can you call his mother's womb a tent? Only something which covers
25 from above and not from below can be called a tent, as it is written, "For a tent over the tabernacle" [Exod. 36:14]; it must provide shelter in the same way as all tents—above a man and not below or under him. But when Jesus was in his mother's stomach, her womb surrounded him above and below, and he was wrapped in the placenta
30 from head to toe. It also says, "His going forth is from the end of the heaven, and his circuit (*tequfato*), etc." [Ps. 19:7]. (*Tequfato* in Latin should not be *decursum eius* like *meruzato* [his running].) We see, on the contrary, that the belief in his divinity is held by a minority. Know too that it is because of this that David said, "The fear of the Lord is
35 pure, enduring for ever" [Ps. 19:10]; this excludes the fear of Jesus which is impure because he came from a filthy place.

[144]

"The king shall rejoice in your strength, O Lord" [Ps. 21:2].
The heretics say that this psalm was said of Jesus' father, praising
him for making Jesus king in the world, while "the king" is Jesus.
The answer is: The phrase, "The king shall rejoice in your strength"
5   indicates that the Lord and not Jesus has strength. If it had said, "O
king, rejoice in my strength," then I would have admitted that the
Lord and the king mentioned here are identical, but the phrase "the
king shall rejoice" indicates someone other than the Lord. "You have
given him his heart's desire, and have not withheld the request of his
10 lips" [Ps. 21:3]. Now, it is impossible to say this of the divine element within him, because that would imply that there were two
deities, one of whom gave the other. On the other hand, if you argue
that this refers to his human aspect, then the fact is that this was not
so, for he prayed for his life and salvation many times without being
15 answered, as it is written in the chapter beginning, "Hear righteousness, O Lord," "Deliver my soul from the wicked with your sword"
[Ps. 17:13]. Similarly, it says in the following psalm, "Be not far from
me, O Lord; O my strength, hasten to help me. Deliver my soul from
the sword, my beloved from the power of the dog" [Ps. 22:20-21].
20 Thus, we see that the request of his lips was withheld and his heart's
desire was not given him. Moreover, in the psalm beginning, "In you,
O Lord, do I put my trust," it says, "For I have heard the slander of
many . . . they devised to take away my life. . . . My times are in your
hand; deliver me from the hand of my enemies and from them that
25 persecute me" [Ps. 31:14-16]. But he was not saved from the sword
or from the hand of the enemies who pursued him in order to take his
life. "He asked life of you, and you gave it to him, length of days for
ever" [Ps. 21:5]. If this refers to his divine aspect, who gave him this?
After all, they say that he was God from time immemorial. If, on the
30 other hand, this was said of his human aspect, then we see that length
of days was not granted him; indeed, he lived less than half of a
normal life span, for it says that the years of a man's life are seventy,
and he lived but thirty-two. Furthermore, no one can argue that Jesus
did not die, for the essence of their faith is that Jesus experienced
35 death for them.

[145]

"My God, my God, why have you forsaken me? Why are you
so far from helping me and from the words of my cry?" [Ps. 22:2]. The
heretics say that Jesus said this psalm at the time of his hanging. Indeed, in their books it says, "My God, my God, remember me; why
5 have you forsaken me?" and it is also written in the heretics' books,
"My God, my God, look at me. Why have you forsaken me? Why are
the words of my transgression far from my salvation?" You see then
that Jesus himself admits that he is a sinner, and so how can you say
that he is God? We see also that Jesus was complaining that God for-
10 sook him; consequently, he could not have been a righteous man, for
Ecclesiastes said, "I have never seen the righteous forsaken, nor his
seed begging bread" [Ps. 37:25].

Ask the heretics who say that Jesus came to redeem the world
by his death why he cried out for help. Did he forget why he came to
15 the world or did he change his mind and regret his decision when he
experienced his tribulations?

"My God, my God, why have you forsaken me?" [Ps. 22:2].
The heretics say that he addressed two powers—the father and the
spirit—and that is why he cried out, "My God, my God," when he
20 was hanged, as is explained in the text. If so, then he was a wicked
man since he was forsaken, as the saying goes, "What God does not
want and forsakes is taken by the demons." Moreover, if he was
God, why did he cry out as he did? Why, all of these troubles came
upon him in accordance with his own will; they were proper in his
25 estimation, and he accepted everything with love.

"I am a worm, and no man" [Ps. 22:7]. They say that he said
this because of his great modesty. "But you are he who took me out
of the womb" [Ps. 22:10], i.e., from my mother, Mary. "Many bulls
have surrounded me" [Ps. 22:13]; these are the Jews who judged him.
30 "Like a lion my hands and my feet" [Ps. 22:127]. In their books it
says, "*Foderunt* my hands and feet," and they say that this refers to
the nails, for he was nailed to the cross through his hands and feet
when he was hanged. The answer is: The practice of pushing nails
through the hands and feet of people who were stoned and hanged did
35 not exist among the Jews. "I may tell all my bones" [Ps. 22:18]; in

their books it says, "They counted all my bones." "They divided my garments among them" [Ps. 22:19]; they say that when they hanged him they divided his clothes among them. "All those that are fat on earth shall eat and worship; all those that go down to the dust shall
5 bow before him, and none shall keep alive his own soul. Posterity shall serve him; it shall be recounted to the Lord for a generation. They shall come and declare his righteousness unto a people that shall be born, that he has done this" [Ps. 22:30–32]. These verses are written in their books as follows: "All they that have gone down to
10 the dust shall bow before him and he shall keep his soul alive for himself." (They read *lo* instead of *lo'*). This, then, is how they explain it: Jesus said, "For the kingdom is the Lord's and he is ruler among the nations" [Ps. 22:29] and not only among the Jews as had been the case until now, and just as the Gentiles were permitted to eat all the fat
15 things on earth until now, so they are still permitted to do so provided that they bow down to their father in heaven. "All those that have gone down to the dust shall bow before him" refers to Jesus, who redeemed the souls which descended to hell. And the apostles will "declare his righteousness unto a people that shall be born."
20   The answer is: How can you say that Jesus said, "My God, my God, why have you forsaken me?" After all, it says in the Gospels that the spirit came from heaven, entered Mary, and took on flesh. According to this, when God left that body what speech or spirit would remain within it? If, however, you will say that Jesus had a
25 body and soul like ordinary men and possessed divinity in addition, then why should the divinity have had to enter Mary in the filthy place? The spirit could simply have entered him after his birth. If it is true that it entered after his birth, then a similar phenomenon is found among other men as well such as Moses, Elijah, and other prophets.
30 Similarly, it says with regard to David, "Do not take your holy spirit from me" [Ps. 51:13]. Now, should we say that they were divine because they possessed the holy spirit? If you then say that you affirm Jesus' divinity because of the public miracles he performed, then we may point out that Moses also performed many miracles. Similarly,
35 Elijah ascended to heaven in a storm in the presence of all, something that Jesus did not do; indeed no one saw his ascent, except that they

maintain that Mary Magdalene and Peter the ass saw it and testified that he ascended.

You may then argue that you believe in his divinity because the prophets spoke of him, but the fact is that you will not find a
5   single instance in all the prophets of a prophet speaking of Jesus son of Mary. Even in those places where you maintain that a verse speaks of Jesus, such as the verse in Jeremiah, "And his powerful one shall come from himself, and his ruler shall proceed out of his midst" [Jer. 30:21], and "A woman shall compass a man" [Jer. 31:22], indeed in all
10   those places where you claim to have found even the name of a deity, you cannot show that it refers specifically to him. You may then point to the fact that Isaiah said, "Behold, the young woman is pregnant . . . and she shall call his name Immanuel" [Isa. 7:14] and argue on this basis that he is called God. On the basis of this sort of argument,
15   however, I could find you other gods, such as Samuel son of Elkanah. Samuel, after all, was born to Hannah, who had been barren, in accordance with God's decree, and Samuel can mean "his name is God" (in the language of the priests, *nomen suum Deus*). Similarly, Ezekiel means strong God—in their language, *omnipotenti Deo*—Uzziah
20   means *forte Deo,* and the same can be said of many other names in Scripture. You may then argue that his name indicates his nature, for Jesus means savior in Hebrew. The answer is: It never was nor can it ever be that a Hebrew word without an 'ayin should be derived from the word meaning savior. Furthermore, you could apply a similar
25   argument to the name Joshua and say that it means "God saves." If you then maintain that there is a distinction because we find that all of these had fathers while Jesus did not, then the case of Elijah can prove the contrary, for you will find no mention of his father in all of Scripture. Consequently, I could maintain that he was born without a
30   father and ask you to accept him as a god, for this characteristic is not more typical of Jesus than of other men.

"My God, I cry in the daytime, but you do not respond" [Ps. 22:3]. They say that Jesus said this. Thus, their own words contradict each other, because in the previous psalm it says, "You have not
35   withheld the request of his lips" [Ps. 21:3], while here it says, "But you do not respond." "But you are holy, O you who dwell amid the

praises of Israel" [Ps. 22:4]. Thus, Jesus himself taught that God, who is holy and sacred, dwells amid the praises of Israel and not of Christendom. If he then says that "Israel" is Christendom, the answer is: We have been called by this name since the days of Jacob
5 our father; indeed, the name Israel is derived from him. They, on the other hand, are not descendants of Jacob but children of Edom. Some of them, incidentally, say that they have a tradition that they are descendants of Japheth while we are descended from Shem, but in any case they were never called Israel. If you argue that they are called
10 Israel because they are princes of the Lord (*sarei el*) and believers, then all the generations who were called Israel before the advent of Jesus must have been princes of the Lord and believers; why, then, did they all go down to hell? You may then maintain that they are called Israel because of their vision and belief, but the fact is that we behold and
15 believe in the God of heaven and not they. Moreover, the name is read Yisrael and not Yishrael.

"Our fathers trusted in you" [Ps. 22:4]; this shows that he had a father. "I am a worm and no man" [Ps. 22:7]. Thus, he admits that worms will cover his flesh, and if he were God he should not
20 have said something that is not so even out of modesty. This, rather, is what he should have said: I am God and no man, but I suffer all this in my humility and permit all those who behold me to mock me in order that I may redeem you. In this way, there would have been both humility and revelation of his name. "I was cast upon you from the
25 womb; you are my God from my mother's stomach" [Ps. 22:11]; but not in the womb or in the stomach. Moreover, if this were said about the hanged one, the problem would be their belief that he was born out of the forehead of a harlot, for the verse says that he was born out of a woman like all children; thus, your books lie when they say that the
30 spirit entered Mary. "Be not far from me, for trouble is near; for there is none to help" [Ps. 22:12]. This indicates that if there were someone to help, he would have gladly agreed to be saved; thus, his death occurred against his will and was regarded as "trouble." How, then, can you say that he willed it? "Bulls have surrounded me" [Ps.
35 22:13]; now, where do we find that the people of Israel are called bulls? The Romans and other nations are called that, as Isaiah said,

"For the indignation of the Lord is upon all the nations. . . . And the wild oxen shall come down with them, and the bullocks with the bulls" [Isa. 34:2–7]. Similarly, Daniel explained all the animals and beasts in the book of Daniel as symbols of the nations.

5   "My heart is melted like wax" [Ps. 22:15]. Why was he afraid? After all, they say that this was his will. Furthermore, he could have objected had he wished. "Like a lion (*ka'ari*) my hands and my feet" [Ps. 22:17]. They are mistaken when they say that what is written is *karu, foderunt* in the priests' language, and this is explained
10 in the interpretation of the psalm. "Deliver my soul from the sword" [Ps. 22:21]. This would be the prayer concerning which it was said above, "I cry in the daytime, but you do not respond," for he was certainly not answered since he was not saved from them. It is, of course, necessary to explain this cry of deliverance as a plea for help
15 during his life, for after his death he was not given over into their hands. Moreover, they contradict themselves, for earlier it said, "You have not withheld the request of his lips" [Ps. 21:3]. "From the horns of the wild oxen have you answered me. I will declare your name unto my brethren; in the midst of the congregation will I praise
20 you" [Ps. 22:22–23]. Thus, the hanged one had brothers. Indeed, even in the Gospels it says that he had brothers named Simon and Jacob; consequently, Mary was not a virgin. Moreover, would God express himself this way? "My name will be declared" is what it should have said. Moreover, does God have brothers? And when was the verse
25 "In the midst of the congregation will I praise you" fulfilled? After he was killed, he never entered the congregation again. "You that fear the Lord, praise him; all the seed of Jacob, glorify him; fear him all the seed of Israel" [Ps. 22:24]. According to their belief that Jesus came to save the world and to call a halt to a situation in which all
30 men, good and evil, descended to hell, why did he warn the seed of Jacob and Israel more than other nations? "All those who go down to the dust shall bow down before him" [Ps. 22:30]. According to the view that Jesus said this, it should have said, "Shall bow down before *me*," since he and not his father redeemed them by sacrificing his life.
35 As for the phrase, "And he did not keep alive his own soul" [ibid.], if it refers to his lifetime, we know that this was true since he died and

was buried. If, on the other hand, it refers to his soul, then we must
conclude that the same was done for his soul as for the others which
he took out of hell, and he did not bring them to life either. "Descendants shall serve him" [Ps. 22:31]. Does God have descendants? You
5   may argue that he says this of his believers, but nowhere in all of
Scripture does God call his believers seed, for that term is applicable
only to physical descendants, as it says, "The seed of Abraham my
friend" [Isa. 41:8]. The true explanation of the psalm is that David
said it of his war with the Amalekites after they invaded and
10   despoiled both the land of the Philistines and that of Judah and left
Ziklag in flames.

[146]

["For he has founded it upon the seas . . ."] [Ps. 24:2]. The
heretics explain this as a reference to their baptismal waters. "Lift
up your heads, O gates . . ." [Ps. 24:7]. This is what Jesus said when
15   he approached hell in order to take out the souls. The answer is:
According to your view, this is what it should have said: "For he has
founded it upon the waters, and one who immerses himself in them
will ascend to the mountain of the Lord." Alternately, it should have
said, "Who shall ascend to the mountain of the Lord? One who is
20   immersed in them." However, once he says, "Who shall ascend to
the mountain of the Lord? . . . He who has clean hands and a pure
heart" [Ps. 24:3-4], this indicates that one who has clean hands will
ascend the mountain and that he will do so because he has clean hands
and not because God "founded it upon the seas." Moreover, why,
25   according to you, does it say, "They shall seek your face, O Jacob.
Selah" [Ps. 24:6]? It should have said, "O Christians," for they are
not called Jacob nor are they among his descendants; they are, rather,
descendants of Esau and are called Edom. There are "scholars"
among them who actually say that they are descendants not of the
30   patriarchs but of Japheth, while the patriarchs and the Jews are
descendants of Shem and the Slavs are the descendants of Canaan.
Indeed, this is probably true, as it is written, "The descendants of
Japheth: Gomer and Magog. . . . And the descendants of Gomer:
Ashkenaz and Riphath" [Gen. 10:2-3], and the Gentiles are called

Ashkenazim while their land is commonly called Ashkenaz. It is true
that some of them speak French, but they are a minority; the main
body of the Gentiles consists of Ashkenazim. Israel, on the other
hand, is descended from Shem, as it is written, "This is the line of
5   Shem, Shem begat . . ." until "Terah . . . begat Abram" [Gen.
11:10-26]. "Lift up your heads, O gates . . . and the king of glory shall
come in" [Ps. 24:7]. According to you, then, Jesus himself descended
to hell, and yet it says, "You will not permit your pious one to see the
pit" [Ps. 16:10], a verse which they read, "You will not permit your
10   holy one to see hell." Now, they refer both this verse and the preceding one, which reads, "Therefore, my heart is glad and my glory rejoices; my flesh also shall rest in hope" [Ps. 16:9] to Jesus, and their
words consequently contradict each other. Moreover, when he
asked, "Who is the king of glory?" [Ps. 24:10], the answer should have
15   been, Jesus is the king of glory. If he then asks who says, "Who is
the king of glory?" answer that it is the cloud of the Lord's glory
which filled the Temple.

[147]

"Give them according to their deeds, and according to the
wickedness of their endeavors. . . . Because they regard not the
20   works of the Lord" [Ps. 28:4-5]. These words contradict the words
of the Gospels in which it says that Jesus in the hour of death said,
"Father, forgive them for what they did to me, for they know not what
they do" [Luke 23:34], and yet here he takes them to account for what
they did. With regard to the phrase, "My flesh rejoices" [see Psalms
25   28:7], their writers have misled them. Indeed, their "scholars" admit
that this is not the phrase of Jerome who translated the Hebrew into
Latin. The fact is that others translated Psalms in accordance with
the general meaning rather than literally, and it was they who misled
them.

[148]

30   "Into your hand I commit my spirit" [Ps. 31:6]. They say that
Jesus said this when he expired. "I hate those who guard worthless
vanities" [Ps. 31:7]. This refers to those who guarded his grave.

"You have seen my suffering" [Ps. 31:8]. They wrote, "My humility." "Have mercy upon me, O Lord, for I am in trouble" [Ps. 31:10]
when handed over to be crucified. "For my life is spent with grief, and
my years in sighing; my strength fails because of my iniquity" [Ps.
31:11]. They wrote, "My strength fails because of the suffering," for
they could not bring themselves to say that there was iniquity in
Jesus. "I was a reproach among all my enemies . . . when they took
counsel together" [Ps. 31:12–14]. They wrote, "When they came together." "My times are in your hand" [Ps. 31:16]. They wrote, "My
fate is in your hand."

    The answer is: You are quite right that the psalm speaks of
Jesus. "Incline your ear to me; deliver me speedily. Be my strong
rock, a fortified citadel to save me" [Ps. 31:3]. Now, this contradicts
their Torah where they wrote that Jesus died in accordance with his
will, and yet here it says that he prayed for salvation. Moreover, in
the Gospels themselves it says that Jesus prayed to his father that he
remove the bitter cup from him. You may then argue that he prayed
and cried not because he wanted to be saved but because people normally pray when they are in trouble; thus, he too prayed because he
behaved like an ordinary mortal in every respect. If so, you contradict
your statement that it was concerning him that David said, "The king
shall rejoice in your strength, O Lord. . . . You have given him his
heart's desire and have not withheld the request of his lips" [Ps.
21:2–3]; here, after all, the request of his lips was withheld. You may
then say that he prayed that he not tarry in the grave after death, but
why should he have prayed about what would happen to him after
death if he was God? It is one thing to say that during his lifetime
when he was on earth, he prayed like everyone else, but he should not
have prayed about what would happen after death, since by then he
would return to pure divinity and be separated from human beings.
"Into your hand I commit my spirit." If he was God and his spirit and
soul were divine, then to whom was he to commit his spirit? "My
strength fails because of my iniquity." This shows that Jesus sinned
and was full of iniquity like other people. Moreover, even according
to their version which reads, "In poverty," the reference must be to
the poverty in righteousness and wealth of sin which characterized

him, for wherever it says "poor" they say it means spiritually poor. "Deliver me from the hand . . . of my persecutors" [Ps. 31:16]; this must refer to his lifetime, for who persecuted him after death? "You shall hide them in the secret of your presence" [Ps. 31:21]. They say
5   that Jesus said this of those who fought and pursued him. Thus they deny their own Torah, which says that when he was crucified Jesus said to his father, "Father, forgive them, for they do not know or understand what they do" [Luke 23:34].

[149]

We have been admonished to observe the Torah of Moses
10 even at the end of days, as it is written, "Remember the Torah of Moses my servant." And it says, "Behold, I am sending, etc." until "the terrible [day of the Lord]" [Mal. 3:22-23].

[150]

"For Solomon: Give the king your judgments, O God, and your righteousness to the king's son" [Ps. 72:1]. This is how David
15 prayed for himself (for he was a king) and his son Solomon. The heretics, however, explain the entire psalm as a reference to Jesus; they say that David spoke of him and that "king" and "king's son" refer to him. "They shall fear you with the sun" [Ps. 72:5]; i.e., he existed before the sun and "before the moon" [ibid.], which is why it says
20 *velifnei* [ibid.], which they translate as *ante* in their language. They also say that the verse, "His name shall endure forever; his name shall be continued before the sun" [Ps. 72:17] refers to Jesus who existed before the sun. The answer is in this very passage, for what hint of Jesus is there here? Using your method, any nation could say that this
25 was said about their god. Moreover, should David have prayed that God give Jesus his judgments and righteousness? You may then maintain that David said this as a prophecy and not as a prayer, but if so he should have said "you will give." Moreover, the word *endet,* which they use to translate "They shall fear," means destruction;
30 thus, David prophesied that the fear of Jesus would be destroyed with the sun, for that is what it says. Furthermore, it turns out that you are saying that Jesus did not exist before the sun but only with it,

and the sun and moon were hung out on the fourth day; thus, Jesus
was not the primeval Creator. "And before the moon from generation
to generation" [Ps. 72:5]; now, before there was a moon, what sort
of generations were there?

5   Furthermore, here is another approach. "Give the king your
judgments, O God, and your righteousness to the king's son." The
heretics say that the king and his son refer to the father and the son.
This is how you should answer them: According to you, the king is
the father and the king's son is the son. Now, if you were to say that
10 the psalmist prayed to the father to give some of his righteousness to
the son, that would sound plausible, but in fact the prayer is that he
give his judgment to the king, i.e., the father, and who can be greater
than the father? Moreover, it says, "In his days shall the righteous
flourish" [Ps. 72:7]; this phrase is apparently restricted to the time
15 that he will live, and this implies that there will be days when he will
not live. Furthermore, what is the meaning of "All kings shall bow to
him and all nations shall serve him" [Ps. 72:11]? After all, Jews,
Ishmaelites, Tatars, indeed, most nations do not bow down to him. It
also says, "He shall come down like rain upon that which is cut" [Ps.
20 72:6]; thus, the fear of Jesus is only as useful as rain falling upon a
sheep that has been sheared, and such rain is actually harmful. "And
abundance of peace so long as the moon endures" [Ps. 72:7]; now,
what peace was there in the time of Jesus or thereafter? "And he shall
have dominion from sea to sea" [Ps. 72:8]—but not in the sea.
25 Consequently, even according to your own views Jesus would have
no dominion in heaven or in the seas, but only on dry land. "And he
shall live, and to him shall be given the gold of Sheba" [Ps. 72:15]. Did
David, then, pray for Jesus' life and riches? Why, everyone [knows
that Jesus was killed and that he was never rich]. "He shall pray for
30 him continually" [ibid.]; it seems to me that they have distorted this
verse and written, "They shall pray to him." "His name shall be continued before the sun" [Ps. 17:15]. The verses thus contradict each
other; above it says, "With the sun" [Ps. 72:5], and here "Before the
sun," which they take as "Earlier than the sun." Finally, it says,
35 Blessed be the Lord . . . God of Israel" [Ps. 72:18], and not, "Blessed
be Jesus, God of Christendom."

[151]

"Evil men have risen against me" [Ps. 86:14]. The heretics say that these men are the Jews who killed Jesus. The answer is: Here we find that Jesus was a sinner, as it is written, "For you, Lord, are good and forgiving" [Ps. 86:5], and forgiveness must be for sin.

5 Elsewhere too we find that he, like other human beings, was made of body and soul without any divine spirit, for he, Peter, and John were once walking along, and they reached the foot of a mountain in the evening. They asked him, "Where shall we go, and where shall we spend the night?" for they saw no house or village, and they had to

10 climb to the other side of the mountain. They were therefore afraid that night would fall before they reached a village. Jesus then told them, "When we reach the top of the mountain we shall look in all directions to see where there is a lodging place, and we shall go there." It is clear from this that he did not even have the spirit of

15 prophecy, for he didn't know what was on the other side of the mountain.

[152]

"The Lord said unto my lord, Sit at my right hand until I make your enemies your footstool. . . . [Ps. 110:1]. The heretics say that David spoke prophetically and said that the father told his son Jesus,

20 "Sit at my right hand." And they wrote, "With you ('*immekha*) there is willingness at the beginning of the day of your power" [Ps. 110:3], i.e., that the world was created with him. "From the womb, from the morning, you have the dew of your youth" [ibid.]. They say that "From the morning" refers to the morning star and that the verse

25 means that he was before the stars. The answer is in this very passage: "The Lord said unto my lord"; which of them would David call simply *domino* and which would he call *domino meo*, i.e., my lord? "The Lord shall send the rod of your strength" [Ps. 110:2]; this implies that he was not God and that the only strength and glory he

30 had was what was sent to him by someone else. You may argue that he was both sender and messenger, but then it should have said, "I will send the rod of my strength from heaven." "Your people ('*ammekha*) are willing." At the outset, the first writer made a slight

error and wrote, "With you (*'immekha*) there is willingness," in
accordance with his understanding of the verse. Then, they transformed this into a major error, when their later authorities wrote that
it refers to the beginning of time. The truth is that as a first interpre-
5 tation we can explain "Your people is willing" quite well as follows:
Abishai told David, "Your people is willing; the people of the land
are prepared to fight their battles on the day of your power." Now,
with regard to their version, "I have given birth to you before the
morning star," they can be refuted on the basis of their own words,
10 for he was not born until his mother Mary came and gave birth to him.
"Rule in the midst of your enemies" [Ps. 110:2]. We see, however,
that his enemies ruled over him and not he over them. Moreover, even
according to their exegesis, it can be shown that this was not necessarily said of Jesus. I say, rather, that it was said of one of the gods of
15 the other nations since these gods were also born, for what hint of
Jesus is there here? Moreover, where does it say here that one should
believe in him or accept him as a god?

Here is another approach to their exegesis of "The Lord said
unto my lord. . . ." The answer is: Where do you find a father calling
20 his son "My lord"? This is certainly not the proper way to speak.
Moreover, to what army did Jesus go that they volunteered to go with
him, who were the kings that fought with him, and in what sense was
he told, "Sit at my right hand"? This, then, is what the psalm means:
David said, "The Lord said to my lord Abraham, 'Sit at my right
25 hand,' " for Abraham was David's ancestor, and it is common for
people to refer to their ancestors as lord. Now the Lord told
Abraham, "I am your shield" [Gen. 15:1], and since a man holds a
shield with his left hand, he sits to its right. Consequently, God. i.e.,
the shield, sits to Abraham's left, while Abraham sits to the right of
30 God. Specifically, it was at the time of the wars of Amraphel and his
friends that this was said to Abraham. "The Lord shall send the rod
of your strength" [Ps. 110:2] means, "Do not fear because they are
many and you are few; the Lord will send you a rod of strength and
you will rule over them." "Your people are willing" refers to Aner,
35 Eshkol, and Mamre who were his people, as it is written, "And they
were the confederates of Abraham" [Gen. 14:13]. They are the ones
who volunteered to go with him in that army, as it is written, "And

the portion of the men that went with me, Aner, Eshkol, and Mamre"
[Gen. 14:24]. Moreover, they went with him willingly, as it is written, "He armed his trainees, who were born in his house" [Gen.
14:14]; thus, they must have gone on their own and willingly. "In the
5   beauties of holiness" [Ps. 110:3], i.e., in the mighty deeds of the Holy
One, blessed be he. Now, what brought this about? It was "the dew
of your youth" [ibid.], the merit which God recognized in me "from
the womb, from the morning" [ibid.], i.e., soon after leaving the
womb. "The Lord has sworn and will not repent" [Ps. 110:4] that the
10 priesthood of Melchisedek will be yours "in accordance with the
matter of Melchisedek" [ibid.], i.e., in light of the blessing with
which Melchisedek blessed Abraham even before blessing God, as it
is written, "Blessed be Abraham to the most high God, [possessor
of heaven and earth. And blessed be the most high God, who has
15 delivered your enemies] into your hand . . ." [Gen. 14:19-20]. "The
Lord at your right hand shall strike down kings in the day of his
wrath" [Ps. 110:5], as it is written, "And he divided himself against
them by night . . . and smote them" [Gen. 14:15]. All of this is what
David said the Lord did for his ancestor, and after that he began to
20 pray for himself: "He shall judge among the nations and fill with dead
bodies" [Ps. 110:6]; i.e., this is how God will carry out judgment for
me and kill many people. "He shall wound the head of the land of
Rabbah" [ibid.]. This refers to the head of Rabbah in Ammon who
raised his head against the fortress guarding the river from which he
25 drank [cf. Ps. 110:7], i.e., against the power of the fortress guarding
the water in Rabbah, as it is written, "And Joab sent messengers to
King David, and said, I have fought against Rabbah, and have taken
the city of waters" [2 Sam. 12:27].
       You may then question the heretics further: You say that the
30 father, the son, and the holy spirit are one. The truth is, however, that
one God could not have spoken this way; there would have had to be
two. After all, this verse indicates that one is afraid and the other is
strengthening him by saying, "Sit at my right hand and do not fear."
You see, then, that there are two, a strong one and a weak one. More-
35 over, the verse implies that one is sitting and the other is standing,
and the former is telling the latter to sit at his right hand; conse-

quently, there must be two. Finally, according to your view that the
two are one, why didn't he say, "Let us sit until we make our enemies
our footstool"? It must follow, then, that they do not constitute a
single God and master.

5   Moreover, here is another answer to their statement that he is
God: This statement is tantamount to a denial of God, for it is written
in the Torah, "See now that I, I am he, and there is no god beside me; I
kill, and I make alive, I wound and I heal, and there is none that can
deliver out of my hand" [Deut. 32:39]. He may then argue that "I, I am
10 he" implies that there are two, the father and the son. The answer is
that this phrase really means, "I am he who revealed himself at the
sea, and I am he who revealed himself at Mount Sinai"; i.e., even
though he appeared as a powerful warrior at the sea and as an old man
who sits, studies, and teaches at Mount Sinai, do not say that there
15 are two powers, for the Lord, on the contrary, is one.
          "The Lord said unto my lord, Sit at my right hand" [Ps. 110:1].
The heretics say that the father told the son, "Sit at my right hand until I made your enemies your footstool" [ibid.]; the enemies, they
say, are the Jews who hanged him. The answer is: David said this
20 verse, and how could the Jews have become his enemies in the time of
David? Why, he was neither born nor handed over to them nor hanged
at that time. And if his enemies are the demons in hell who had dominion over both righteous and evil men, then why did he descend to
hell to steal from Satan those souls which the latter had been given as
25 a present? He should have waited until his father fulfills his oath of
making the demons his footstool. If, however, the plain sense of the
passage refers to the future and it was concerning the future that
David was prophesying, then I should like to ask you about this matter of sitting. Just how did he sit near his father before he was born?
30 Furthermore, what did he do before he was commanded to sit? Did he
lie down or stand? If he stood, how did he stand? Was it in front of his
father, behind him, beside him or in the air? Then his father told him,
"Sit at my right hand." Let me ask you something. Did he sit or not? If
you say he did, then you are describing two powers sitting next to
35 each other. If he didn't, then he disobeyed his father's commandment.
Moreover, according to your view that the father told his son, "Sit at

my right hand," it follows that the son is powerless to make his
enemies his footstool without the father's help. It also follows that
the father perpetrated a major betrayal of his son; the son went down
on the assumption that his father would make his enemies his foot-
5 stool, and the opposite occurred—he was made the footstool of his
enemies.

The truth is that David said this passage about himself. Its
meaning, then, is as follows: The Lord said unto me concerning my
lord Saul who was pursuing me, "Sit at my right hand (*yemini*) and I
10 shall make your enemy Saul your footstool." If you will ask how
David could sit at the right hand of God, the answer is that he could
do so in the same sense that it is written in the previous chapter, "For
the Lord shall stand at the right hand of the poor to save him from
those that condemn his soul" [Ps. 109:31]. Alternately, it may mean,
15 "Sit with the help of Saul the Benjamite," for it is written, "And Saul
answered and said, "I am a Benjamite (*yemini*)" [1 Sam. 9:21]. It
should be noted that the word "to my lord" really means "concerning
my lord" as in the phrase, "The Lord will fight for you" [Exod.
14:14]. One can also interpret "sit at my right hand" in the sense of
20 "wait for the salvation of my right hand, which will punish the
enemies of Israel," as it is written, "Your right hand, O Lord, is
glorious in power; your right hand, O Lord, has dashed the enemy in
pieces" [Exod. 15:6]. Moreover, we find that the word for sitting
(*yeshivah*) is used in the sense of waiting with regard to redemption
25 and a king, for it is written, "For the children of Israel shall abide
(*yeshevu*) many days without a king . . ." [Hos. 3:4].

"From the womb of morning" [Ps. 110:3]. Jesus, however,
came from a womb of impurity when he was born, as it is written, "If
a woman conceives and bears a male, then she shall be impure seven
30 days; according to the days of her separation for impure discharge
shall she be impure" [Lev. 12:2]. You may argue that he was born in a
holy and pure place, but it is written, "In the midst of years (*shanim*)
give him life" [Hab. 3:2], and they translate it, "In the midst of two
(*shenayim*)," an ox and a donkey. It follows, then, that he was born in a
35 place of dirt, filth, stench, and refuse—in a manger. "You are a priest
forever" [Ps. 110:4]. If he is a priest, i.e., a servant, then he is not

God. "He shall drink of the brook in the way" [Ps. 110:7]; this refers
to a stinking and muddy brook flowing along the way. Moreover, even
if you argue that it is a stream of fresh water along the way which is
flowing from its own source and it is this which he will drink, one can
5   still ask why he should "lift up his head" [ibid.] because of this. On
the contrary, such a thing should have made him ashamed and caused
him to bury his head on the ground. He should not have lifted up his
head; rather, he should have mourned and covered his head at having
to drink lest he die of thirst. Why, this would mean that Moses was
10   greater than he, as it is written, "And he was there with the Lord
forty [days and forty nights; he did not eat bread] or drink water"
[Exod. 34:28]. Moreover, Adam was greater than he, for God took
him out of pure, holy earth; he had no father or mother and did not
stink in a woman's stomach.

SONG OF SONGS

[153]

The heretics speak defiantly concerning the verse, "Go forth, O
daughters of Zion, and behold King Solomon with the crown wherewith his mother crowned him in the day of his wedding . . ." [Song of
5 Songs 3:11]. They say that every "Solomon" in the Song of Songs is
sacred and that this verse refers to the mother of Jesus. This is how
you should answer them: What was the crown with which his
mother crowned him? If anything, Jesus crowned his mother and not
she him. Moreover, if this were said of Jesus it would prove that he
10 had a sister, for it says, "I have come into my garden, my sister, my
beloved" [Song of Songs 5:1]. Furthermore, what is "the day of his
wedding"? After all, you say that he attained kingship when he died,
and then his mother was not with him.

This, then, is the meaning of the passage: It is indeed sacred,
15 and it means, "Go forth, O daughters of Zion, and behold him with
the crown wherewith the Torah crowned him," for Torah is called
mother, as it is written, "For it will be called mother of wisdom"
[Prov. 2:3]. The crown is the crown of gold which was made for the
ark in honor of the Torah. "The day of his wedding" refers to the
20 building of the tabernacle when God took Israel as his bride, as it is
written, "And I will betroth you in faithfulness, and you shall know
the Lord" [Hos. 2:20]. Moreover, they maintain that Jesus said, "Ego
non cognosco patrem, ego non cognosco matrem et non fratres nec
sorores ni filios quam Israel," which means: He has no father or
25 mother, no son or daughter, but Israel.

[A CRITIQUE OF THE GOSPELS AND CHRISTIANITY]
[154]

Be diligent in your study of Torah so that you may be able to answer a heretic.

5   It is written in those sinful notations (*'avon gilyon*) which they call *Evangelium* that Jesus' genealogy can be traced to kings. Thus, they say that so-and-so begat so-and-so until "Mattan begat Jacob, and Jacob begat Joseph the husband of Mary of whom was born Jesus, who is called Christ" [Matt. 1:15-16]. Now, this is how we answer them: If she had not yet had sexual relations nor was she even 10 married to her husband, then why is he called her husband? It should have said "the betrothed of Mary," in which case they would not be stating an obvious falsehood in their liturgy when they say that he never had relations with her. Moreover, if they want to inform us that he is from a royal family, why was his genealogy related to that of 15 Joseph, who was not his father and to whom he had no blood relationship at all? Rather than telling us the genealogy of Joseph, he should have told us that of Mary by saying that so-and-so begat so-and-so until "So-and-so begat Mary who gave birth to Jesus." The fact that this was not done shows that they did not know Mary's genealogy 20 and that she was not of royal descent. If the heretic then argues that she was a relative of Joseph, you can find the answer to this in our earlier discussion of the passage, "And there shall come forth a rod out of the stem of Jesse . . ." in Isaiah.

      This, then, is how Jesus' genealogy is written: "These are the 25 generations of Jesus, the son of David, the son of Abraham. Abraham begat Isaac, and Isaac begat Jacob, and Jacob begat Judah and his brethren. And Judah begat Peretz and Zerah of Tamar, and Peretz begat Hezron, and Hezron begat Ram. And Ram begat Aminadab, and Aminadab begat Nahshon, and Nahshon begat Salmon. And Salmon 30 begat Boaz, and Boaz begat Obed of Ruth, and Obed begat Jesse. And Jesse begat King David, and David begat Solomon of Uriah's wife. And Solomon begat Rehoboam, and Rehoboam begat Abiah, and Abiah begat Asa. And Asa begat Jehosaphat, and Jehosaphat begat Jehoram, and Jehoram begat Uzziah. And Uzziah begat Jotham, and

Jotham begat Ahaz, and Ahaz begat Hezekiah. And Hezekiah begat
Menasheh, and Menasheh begat Amon, and Amon begat Josiah. And
Josiah begat Jechoniah and his brothers who were in the Babylonian
exile. After they were exiled to Babylonia, Jechoniah begat Shealtiel,
5 and Shealtiel begat Zerubabel. And Zerubabel begat Abner, and
Abner begat Eliakim, and Eliakim begat Azor. And Azor begat Sadok,
and Sadok begat Yakhin, and Yakhin begat Elihu. And Elihu begat
Eleazar, and Eleazar begat Mattan, and Mattan begat Jacob. And Jacob
begat Joseph the husband of Mary of whom was born Jesus, whom
10 people call Christ" [Matt. 1:1-16]. And it is written, "All the generations from Abraham until the kingdom of the house of David are fourteen generations, and from King David until the Babylonian exile are
fourteen generations, and from the Babylonian exile until Jesus there
are fourteen generations" [Matt. 1:17]. This is Jesus' genealogy in
15 that Gospel of theirs which was written by Matthew.

In Luke, however, it is written as follows: "Jesus apostasized, and when he prayed, the heaven was opened and the holy spirit
descended upon him in the shape of a dove. A voice then came from
heaven and said, You are my beloved son, for I am well pleased with
20 you. And Jesus grew to the age of thirty, and a wise man was Jesus
son of Joseph son of Heli son of Mattat son of Levi son of Malki son
of Natni son of Joseph son of Mattat son of Amos son of Nahum son
of Hasal son of Nagi son of Maot son of Mattat son of Shimi son of
Joseph son of Judah son of Johanan son of Dosa son of Zerubabel son
25 of Shealtiel"—in the book of Luke, then, he counted twenty-two generations from Joseph the father of Jesus to Shealtiel while in Matthew
he counted but fifteen—"Shealtiel son of Neri son of Malki son of
Addi son of Cosam son of Elmodad son of Ezer son of Jose son of
Eliezer son of Joram son of Mattathias son of Levi son of Simon son
30 of Judah son of Joseph son of Joram son of Eliakim son of Melea son
of Mani son of Mattathias son of Nathan son of David" [Luke
3:21-31]. You see, then, that the names and calculations differ according to their own lie and error, for I have written his genealogy as
it is found in the books of Luke and Matthew.
35 Furthermore, it is written in the book of John that "Philip

found Nathaniel and told him, We have found that which is written in the Law and the Prophets in Jesus son of Joseph of Nazareth. And Nathaniel said to him, Can a good thing come out of Nazareth? So Philip told him, Come and see Jesus [John 1:45‒46], and when he came
5 before him, he said, Indeed, this is truly the son of Joseph." You see, then, that both Philip and Nathaniel testified that he was the son of Joseph, and yet the Christians say that he had no father although the above passage is written clearly in the Gospels.

[155]

Be diligent in the study of Torah in order to be able to answer
10 a heretic and question him. When you speak to them, do not allow your antagonist to change the subject, for it is the usual method of the assertive and impatient Gentile to skip from one subject to another. He does not continue to stick to the point, for when he realizes his inability to verify his statements, he begins to discuss other matters.
15 One who argues with them should be strong-willed by asking questions or giving responses that deal with the specific issue at hand and not permitting his antagonist to extricate himself from that issue until it has been completed. Then, you will find the Gentile thoroughly embarrassed; indeed, he will be found to have denied their
20 central dogmas, while all Israel "will speak lovely words" [Gen. 49:21].

[156]

Now, the children of the living God should study the following and make no mistake. First, ask them from what people they come. If they answer that they are of the seed of Israel, silence them
25 by asking: How do you explain Isaiah's statement, "Who caused Jacob to be despoiled and gave Israel to the robbers? Was it not the Lord, against whom we have sinned, in whose ways they would not walk nor be obedient to his law" [Isa. 42:24]? And he said, "Therefore I have profaned the holy princes and have given Jacob to the curse . . .

[Isa. 43:28]. It follows that if you are from Jacob, then you must be sinners. Moreover, when were you despoiled or given over to robbers? Why, you have been living comfortably and quietly since your youth and have not been "emptied from vessel to vessel," nor have
5   you been exiled.

You can question the heretics further on the basis of Hosea's prophecies, for it is written, "Though you, Israel, play the harlot, let not Judah sin" [Hos. 4:15], and it is written, "Israel has gone astray like a straying heifer" [Hos. 4:16]. Moreover, it says , "Do not re-
10 joice, Israel, in happiness like other peoples, for like a wanton you have forsaken your God" [Hos. 9:1], and it says, "Ephraim besets me with treachery, the house of Israel besets me with deceit" [Hos. 12:1]. It also says, "Ephraim, you have played the wanton; Israel, you have defiled yourself" [Hos. 5:3]. Thus, he calls them wanton, stray-
15 ing, and defiled. Furthermore, it is written, "I found Israel like grapes in the wilderness, I looked upon your forefathers with joy like the first ripe figs; but they went to Baal-peor and consecrated themselves unto that shame, and they became as abominable as that which they loved" [Hos. 9:10]. Now, if you are Israel, when did your fathers
20 worship Baal-peor? The truth is that you are simply looking for trouble, for it says, "When Israel was a child, I loved him, and I called my son out of Egypt" [Hos. 11:1]; now, who was in Egypt, we or you? It is also regarding us that the prophet concluded, "Return, O Israel, unto the Lord your God, for you have stumbled in your
25 iniquity" [Hos. 14:2]; where, then, did you stumble? We, on the other hand, have stumbled in many exiles. Furthermore, it is concerning us that it says, "I will heal their backsliding, I will love them freely, for my anger is turned away from them" [Hos. 14:5]; you, however, do not require healing since you were not afflicted like us. It is then writ-
30 ten, "I will be as the dew unto Israel" [Hos. 14:6].

Moreover, Isaiah said, "One shall say, I am the Lord's, and another shall call himself by the name of Jacob; another shall subscribe with his hand unto the Lord, and call himself by the name of Israel" [Isa. 44:5]. If they then answer you that this was not said of
35 Israel alone but of other nations or of the children of Esau as well, then tell them the following prophecy which Isaiah said: "Come near,

you nations, to hear, and hearken, you people; let the earth hear, and
all that is in it, the world and all that comes forth from it. For the
anger of the Lord is upon all nations, and his wrath upon all their
hosts; he has destroyed them, he has delivered them to the slaughter.
5   Their slain shall be cast out, and their stench shall come up out of
their carcasses, and the mountains shall be melted with their blood.
And all the host of heaven shall be dissolved, and the heavens shall be
rolled up as a scroll, and all their host shall fade away, as the leaf falls
off from the vine, and the ripening fruit from a fig tree. For my sword
10   shall be bathed in heaven; behold, it shall come down upon Idumea,
and upon the people of my curse, to judgment. The sword of the Lord
is filled with blood, it is gorged with fat, and with the blood of lambs
and goats, with the fat of the kidneys of rams; for the Lord has a
sacrifice in Bozrah, and a great slaughter in the land of Idumea. Wild
15   oxen shall come down with them, and the bullocks with the bulls; and
their land shall be soaked with blood, and their dust sated with fat.
For the Lord has a day of vengeance, a year of recompense for the
controversy of Zion. Idumea's streams shall be turned into pitch, and
its dust into brimstone, and its land shall become burning pitch. It
20   shall not be quenched night or day; its smoke shall go up forever;
from generation to generation it shall lie waste; none shall pass
through it for ever and ever" [Isa. 34:1-10]. It follows, then, that if
you are of Esau's descendants or of other nations, all these punishments will befall you.

[157]

25   You can also respond to their arguments regarding the stain
of their baptism. Their Torah says that only one who has been immersed in water can be saved from hell, and they cite supporting
evidence from the following verse: "Then will I sprinkle pure water
upon you, and you shall be pure"[Ezek. 36:25]. The answer is: You
30   don't do that, i.e., you do not sprinkle water upon yourselves; instead, you are thrown into water, and the verse does not say that.
Moreover, what sort of sin and impurity is removed by the stain of
their baptism? What impurity or sin can be found in the small children whom they baptize? If, however, this baptism relates to future

sins, then it follows that they needn't be scrupulous in doing good
deeds, nor need they avoid sin, for everything is taken care of by this
baptism. On the other hand, if their baptism is simply based on imita-
tion of Jesus' baptism (for John the Baptist, whom they call *Baptista,*
5   baptized him, and Jesus also baptized himself and other Jews who
erred by following him), then they should have imitated that baptism
in all its particulars. In fact, however, Jesus and John were baptized in
the Jordan, which consists of fresh water, while they are baptized in
drawn water to this day. Furthermore, just as they derive the require-
10 ments of baptism from Jesus' behavior, i.e., from the fact that he
baptized himself, in the same manner they should derive the requirement of circumcision, for Jesus and John were both circumcised. If
your antagonist then argues that when Jesus came he renewed the
Torah, abandoning circumcision and enjoining baptism in its stead,
15 this would give the lie to his own Torah, for it is written in the book
of Matthew, "I have not come to destroy the law of Moses . . ."
[Matt. 5:17], as I have explained above. And in the Torah of Moses it
says, "On the eighth day the flesh of his foreskin shall be circumcised" [Lev. 12:3], and it is written, "Take care to observe the entire
20 Law which I command you this day; do not add to it or diminish from
it" [Deut. 13:1]. It would follow, then, that Jesus annulled the law of
Moses and thereby gave the lie to his own Torah where he wrote,
"Not one thing will pass from the Law" [Matt. 5:18], for he added and
diminished from the Law in several places.

25   We find, moreover, that David prayed for those forced converts in the exile who would be baptized against their will, for it is
written, "Save me, O God, for the waters have come unto my soul"
[Ps. 69:2]. Now, when was David drowning that he had to pray to be
saved from water? Furthermore, what sort of water reaches the soul?
30 After all, if a man drowns in the sea or in a river, his soul is not destroyed even though his body dies. What, then, was the water concerning which David prayed? He must have been referring to baptismal water which does, indeed, reach the soul. Similarly, he says near
the end of the book of Psalms, "Save me, and deliver me out of much
35 water" [Ps. 144:7]. He also says, "Let not the waterflood overflow
me, neither let the deep swallow me up, and let not the pit shut her

mouth upon me" [Ps. 69:16]; this refers to the water of their baptismal stain, while the pit refers to hell. David also prayed concerning the forced converts in the following verse, saying, "For this shall everyone who is godly pray unto you in a time when you may be
5   found; surely in the flood of great waters they shall not come near to him" [Ps. 32:6].

[158]

Moreover, it says in the Torah, "You shall follow the Lord your God . . ." [Deut. 13:5], and yet they do not follow the ways of their god Jesus by circumcising themselves and observing the Sab-
10   bath and festivals as he did (for he did observe all these commandments). Your antagonist may maintain that this change results from Paul's statement in the name of Jesus that the Sabbath and festivals should not be observed in light of Isaiah's admonition, "Your new moon and your appointed feasts my soul hates . . ." [Isa. 1:14]. How-
15   ever, this would again contradict the Torah of Paul's teacher Jesus, in which it is written, "Heaven and earth may pass away, but nothing in the Torah of Moses will pass away" [Matt. 5:18].

[159]

It is written in their books: "When the angels who had come to seek Jesus returned, behold, an angel appeared to Joseph in a
20   dream, saying, Arise, and take the young child and his mother, and flee into Egypt and be there until I bring you word, for Herod will seek the young child to destroy him. . . . And Joseph departed into Egypt" [Matt. 2:13-14]. What was the reason for this? If he were God, why should he have been afraid of the king? Why, we see that
25   God's angels and servants were not afraid of flesh and blood; they carried out their divine mission openly, and no man had the power to touch them or harm them at all. With regard to Lot, for example, it says, "And they smote the men that were at the door of the house with blindness" [Gen. 19:11]. In the case of Elisha, it says, "Elisha
30   prayed unto the Lord, and said, Smite this people, I pray you, with blindness. And he smote them with blindness according to the word of Elisha" [2 Kings 6:18]. Elsewhere, it says, "And the king put forth

his hand . . . saying, Take hold of him, and his hand . . . dried up so that he could not pull it in again to him" [1 Kings 13:4].

[160]

It is written in their books: "Then the residents of Jerusalem and all Judea and all the region about Jordan went out to John, and they
5 were baptized in the Jordan" [Matt. 3:5-6], and this baptism is what they call *Taufe* (*Baptisma*). Now, why was this done? Who commanded John to administer this baptism? In what Torah did he find it? Not in the old one nor in the new one. Furthermore, when he did baptize them, he did so in fresh water. Why, then, don't these
10 Gentiles who learned from him do so in fresh water? The fact is that we see that they are not careful about this but immerse themselves in water that has been drawn and with which vessels have been filled.

It is written in their books: "Then Jesus came . . . to the Jordan and John baptized him in the Jordan. . . . And when he came out of the
15 Jordan the heavens were opened unto him and he saw a spirit descending from heaven in the form of a dove alighting upon him. And lo a voice from heaven saying, This is my beloved son in whom I am well pleased" [Matt. 3:13-17]. What was the purpose of this? What sort of god must be sanctified through removal of his impurity just
20 like a human being? Moreover, it is written elsewhere in their books that a spirit had originally entered Mary when she became pregnant. Where, then, had that spirit gone? If you will answer that the spirit became impure in her womb, then it follows that she was impure like other women.

25 Furthermore, there is a warning in their Torah that a man should be baptized only once, and one who does this more than once is considered a heretic. And yet this man, who one would think needed no further sanctity in light of the fact that his divinity made him holy, this Jesus was sanctified at the hands of a man. Indeed, he
30 was sanctified three times. Initially, when he entered his mother's womb there was a holy spirit; then, when he was baptized by John like all other men there was a holy spirit; finally, when he came out of the Jordan there was a holy spirit. Thus, there were three such occasions. Moreover, when people are baptized it is for the sake of the

soul, for the body is considered an empty vessel before that. In that case, why do they baptize the crosses in their houses of abomination as well as all other vessels used for their idolatry such as bells and chalices? Do these too have spirit and soul?

[161]

5   We ask them the following question: After a man has died without baptism, is it possible to baptize him so that he should go to heaven on the strength of this posthumous baptism? Their answer is: He will never go to heaven since he was not baptized during his life-time. We then ask the following question: It is written in their Torah
10   that this is what their saint Gregory said: One time he was walking among the graves of some Muslims and he found inscribed on one grave how long that Muslim had lived, how good, merciful, and upright he had been, how he had loved justice, and the kindness that he had shown toward one poor woman. One of this man's servants
15   had met this woman's son and had an argument with him, and in his anger the servant had arisen, struck her son and killed him. The woman had then come before this Muslim prince and cried out to him. Although he had intended to go out to the army at the very moment that the woman had come before him crying over her son's death, he
20   had turned back toward the woman and asked, "What is the matter, woman?" The woman had then told him, "Please help me, my lord, for this is how one of your servants has wronged me." Immediately, he had commanded that this servant be brought before him and had ordered him on pain of death to go with this woman and be with her,
25   to serve and guard her all the days of her life as if she had been his mother. The Muslim prince had then gone on his way and been killed. When Gregory read of this event he took pity on this man and cried over the grave, praying that the Muslim's sins be forgiven and that his soul be bound up in paradise. And his prayer was granted. Indeed,
30   they say that the Muslim was baptized with the tears that fell on the grave in order not to invalidate what is written in their Torah that one can enter paradise only if one was baptized and that one who was not baptized can never enter. After this, a heavenly voice said, "Gregory, I am warning you not to ask again for the sort of forgiveness which I

have granted to this Muslim because of you, for I shall never again grant any man in the world such forgiveness. Furthermore, you will be taken ill for a long time as a result of the forgiveness which I have granted for your sake." And so it was, for he was overcome by a
5   fever.

Now, this story causes me great wonderment, for I know that first of all it says in their Torah that no one can enter paradise without baptism. How then did this fellow enter? Why, not even one-quarter of the stone covering his body could have been baptized by
10 these tears. Moreover, in light of the fact that there was no longer any spirit within him, even if he had been baptized a thousand times in a thousand ritual baths it would have been to no avail. Furthermore, even granting your contention that the baptism was a baptism of forgiveness resulting from the tears, why should a heavenly voice
15 have told him never to consider doing such a thing again, i.e., never to beg for mercy for any man who has already died, whether through tears or any other medium? Should God not have rejoiced with this Gregory, regarded him even more favorably and done good things for him because an additional soul would be saved? If you put me off by
20 arguing that that Muslim never entered the kingdom of heaven but was merely spared the suffering of hell because of Gregory's prayer, then why is it told that he was forgiven because of the prayer and baptized by those tears? It should have been said that because of the prayer and tears his sins were forgiven so that he was not punished
25 in hell, but the mention of baptism makes it clear that the entire forgiveness was dependent upon that baptism.

[162]

It is written in their books that "Jesus was led into the wilderness where Satan tempted him. And Jesus fasted forty days and forty nights, and afterwards he was hungry. The tempter then came
30 and said, If you are the son of God, command that these stones be made bread. But Jesus answered and said, Man shall not live by bread alone, but by every word that proceeds out of the mouth of God shall man live. Satan then took him up into the holy city, and set him on a pinnacle of the temple, and said to him, If you are the son of God, cast

yourself down, for it is written, He shall give his angels charge concerning you to guard you in all your ways. Jesus answered him, Do
not tempt the Lord your God. Again, Satan took him up to an exceedingly high mountain and showed him all the kingdoms of the world.
5   He then said to him, All this will I give you if you will fall down and
bow to me. Jesus said to him, You shall fear the Lord your God, and
him shall you serve. Then Satan left him" [Matt. 4:1-11]. Now what
was the need for relating that he fasted forty days and forty nights?
What sort of praise of God is it to say that he needs food and drink?
10 Why, all the angels of our God who serve him need no food or drink.
Moreover, Moses, who was flesh and blood, was sustained by the
glory of the divine presence forty days and forty nights without eating bread or drinking water, and so was Elijah. Furthermore, the Jews
were unable to look upon the countenance of Moses until he placed a
15 veil over his face because he had approached his Creator; how much
more, then, should this be true of this man, who called himself God.
Also, why did he become hungry? If you say that it was because of his
flesh, the flesh could not fast forty days and forty nights if not for the
holy spirit. It was the holy spirit, then, which gave him the strength
20 to fast forty days and forty nights; in that case, why did it not sustain
him indefinitely without food or drink and without hunger or thirst?
In addition, when Satan told him, "If you are God, make these stones
into bread and eat it," why did he reply, "Man shall not live by bread
alone"? This is a faulty response, for Satan could have answered him,
25 "It is precisely because man does not live by bread alone but rather by
every word that proceeds out of the mouth of God that you should
make bread out of these rocks, for man lives by what proceeds out of
the mouth of God whether from wood or from rocks." Moreover,
why did Satan tempt him in all these ways? After all, everyone knows
30 that Satan is an evil angel who knows both manifest and hidden things
just as any other angel does, and if it had been true that Jesus was
divine, why should Satan have troubled him so much and not been
afraid of him?

[163]

It is written in their books: "Joseph took his wife and knew her not till his firstborn son was born, who was called Jesus" [Matt. 1:24-25]. The Latin is: "Joseph accepit conjugem suam et non cognovit eam donec peperit filium suum primogenitum qui vocatur Jesus."

[164]

5   It is written in their books: "When he was born from his mother's stomach like other men, her womb opened and she gave birth to a boy, and she called him God" [Luke 2:5-11].

[165]

It is·written in their books: "The father is unbegotten, the son was begotten, and the spirit proceeded from both of them." It
10 follows, then, that the father preceded the son. Moreover, when he says that the spirit proceeded from both of them, this necessarily implies that there was a time when there was a father and no spirit, and yet you say that the three are equal in greatness, age, indeed, in all respects; this contention, then, must be ruled out whether you like it or
15 not. The Latin in the *Quicunque vult* goes as follows: "Patrus ingenitus, filius genitus, spiritus sanctus ab utroque procedit."

[166]

It is written in their books: "When Jesus came down from the mountain, great multitudes followed him. And behold, there came a leper and bowed down to him, saying, Lord, if you wish you can cure
20 me of my leprosy. And Jesus put forth his hand and touched him, and he was immediately cured. And Jesus said to him, See that you tell no man, but show yourself to the priest and bring him the sacrifice for your purification as Moses has commanded in his Torah" [Matt. 8:1-4]. Now, I am surprised at his commanding the leper to go to the
25 priest and bring his sacrifice. Once he was cured by Jesus why should he have to go to the priest? Moreover, from the time of his birth we don't see that he commanded the observance of any other commandments in the Torah, such as those regarding the Sabbath, circumcision, pork, and the mixing of species, and several others
30 which, in fact, he permitted people to transgress after his advent. Indeed, even this commandment was not observed from that day on.

[167]

It is written in their books: "And it came to pass that when
Jesus had finished these words—the solutions which he explained to
his students and all the secrets that he told them—he departed from
there and came to his city Capernaum, he, his brothers, and his stu-
5   dents. He was teaching in their synagogues, and all his listeners
were astonished at him and said, Whence have wisdom and might
come to this man? Is not this the blacksmith's son? And is his mother
not Mary? And his brothers Jacob, Joseph, Simon, and Judah, and his
sisters—are they not all with us? From where has he become expert
10   in all these matters of wisdom? Jesus answered and said to them, A
prophet is not without honor save in his own city and in his own
house. Therefore he did not do many great works" [Matt. 13:53-58;
Mark 6:1-4]. This is what I ask you: Did Mary have sons and
daughters besides Jesus, or did Joseph the blacksmith have sons and
15   daughters from another woman? If you will say that they did have
sons and daughters, fine; that is why Jesus' Jewish acquaintances
said, "We see that his brothers and sisters—Jacob, Joseph, Simon,
and Judah—do not do such wise deeds." But if Joseph had no sons
and daughters besides Jesus, why did the Jews say, "His brothers
20   and sisters are with us"? And why did they call the above-named
people brothers and sisters just as they would the siblings of anyone
else? Also, why didn't Jesus answer them, "Fools, all that you have
said about my having brothers and sisters is a lie; in fact I am not
even the son of the blacksmith, and your astonishment at my wisdom
25   is out of place since all the wisdom in the world is mine"? Instead, he
answered in the manner of jokesters who say that wherever they go
they are honored more than they are at home. Furthermore, who were
the brothers who came with him to Capernaum? You may argue that
they were his students, but it says that he, his brothers, and his stu-
30   dents came to Capernaum. You may then argue that all Israel are considered brothers, but elsewhere in the passage they are called by
their proper name, for this is what it says: "When the people of Israel
saw the signs which Jesus performed, they said to each other,
Whence have wisdom and might come to this man? Is he not the
35   blacksmith's son? And is his mother not Mary? And his brothers and
sisters are all with us."

[168]

It is written in their books that Jesus told the man afflicted by demons who was lying on the bed, "Arise and walk, so that you may know that there is a son of man who has power on earth to forgive sins." Then Jesus told him, "Arise, walk, take up your bed, and go to
5   your house" [Matt. 9:6]. It is written in their book of Mark: "Once he wanted to go to Samaria while there were many people with him, but the Samaritans did not wish to receive him either in the city of Samaria or in the fields . . . and he fed five thousand people who were there from five loaves of bread and two fish. And he told them, Foxes
10 have holes and birds of the air have nests, but I, the son of man, have no place to lay my head" [Luke 9:52–53, 13–17, 58]. It is written further in their book of Mark: "When Jesus saw great multitudes about him, he crossed the Euphrates River. And a certain scribe came and said, I will follow you wherever you go. And Jesus said to him, The foxes
15 have holes etc." [Matt. 8:18–20].

(It says in their books that Jesus complained about his plight and said, "Wolves have holes and birds of the air have nests, but I, the son of man, have no place to lay my head"; i.e., he was so poor. It is written in their books that Jesus cried out to his father after he was
20 crucified and said, "My father, if it is possible, let my trouble come to an end" [Matt. 26:39]. The Latin reads: "Pater mi, si est possibile transeat a me calix iste, verumtamen non sicut ego volo sed sicut tu vis.")

Now, if he was God why did he call himself a man? Why, we
25 find in several passages that Scripture warns us not to compare God to a man, as Balaam said, "God is not a man, that he should lie, nor the son of man, that he should change his mind" [Num. 23:19]. More-over, David said, "Put not your trust in princes, nor in the son of man, in whom there is no help" [Ps. 146:3], and it says, "All men lie"
30 [Ps. 116:11]. It also says, "Cursed be the man that trusts in man and makes flesh his arm" [Jer. 17:5]. Indeed, all these statements are applicable to Jesus, who was called son of man, as it is written in the Gospels that he himself called himself son of man—*fili homo*—at every opportunity. He did, in fact, lie and change his mind, as it is
35 written in their Gospels that Jesus beseeched God and said, "Father,

all things are possible for you; take away this cup from me; nevertheless, not what I will, but what you will" [Mark 14:36]. If he was
God, then he lied, for who could counteract his will? He also changed
his mind, because the purpose of his advent was the suffering of
5 these tribulations, as it is written in the Gospels, "The son of man
came not to be ministered unto, but to minister, and to give his life as
a ransom for many" [Matt. 20:28]; afterwards, however, he said,
"Take away this cup from me," and so he changed his mind. Furthermore, if he performed this sign of curing the man afflicted with
10 demons in order to show his power and greatness, why did he say,
"So that you may know that there is a son of man who has power on
earth"? He should have said "that there is a God who has power on
earth." Moreover, if he was God, why did he lie to that scribe by saying that he had no place to lay his head? Why, it is written, "The land
15 shall not be sold forever, for the land is mine" [Lev. 25:23], and it is
written, "The earth is the Lord's, and the fullness thereof; the world,
and they that dwell therein" [Ps. 24:1]. In fact, he himself told them
elsewhere, "Dominion is given unto me in heaven and in earth"
[Matt. 28:18].

[169]

20   It is written in their books that Jesus passed through a certain
place and found a man "who had been sick for thirty-eight years. And
Jesus said to him, Do you wish to be cured? He told him, My lord,
that is what I would like. And he said to him, Take up your bed and
walk. Immediately the man was cured and took up his bed and
25 walked, and the same day was the Sabbath. The Jews therefore came
to him and said, It is the Sabbath; it is not lawful to do work on the
Sabbath by carrying burdens" [John 5:5-10]. The fact is that they
were right. If he cured the man, all right, but why did he command him
to carry his bed?

[170]

30   It is written in their books, "At that time Jesus said, I thank
you, O Lord of heaven and earth, because you have hidden these
things from the wise and prudent which you have revealed to me, for

so did you will it. . . . Come to me, all you that are weary and heavy-
laden, and I will satisfy you. Place your necks in my yoke and believe
in me, for I am meek and humble, and you will find rest for your souls.
My yoke is soft, and my burden is light" [Matt. 11:25-30]. Now, did
5   he have to say, "I thank you"? If he was God, what sort of thanks
must he give? Everything that is hidden from all the world is known
to him, yet he says, "I thank you. . . ."

[171]

It is written in their books, "At that time Jesus went to and
fro on the Sabbath, and his disciples were hungry and plucked the
10   ears of corn and ate. But when the Pharisees saw him, they said to
him, Behold, your disciples do that which it is not lawful to do upon
the Sabbath day. And Jesus heard it and said to them, Have you not
read what David did when he was hungry, and they that were with
him? How he entered into the house of God and ate the shewbread,
15   which was not lawful for him to eat, and which was permitted neither
to him nor to those that were with him but only to the priests? He
went on to say, Have you not read that it is written how the priests in
the Temple profane the Sabbath and are blameless? But I say unto you
that in this place there is one greater than the temple. Also, you
20   should know the meaning of 'I wish mercy and not sacrifice.' . . .
Moreover, when a man whose hand had withered came before him,
the Jews asked him, Is it lawful to heal on the Sabbath? that they
might accuse him. And he said to them, What man is there among you
who has one sheep which, if it should fall into a pit on the Sabbath, he
25   would not lift out? How much then is a man better than a sheep?
Moreover, is it not lawful to do good on the Sabbath" [Matt. 12:1-12]?
What sort of answer is this that Jesus gave them? If David behaved
improperly, this does not give them the right to pluck those ears of
corn on the Sabbath. Furthermore, if the priests perform the service
30   in the Temple both on week-days and on the Sabbath as they are commanded to do, how does this permit Jesus' disciples to desecrate the
Sabbath by plucking ears of corn? As for his statement, "I wish
mercy and not sacrifice," i.e., that he does not want any sacrifices,
how does this square with his command to that above-mentioned

leper whom he cured to bring a sacrifice in accordance with the commandment given to all lepers in the Torah which was revealed of old? How can he now say, "I wish mercy and not sacrifice"? And as for his statement, "What man is there among you that has one sheep
5 etc.," this is a lie. All people know that Jews are not permitted to raise any animals on the Sabbath either from a well or from a ditch. Why, then, did he answer as he did? By saying this he was actually permitting work on the Sabbath.

[172]

It is written in the same place in their book of Mark that "the
10 scribe told him, Master, I will follow you. One of his disciples then said to him, Allow me first to bury my father. But Jesus answered him, Follow me, and refrain from burying the dead [Matt. 8:21-22]. Now, that man was rich, and Jesus told him, Sell all your possessions and follow me. But the man went to his home and buried his
15 father; he did not sell his possessions and follow Jesus [cf. Matthew 19:21-22]. And Jesus entered a ship, and his disciples followed him. And, behold, there was a great tempest in the sea, and the ship was about to break. The wind came across the sea with great force, yet Jesus was asleep. His disciples came and awoke him . . . and Jesus
20 told them, You are men of little faith; why are you fearful of a little storm" [Matt. 8:22-26]? Now, is there anything worse than what he told that scribe, i.e., "Refrain from burying your father"? Why, there is no greater good deed than burying even those dead who are not one's relatives, and this is certainly the case with regard to one's
25 own father. Furthermore, it says that he was asleep; but if he were God, how could he sleep? It is, after all, written, "Behold, the guardian of Israel shall neither slumber nor sleep" [Ps. 121:4].

[173]

It is written in their Torah in John: "And when the days of her purification were accomplished, they brought him to Jerusalem" [Luke 2:22].
30 [Luke 2:22]. This implies that she was impure like all women who give birth, for it says, "When the days of her purification were accomplished." Furthermore, she brought a sacrifice consisting of two

turtledoves and two young pigeons, which is brought only because of impurity.

[174]

It is written in their books: "Then Jesus went thence, and departed to Tyre and Sidon. And, behold, a Canaanite woman walked
5   behind him and cried out unto him, saying, Have mercy on me, O lord, son of David; my daughter is full of devils. But Jesus answered her not at all. And his disciples came and besought him, saying, Forgive her, for she cries after us. But he answered and said, I am not sent but unto the lost sheep of the house of Israel. Then she came and bowed
10   down to him, saying, My lord, save me. But Jesus answered and said, It is not right to steal bread from the children and give it to the dogs. And she answered, saying, My lord, the dogs eat of the crumbs which fall from their masters' table. Then Jesus answered and said to her, O woman, great is your faith; let it be unto you as you wish. And her
15   daughter was cured at that very hour" [Matt. 15:21-28]. Now, with regard to Jesus' answer, "I am not sent but unto the lost sheep etc.," i.e., that he came to the world only to forgive the transgressions of Jewish sinners, why did he cause them to sin and to stumble and to be blinded if he really came to forgive and pardon Israel (for they did in-
20   deed stumble as a result of his death)? Was there no other nation he could cause to stumble except the one which he had come to save and redeem? Moreover, regarding his statement to the Canaanite woman that "it is not right to steal bread from the children and give it to the dogs," what he must have meant by this metaphor is , "It is not right
25   that I should steal the kindness which I have to perform for the Jews and give it to other nations," i.e., to this Canaanite who is called a dog.

[175]

It is written in their books in the account of Mark: "When they were sitting at the table on the eve of Passover, Jesus took the
30   bread, broke it, recited a blessing, and gave it to his students, saying, Take this bread, for it is my body. In addition, he took the cup, recited a blessing, and gave it to all of them, and they all drank of it. And he

said unto them, This is my blood of the new testament" [Mark 14:22–24]. In what sense was it his body that they ate and drank? Did he cut a piece off his body which he gave to them, or did his body first become bread and wine and he gave them pieces of it? Moreover,
5   where did that body which they ate and drank descend? Did it go on its way separately or was it mixed up in the stomach with all the other food?

[176]

It is written in their books: "When Jesus came with his disciples to a village which was named Gethsemane, he said to his dis-
10   ciples, Sit here until I pray. He took with him Peter and James and John and began to be fearful and to tremble. And he said, My soul is sorrowful unto death; sit here and watch. And he went past them a little, and fell on the ground, and prayed: If possible, let this cup pass from me at this hour. And he said, My father, you are omnipotent;
15   take away this cup from me, but let it be not as I will, but as you will. And he came to his disciples and found them sleeping, and he said to Peter and Simon, Could you not watch with me one hour? Watch and pray, lest you enter into temptation; the spirit is ready, but the flesh is weak. And again he went away and prayed the same prayer, and he
20   returned and found them asleep (for their eyes were heavy with sleep), and they knew not what to answer him. He came a third time and told them, Sit and rest, for this is the hour when the son of man is given over into the hands of evil men. Rise up, let us go, for he that will betray me is at hand" [Mark 14:32–42; cf. Matthew 26:36–46].
25   Now, to whom was Jesus praying? Did he have need of prayer and supplication? Why, it is written, "He speaks and carries out; he decrees and fulfills," and yet it says that Jesus began to be fearful and to tremble and that he told his disciples, "My soul is sorrowful unto death." You may argue that he is referring to the flesh, which was
30   fearful, but it says, "My soul is sorrowful." Moreover, you always argue that this sort of thing refers to the flesh, but is it really possible to maintain such a position? Everyone knows, after all, that the flesh itself does not speak or know anything; it would be like a stone except for the impetus it receives from the spirit. Furthermore, Jesus

prayed that his father remove the cup from him; in effect, then, he was saying, "You can remove it from me, but I cannot." He also said, "Let it not be as I will, but as you will." If so, then the wills are not the same, and if they have two wills, then Jesus could not be God.

5 You also maintain consistently that Jesus accepted all these troubles willingly in order to redeem his children. Well, if that was his desire, then why these supplications? On the other hand, if he did not wish to accept all this, why did he not save his body? In fact, he told them, "The spirit is ready, but the flesh is weak." (It is written in their

10 books: "Jesus said at the time of his crucifixion, My soul hurts unto death, and the flesh is in turmoil" [cf. Mark 14:34]).

     Now, tell me what in man has will and desire; clearly, it is the soul. They call that desire *ratio* in Latin, and no one can be without these three things: body, soul, and *ratio*; *ratio*, moreover, comes from

15 the soul. How, then, did Jesus say, "Let it not be as I will, but as you will"? After all, his soul came from the father, and his father desired that cup. Do not put me off by arguing that Jesus referred to the flesh, because only the spirit and not the flesh has knowledge of good and evil. You may then try to refute me by maintaining that he must have

20 referred to the flesh, for the flesh is naturally fearful and it simply must behave in its natural manner; yet the natural manner of the flesh is to have thoughts of women, to sleep, and to hunger, and so how could the flesh fast forty days and forty nights? If you will argue that no impure thought assailed Jesus' flesh because of the holy spirit

25 within it, then why did that spirit not have the power to save the flesh from fear and hunger? The fact is that we know that he was fearful, hungry, and sorrowful, for he said, "My soul is sorrowful," not "my flesh" but "my soul." Consequently, I am amazed by their contentions in light of the fact that Hananiah, Mishael, and Azariah, who

30 were human beings and were thrown into a burning furnace (which is the most painful sort of death), were neither fearful nor sorrowful; indeed, they remained completely unharmed in both body and soul, and even their clothing was unaffected, as it is written, ". . . upon whose bodies the fire had no power, nor was a hair of their head

35 singed, neither were their garments changed, nor had the smell of fire been passed on to them" [Dan. 3:27]. Jesus, on the other hand, did not

save his soul and body even from fear. If you say that this was in accordance with his will and desire, then why these supplications?

[177]

It is written in their books: "In those days, after that tribulation, the sun shall be darkened, and the moon shall not give her light. And the stars of heaven shall fall, and the powers that are in heaven shall be shaken. And then shall they see the son of man coming in the clouds with a great host and with glory. Then he shall send his angels and gather together his elect from the four winds of the earth, from the uttermost part of the earth to the uttermost part of heaven. Now the following parable is said of a fig tree: When its branch is yet tender and its leaves come forth, know that summer is near; so when you shall see these things come to pass, know that the end is near. Verily I say unto you that this generation shall not pass till all these things be done. Heaven and earth shall pass away, but my words shall not pass away. But of that day and that hour no one knows, not the angels in heaven nor the son, but the father . . . like a man going into exile, and the members of his household do not know on what day or at what hour he will return" [Mark 13:24-35]. Now, it surprises me very much that he should say that the son does not know the day and hour he will come. If he is like his father, who can hide any matter or any act from him? Moreover, he himself would be coming without his own knowledge; it is thus obvious that he is less knowledgeable than his father.

It is written in their book of Mark that when his students asked him when the end would be, he answered that it is hidden from the angels and from the son, but the father and holy spirit know [Mark 13:32]. Now, according to your contention that they are all equal both in power and in knowledge, why is something hidden from one which is known to another? It must be because the son is not preexistent like the father.

[178]

It is written in their books: "And in the sixth hour there was darkness in the land until the ninth hour, and at the ninth hour he cried

out, My Lord, my Lord, why have you forsaken me" [Mark 15:33-34]?
If he was God, why did he cry out that way? Why, all the tribulations
came upon him in accordance with his will and were proper in his
eyes; he accepted everything with love, and all these things befell
5 him through his own will.

[179]

It is written in their book of Mark that an angel came to his
mother Mary to inform her, "Behold, you shall conceive and bring
forth a son, and shall call his name Jesus. He shall be great and shall
be called the son of the highest, and God shall give unto him the
10 throne of his father David. And he shall reign over the house of Jacob
forever, and of his kingdom there shall be no end" [Luke 1:28-33].
Now, why should a son of God need a present? After all, the entire
world is his. Moreover, what sort of honor is it for him to be given
the throne of his father David? Is one kingdom an honor for God?
15 Furthermore, he calls David his father; well, who was created first,
David or his son?

[180]

It is written in their book of Luke: "When he was twelve
years old, he went to Jerusalem with his parents for the festival of
Passover. And when his parents returned, he remained alone in
20 Jerusalem. His parents realized this and were surprised that he had
not returned with them, and so they returned to Jerusalem and sought
him, and they found him among the students. And his mother said to
him, Why have you done this? Your father and I have been seeking
you in sorrow and pain" [Luke 2:42-48]. Who, then, was this father
25 that his mother mentioned? If she meant Joseph, then how can Jesus
be called God? On the other hand, if she was referring to his father in
heaven, then it follows that he was a sinner, for he angered his Creator. Furthermore, does his father in heaven have to look for him?
Why, everything is known to him.

[181]

30 It is written in their books: "In the evening, Jesus went out to

Bethany with his twelve students, and on the next day, when they had left Bethany, Jesus was hungry. And he saw a fig tree from afar off, and he desired it. He then came to see if there were figs there, but when he came to it, he found nothing but leaves on the tree. So he was angered and said, No edible fruit will come out of you for ever"[Mark 11:11-14]. Now, why was he hungry? You may say that it was because of his flesh, but we have seen that Moses, may he rest in peace, who was flesh and blood, was able to fast forty days and forty nights because he had drawn near to the divine presence; why, then, was this fellow, who was himself God according to you, hungry because of his flesh? You may then maintain that the spirit was hungry, but this is preposterous since the spirit doesn't eat anything. A further question may be posed in light of the fact that Jesus went to see if there were any figs on the fig tree. Did he, then, not know if there were figs or not from the original vantage point from which he saw the tree? Perhaps you will again maintain that he said this in accordance with his carnal aspect, but since when does the flesh think about or know anything? It is, after all, well known that it is not the flesh but the spirit which knows or understands anything. Consequently I am amazed at this; if he was God and the spirit of God was in him, why did he not know from his original vantage point that there was no fruit there? Moreover, even if he didn't find fruit, why did he curse the tree? Perhaps he was angry at it and cursed it because it caused him to make the vain effort of getting there; however, it is written that he commanded the apostles, "Love your enemies, and do good to those that hate you. Pray for your oppressors, and bless those who hate you" [Luke 6:27-28]. Now this should certainly be true of this tree, which committed no sin. It didn't send for Jesus and mock him by inviting him to come and eat of its fruit. Why, then, did he curse it and cause it to dry up without a trial or a discussion?

[182]

It is written in their books: "Then the twelve disciples went into Galilee to a mountain where Jesus had commanded them to go. And when they saw him, they bowed down to him, but some of them did not believe in him. And Jesus came and spoke to them, saying, All

power is given unto me in heaven and in earth. Go and teach all nations baptism in the name of the father, the son, and the holy spirit,
and teach them all things which I have commanded you; and lo, I am
with you always until the end of the world" [Matt. 28:16-20]. I am
5 surprised at his statement, "All power is given unto me in heaven and
in earth." Who gave it to him? You may say that his father gave it to
him, but are he and his father two? Why, they are supposed to be one
entity; neither is greater than the other in rule, power, or wisdom.
Moreover, note his statement, "Lo, I am with you always until the
10 end of the world" [Matt. 28:20]; i.e., I will be with you until the end of
the world, but I will not be with you in the world to come.

[183]

It is written in their books: "After he cured the daughter of the
ruler of the synagogue and sent all the members of the household out
of the house except for Peter, James, John, the father of the girl, and
15 her mother, he said to the girl, Arise, I say unto you. And immediately
she arose" [Mark 5:35-42]. It is written further after this: "And he
called the twelve and gave them the power to exorcise impure spirits.
And he commanded them that they should not take their bundle when
they go but only a staff; he commanded that they take no bread in their
20 hand but that they be shod with sandals, and that they not put on two
coats" [Mark 6:7-9]. Yet I find that in another place it says in the
Gospels that all his students were unable to exorcise a spirit from
one little boy, for this is what is written in their books: "And when
Jesus came to his disciples, he saw great multitudes with them, and
25 the scribes were talking with them. And when all the people saw him,
they became silent and fearful, and they ran to greet him. He then
asked them, What things are you discussing with my students? And
one of the multitude answered and said, Master, I have brought you
my son, who is dumb and is perturbed by an evil spirit; he spits and
30 foams at the mouth. I spoke to your disciples that they cast out the
spirit from my son, but they could not. And Jesus answered and told
them, O stubborn generation, how long shall I be with you and how
long shall I suffer your rebelliousness? Bring him to me. They
brought him . . . and he asked his father, saying, When did this impure

spirit come to him? And he said, From childhood. And he removed the impure spirit from the boy" [Mark 9:14–26].

[184]

It is written in their books: "When Jesus went out on his way, a man came running to him with bent knees and begged him, saying,
5 My good master, what shall I do that I may inherit the life of the world to come? Then Jesus answered and said to him, Why do you call me good? There is no one good but God himself. Do you not know the commandments, Do not kill, Do not commit adultery, Do not steal, Do not bear false witness against your neighbor, Do not defraud,
10 Honor your father and mother? He answered him and said, My master, all these things have I observed from my youth. And Jesus felt affection for him and loved him, and he said to him, There is one more thing you must do. Sell everything you have and give to the poor so that you will have treasure in heaven, and follow me" [Mark
15 10:17–21]. Now, he didn't tell him, "Go and be baptized." Rather, he commanded him to observe the ancient commandments, and it was on the basis of those commandments that he promised him life in the world to come.

[185]

It is written in their books: "Now Jesus left Judea and went to
20 Galilee, and he wanted to go to Samaria. Then he came to a city of Samaria called Sychar, near the parcel of ground in Shechem that Jacob gave to his son Joseph. Now Jacob's spring was there; and Jesus was tired and sat on the spring, and at the sixth hour of the day a woman of Samaria came to draw water. Jesus said to her, Give me
25 water to drink (for his disciples had gone away to the city to buy food). Then the woman of Samaria said to him, How can you drink with me when you are a Jew and I am a woman of Samaria, and Jews refuse to benefit from dealings with Samaritans" [John 4:3–9]? Now, if he was divine, why was he tired and why did he have to drink? You
30 may argue that the flesh was tired, but this can never happen without the spirit; for the nature of man is that he becomes tired only when the flesh and spirit are combined. On the other hand, flesh which con-

tains the holy spirit within it should never be tired. Moreover, why
did the woman say, "Why, Jews do not benefit from dealings with
Samaritans"? The fact is that we drink water with people of all
nations. Now, from the expression she used you can understand that
5   he asked her for something shameful, namely, to have relations with
her. If you will argue that this is not true, then how do you explain a
subsequent verse which says that when his disciples returned from
the city and found him talking to the woman, they were amazed [John
4:27]? What were they amazed about? It must be that they suspected
10   him. Now, if his students who were with him day and night and grew
up with him nevertheless suspected him, then we who never saw him
are certainly justified in doing so.

[186]

It is written in their books: "A marriage took place in Canaan
of Galilee, and the mother of Jesus was there. And Jesus was called
15   there with his disciples, and wine was lacking. Then his mother,
Mary, said to Jesus, They have no wine. And Jesus said to her, What
have I to do with you, woman? My hour has not yet come. . . . After
this he went down to Capernaum, he, his mother, his brethren, and
his disciples; and they remained there a short time, and it was close
20   to Passover" [John 2:1-4, 12-13]. Now, they say that Jesus' mother is
not called "woman" or "wife" in their Torah, yet here her own son
called her "woman"; and if he is divine, he could never say something false and deceptive. I should also like to comment on his statement, "What have I to do with you?" which means, "What do we
25   care if the wine is missing?" Who should care if not the one who
made the feast, and he was the one who made the feast.

[187]

It is written in their books that "a man said to him, Your
mother and brothers are standing outside, seeking you. . . . Jesus then
stood up and sat by the sea side, and great multitudes were gathered
30   together unto him, so that he went into a ship while the whole multitude stood on the shore. He spoke many parables to them, and he told
them the following parable. A sower went forth to sow. Some seeds

fell by the wayside, and the fowls came and devoured those seeds. . . . Some seeds fell into fertile ground and brought forth fruit, some a hundredfold, some sixtyfold, and some thirtyfold. He who has ears to hear, let him hear. And his disciples came and said, Why do you
5   speak in parables to the multitudes? Jesus answered and said to them, It is given unto you to know the mysteries of the kingdom of heaven, but not to them. Whoever has, to him shall be given, and he shall have in abundance; but whoever has not, from him shall be taken away even what he has. Therefore, I speak to them in parables,
10   because they do not see or hear or understand, so that in them may be fulfilled the prophecy, By hearing you shall hear but not understand, and seeing you shall see but not perceive, for this people's heart has grown fat, etc. But blessed are your eyes, for they see, and your ears, for they hear. Now I shall explain to you the truth in the parables, and
15   you shall listen. This is the meaning of this and that is the meaning of that, and he explained everything to them" [Matt. 12:47-13:18]. I see, then, that on this one occasion he did not speak in a devious manner.

[188]

You have said that the father, the son, and the holy spirit are one entity. This contention might at least seem plausible with regard
20   to the father and the holy spirit, for neither one nor the other eats, sleeps, becomes fearful, or gets tired. But how is it possible for the son to be like the father and the holy spirit when he ate and slept and grew tired and was afraid? He grew tired, as it is written in their Torah, "And he came to Jacob's well and was tired, and he asked the
25   Samaritan woman for water" [John 4:5-7]. He was afraid, as it is written, "My Lord, my Lord, why have you forsaken me" [Matt. 27:46]? He slept, as it is written in a passage which I have already discussed, "The wind came across the sea, yet Jesus was asleep. His disciples came and awoke him" [Matt. 8:24-25]. If you argue that the
30   three are considered one because of the holy spirit that was in the flesh, then the same should be said of every prophet who had the holy spirit. Indeed, even Adam, into whose nostrils God infused the spirit of life, should be called a god. If you argue that Adam performed no marvelous deeds, then I could cite Elijah and Elisha, who did. More-

over, even according to you, the flesh died at the very moment when
the holy spirit departed, and you admit that after the flesh died he
could not do good or evil; after his death, then, how could all three be
considered one? Now, once we find a separation in this entity, how
5   can we say that he is one?

      Furthermore, with regard to all things he did and said which
are inappropriate for God, you immediately put me off and try to say
the he said this in accordance with the flesh. If so, then the flesh and
holy spirit are not one thing. You should also know that the flesh
10   does not know or understand; it is, rather, the soul which calculates,
sins, desires, and covets. Moreover, it is written, "Do not desire
your neighbor's home; do not covet, etc." [Exod. 20:17; Deut. 5:18];
now, once the Torah has warned us in these commandments of "Do
not desire" and "Do not covet," it follows that he who desires and
15   covets will be punished. What, then, desires and covets? It must be
the soul, for if you say it is the flesh, then you can be refuted by the
following verses: "My soul is eagerly awaiting your salvation, O
Lord" [Ps. 119:81], "With my soul have I desired you in the night;
with my spirit within me I will seek you early" [Isa. 26:9], and "The
20   soul that sins, it shall die" [Ezek. 18:4, 20], i.e., it shall fall into hell.
Further evidence that the flesh knows nothing may be cited from the
statement of their saint Paul in the *Evangelium* that the soul constantly
warns the body not to sin [Gal. 5:17]. It is also written in their Torah,
"Do not enter my sanctuary with raised hands." Now, what is meant
25   by raised? It means that if a person hates his neighbor and plans to
kill him, then his hands are considered raised; even if he did not
actually kill him, their Torah considers it as if he did. You may then
argue that the heart, which is flesh, is what plans to kill him, as it is
written, "Many are the thoughts in the heart of a man" [Prov. 19:21].
30   The fact remains, however, that it says, "My soul is eagerly awaiting" [Ps. 119:81], and "With my soul have I desired you in the night"
[Isa. 26:9], and "All the labor of man is for his mouth, and yet the soul
is not satisfied" [Eccles. 6:7], and "If your soul wishes, etc." [Gen.
23:8]; it follows, then, that all desires depend upon the soul. More-
35   over, if the flesh sins without the spirit, why is the soul punished?
Does one sin while the other is then punished? The situation, rather,

is that they both sin together. This may be compared to the parable of the lame man and the blind man who were guardians of an orchard. A king once had a very beautiful orchard in which many types of fruit were planted, and the guardians of this garden used to eat the fruit be-
5   cause it was tasty and attractive. The king was simply unable to find faithful guardians who would guard the orchard without eating the fruit. Finally, an idea struck him, and he brought a lame man and a blind man into the orchard; he figured that the lame man would not be able to climb up the trees, while the blind man would not be able to find the fruit even if he came up. After a while, the lame man and the blind man took counsel together, and the blind man took the lame man on his shoulders and carried him so that he could take the fruit from the trees; thus, they both sinned.

[189]

Moreover, I am surprised by the whole story of this Jesus.
15   Why did he have to be born to a woman, why did he suffer all the pain, tribulations, and shame which they inflicted upon him, and why did he die? This, then, is the answer which they give us: All this happened as a result of Adam's sin. When Adam violated the command of his Creator, he was given over into the hand of Satan, for the power that
20   God gave Satan was such that any creature who transgresses divine commandments is given over to him. Consequently, when Adam sinned as a result of the fruit that he ate, he was immediately handed over into the hand of Satan. Furthermore, because of that same sin, all men born after him, whether good or evil, were handed over into the
25   hand of Satan, for far be it from God to do evil by committing robbery or injustice against any of his creatures, whether it be Satan or anyone else. Eventually, however, the mercy of the Creator overcame his wrath and he had compassion for all his creatures, who had descended to hell. He then decided, "I shall go down and redeem those
30   who have been given over into the hand of Satan." In what manner did he do this? He took a man away from Satan that he had made out of himself, and that man was Jesus whom they call son of God. He had sent him to earth in the womb of a woman just like other men, but this man was free of sin and iniquity. Now when Satan had seen that he

had died, he had decided to take him as part of his portion and to treat
him in the same way he had treated the other sinners. At this point,
God told him, "Since you have taken an innocent man against whom
you have no valid claim, it is fair and proper that I wrest from you
5 those sinners who have been given over into your hand." And this is
precisely what he did; he descended to hell, from where he took those
who had been given over to Satan. This, then, is the reason for all that
he did.

Now I have the following comments: If this were true, I
10 would be amazed at the implausibility of doing all this. Why, everyone knows that Satan is an evil angel who knows both the past and the
future; how, then, do you say that God hid this from him? Moreover,
according to your contention that he did hide it from him and that
Satan did not recognize his Creator because the latter had made a
15 carnal garment which made him like an ordinary man, then how did
Satan sin by this act? After all, what he did was done by mistake. Is
God to be praised for dealing with his creatures through stratagems,
indirection, and trickery? This is not acceptable even from flesh and
blood, who often behave improperly toward one another. If a man in-
20 advertently behaves improperly toward his master, the master may
not grab his present away from him; now this applies a fortiori to the
Creator, who is praised for giving his creatures the benefit of the
doubt and acting more compassionately than strict justice requires.
Moreover, we find in the Gospels that Jesus exorcised demons from
25 several people and thus stole Satan's present for no reason. After all,
Satan had previously been given control over them, and he had done
nothing wrong; so why did Jesus steal his present, expel him, and
push him away from the body without trial or discussion? What he
should have done was make such a stipulation in the first place.
30 When he gave Satan power over Adam, he should have told him, "I do
not want you to have power over this man," just as he told the
demons which he took out of those people for whom he performed
wonders.

I am also surprised at why he delayed this redemption so long
35 and why he gave the Torah earlier when there was no reward for it
(since you say that everyone descended to hell). Consequently, I

think that it would have been proper to redeem the nation from hell first and then give them the Torah.

[190]

Furthermore, they say that before Jesus came to the world all creatures descended to hell whether they were good or bad. But I say:
5 How can they make such an assertion? Why, they say that before Jesus came to the world the story of Lazarus took place, and this is how that story is written: "There was a certain very rich man whose name was Dives who was clothed in purple garments and ate sumptuously. And there was a certain poor man named Lazarus who lay at
10 the gate of the rich Dives, and he used to cry out continuously to the rich man, begging him to show him some kindness; but the latter refused. Finally, they both died. The rich man went to hell, and Lazarus went to the bosom of Abraham. And when the rich man saw that Lazarus was sitting in the bosom of Abraham without pain, indeed, in
15 contentment, gladness, and joy, while he himself was sentenced to great torment with fire and flame in his mouth, he cried out and said, My master Abraham, tell my brother Lazarus to dip his little finger in water and drop it on my mouth, for I am tormented by the great flame coming out of my mouth." Now, since Abraham and Lazarus were
20 not in hell, how can they say that everyone descended to hell?

"There was a certain very rich man whose name was Dives, etc." until "and drop the water on my mouth, for I am tormented by the fire and flame coming out of my mouth," as I have written just above. "And Abraham answered, saying, You remember that in your
25 lifetime you had everything your heart desired while your brother Lazarus was in great torment from illness and hunger; yet when he asked you for the crumbs that fell from your table, you hadn't sufficient compassion to give them to him. So now he will be happy and content while you will suffer torment. Then Dives said, I beg you to
30 send him to my father's house, for I have five brethren there, so that he may warn them, lest they also come into this great torment in which I find myself. Abraham then answered and said to him, They have Moses and the prophets; let them hear them. Dives answered and said to Abraham, They will not listen to Moses and the other pro-

phets, but they will listen to the dead that you would send to warn them; they would then believe and be saved from this great torment. And Abraham told him, If they will not listen to Moses and the prophets, then they will not listen even to the dead that I might send

5   there" [Luke 16:19–31]. It is apparent, then, that Abraham and Lazarus were in paradise. Moreover, Abraham said that they should listen to Moses and the other prophets; this shows that if they would listen to the Torah of Moses and the commandments of the prophets, then they would come to paradise.

[191]

10   It is written in their books that Jesus said, "I and my father are one" [John 10:30], but elsewhere it is written that he said, "My father is greater than I" [John 14:28]. Thus, he contradicts his own words. Now, they say that he made this last statement with regard to the flesh, but I answer that since they assert that the three parts are

15   one and that none is greater than the other either potentially or actually, then if one part took on flesh in the same way that a man would put on a garment, what inferiority would be attached to that part which took on the flesh and why should he be weakened or diminished for that reason? Furthermore, one can respond to those heretics

20   who say that we are in exile because we sinned in connection with Jesus' death not only by pointing out that we had been in exile before his birth but also by citing the statement in their books that at the time of his death he asked his father, "Father, forgive them, for they know not what they do" [Luke 23:34]. I may conclude, then, that if the

25   father and son are one entity and possess a single will, this sin must have been entirely forgiven.

[192]

It is written in their books that "the hour will come in which all that are in the graves shall hear his voice. And the good will arise to the resurrection of life, and the evil to stand in judgment. I can do

30   nothing of my own self; as I hear, I judge, and my judgment is just, for I seek not my own will but the will of him who sent me" [John 5:28–30]. Does this mean that they have two wills, so that one wants

what the other does not? According to them, the two are one entity,
yet one says, "I seek not my own will"; i.e., only his father's will
was fulfilled in this matter, but his was not. Moreover, if they say
that he was the Messiah in accordance with the verse, "And the spirit

5   of the Lord shall rest upon him, etc." [Isa. 11:2], how could he say
that he can do nothing of his own self? "As I hear I judge"; but after
the above verse in Isaiah it says, "And he shall be of quick understanding in the fear of the Lord; he shall not judge according to the
sight of his eyes nor reprove according to the hearing of his ears. But

10 with righteousness shall he judge the poor, etc." [Isa. 11:3-4].
Furthermore, if they say that this Messiah of theirs was God, why
does it say, "And the spirit of the Lord shall rest upon him"? This indicates that he himself was not God. Moreover, if the word spirit had
been written three times in this verse, then one could argue, as they

15 do, that it refers to the father, the son, and the holy spirit, but now
that it says "spirit" four times in the verse, who was the fourth?

[193]

The following constitutes an answer to the heretics: Enoch
and Elijah ascended to heaven just as you say this Jesus did, and yet
we do not believe in them. Moreover, even according to your conten-

20 tion that he is called son of God, we find that the children of Israel are
also called sons of God, as it is written, "You are the children of the
Lord your God" [Deut. 14:1], and "Israel is my firstborn son" [Exod.
4:22]; nevertheless, no one should believe in them. The Jews are also
called holy, as it is written, "You shall be holy" [Lev. 19:2], and it is

25 written, "And you shall be holy" [Lev. 11:45]. Even if you marvel at
his making water into wine [John 2:7-9], his satisfying the hunger of a
thousand men with five loaves of bread [Matt. 14:19-20], his resur-
recting of a dead man [Luke 7:14-15; John 11:44], his curing of the sick
[Matt. 4:23 and passim], and his walking on water [Matt. 14:25; Mark

30 6:48; John 6:19], the fact is that Moses turned water into blood [Exod.
4:9; 7:20], sweetened bitter water [Exod. 15:25], led the Jews through
a sea that had become dry land [Exod. 14:22], and hit a rock, causing it
to bring forth water [Exod. 17:6; Num. 20:11]. In addition, Elisha
filled several vessels from one jug of oil [2 Kings 4:3-6], cured

Naaman of his leprosy [2 Kings 5:14], resurrected two dead people, once while he was alive and once after his death [2 Kings 4:35; 13:21], and Elijah performed similar miracles. Ezekiel, in fact, resurrected several thousand people [Ezek. 37:7–10]. And if Jesus fasted forty
5   days and forty nights [Matt. 4:2], Moses did this three times, and Elijah too fasted forty days and forty nights [1 Kings 19:8].

[194]

Now here is another refutation of the heretics: It is written in the fifth book of Mark that Jesus' disciples asked him when the day of the resurrection would be. Jesus answered them, "No creature
10 knows that day or hour, not the angels above nor any man, but God alone" [Mark 13:4, 32]; he thus excluded himself from the category of the divine. It is also written in the fifth book of John: "Now I shall see those men who love me, and if I wish, I shall carry out my judgment with the permission of God. But I am not alone; rather, it is I and he
15 who sent me" [cf. John 14:23–24; 5:30]. It is also written that trust-worthy people affirmed that he testified about himself, saying, "God sent me" [cf. John 5:31–33]. Thus, if you say that he is God, then you have in effect denied God, for it is written in the Torah, "See, then, that I, I am he; there is no god beside me" [Deut. 32:39]. The counter-
20 argument that they are one may be refuted by reference to Jesus' statement, "It is I and he who sent me; he has not left me alone"; this implies that they are two.

[195]

Moreover, you say that he came to purify people from sin, to take them out of hell, and to atone for sins, yet by his death he added
25 an immense sin to the Jews in that they hanged him; this sin of hang-ing a god was of a magnitude unparalleled either before or since. Furthermore, did sins end because of this? Why, people murder and commit adultery and steal every day. In addition, even if Jesus agreed to suffer his own death in order to redeem the sinners from hell, why
30 were his servants killed? Who gave their killers permission and power to kill them? It couldn't have been Jesus, because he would not pervert justice.

[196]

Gregory interpreted that we should placate our Creator for saving us from the impure water that was sanctified falsely through the god who can be represented by an image.

[197]

It is written in their books that Jesus said to Peter the ass, "Peter, one of us will betray me this night, and I will be held and suffer punishment" [cf. Matthew 26:21]. Peter then said to him, "Since you know the future, you must be God; why, then, didn't you tell me until now?" And Jesus said to him, "Tell no man that I am God [cf. Matthew 16:20], for from the time that I have abandoned the Torah of my birthplace, I have rebelled against my Creator and against his Torah."

[198]

It is written in their books: "Jesus was sitting at a spring of water, eating bread and drinking water, when a man came to him and said, My lord, I have heard that you are a god and that you can help me out of my difficulty. And Jesus answered, Woe to the man who was born with eyes to see but cannot see with them. Once you see that I have flesh and blood like any other man, how can I be God?"

[199]

It is written in their books that "Jesus was walking on the road and a man came to him. Jesus said to him, If you want to see the difference between the power of God and that of man, climb up on this tree. He then said, Give me your hand, and Jesus raised his own hand toward that of the other man above. Jesus then said to him, Just as I am unable to touch your hand above, so am I unable to save you."

[200]

It is written in their books that Mary was lying in the bosom of Jesus and he was eulogizing her, for she was about to die. Now, if he was God, why did he kill his mother? After all, it is written,

"Honor your father and your mother" [Exod. 20:12]. Even if you argue that an angel killed her, the fact would remain that that angel was his messenger and since he could protest but did not, it is as if he himself killed her.

[201]

5   It is written in their books: "Just as Jonah was in the whale's stomach three days and three nights, so shall Jesus be in the earth three days and three nights" [Matt. 12:40]. But it is impossible for Jesus to have been in the heart of the earth for three days and three nights since he was crucified on Friday evening and arose early Sun-
10   day morning, and even if they should argue that part of the day is considered like the whole day, there would still be only three days and two nights.

[202]

         It is written in their book of Luke: "When Jesus was brought to be hanged, they hanged him between two thieves; one was to his
15   right and the other to his left, and he was in the middle. . . . The one who was hanged to his left mocked him, saying, If you are the Messiah, save yourself and us. But the one who was hanged to his right said, You did not fear God, and that is why you are enduring this suffering; we are being judged according to our deeds, but this man be-
20   tween us did nothing wrong. And he said to Jesus, My lord, be kind to me when you come to heaven. And Jesus said to him, Verily I say unto you, today you shall be with me in my place" [Luke 23:32–43]. Now, if he was divine, why did he allow himself to undergo such a peculiar shame of being hanged between thieves and on a stalk of cabbage?

[203]

25   It is also written in their books: "Anyone who believes in Jesus even like a seed of millet can move a mountain with his speech" [Matt. 17:20]. We see, however, that even their saints cannot do this, and surely not the rest of the people; thus, none of them believe in the Creator.

[204]

It is written in the Torah, "Follow the majority" [Exod. 23:2],
and this is the general custom. Now, only eleven nations have erred
after the belief in Jesus, and all of them together do not equal the one
nation of Ishmaelites. Thus, sixty nations including the Ishmaelites
5   all testify that their religion is vanity, and we, the children of Israel,
also testify that the hanged one was a human being born of a mother
and father. Now you contend that he was the Creator, that he had
mercy upon his creatures who were in hell because of Adam's sin,
and that he took upon himself suffering and death to save his
10   creatures from the judgment of hell, God forbid. If so, then he should
have overridden his stern judgment in favor of his mercy—for he may
do this—and caused all nations to believe in him so that they would
be saved; as it is, only a minority believe in him. Thus, it is evident
that their assertions are false. One can also point out that "a matter
15   is established by two witnesses" [Deut. 19:15], and there are two
witnesses for our Torah since both you and the Ishmaelites admit
that our Torah is true. However, neither we nor the Ishmaelites admit to the truth of your Torah, and neither we nor you admit to the
truth of the Torah of the Ishmaelites. Consequently, there are two
20   witnesses that our Torah is true and that our God is true and eternal.
Blessed is he who chose us.

[205]

It is written in their books: "When Mary gave birth to Jesus,
Augustus, who was king at that time, searched for him in order to
destroy him from the world, and his mother hid him in the manger of
25   an ass" [cf. Luke 2:1-7]. Now, why did he not protect himself?
Indeed, why did he not reveal himself to those searching for him and
tell them, "Here I am, but there is nothing you can do to me, for I have
been born and shall live for thirty-three more years"? Similarly, when
he grew up and claimed to be son of God and was therefore sentenced
30   to death in accordance with the judgment applicable to one who
entices people toward idolatry, why did he fly up into the sky in order

to save himself from death until Judas Iscariot came, flew up to him, and brought him to the ground against his will and in a manner not conducive to his benefit so that they could hang him? He should have said, "Here I am; do with me whatever you like, for the purpose of

5   my advent was to accept suffering and death in order to save the world from the judgment of hell." Moreover, why did he wait until he was an adult and intellectually mature before performing his wonders? He should have performed wonders while *in utero* and in his infancy when he was two or three years old; then everyone would

10   have believed in him and been saved from hell. In fact, you should know that he was a sorcerer and that all his wonders were performed through sorcery; consequently, he was condemned to death legally and properly, just as we were commanded by our Lord God, may his name be blessed and exalted forever.

[206]

15   Ask them further: Why was there no prophecy either among Israel or among other nations from the time that Jesus was hanged? It must be that the spirit of falsehood prevailed over the world to such an extent that the spirit of prophecy refrained from coming.

[207]

It is written in the book of Simon son of Cepha, i.e., Peter, that

20   Jesus told Peter the ass: "Satan is involved in an attempt to kill you, but I, Jesus, shall pray to God that he refrain from shortening your days" [cf. Luke 22:31-32]. Now, if he himself were God why should he have had to pray to others for Peter? Moreover, he himself did not call himself God but only prophet or servant or messenger of God, for

25   when he came into his country or sat with the people of his country, he told them, "Fear God, the Lord of lords." And they marveled at him, saying, "What should we do with this son of a carpenter whose mother's name is Mary and whose brothers Simon and Jacob are with us in Nazareth which is in the Galilee in the land of Israel?" Now,

30   when he saw that they recognized him and recited his genealogy, he said, "A prophet is not held in contempt or abused save in his own country and in a place where he is recognized," and he fled

immediately because King Herod was trying to kill him [cf. Matthew 13:54-58; Mark 6:1-5]. Thus, he testifies about himself that he is a prophet and not a god, for he said, "A prophet is not held in contempt save in his own country." In addition, it says at the end of their in-
5   valid book: "Jesus son of Joseph from the city of Nazareth" [John 1:45]. It also says in the third book of John: "I have not spoken on my own, but God has sent me so that he might give a man what to say" [John 12:49]; thus, he calls himself a messenger. He also said that he did not speak on his own; this too shows that he was not God.
10 Furthermore, in the third book of Matthew he testified about himself that he was born from the stomach like all people and that he is the servant of God, as Isaiah said, "Behold my servant, I shall support him" [Matt. 12:17-18; Isa. 42:1]. All this is explained above in its proper place in Isaiah.

[208]

15   It is written in their book of Mark that an angel came to inform Mary, "Behold, you shall conceive and bring forth a son, and shall call his name Jesus. He shall be great and shall be called the son of the highest, and God shall give unto him the throne of his father David" [Luke 1:28-32]. The angel should have said that he will be God and
20 will rule over the entire world, over those things that are above and those things that are below. What sort of honor is it for God to sit upon the throne of David? Moreover, if he were God, why should he have needed a present from others? Furthermore, who came first, he or his father David? Why, according to you, he preceded all the
25 prophets.

[209]

Ask them: If the Christian priest is supposed to take the place of the biblical priest, why doesn't he get married and have children like Aaron the high priest? Moreover, the first commandment given to Adam dealt with being fruitful and multiplying, yet you refrain
30 from this and instead pursue fornication and wine, which capture your fancy.

[210]

Ask the heretics: You know that a dead man is impure and
defiles all who carry or touch the body and everything in the tent
where it is, and yet you defile priests constantly by bringing them
into your houses of idolatry. Thus, you are corrupt in all your words
5 and deeds, and your affairs are vain and exceedingly evil. In addition,
it is written, "Those who sit among the graves, who eat swine's
flesh and broth of abominable things" [Isa. 65:4]. Now, this is the
interpretation: "Those who sit among the graves"—who bury their
corpses in their houses of idolatry and defile themselves. And who
10 are the ones who do this? Those "who eat swine's flesh." It is also
written, "Those who eat swine's flesh, and the abomination, and the
mouse, shall be consumed together, says the Lord" [Isa. 66:17].

[211]

With regard to their questioning us as to whether there are
proselytes among us, they ask this question to their shame and to the
15 shame of their faith. After all, one should not be surprised at the bad
deeds of an evil Jew who becomes an apostate, because his motives
are to enable himself to eat all that his heart desires, to give pleasure
to his flesh with wine and fornication, to remove from himself the
yoke of the kingdom of heaven so that he should fear nothing, to free
20 himself from all the commandments, cleave to sin, and concern himself with worldly pleasures. But the situation is different with regard
to proselytes who converted to Judaism and thus went of their own
free will from freedom to slavery, from light to darkness. If the
proselyte is a man, then he knows that he must wound himself by re-
25 moving his foreskin through circumcision, that he must exile himself
from place to place, that he must deprive himself of worldly good and
fear for his life from the external threat of being killed by the uncircumcised, and that he will lack many things that his heart desires;
similarly, a woman proselyte also separates herself from all
30 pleasures. And despite all this, they come to take refuge under the
wing of the divine presence. It is evident that they would not do this
unless they knew for certain that their faith is without foundation and

that it is all a lie, vanity, and emptiness. Consequently, you should be ashamed when you mention the matter of proselytes.

[212]

They bark their assertion that it is improper for the uncircumcised and impure to serve Jews. Tell them: On the contrary, if not for
5   the fact that they serve Jews they would have been condemned to destruction, for it is written in Isaiah, "Arise, shine, for your light has come. . . . For the nation and kingdom that will not serve you shall perish; yea, those nations shall be utterly wasted" [Isa. 60:1, 12]. On the other hand, as long as they serve Israel they have some hope, as it
10   is written, "And strangers shall stand and tend your flock, and the sons of foreigners shall be your farmers and vintners" [Isa. 61:5]; consequently, they should serve us all the time, so that they may fulfill the prophecy, "The elder shall serve the younger" [Gen. 25:23]. It was for this reason that the Torah said, "You shall not eat anything
15   that dies of itself; you shall give it to the stranger that is in your gates, that he may eat it, or you may sell it to a Gentile" [Deut. 14:21]. The Torah told us to sell such meat to Gentiles because they will serve us, and God does not withhold the reward of any creature. This, in fact, is what we do; we give over to them the animals which
20   are ritually unfit for our use, and we sell them the hind portions of animals for this same reason.

[213]

They abuse us by saying that they do not have sacrifices and burnt offerings of the kind that once existed among Jews, but they do have sacrifices and burnt offerings in that they sacrifice the flesh of
25   the hanged one and eat it. Respond by pointing out that sacrifices and burnt offerings should not be brought here but only in Jerusalem. So it is written in Deuteronomy, "Take heed to yourself lest, etc." until "all that I command you" [Deut. 12:13-14], and David too said in the book of Psalms, "For you desire not sacrifice, etc." until "Then shall
30   they offer bullocks upon your altar" [Ps. 51:18-21]. Thus, it is not God's will that they bring sacrifices and burnt offerings except in Jerusalem when it is built up, and as long as it is destroyed and we are

not in it, sacrifices and burnt offerings may be brought only in the
form of a broken spirit and heart. Now, then, according to your contention that you bring a sacrifice every day both outside Jerusalem
and during the period of its destruction, you should know that there is
5   a false doctrine among you and that you will ultimately have to stand
judgment. Consequently, in the future, when our Temple is rebuilt
speedily and in our own time, then we will bring sacrifices and burnt
offerings, "bullocks upon your altar." It is also written, "All the
flocks of Kedar shall be gathered together unto you; the rams of
10 Nevayot shall minister to you. They shall come up with acceptance
on my altar, and I will glorify the house of my glory" [Isa. 60:7].
Finally, it is written, "Behold, I will send my messenger . . . and he
shall purify the sons of Levi and purge them as gold and silver, that
they may offer unto the Lord an offering in righteousness. Then shall
15 the offering of Judah and Jerusalem be pleasant unto the Lord, as in
the days of old, and as in former years" [Mal. 3:1-4].

[214]

A heretic asked: How can you atone for your sins now that
you do not bring sin and guilt offerings as the Lord commanded? This
is the way to answer. Let me compare this to a man who sinned
20 against the king of France, and the king required him to bring a sin
offering. However, he told him, "Be very carefeul not to bring me this
sin offering except in my home in Paris and nowhere else." But Paris
was then destroyed and with it the king's home, and the king then
went to live in Orleans; now, how could one argue that this man
25 sinned if he failed to bring his sin offering? Similarly, God commanded, "Do not offer your burnt offerings . . . except in the place
which the Lord shall choose" [Deut. 12:13-14], and now that that
place which he chose was destroyed, how can we be faulted? When it
is built, we shall make it up. It is also written, "When you build the
30 walls of Jerusalem, then shall you be pleased with the sacrifices of
righteousness, with whole burnt offerings; then shall they offer
bullocks upon your altar" [Ps. 51:20-21]. It is also written, "All the
flocks of Kedar [shall be gathered together unto you; the rams of
Nevayot shall minister to you. They shall come up with acceptance

on my altar, and I will glorify the house of my glory]" [Isa. 60:7]. But
people will not sin in the messianic age; consequently, these verses
must refer to making up sin and guilt offerings which they failed to
sacrifice while they were in exile. Similarly, during the additional
5 prayer that we recite on Sabbaths, holidays, and new moons, we say,
"We will sacrifice to you the additional sacrifice of this particular
day," for we shall make up everything. Furthermore, we find that
prayer is in place of sacrifice, as it is written in Daniel, "The God
whom you serve continually" [Dan. 6:17, 21], and he did no more than
10 pray. Moreover, it is written in Isaiah, "I will bring them to my holy
mountain, etc." until "for all people" [Isa. 56:7]; it follows, then, that
prayer is in place of sacrifice and that in the future we shall offer
burnt offerings and sacrifices. This, too, is the meaning of "We shall
take the place of bullocks by the offerings of our lips" [Hos. 14:3].
15 One can also respond by saying that the exile itself atones for sin, as
it is written, "And I will scatter you among the nations and disperse
you in the countries, and will consume the sin out of you" [Ezek.
22:15].

[215]

It is possible to prove to the heretics that Jesus of Nazareth
20 was an actual human being and not God, for it is written in the
Gospels that Jesus told his disciples, "The time now nears when the
son of man will be betrayed into the hand of sinners" [Mark 14:41].

[216]

We ask you heretics how you can talk about fear of God and
exalt yourselves by referring to Scripture when you don't believe
25 properly. The Jew shall raise his voice and say: It is our duty to
observe the Torah; it is we who have this obligation, as it is written,
"In Judah is God known, his name is great in Israel" [Ps. 76:2]. But
concerning you it says, "But unto the wicked God says, What affair
is it of yours to declare my statutes and to take my covenant into your
30 mouth?" [Ps. 50:16]. Thus, since he did not give you a law and a Torah
and you were not ordered to observe the commandments, you have no
special relationship to the Creator and no reward for observing the
commandments.

[217]

The heretics contend that they beseech the saints, who are dead corpses, so that these saints may pray for them before God. The answer is: It is written, "The dead praise not the Lord" [Ps. 115:17]. If he says that this refers to the dead who are in hell, tell him: It is 5 written, ". . . nor any that go down to Dumah" [ibid.] This refers to those who were handed over to the angel in charge of hell whose name is Dumah, but the first part of the verse refers simply to those who are dead and who lie in their graves in the earth. Moreover, at the end of the psalm beginning "A psalm at the dedication of the Temple, by 10 David," it is written, "Shall dust praise you? Shall it declare your faithfulness?" [Ps. 30:10], and they even maintain that Jesus said this psalm. Furthermore, it is written in Isaiah in Hezekiah's prayer, "For the grave cannot praise you; death cannot celebrate you. They that go down into the pit cannot hope for your truth. The living, the living, he 15 shall praise you, as I do this day" [Isa. 38:18-19]. We see, then, that praise and prayer can come only from the living, as it is written, "The living, he shall praise you, as I do." Moreover, they are of the opinion that the dead hear and understand the prayers that they recite before them, yet it is written, "Who can tell a man what shall be after him 20 under the sun?" [Eccles. 6:12], and Isaiah too warns in several places that one should not pray or bow down to anyone but God. As for their assertion that God performs wonders for the saints after their death, it says in Psalms in the chapter beginning "A song and psalm of the sons of Korah," "Will you perform wonders for the dead? Shall the 25 dead arise and praise you? Selah" [Ps. 88:11]. This also shows that there is no praise and prayer except by the living. It also says, "Shall your loving-kindness be told in the grave, etc. But I have cried out unto you" [Ps. 88:12-14], i.e., because I am alive and standing before you. (All these verses are written together in the chapter beginning, 30 "A psalm of the sons of Korah . . ., a maskil of Heman the Ezrahite.") It is also written, "I shall not die, but live, and declare the works of the Lord" [Ps. 118:17]; this indicates that a person recites praise to God only while he is still alive.

The heretics ask us: Why do you not seek the aid of the great 35 the way we do (for they seek the aid of their saints)? Answer them:

Fools! All your requests and deeds anger the Lord. Are these saints any better than angels? Well, see what the angel told Manoah. When the latter tried to honor him, he was told, "If you offer a burnt offering, offer it to the Lord" [Judg. 13:16]; the angel, then, did not want to
5   be honored. The heretic may then tell you: The fact remains that saint so-and-so does remarkable deeds such as curing the blind, strengthening the weak, and freeing the imprisoned. This is how you should answer him: Let me tell you a parable so that you may understand this matter by analogy. This is similar to a trustworthy man to whom
10 people generally entrust things without witnesses; one day, however, a man came and entrusted something to him in the presence of witnesses, and the witnesses later died. The wife of the trustee said to him, "Since this fellow entrusted something to us in the presence of witnesses and thereby shamed us, let us deny that he gave it to
15 us." The trustworthy man answered her, "Shall we lose our faithfulness just because this fellow behaved improperly?" Similarly, a sickness has a specific time allotted to it, and it is faithful; it will not endure past its time and give the lie to its faithfulness even if it turns out that the sick man will be cured when he goes to some idolatrous
20 practice. This is the interpretation of the statement, "You have saved us from evil and faithful diseases," in which we thank God for saving us from being afflicted with impure issue, leprosy, and skin disease as they are, for the Lord is the one who cures us. He may then ask: Why didn't the end of this disease come before he came to this saint?
25 Why is it that he was cured at the very moment that he came to the saint? Answer him: This is done to mislead you, as Job said, "He misleads nations and destroys them, he spreads out for the nations and leads them" [Job 12:23]; i.e., he spreads out a trap and leads them into it to be caught. Moreover, Isaiah said, "I am sought by
30 them that asked not for me; I am found by them that sought me not. I said, Behold me, to a nation that was not called by my name. I spread out my hands all day unto a rebellious people which walks in a way that is not good, after their own thoughts . . . who eat swine's flesh, and broth of abominable things is in their vessels, etc." [Isa. 65:1-4].
35 Now, all this was said about you and you cannot deny it, because no nation in the world eats swine except for you.

It is written in their books that there was a certain house of
priestesses, and in it there were priestesses who were all virgins and
from whom the Romans remained separate. Then, one of them en-
gaged in sexual relations. (The report concerning such behavior was
5   true.) The Romans then gathered together and wanted to kill the one
who prostituted herself, but all the other priestesses said, "Our
sister did not engage in licentious behavior." The Romans then said,
"This is how we shall know. If she will fill a sieve with water and
bring it from the river without a single drop falling through the holes,
10   then the veracity of your words will have been established by a test
and it will be clear that she is innocent." They gave her time to pray
that she be saved through a miracle, and the priestesses bowed down
before their idols; and a miracle took place so that she was able to
bring the sieve full of water, even though it was clear that she was
15   guilty. Now, all this took place before the hanged one was born.
Thus, there is proof from their own erroneous literature that their
being cured by their saints does not result from their idolatry; rather,
there was a decree by God that a cure be effected through this thing,
in this matter, and at this time, for this prostitute was saved before
20   the birth of Jesus.

[218]

Now, with regard to their statements about the saints whom
they call *apostoli,* who were Jesus' messengers and students and who
went throughout the world to convert the nations to belief in Jesus, if
there were substance to their contentions and the matter had really
25   been the will of God, then how could their opponents have killed
them? Look at what it says with regard to Moses and Aaron, who
went to Pharaoh at God's behest and effected several wonders and
plagues aganst him, his people, and all his servants, and yet they
emerged unscathed. A similar situation obtained in the case of
30   Jeremiah, who was saved by God although his life was threatened
several times, as it is written, "For, behold, I have made you this day
a fortress, an iron pillar, and brazen walls against the whole land,
against the kings of Judah, against its princes and priests, and
against the people of the land" [Jer. 1:18]. So too it is written in

Ezekiel, "Do not fear them, though briars and thorns be with you and you dwell among scorpions; be not afraid of their words, nor be dismayed at their looks" [Ezek. 2:6]; i.e., even though they are a rebellious people, do not fear them, because they will not be permitted to
5 harm you. We find a similar phenomenon in connection with Jeroboam when he made the calves of gold "and set one in Beth-el and the other in Dan. . . . And he ordained a feast for the people of Israel . . . and he went up to the altar to offer incense. And behold, there came a man of God out of Judah by the word of the Lord unto Beth-el, and
10 Jeroboam stood by the altar to burn incense. And he cried out to the altar by the word of the Lord and said, Altar, altar, thus said the Lord: Behold, a child shall be born to the house of David, Josiah by name; and upon you shall he slaughter the priests of the high places that burn incense upon you. . . . And Jeroboam put forth his hand, saying,
15 Take hold of him; and his hand, which he put forth against him, dried up, so that he could not pull it in again toward him" [1 Kings 12:29, 32–33; 13:1–4]. Now, if these *apostolus* came by the word of God why did such misfortune befall them?

[219]

As for their contention that they bestow divine honors upon
20 the idols in their houses of abomination because these idols are the image of their god, the fact remains that it says, "I am the Lord; that is my name, and my glory will I not give to another, nor my praise to graven images" [Isa. 42:8]. It also says, "Assemble yourselves and come; draw together, you that have escaped from the nations. Those
25 people are ignorant who carry the wood of their graven image and pray unto a god that cannot save. . . . I am the Lord, and there is no other god (*elohim*) beside me; a just God and a savior; there is none beside me. Look unto me and be saved, all the ends of the earth; for I am God, and there is none else. I have sworn by my own self; the
30 word has gone out of my mouth in righteousness and shall not return, that unto me every knee shall bow, every tongue shall swear" [Isa. 45:20–23]. The real interpretation of this passage is that there is not even another *elohim*, i.e., a prince, master, or proud man like the saints, to whom people should pray or bow, except God himself. A

similar use of the word *elohim* can be found in the verse, "And you will be an *elohim* to him" [Exod. 4:16], where it is translated "master." "Those who carry the wood of their graven image" refers to a cross upon which an image is drawn; they carry the wood, praying to the
5 god in whose image this cross is made, but he "cannot save." It is, in fact, impossible to argue that the verse refers to another people who carry the wood of their graven image and pray to the wood itself, for if so, it should have said, "Those who carry the wood of their graven image and pray to it." It must be, then, that the verse is referring to
10 that nation which believes in Jesus, for they carry the wood and the idol in order to show the image of their deity, but they do not pray to the wood and idol themselves but to the one in whose image and likeness this wood and idol were made. You see, then, that the prophet testifies that this is a god that cannot save. "Unto me every
15 knee shall bow"—to me alone and not to the dead. In fact, it is because of their contention that they carry a likeness of the Deity that Scripture says, "To whom will you liken me and make me equal, and compare me, that we may be alike? They pour gold out of a bag and weigh silver in the balance, and they hire a goldsmith; he then makes
20 it a god and they bow down and worship" [Isa. 46:5-6]. The verse means that the goldsmith makes it into the likeness of a god. "They bear it upon the shoulder; they carry it. . . . It does not move from its place; they cry out unto it, yet it cannot answer" [Isa. 46:7]. The passage continues, "Remember this and show yourselves men;
25 bring it again to mind, you transgressors. Remember the former things of old, for I am God" [Isa. 46:8-9]; but he who came recently and of late is not God, as it is written, "Am I a God from near?" [Jer. 23:23].

[220]

Ask them: How old was Mary when she gave birth to the
30 hanged one? It says in their Scriptures that she was thirteen years of age. Now, according to your assertion that he was born without a father, why did he show his power through a thirteen-year-old, who was prepared for conception and pregnancy? He should have shown his power through a three- or four-year-old, who cannot normally

conceive, and then everyone would have been able to recognize the miracle, namely, that something new has been done which has never been heard of before. The truth is that you should know with certainty that Joseph had relations with her in the normal manner and she
5 bore his child.

[221]

One should ask the heretics: Why do you uproot even one letter from the Torah of Moses? The fact is that Jesus himself said that he "did not come to destroy the Torah of Moses or the words of the prophets, for as long as heaven and earth exist, not one letter or
10 punctuation mark will be uprooted or pass away" [Matt. 5:17-18]. If so, then, how do you ignore commandments like the Sabbath and circumcision?

[222]

It is written in their books:"Just as the flesh and spirit together constitute a man, so do God and man together constitute the
15 Messiah (*Christus*)." The following is the Latin: *Sicut anima et caro unus est homo, ita Deus et homo unus est Christus.* If so, then when the man was killed so was the divinity.

[223]

It is written in the book of Luke in the Gospels: "Whoever sins against the father will find forgiveness, and whoever sins
20 against the son will find forgiveness; but he who sins against the impure spirit will not find forgiveness either in this world or in the world to come" [Luke 12:10]. But if the three are one, why shouldn't the person who sinned against the impure spirit find forgiveness?

[224]

It is written in their book of Alexander: "When Mary gave
25 birth to her son Jesus in a hole in Bethlehem it was very dark there. As soon as Jesus was born there came to the hole a light greater than the darkness, but afterwards there returned a darkness greater than the light. Then, Joseph son of Pandera came and took the child and put

him in a manger, which they call *Krippe*, where an ox and a donkey ate together. Then three kings came there, and his mother commanded that he be circumcised. The kings answered, 'We shall not circumcise him because he is divine.' But his mother, Mary, answered
5 them and said, 'Once he came from the seed of the Jews out of four loins, he must be circumcised.' "

[225]

Ask them: If the night is part of the following day, as it is written, "And it was evening, and it was morning—one day" [Gen. 1:5], and "From evening unto evening shall you celebrate your
10 Sabbath" [Lev. 23:32], then why do you eat meat on the evening before Friday, which is your fast day?

[226]

In addition, ask them why they fast on Friday. If it is because Jesus was hanged on that day, then they should have made it a joyous festival since they maintain that they were saved from hell through
15 his hanging and torments. The truth is that they mourn because they know that all who believe in him will go down to hell, to a place of obstacles and stumbling.

[227]

There was once an emperor who wanted to test and determine which faith is good and true and in which there is genuine fear of the
20 Lord—the faith of Israel, the faith of the Christians, or the faith of the Muslims. So he took one Jew, one Christian, and one Muslim and put each of them in a separate jail cell, and then he went to each one separately with an ultimatum that he change his faith for another or be decapitated. First he went to the Jew and told him that he must
25 choose the Christian faith or the Muslim law or be cut to pieces limb by limb. But the Jew answered the emperor and said, "Heaven forbid that I should leave my God, my creator and protector, who is the living God and eternal king, and cleave to a belief in a dead carcass. Know that for the Torah of our God, for the unity of our king and for
30 the sanctification of the name of our creator I shall willingly suffer a

thousand deaths and fulfill the verse, 'For your sake are we killed all day long' " [Ps. 44:23]. Now when the emperor saw that he was unable to force him to abandon his religion and that he did not budge from his Torah, he took him to the edge of his grave and held a sword
5 to his neck to threaten and torment him, but he paid no heed to the command that he abandon his God.

Then the emperor left him alone and went to the Christian priest, and he told him the same sort of thing—to change his religion and choose Judaism or Islam or else suffer a painful death. But the
10 wicked man refused to do this; instead, he remained deeply attached to his false faith, crying and begging the emperor to allow him to remain loyal to his religion since it is the true one and arguing that this was why Jesus suffered death—to redeem him and other sinners like him and admit them to his heavenly abode. He screamed very
15 much and would not stop talking. The emperor, however, became very angry at him and decided to cut off his talk and reaffirm the decision that if he changed his faith his life would be spared and if not, his only fate would be death. Now, when the priest saw that the emperor had shown his wrath and that the evil decree had been fully
20 turned against him, he chose to live. He therefore said that since he was being forced to abandon his faith, he would prefer to be a Jew, for there is no value or substance in the Muslim faith. After all, their god Muhammad got drunk from wine and was thrown into the garbage, and when the pigs came and passed through the dump, they found
25 him, dragged him, surrounded him, killed him, and ate him; how, then, could he be divine? Thus, the faith of Israel is superior to this.

The emperor then left him and went to the Muslim with the same ultimatum—either to utterly abandon his faith and choose either Judaism or Christianity or to suffer a bizarre death. The man became
30 terribly upset, tears fell from his eyes, and he stretched his hands out while crying and said, "Why should my lord do this to me? Why should I be forced to abandon the faith in which I was born and raised, especially since my Torah is true and straight, pure and unsullied, lovely and clear? Indeed, none of the Torahs are as pure and precious
35 as our exalted Torah. I shall remain loyal to it till the bitter end." The emperor grew angry at his words and commanded that he be decapi-

tated; but when the man saw the executioner brandish his sword, his heart trembled, and he asked to be given time till the morrow to make his choice. This request of his was granted and his desire fulfilled. On the morrow, he cried out in a loud voice and said, "The Lord, God
5 of my father Abraham the father of Ishmael, the God of Israel, he is the perfect God, the creator of heaven and earth, and him shall I choose as my allotted portion; I am his servant and he is my God, while the belief in Jesus is evil, wanton, worthless. The Torah of his believers, rather than being perfect, is a shame and a disgrace, a lie
10 and a betrayal, for he was crucified and hanged and was thus unable to save himself; how then can he save his people? When he was still alive, he could not escape or get away from his enemies; how then can he do anything for his worshipers after his death? I take an oath that I shall be a Jew."
15   Now, when the emperor heard that the Jew was willing to die for his Torah and would not move from his faith one bit, while the priest and the Muslim both denied their vain beliefs and accepted our faith, he himself chose our religion; he, the priest, and the Muslim were all converted and became true and genuine proselytes.

[228]

20   Ask the heretic: After all, you believe that God shows mercy toward all his creatures, and all his attributes reflect kindness and justice toward them. Indeed, it is with confidence in these attributes that we come before him daily, as David said, "Have mercy upon me, O God, according to your loving-kindness; according to the multi-
25 tude of your mercy blot out my transgressions" [Ps. 51:3]. [This is the Latin: "Miserere mei Deus secundum magnam misericordiam tuam et secundum multitudinem miserationum tuarum dele iniquitatum meum."] Moreover, God said, "For I do not wish the death of him who dies, but rather that he return from his ways and live"
30 [Ezek. 18:32, 23], and you too believe that because of his great mercy his hand is stretched out to accept those who repent. If so, how can it even enter your mind that God behaved so cruelly toward Adam, catching him as a result of a minor accusation—the biting of a single apple—and removing him from both this world and the world to

come? And this applied not only to him but to all those born after him, including all the righteous and just men who ever lived. Furthermore, Adam sinned inadvertently since he had no discernment yet, as it is written, "And the eyes of both of them were opened, and they knew
5   that they were naked" [Gen. 3:7]; this refers to the opening of the eye of wisdom. In addition, the murder of Abel was a thousand times worse than this transgression, yet no such punishment resulted from it. Finally, look what is written regarding the six hundred thousand men who denied God and made the calf: "But he is full of compassion
10   and he forgave their iniquity, etc." [Ps. 78:38]. [And this is the Latin: "Et ipse est misericors et propitius fiet peccatis eorum et non mitterit repudium eis et abundabit ut averterit iram suam et non accendet omnem iram suam."] Now, since God is merciful and does not destroy a man because of his sins, how can you believe that he
15   destroyed and threw into hell, into the pit, all the souls that were born from Adam until the advent of Jesus?

[229]

You can also refute the heretic by asking him how he can say that one who was born was divine. After all, no one born from a woman can be without sin, as David said, "Behold I was shapen in
20   iniquity, and in sin did my mother conceive me" [Ps. 51:7]. And this is the Latin: "Ecce enim in peccatis conceptus sum et in iniquitatem concepit me mater mea."

[230]

"Tantum fidem ego non invenio inter populos gentiles Edom solum granum sinapis." The translation of this is: The congregation
25   of Edom does not possess faith which is the equivalent of even a mustard seed.

[231]

When they defile the abominable bread and make it impure, they say the following: "Hoc est enim corpus meum." Translated, this means: "I alone am the body and blood." Moreover, when they
30   baptize their children in the impure waters, they say, "Offerentia

Satanae"; i.e., let this be an offering to Satan. The following is called
the Credo in their language: "Credo in Deum patrem omnipotentem
creatorem coeli et terrae et in Jesum Christum filium eius" (some say
at this point: "unicum dominum nostrum qui conceptus est de spiritu
5   santo natus ex Maria virgine"—this is as far as the additional
passage extends) "passus Pontio Pilato, crucifixus, mortuus et
sepultus, descentus ad infera, tertia die resurrexit a mortuis,
ascendit ad coelum, sedet ad dexteram Dei patris omnipotentis."
This means the following: I believe in God the ruling father, creator
10 of heaven and earth, and also in his son Jesus who suffered agonies at
the hand of the procurator Pilate. He suffered, and he was killed and
buried, and on the third day he arose from the dead—he who sits at
the right hand of God the ruling father. [The German translation is:
"Ich glaube an Gott Vater gewiltig Schöpfer Himmel und Erde und an
15 seinen Sohn Jesu der hat gelitten von dem Fürsten Pilatus den Marter.
Er ist gepeinigt und getötet und begraben. Am dritten Tag stund er
auf von seinem Tode, der sitzt zu der Rechten Seiten Gottes Vater
gewiltig."] Now, one may ask that since they say that they believe in
God and in Jesus, it follows that Jesus is not God. Moreover, they say
20 that he sits at the right hand of God; this indicates that he himself is
not God. Otherwise, they should have said, "He who sits on a lofty
and exalted throne" [Isa. 6:1]; only that would indicate that he himself is divine.

They say the following daily in the Prima prayers: "Christi
25 fili Dei, vae vae, miserere nobis, miserere nobis. Offerimus tibi
Domine calicem salutaris secundum ordinem Melchisedek et secundum ordinem Moysi et Aaron in sacerdotibus eius et Samuel inter eos
qui invocant nomen Domini." That is what they call *Stillmess*; they
teach it only to those who are ordained as priests, and those priests
30 whisper it silently in their house of prayer. [The following is its German translation: "Christus des lebende Gottes Sohn, erwärm dich
über uns, der sitzt zu der rechten Seiten seines Vaters, erwärm dich
über uns. Wir opferen dem Herren dakenlich der salbet. . . . Aharon in
ihr Priesterschaft und Samuel der Rufer in Namen Gottes."] Now,
35 how can you say that this is God when the priest himself says that it
is just an offering and when you yourself made the wine and baked the

bread? How can you say that this made you, established you, formed you, and created you? During the swallowing of the bread he says, "I will take the cup of salvation and call upon the name of the Lord" [Ps. 116:13]. The Latin is: "Calicem salutaris accipiam et nomen Domini invocabo." At that point he drinks the wine which he had smelled when it was in the chalice.

[232]

It is written in their books: "If a Jew smites you on the cheek, offer him the other and do not smite him at all" [Matt. 5:39; Luke 6:29]. The Latin reads, "Si quis percussit maxillam praebe aliam."

The water of apostasy is called "the evil water." In Latin: "Forsitan pertransisset anima nostra aquam intolerabilem" [Ps. 124:5].

It is written in their books: "Accursed are all those who boast of their idols and bow to them, but your ancestral law is holy and the commandments are just and good" [cf. Romans 7:12].

It is written in their books: "The Jews did not kill Jesus because he desecrated the Sabbath but because he said he was a god" [cf. Matthew 26:62-66].

It is written in their books: "Priests, do not speak to the Jews about matters of faith, for the Jews are the root of Christianity, and if the roots flourish so does the branch."

It is written in their Scriptures: "Jesus told his apostles, I, Jesus, was born of the woman, Mary, and I am also the son of Joseph. He who wishes to believe may believe."

It is written in their books that Saint Peter told them: "We do not know if we have been delivered or not, if we have achieved redemption or not, if we have salvation from the Lord or not."

It is written in their books that they are not suppposed to persecute Jews but only Muslims.

It is written in their books that they are supposed to compel only Muslims and not Jews to worship their god.

It is written in their books that Saint John said: "We must honor the Jews, for our salvation comes from them." The Latin is: "Nostra salus ex Judaeis est" [John 4:22].

[233]

The heretics say that if a man worships Jesus of Nazareth instead of the honored and awesome Lord because of that man's great love, then he should not be punished for this. They say that this is similar to a man who was told that so-and-so is the king of France and who consequently served that man with all his heart in accordance with the honor due him. Now, even if the man who was pointed out is not the king, the fact remains that this fellow thought he was, and if the king should hear about it he would not be angry. Answer this heretic: If the king issued a command and proclaimed that he would behead anyone who would serve a man other than the king, then people would have to be careful about this. Well, this is what God said: "He that sacrifices unto any god save unto the Lord alone shall be utterly destroyed" [Exod. 22:19].

[234]

It is written in their Gospels that Jesus called himself a camel, for when he said, "Woe unto you, hypocritical Pharisees and Sadducees, for you have mercy on the gnat and swallow the camel" [Matt. 23:23-24], he meant, "I am the camel. Now, those prophets who are as significant as gnats you leave alone and tell nothing; indeed, you even accept their prophecies. But as for me who am as important as a camel and who came to suffer tribulations for your sake—just as a camel bears the burden willingly, so did I descend willingly to suffer tribulations and so redeem the world—you swallow me up; i.e., it is your intention to kill me."

[235]

Jesus had three brothers, and he was the fourth and last. So it is written in the Gospel of John the Baptist in connection with the hanged one's burial. It says that he cried out and said, "I have three brothers and none of them has been beset by evils as I have." It is also written that Pilate told Jesus, "Why do you maintain that you are the son of God? Your brothers make no such pretensions." The accursed one then answered him: "They are indeed my brothers in that they were born of my mother, but I was not born from a drop of semen as they were, nor am I flesh and blood like them."

[236]

The heretics criticize us in connection with the *Beichte* for not confessing the way they do, and they cite proof from the book of
5 Proverbs: "He that covers his sins shall not prosper, but he who confesses and forsakes them shall have mercy" [Prov. 28:13]. This is how you should answer him: On the contrary, one should conceal one's sins from another man and not tell him, "This is how I have sinned," lest the listener be tempted to commit that sin. One should,
10 rather, confess one's sins to God, as David said, "I acknowledge my sin to you, and my iniquity have I not hidden. I said, I will confess my transgressions unto the Lord, and you have forgiven the iniquity of my sin. Selah" [Ps. 32:5]. It was concerning one who conceals his sin from God that Solomon said, "He that covers his sins shall not
15 prosper." Indeed, this refers to the nations of the world, who conceal their sins from God, for adultery, fornication, and murder are found among them. In fact, all the commandments that God ordained are hidden among them, for they concoct different interpretations so that they can change such commandments as circumcision, the prohibi-
20 tion of swine, suet, and blood, indeed, all the prohibitions in the Torah. Not only that, it was because of the fact that they wallow in fornication and yet their Torah forbade them from marrying that they agreed to require men to come and tell their sin and publicize their adultery so that they might know which women are having extra-
25 marital affairs. They then tell those women that they would like to do the same, and the women cannot deny anything because the adulterer has already identified them. This is certainly the explanation, because otherwise why doesn't the pope, who is regarded as the vicar of their god and who has the power to forbid and permit, give nuns the
30 authority to hear the confession of women? It would clearly be more proper and acceptable for women to confess to women and men to men so that they would not be seduced into fornication and adultery.

Moreover, neither alternative will really help, for only God himself can pardon and forgive. Even Moses, who was the greatest of

the prophets, did not have the power to pardon and forgive; in fact,
even after three thousand Israelites were killed at his direction because of the sin of the calf, he had to pray forty days and forty nights
in order to obtain forgiveness from God. Similarly, David said,
5   "There is forgiveness with you so that you may be feared" [Ps.
130:4], i.e., because forgiveness is with you and there is no one who
can forgive except you. We may therefore infer that it is not proper
for a sinner to give an account of his deeds before anyone but God. If
he will argue that Achan confessed, tell him that he confessed before
10   all of Israel because the occasion demanded it. One can also answer
the general accusation by pointing out that we confess all our sins out
loud every year on the Day of Atonement.

[237]

The heretics ask: We baptize both males and females and in
that way we accept our faith, but in your case only men and not
15   women can be circumcised. One can respond: Women are accepted
because they watch themselves and carefully observe the prohibitions connected with menstrual blood.

[238]

The heretics ask: Why are most Gentiles fair-skinned and
handsome while most Jews are dark and ugly? Answer them that this
20   is similar to a fruit; when it begins to grow it is white but when it
ripens it becomes black, as is the case with sloes and plums. On the
other hand, any fruit which is red at the beginning becomes lighter as
it ripens, as is the case with apples and apricots. This, then, is testimony that Jews are pure of menstrual blood so that there is no initial
25   redness. Gentiles, however, are not careful about menstruant women
and have sexual relations during menstruation; thus, there is
redness at the outset, and so the fruit that comes out, i.e., the
children, are light. One can respond further by noting that Gentiles
are incontinent and have sexual relations during the day, at a time
30   when they see the faces on attractive pictures; therefore, they give
birth to children who look like those pictures, as it is written, "And
the sheep conceived when they came to drink before the rods" [Gen.
30:38–39].

[239]

The heretics say that the priest holds in his hand the actual body of Jesus just as it was on the cross. This is how you should answer them: That which the priest holds in his hand is the work of man, and the prophets say, "We shall not say any more to the work of
5 our hands, You are our gods" [Hos. 14:4], and "We shall no longer worship the work of our hands" [Mic. 5:12]. In fact, Jeremiah was referring to this Christian practice when he said, "Shall a man make gods unto himself when they are no gods?" [Jer. 16:20].

[240]

This is how the heretics should be refuted with regard to their
10 practice of taking the bones of the dead as holy relics: The fact is that God has declared them impure, as it is written, "Whoever in the open field touches one who is slain with a sword, or a dead body, or a bone of a man, or a grave, shall be impure seven days" [Num. 19:16]. Thus, they are themselves impure and they also impart impurity to others;
15 indeed, even the bones of Abraham, Isaac, Jacob, and all righteous men convey impurity just like those of other men, for Scripture makes no qualifications here. It was, in fact, for this reason that God destroyed the graves of the righteous, because he knew that the nations of the world would err by worshiping their remains. Thus, it
20 is written with respect to Moses, "No one knows his burial place until this day" [Deut. 34:6], and although everyone knows that the patriarchs lie in a cave at Hebron, no nation can enter there. Why is that so? It must be for the reason I have indicated.

[241]

The heretics provoke us by pointing out that we are the least
25 numerous of the nations; they say that falsehood cannot stand and that we are unsuccessful because our faith is false. The answer is: That is why it says, "It is not because you were more in number than any people that the Lord desired you and chose you, for you are the fewest of all people. But it was because the Lord loved you and be-
30 cause he would keep the oath which he had sworn unto your fathers" [Deut. 7:7-8], and it says, "For you are a holy people unto the Lord

your God; the Lord has chosen you to be his special people" [Deut. 7:6].

[242]

The heretics provoke us by discussing the length of our exiles, and they say: The exile in Egypt lasted four hundred years,
5   and the Babylonian exile lasted seventy years. Why, then, does this exile last so long? It is evident that if you were going to be redeemed, you would have been redeemed already. It must be, then, that because of your sin against Jesus, you will remain in exile and will never be redeemed. This is how you should answer them: The earlier exiles
10 were given an explicit time limit which applied whether the Jews had repented of their sins or not, and as a result they were redeemed when that time came. This exile, however, is dependent upon repentance; if they repent, the time will be shortened, as it is written, "And you shall return unto the Lord your God . . . and the Lord your
15 God will return with your captivity and have mercy upon you, and he will gather you from all the nations to which the Lord your God has scattered you. If any of you be driven out unto the outmost parts of heaven, from there will the Lord your God gather you, and from there will he fetch you" [Deut. 30:2-4]. Nevertheless, God has set a time
20 limit to our exile, but it is hidden from us, as it is written, "I the Lord will hasten it in its time" [Isa. 60:22]. What is meant by "I will hasten it in its time"? What God meant was the following: If they repent, I shall hasten it, and if they do not repent, it will come in its time. This shows that the exile does have a time limit, and even if they do not
25 repent the redemption will come in its time; that time will not pass. However, God has not revealed the appointed time for the redemption except to his own heart, as it is written, "For the day of vengeance is in my heart" [Isa. 63:4]. Now, it is because of the heretics and apostates among us that we must suffer the exile until that appointed
30 end, for all Israel are responsible for one another. This will last until they are almost all destroyed and then they will repent, as it is written, "When you are in tribulation and all these things have come upon you, in the end of days, then you will turn to the Lord your God and be obedient to his voice. For the Lord your God is a merciful God; he will

not forsake you or destroy you, nor will he forget the covenant of
your fathers which he swore unto them" [Deut. 4:30–31]. Similarly, it
says in the book of Malachi, "Behold, I will send you Elijah . . . and he
shall turn the heart of the fathers to the children, and the heart of the
5   children to the fathers" [Mal. 3:23–24]. You see, then, that they are all
to repent before the appointed end hastens to come.

      The heretics harass us by noting that God has delayed the end
of this exile longer than those of the others. But this is not surprising, for God does not punish a nation until the measure of its sins has
10 been filled, as it is written, "In measure, when it is sent forth you will
contend with it" [Isa. 27:8]. Similarly, he told Abraham, "And the
fourth generation shall return here, for the iniquity of the Amorites is
not yet complete [Gen. 15:16], and I do not wish to destroy the
Amorites until their measure has been filled." That is why that exile
15 lasted only four hundred years, for in that period of time the measure
of two nations—the Egyptians and the Amorites—was filled, and
they became deserving of destruction; it should be noted, furthermore, that it took a long time for it to be filled since it dates back to
the generation when nations were separated. Now, until the genera-
20 tion when the Babylonian exile ended there was no further destruction of any nation, and that redemption was also not accomplished
"with a high hand"; indeed, that is why the exile lasted only seventy
years. This redemption, however, will involve the ruin, destruction,
killing, and eradication of all the nations, them, and the angels who
25 watch over them, and their gods, as it is written, "The Lord shall
punish the heavenly host in heaven and the kings of the earth on the
earth" [Isa. 24:21]. Jeremiah too said, "Fear not, my servant Jacob,
said the Lord, for I am with you; for I will make a full end of all the
nations whither I have driven you, but with you I will not make a full
30 end" [Jer. 46:28]. You see, then, that God will destroy all the nations
except Israel, as God promised us through Moses, "And yet for all
that, when they will be in the land of their enemies, I will not abhor
them or reject them by destroying them utterly, thereby breaking my
covenant with them" [Lev. 26:44]. Similarly, it is written by the
35 prophets, "And it shall come to pass, that as you were a curse among
the nations, O house of Israel and house of Judah, so will I save you

and you shall be a blessing; fear not, and let your hands be strong"
[Zech. 8:13]. Therefore, we should be strong in our faith. Moreover,
we are suffering in exile in accordance with the verse, "I will sift the
house of Israel among all nations as things are sifted in a sieve"
5 [Amos 9:9], and in that very prophecy our consolation is recorded, as
it is written, "I shall return with the captivity of my people Israel . . .
and I shall plant them upon the land . . . which I have given them, said
the Lord your God" [Amos 9:14-15].

The heretics say that our exile is so long because we do not
10 believe in the Torah of Jesus. This is how you should answer them:
After all, the Muslims do not believe in your Torah and your faith, and
yet they are not in exile. Moreover, why did we suffer exile before
Jesus was born? No, we shall not abandon our Torah, which was
given to us through Moses to the accompaniment of thunder and
15 lightning in the presence of all living creatures, for the sake of your
Torah, which was given to you in secrecy and in silence without the
knowledge of anyone but the mother of Jesus. Consequently, we
could say that sinful men simply made it up for the purpose of throw-
ing off the yoke of the kingdom of heaven and of the commandments
20 so that they might eat pork, drink wine of libation, and commit
adultery. In fact, all the bodily pleasures which are prohibited in our
Torah are permitted in theirs.

[243]

The fear of our God and his holy Torah must not be changed
for any other, for he has given us a true Torah that will stand till the
25 final generation, as it is written, "Listen, my people, to my Torah;
incline your ears to the words of my mouth. I shall open my mouth in
a parable; I shall utter dark sayings of old, which we have heard and
known, and our fathers have told us. We shall not hide them from
their children, telling the last generation the praises of the Lord and
30 his strength and the wonderful works that he has done" [Ps. 78:1-4].
Thus, there is a tradition passed down from the fathers and sons to
be firm in the ancient Torah, as it is written, "Only take heed to yourself, and guard your soul diligently, lest you forget the things which
your eyes have seen, etc." [Deut. 4:9]. It also says, "Now hearken, O

Israel, unto the statutes, etc." [Deut. 4:1]. It is also written, "I am the
Lord your God who has taken you out of the land of Egypt, etc."
[Exod. 20:2; Deut. 5:6]. And it is written, "You shall know no god but
me, and there is no savior beside me" [Hos. 13:4]. Finally, it says,
5   "Remember the Torah of Moses my servant, etc." [Mal. 3:22]; now,
this makes it clear that there is no Torah except that of Moses.

[244]

The heretics anger us by charging that we murder their children and consume the blood. Answer by telling him that no nation
was as thoroughly warned against murder as we, and this warning
10   includes the murder of Gentiles, for in connection with "Do not
covet" [Gen. 20:17], it says "your neighbor," but in connection with
"Do not murder," "Do not commit adultery," and "Do not steal"
[Gen. 20:13-15], it does not say "your neighbor." This shows that
"Do not murder" refers to any man; thus, we were warned against
15   murdering Gentiles as well. What is the reason for this? "For in the
image of God did he make man" [Gen. 9:6]. And it says, "Whoever
sheds a man's blood, by man shall his blood be shed" [ibid.]; this
indicates that all men are included. It also says, "When you come
near to a city to fight against it, then proclaim peace unto it" [Deut.
20   20:10]. Now, God's command, "Do not leave a soul alive" [Deut.
20:16], refers only to the seven nations; the reason is that it is
written, "Do not leave a sorceress alive" [Exod. 22:17], and all of
them were sorcerers, as it is written, "When you come into the land
which the Lord your God is giving you, you shall not learn to act in
25   accordance with the abominations of those nations. There shall not
be found among you anyone that makes his son or daughter pass
through the fire for Moloch, or a diviner, an observer of times, an
enchanter, or a sorcerer. . . . For these nations, which you shall
possess, hearken unto observers of times and unto diviners. . . . "
30   [Deut. 18:9-14]. Moreover, we were also warned against blood more
than any nation, for even when dealing with meat that has been
slaughtered properly and is kosher, we salt it and rinse it and bother
with it extensively in order to remove the blood. The fact is that you
are concocting allegations against us in order to permit our murder;

this is in accordance with David's prophecy in Psalm 44 that you would abuse us, permit our murder, and kill us because of our fear of God, and he prayed for us saying, "You are my king, O God; command the deliverance of Jacob" [Ps. 44:5].

[245]

5   The heretics criticize us by saying that the Talmud distorts and spoils our entire Torah and prevents us from realizing the truth by leading us astray. The answer is that the Talmud is a fence and hedge around the entire Torah, for all the commandments are spread through the twenty-four books of the Bible, a little here and a little
10   there, and one who learns a particular commandment is likely to forget it before he reaches the next. Consequently, the sages established tractates and arranged all the laws which belong together in the appropriate tractate; for example, all the laws of the Sabbath are set down in the tractate *Shabbat,* all the laws of Passover are explained
15   in the tractate *Pesahim,* all the laws of levirate marriage are found in the tractate *Yevamot,* and similarly, each tractate has its own relevant commandment set down in it. You may also answer that even they would not be able to remain steadfast in their faith if not for the Talmud, for it is written, "An Ammonite or Moabite shall not enter
20   into the congregation of the Lord" [Deut. 23:4], and it is the Talmud which explains that this refers to a male Ammonite but not to a female, to a male Moabite but not to a female. Now, since they do not study the Talmud and are consequently ignorant of this interpretation, how do they explain how David entered the congregation of the
25   Lord or, indeed, how Jesus, who they say was descended from David, could have entered it?

COMMENTARY

COMMENTARY

Page 41

2   ***The Book of Polemic*** The Hebrew word *nizzaḥon* is usually translated "victory." Wagenseil, for example, begins his introduction to N.V. with the phrase, "Nizzachon, quod victoriam notat . . . ." M. Steinschneider, however, pointed out that its meaning in this context is polemic (*Jewish Literature from the Eighth to the Eighteenth Century* [New York, 1965; 1st ed., London, 1857], p. 317). See also Loeb in *Revue d'Histoire des Religions* 17 (1888): 329, note 5, and Rosenthal in his introduction to *Sefer Yosef HaMeqanne,* p. 13.

5   ***He who gives power to the weak. . . .*** The same invocation of divine aid appears in Meir of Narbonne's *Mil. Mizvah* (Parma ms., p. 120a) and Moses of Salerno's *Ta'anot* (Pos. ms., p. 55).

7   **Bereshit** This and subsequent Hebrew headings refer to divisions made in the Pentateuch for use in the synagogue. *Bereshit* = Genesis 1:1—6:8.

10-11   ***The son, the holy spirit, and the father*** The Hebrew word *bereshit* begins with the three letters *bet, resh,* and *aleph* which are, respectively, the first letters of the words *ben* (son), *ruaḥ* (spirit), and *av* (father). That Christians were familiar with these Hebrew terms is evident from the fact that the words *abba, ben,* and *ruaḥ* appear in a Latin poem dating from the eleventh century or earlier; moreover, in a declaration made in 1236 Frederick II remarked that the Hebrew word for Bible is *Berechet* (references in Merchavia, *HaTalmud BiRe'i HaNazrut,* pp. 219, 222). The christological interpretation of the phrase "in the beginning" was widespread in a different form; see the references in Williams, p. 29, note 3, and cf. the *Dialogus* . . . attributed to William of Champeaux, PL 163.1057, Peter of Blois, *Contra Perfidiam Judaeorum,* PL 207.828, 830, and the *Tractatus* in *TNA* 5.1509-11 = PL 213.750-51. For another Christian use of acrostics in the Hebrew text of the Bible, cf. p. 60, and see Walter of Châtillon, *Tractatus,* PL 209.440-41, for references to the Hebrew names of Exodus, Leviticus, Numbers, and Deuteronomy. On Christian familiarity with Hebrew in the early Middle Ages, see Matthias Thiel, *Grundlagen und Gestalt der Hebräischkentnisse des Frühen Mittelalters* (Spoleto, 1973). For the late thirteenth century, see B. Blumenkranz's discussion of the Hebrew material in Ermengaud's *Breviari d'Amor,* "Écriture et Image dans la Polémique Antijuive de Matfre Ermengaud," *Cahiers de Fanjeaux* 12 (1977): 307-08.

12   ***Now finish the word*** The central point, of course, is that it is arbitrary to confine an abbreviation to the first three letters of a six-letter word. The author may be reflecting the common Jewish practice of multiplying an alleged trinitarian

L

reference so that it refers to more than three, thereby rendering it useless to the Christian polemicist. On this practice, see appendix 1. It is possible that he also had a specific abbreviation in mind, but it is difficult to determine just what it was. Many interpretations of this sort are cited by the thirteenth-century Isaac b. Judah Halevi, *Pa'neah Raza* (Jerusalem, 1965), pp. 15 ff. See also *Torah Shelemah* ad loc., pp. 18, 20. For various polemical possibilities, see J.D. Eisenstein, *Ozar Vikkuhim*, New York, 1928, p. 236.

19   **Bet** This is the second letter of the Hebrew alphabet and has the numerical value of two. Many Jewish explanations for beginning with a *bet* may be found in Isaac Halevi, *Pa'neah Raza,* pp. 1-15; in addition, the *Zohar* quotation discussed in G. Scholem, *Major Trends in Jewish Mysticism* (New York, 1961), p. 222, may be of some interest in this connection.

25   ***Where is the trinity?*** Cf. p. 51.

Page 42

2   ***The two attributes law and mercy*** On the place of divine attributes in Ashkenazic Jewish thought, see Yosef Dan, *Torat HaSod shel Hasidut Ashkenaz* (Jerusalem, 1968), pp. 94-103. However, the specific relationship that the Christian here ascribes to law, mercy, and grace (or loving-kindness) is anomalous, and in response to an inquiry, Prof. Scholem wrote me that there is no doubt "that the Christian speaking there mixed it all up." For the relationship between attributes and the hypostases or *personae* of the Trinity, see appendix 5.

5   **Aleph** The first letter of the alphabet, with a numerical value of one. The answer given here does not attempt a direct explanation of why the Torah begins with a *bet*. That the issue is an ancient one is evident from the fact that such an explanation is suggested in a nonpolemical context in *Yer. Hagigah* 2, f. 77c, where *bet* is said to have been chosen rather than *aleph* because the former is the first letter of the word "blessing" (*berakhah*) and the latter, of the word "accursed" (*arurah*). See also Abraham ibn Ezra's introduction to his commentary on the Pentateuch, where this talmudic explanation is rejected.

8   ***Unequal in age*** On the arguments from equality of age and inseparability, see p. 137 and the notes there.

12   ***One could make a decree which the other might annul*** This theoretical argument from the possibility of contrary wills in the persons of the Trinity is really more valid as an argument against polytheism than against trinitarianism; indeed, it reveals a Jewish tendency to think of Christianity as polytheism (cf. the notes to p. 75). It is interesting that this problem of contrary wills is raised by other polemicists in connection with the statement in Luke 12:10 and Matthew 12:31-32 that one who speaks against the son (or, as it is quoted by Jewish polemicists, the father or son) will be forgiven, but one who speaks against the holy spirit will not. See the notes to p. 215.

16   ***Why is the word "God" written in the plural?*** On this passage, see appendix 1.

L

21-22   ***An expression of respect*** Cf. *Mil. Hashem*, p. 45, for the view that the plural in Genesis 1:26 is a sort of plural of majesty. See also ibid., p. 41, for the argument that the plural *Elohim* reflects ordinary Hebrew usage as in Genesis 42:30 and Isaiah 19:4.

30   ***"Let us make man"*** This is a *locus classicus* of trinitarian exegesis that is reflected in the Talmud (*Yer. Berakhot* 9.1, f. 12d, *Midrash Bereshit Rabbah* 8:8 [Theodor-Albeck, p. 61], *B. Sanhedrin* 38b). Note especially the rabbinic remark that Moses was reluctant to write this phrase until God told him, "Write, and let him who wishes to err err" (*Ber. Rab.* 8, quoted in *Ver. Israel*, p. 231). The Jewish view that God was speaking to the angels (*B. San.* 38b; *Targum Jonathan* ad loc.; Rashi ad loc.; R. Joseph Bekhor Shor ad loc. [*Perush 'al HaTorah*, Jerusalem, 1956/57, p. 3]; *Sefer Yosef HaMeqanne* in *Mimizrah u-Mima'arav* 4:19 = Rosenthal, pp. 31, 32; Meir of Narbonne, Parma ms., p. 107b) was well known to Christian writers. The usual response was that God and the angels do not share the same image; indeed, Paul Alvarus wrote that the Jews are really defending polytheism by arguing that the angels are like God. See his Epistle 18 to Bodo-Eleazar (PL 121.493-94 = Madoz's critical edition, p. 245, cited in *Juifs et Chrét.*, p. 227). For this argument against the contention that God was addressing the angels, see also Peter Chrysologus, *Sermo* 131, PL 52.560 (cited in *Auteurs*, p. 26); Bede, *In Genisim, CC, Ser. Lat.*, 118 A, p. 25; *De Fide Cath.* I.3.5, PL 83.445 = Eggers, pp. 20-22; *Gloss* ad loc.; the *Dialogus* attributed to William of Champeaux, PL 163.1058-59; the *Tractatus* in TNA 5.1511 = PL 213.751-2; Peter of Blois, *Contra Perfidiam Judaeorum*, PL 207.830-31; Walter of Châtillon, *Tractatus*, PL 209.450 (allegedly said in an actual debate with a Jew); Alan of Lille, *Contra Haereticos*, PL 210.403. For other references, see Williams, pp. 73, 119, 175, 300. On this verse as evidence of the Trinity, see also appendix 1, note 4.

   Other Jewish arguments maintained that the plural represents a sort of majestic plural (*Mil. HaShem*, p. 45; *Mil. Mizvah*, loc. cit.), that a plural often appears instead of a singular (Num. 26:8) and vice versa (Joshua 2:4—R. Joseph Bekhor Shor ad loc.), that it was Moses who was speaking and saying that God commanded us to make man, i.e., to multiply (R. Yom Tov of Joigny quoted in *Sefer Yosef HaMeqanne*, loc. cit.), and even that the verb in Genesis 1:26 is really singular, with a *nun* taking the place of an *aleph*, as in Song of Songs 1:4 (ibid.).

30-31   ***The Holy One, blessed be he, told the earth. . . .*** The most commonly cited reference to this interpretation in Jewish sources is the twelfth-century *Sefer HaBerit* of R. Joseph Kimhi (*Mil. Hovah*, p. 23b = Talmage's ed., p. 32) which is quoted approvingly by Nahmanides in his commentary ad loc. (*Perush HaRamban 'al HaTorah*, edited by Ch. Chavel [Jerusalem, 1962], p. 27). The same interpretation is briefly noted by Meir of Narbonne, loc. cit. R. David Kimhi quotes his father's view in his own commentary to Genesis ad loc. and points to a parallel in *Bereshit Rabbah* 8 ("He consulted with the 'works' of heaven and earth"— במלאכת השמים והארץ נמלך). Moreover, it should be noted that Joseph Kimhi himself does not present this as an original interpretation. The truth is that this explanation is clearly stated by Philo; see S. Belkin, "HaMidrash HaNe'elam

L

U-Meqorotav BaMidrashim HaAlexandroniyyim HaQedumim," *Sura* 3 (1957/58): 12. Belkin also points to *Midrash HaNe'elam* 16:1, where the same explanation is cited clearly and at length אמר לון [לשמיא, ארעא, ומייא] קודשא בריך הוא, לא) שום חד מנכון יכיל למעבד בריה דא [אדם] בלחודוי . . . אלא כולכון התחברון כחדא ואנא עמכון ונעביד אנשא . . . גופא יהא דילכון תלתיכון ונשמתא דילי. ולפיכך קרא לון קודשא בריך הוא ואמר לון נעשה אדם אנא ואתון, אנא נשמתא ואתון גופא). Belkin's argument for the antiquity of the *Midrash HaNe'elam* cannot, however, be made to depend on this parallel since the author could have taken this interpretation from either of the Kimḥis or, more likely, from Naḥmanides. (That there is a Zoharic parallel to Naḥmanides was noted as early as the sixteenth century; see Abraham Zacuto's *Sefer Yuḥasin,* edited by H. Filipowski [Frankfurt, 1924], p. 224.) Such a Jewish interpretation of Genesis 1:26 is also reflected in *Trypho,* chapter 62, where Justin cites the plural in Genesis 3:22 in order to show that the plural in 1:26 must have been addressed to "one endowed with reason." This citation is necessary, he says, in order to refute the view "that God said, 'Let us make man' to the elements, that is, to the earth or other similar substances of which we think man was composed." It is likely that Justin's source for such a view was Philo himself.

Page 43

12-13   *You can put off such a heretic. . . .* Cf. p. 77 for a similar satirical story about Jesus. For other examples of satirical and even vituperative anti-Christian remarks in N.V., cf. pp. 58-59 (on Genesis 40:10), p. 59 (on Genesis 47:31), pp. 68-69. See *Juifs et Chrét.,* pp. 220-21.

28-29   *Why did he cover himself with flesh?* The argument that the Christian revelation should have been public and undeniable recurs on pp. 104, 146, 148, and 204. In Origen's *Contra Celsum* 2:72 (Chadwick's trans. p. 121), the following Jewish argument is cited: if Jesus wanted to remain unrecognized, why did a celestial voice announce him as a son of God, and if he wanted to manifest his divinity, why did he allow himself to be executed? See E. Bickerman, "Latens Deus . . . ," *HTR* 39 (1946): 170. In the so-called *Vikkuaḥ LehaRadaq* (*Mil. Ḥovah,* pp. 16b-17a = Talmage's ed., p. 91), the author insists that there should have been clear, demonstrable proof of the virgin birth. Mary, he suggests, should have given birth at an unnaturally young age; then, "the adversary would have had to be silent and everyone would have declared, 'This is a great miracle the likes of which the world has never seen' " (לא היה פתחון פה לבעל הדין לחלוק והיו אומרים כל העולם זה פלא גדול לא נעשה כמוהו מעולם). So also below, pp. 214-15. This assertion that the manner of the alleged Christian revelation was unfair because it was unclear and misleading may constitute a conscious reversal of a Christian argument against the Jews, for Tertullian had argued that the *Jewish* revelation was unfair because it was restricted to one nation ("Cur etenim Deus, universitatis conditor, mundi totius gubernator . . . legem per Moysen uni populo dedisse credatur, et non omnibus

L

gentibus attribuisse dicatur?"). See his *Adversus Judaeos*, chapter 2, PL 2.599 = Tränkle, p. 4, and cf. N.V., p. 203, for another reversal of this argument.

Page 44

6-7   ***How could this man be God, for he entered a woman.*** .... On this argument, see appendix 2.

19-20   ***Unaccompanied by pain or the defilement of blood*** The reference to pain is not a superfluous flourish since the absence of blood would not in itself establish the absence of impurity (at least not to Jewish ears); cf. Rashi on Leviticus 12:2, s.v. *kimei*, and on *Niddah* 21a, s.v. *ve'im*. On the association of the pain of childbirth with the need for sacrifice, see B. *Niddah* 31b.

20   ***You yourselves admit.*** .... See Luke 2:22-24. The argument from Mary's *ritual* impurity may also be an attempt to counter the sort of argument raised by Odo of Cambrai (PL 160.1111-12, cited in appendix 2) which maintained that there is nothing wrong with contact with objects that are physically unclean. The same Jewish argument is found below, pp. 183-84, in the *Vikkuaḥ LehaRadaq*, Talmage's ed., p. 92, and in Rome ms. 53, p. 24a = Pos. "Mordecai of Avignon" ms., p. 28 = Rosenthal's "Menaḥem," p. 70.

26   ***"Lichtmess"*** Candlemas (February 2). In the Middle Ages, the procession on Candlemas left the church and went to the cemetery surrounding it, thus making the festival more conspicuous to Jews. See *Catholic Encyclopedia* III (New York, 1908), pp. 245-46.

Page 45

1-2   ***Without the second name*** See p. 78 (on Deut. 6:4) for the same sort of response.

12-13   ***The stones of the Sambation River rest . . . on our Sabbath*** See B. *Sanhedrin* 65b and *Bereshit Rabbah* 11:6 (Theodor-Albeck, p. 93) for a reported conversation between Tineius Rufus and R. Akiba in which the latter cites this legendary river to prove which day is the Sabbath. Meir of Narbonne cited this argument along with references to two other phenomena (one of them based on B. *Sanhedrin*, loc. cit) that allegedly take place only on the Jewish Sabbath; see *Mil. Miẓvah*, Parma ms., p. 88b. Further references regarding the Sambation legend may be found in L. Ginzberg, *Legends of the Jews* (Philadelphia, 1928), 6:407-9.

17-18   ***Changed the Sabbath to Sunday*** Cf., for example, Raban Maur's *De Clericorum Institutione* 2:42, PL 107.356, for a discussion of the priority of Sunday over Saturday (cited in *Auteurs,* p. 176).

20   ***You violate and contradict the words of Moses*** Cf. p. 96. The same argument is found in *Sefer HaBerit, Mil. Ḥovah,* p. 21a = Talmage's ed., p. 26: "The Christians do all sorts of work even on Sunday, which is their Sabbath." Note especially a

L

strikingly similar passage in Rupert's *Annulus seu Dialogus Christiani et Judaei,* PL 170.590, where the Jew argues: "You observe neither the Sabbath nor the day which you call *Dominicus*" ("Tu neque Sabbatum custodis, neque illum diem quem Dominicum dicis. Negotiaris enim, ambulas, et circa res quaslibet exerceris"). The reading "Dominica" in N.V. is uncertain. This Jewish argument is reversed in the *Tractatus* in TNA 5.1517-18 = PL 213.757-8, where the author argues that *Jews* do not observe the Sabbath laws properly since they take walks in violation of the biblical injunction that they sit home [Exodus 16:29]. By such behavior, they reject the plain sense of Scripture in favor of the interpretation of their rabbis.

23-24   **The man found gathering sticks** Numbers 15:32-36.

27-28   **The work was completed during the seventh day** In other words, some work was done on the seventh day. The Septuagint reading, "And on the sixth day God finished," is cited in *B. Megillah* 9a, where Rashi comments that the change was made "so that no one should conclude that he did work on the Sabbath." For various approaches to this verse, see Rashi and Ibn Ezra ad loc.; *Leqet Qazar, Michael* 4 (1976): 63; *Sefer Yosef HaMeqanne* in *Mimizraḥ u-Mimaʿarav* 4:20 = Rosenthal, p. 34. The Christian argument cited here is found in *De Fide Cath.* II.15.2, PL 83.522, and in Bede [pseud.], *Quaestiones super Genesim,* PL 93.260 (probably written by Wigbod. See C.H. Jones's introduction to Bede's *In Genisim,* p. iv.), and in the *Tractatus* in TNA 5.1516 = PL 213.756. See also Williams, p. 396.

Page 46

10   **He foresaw that Jesus would attempt to mislead the world** The view that the Bible contains various warnings against believing in Jesus is rather common in N.V. Cf., for example, the list of such warnings on p. 147, as well as the comment on p. 64·(on Exodus 12:22). See also *Sefer Yosef HaMeqanne* in *Mimizraḥ u-Mimaʿarav* 4:18 = Rosenthal, p. 30 (and cf. note 2 there) for the view that the second day of creation was not proclaimed "good" because water was created then and God knew of the baneful effects that belief in baptismal water would have. Cf. *Festschrift A. Berliner's,* p. 86, for Yosef's argument that certain laws were given in specific ways as a warning against Christianity, and see also Rosenthal's introduction to *Sefer Yosef HaMeqanne,* p. 25. This is, of course, a reversal of the basic Christian argument that the Old Testament prefigures Jesus. As I indicated in the Introduction, it is often difficult to tell when a polemicist was serious about such an interpretation and when he was just being playful. It should be noted, however, that in some sources this sort of interpretation follows a Christian question about how the Torah could have omitted all reference to Jesus; see Meir of Narbonne, *Mil. Mizvah,* Parma ms., pp. 39a-b, 110a; Moses of Salerno, *Pos.* ms., p. 42.

        This specific argument about the tree of life was undoubtedly inspired by a Rabbinic statement that God inflicted death on the world because he foresaw that Nebuchadnezzar and Hiram would assert their own divinity. See *Bereshit Rabbah* 9:5 and *B. Bava Batra* 75a-b. Elsewhere, the author applies Numbers 24:23 to Jesus'

L

pretensions of divinity. Here too his source was a talmudic passage that Rashi had referred to the similar contentions of Pharaoh and Hiram. See p. 86, and cf. Rashi to *Sanhedrin* 106a s.v. *shemeḥayyeh.*

15 **Lekh Lekha** Genesis 12:1—17:27.

16 *Melchisedek* See Hebrews 7 for a full description of the analogy between Jesus and Melchisedek based especially on Psalms 110:4. On the typological interpretation of Melchisedek, see G. Bardy, "Melchisédech dans la tradition patristique," *Revue Biblique* 35 (1926): 496 ff., and 36 (1927): 25 ff.; Marcel Simon, "Melchisédech dans la polémique et la legende," *Rev. d'hist. et de phil. rel.* (1937): 58–93, reprinted in his *Recherches d'Histoire Judéo-Chrétienne* (Paris, 1962), pp. 101-26.

18 *The bread refers to his body* The view that the bread and wine in this verse prefigure the sacraments was first expressed by Clement of Alexandria, *Stromata* 4.25, cited in Simon, *Recherches,* p. 106, *Ver. Israel,* p. 110. For later acceptance of this view, cf. pseudo-Bede's commentary ad loc., PL 91.233, interlinear gloss ad loc. ("Haec sacramenta nostrorum sacramentorum figura fuerunt"), the letter of "R. Samuel of Morocco," chapter 19, cited in Williams, p. 231, and Peter of Blois, *Contra Perfidiam Judaeorum,* PL 207.859.

20 *Therefore, they ask. . . .* On the tactic of inquiring about the reason for a commandment in order to set up an allegorical interpretation, see appendix 3.

22–23 *Libations and meal-offerings* This interpretation is taken from *Bereshit Rabbah* 43:6 (Theodor-Albeck, pp. 420-21).

24 *If the heretic will then ask. . . .* See appendix 3. The view that the Jews were commanded to bring sacrifices in order to save them from idolatry is found in various Christian works. See *Trypho,* chapters 19, 22, 92; *Didascalia* 6:17:1 (cited in *Ver. Israel,* p. 114); *Trophies of Damascus* 1:3:2 (cited in Williams, p. 164); Isidore's *Quaestiones in Leviticum* (PL 83.337) and Damian's *Antilogus* (PL 145.58-59); Rupert's *Dialogus,* PL 170.583. Maimonides expressed a related view in his *Guide of the Perplexed,* 3:32. (An alleged midrashic parallel to Maimonides' position which was cited in the Middle Ages is imprecise though it is defended by M. Margulies, *Midrash VaYiqra Rabbah* [Jerusalem, 1953], p. 517; see David Hoffman, *Sefer VaYiqra* [Jerusalem, 1953], pp. 60-61). In general see Hebrews 10, and cf. *Ver. Israel,* pp. 201-2; *De Fide Cath.* II.17, PL 83.526-27.

Page 47

4 *It would be more fitting to sacrifice the sinner* Cf. Naḥmanides' commentary to Leviticus 1:9.

8 *This verse implies. . . .* Why should a Christian ask this question in a polemical context? It may simply be part of the tendency to ask the Jews embarrassing questions about the partriachs; see, for example, p. 56 and the notes there. It is also possible that the purpose was to show that the verse means not so much that Abraham believed in a particular promise but that he had a general faith in God. This could then be used to show that Abraham was justified by faith (cf. Galatians

L

3:6 and Romans 4:9). On this subject, see pp. 47–48 (on Genesis 17:24) and the notes there.

15-16   **This caused him to understand.** . . . One point of this response may be to show that asking for a sign as proof is not an indication of faithlessness; see 1 Corinthians 1:22.

18   **The four exiles** Cf. p. 123 (on Amos 2:6). The relevant exiles could be the exile in Egypt, the exile of the northern kingdom of Israel, and the destruction of the two temples. For the various "exiles," see *Midrash 'Eser Galuyot*, ed. L. Grünhut in *Sefer HaLiqqutim* (Jerusalem, 1900), 3:2–22. (This midrash omits the exile in Egypt.) However, see David Kimhi's commentary on Psalms 13:2 where he cites a midrash which allegedly says that the phrase "till when" is repeated four times because of the "four exiles." Now, the usual text of that midrash, a text cited by Rashi ad loc., says "four kingdoms." It is thus probable that "exiles" here is synonymous with "kingdoms" and simply refers to periods of foreign domination; cf. the quotations in M. Kasher, *Haggadah Shelemah,* 3rd ed. (Jerusalem, 1967), p. 95.

22   **The heifer in this vision is Egypt.** . . . Rashi (on Gen. 15:10) wrote, "The explanation lies in the fact that the Gentile nations are compared to bulls, rams, and goats, as it is written, 'Many bulls have surrounded me' [Ps. 22:13], and it is written, 'The ram which you saw with horns represents the kings of Media and Persia' [Dan. 8:20], and it is written, 'The rough goat is the king of Greece' [Dan. 8:21]. Israel, on the other hand, is compared to a dove, as it is written, 'My dove in the clefts of the rock' [Song of Songs 2:14]. That is why he cut the animals— in order to indicate that the nations will cease to exist. But he did not cut the bird, in order to indicate that Israel will exist forever."

The other sources of N.V. are *Bereshit Rabbah* 44:15 (Theodor-Albeck, p. 437), *Pirqei deRabbi Eliezer* 28 (cf. A. H. Silver , *A History of Messianic Speculation in Israel* [Boston, 1959], pp. 37 ff.), *Leqaḥ Tov,* ed. S. Buber (Jerusalem, 1960), pp. 69–70 (cf. Kasher's notes in *Torah Shelemah* ad loc., pp. 646–47), and perhaps the material preserved in the later *Midrash HaHefeẓ* (see M. Havazelet, "Allusions to Christianity and Islam in Midrash HaHefeṣ," *Augustinianum* 9 [1969]: 362–65). In *Bereshit Rabbah*, however, the heifer is Babylonia while the turtledove (*tor*) and pigeon are Edom (=Rome); in *Midrash HaHefeẓ*, the heifer is Babylonia while the turtledove and pigeon are Edom and Ishmael. In *Pirqei deRabbi Eliezer*, the explanation of the turtledove and pigeon is the same as in N.V. down to the proof-text and the Aramaic interpretation, but the heifer is regarded as the fourth kingdom, i.e., Edom. *Leqaḥ Tov* is the only source which agrees with N.V. that the heifer is Egypt (with the same proof-text), but it takes both the turtledove and pigeon as references to Israel. Thus, the passage in N.V. probably goes back to an eclectic one taken from a variety of sources. An even more elaborate polemical treatment of Genesis 15, which also sees it as a symbol of the various exiles, is found in Mordecai of Avignon, *Maḥaziq Emunah*, Vatican ms., pp. 3b–4a.

(It is of some interest that Rashi's explanation of the cutting up of all the

L

animals except for the bird is paralleled to some extent in Muslim polemic; there, of course, the bird represents Islam. See E. Strauss, "Darkhei HaPulmus HaMuslemi," *Sefer HaZikkaron LeBeit HaMidrash LeRabbanim BeVinah* [Jerusalem, 1946], p. 190).

23-24   **The kingdom of Greece** Rome does not appear in this passage, and the author undoubtedly considered it a part of the kingdom of Greece. Cf. p. 132. This was the view of Abraham ibn Ezra; see his commentary to Daniel 2:39, Genesis 27:40, Zechariah 11:5 (cited and discussed in G. Cohen, ed., *The Book of Tradition* [Philadelphia, 1968], pp. 237-38. See also Cohen's "Esau as Symbol," pp. 46-48). Despite some ambiguities, this was probably the view in *Leqaḥ Tov,* loc. cit.

32   **One may ask. . . .** The question is probably based on the Christian contention that Abraham had been justified by faith before his circumcision; God did not command circumcision earlier so that this would be clear. For this contention, see Romans 4:9 ff., and cf. Galatians 3:6, 17 (cited in *Ver. Israel*, pp. 106-7). For this argument as proof that circumcision is not essential, see Zeno's work on circumcision (PL 11.345-54 = crit. ed. by Giuliani [Verona, 1883], pp. 91-100, cited in *Judenpredigt*, p. 29) and Rupert's *Dialogus*, PL 170.563. Various Christian writers had pointed to the righteous figures in Genesis who were never circumcized (see *Judenpredigt*, p. 12; Simon, *Recherches,* p. 105). Cf. also *De Fide Cath.* II. 16, PL 83.524-26, Peter the Venerable, *Tractatus*, PL 189.584, and Williams, pp. 180, 302. On the general attitude of the church fathers toward circumcision, see *Judenpredigt*, pp. 145-48, and *Ver. Israel*, pp. 198-99. See also the discussion by Yosef HaMeqanne, Rome ms., pp. 11a-b. This commandment to Abraham was also cited by Christians as evidence that God can reveal new laws and that he can consequently change old ones; see Peter the Venerable, *Tractatus*, PL 189.571-72, 584. This was an important Muslim argument; cf. M. Perlmann, *Ifham al-Yahud* (New York, 1964), p. 34.

Page 48

4   **Vayera Elav** Genesis 18:1-22:24.

6   **The heretics say. . . .** See appendix 4.

9   **Refute him with his own words** N.V. and other Jewish polemicists frequently granted a Christian premise or exegetical formula for the sake of argument and then turned it around to show that this very premise or exegesis can prove an anti-Christian position. Cf. p. 75 (on Deuteronomy 18:18), p. 59 (on Genesis 48:2), *Mil. HaShem*, p. 140 (on Prov. 30).

Page 49

4   **Does God eat and drink?** The author undoubtedly believed that even angels could only have pretended to eat (cf. *B. Bava Meẓi'a* 86b; Josephus, *Antiquities* 1:197); the point is that Abraham believed that they were ordinary human beings. Note that some Muslim polemicists pointed to this passage as a problem for Jews since the Jews themselves maintain that angels do not eat (Strauss, "Darkhei HaPulmus HaMuslemi," p. 186).

L

10		***When he will eat and drink*** Other Jewish polemicists maintained that Jesus' eating during the incarnation is absurd. See *Sefer Nestor HaKomer*, ed. A. Berliner (Altona 1874/75), p. 1, and Kimḥi's *Sefer HaBerit, Mil. Hovah*, p. 22a = Talmage's ed., p. 29.

16		***Who performed three missions*** Rashi on Genesis 18:2 writes that one was sent to inform Sarah, another to destroy Sodom, and the third to cure Abraham and save Lot (two missions of the same type). Cf. *B. Bava Meẓi'a* 86b, and *Bereshit Rabbah* 50:2 (Theodore-Albeck, p. 516). Ibn Ezra (on Gen. 18:1) and Joseph Kimḥi (*Sefer HaBerit, Mil. Hovah*, p. 31b = Talmage's ed., p. 51), like N.V., mention only the saving of Lot as the mission of the third.

17-18		***One angel does not perform two missions*** *Bereshit Rabbah*, loc. cit.

20-21		***The third was no longer with them*** The fact that only two men came to Sodom was cited by other polemicists to disprove the trinitarian exegesis directly. Saadia, quoted by Jacob ben Reuben, points out that this in itself shows that the three men did not represent the three persons of a unified God (*Mil. HaShem*, p. 48). A full expression of this argument is found in *Sefer HaBerit, Mil. Hovah*, p. 32a = Talmage's ed., pp. 51–52, and it also appears in Ibn Ezra (on Genesis 18:1)and *Sefer Yosef HaMeqanne* in *MiMizraḥ u-MiMa'arav* 4 (1889), ad loc. = Rosenthal, p. 39. Some Christians regarded the two angels as the father and son; see Williams, p. 320.

28		***He said this to their leader. . . .*** So too Kimḥi in *Sefer HaBerit, Mil. Hovah*, p. 32a = Talmage's ed., p. 51. This explanation and the subsequent one that Abraham was addressing God are found in the same order in Rashi on Genesis 18:3.

Page 50

1-2		***They say in the Gospels. . . .*** See appendix 4, note 1.

6		***They are four*** On this "additive" interpretation, see appendix 1.

20		***An a fortiori argument*** So too Jacob ben Reuben, *Mil. HaShem*, p. 48.

28		***Where do we find that bowing means prayer?*** So Kimḥi in *Sefer HaBerit, Mil. Hovah*, p. 31b = Talmage's ed., p. 51.

Page 51

16		***"Then the Lord caused to rain. . . ."*** This argument was posed by a "heretic" cited in *B. Sanhedrin* 38b; the answer, based on an analogy with Genesis 4:23, was that this sort of expression is characteristic of Scripture. Cf. also *Torah Shelemah* ad loc., p. 811. The Council of Sirmium anathematized those who refused to accept this verse as a christological proof. ("Si quis hoc dictum: 'pluit Dominus ignem a Domino' non de patre et filio accipiat, se ipsum a se ipso pluisse dicat, anathema est.") Simon (*Ver. Israel*, p. 231) thinks that this was aimed against Jews, while Blumenkranz maintains that it refers to Arians (*Auteurs*, p. 65, n. 3). This verse is also cited in *Trypho*, chapters 26, 129; *The Dialogue of Athanasius and Zacchaeus*, cited in Williams, p. 120; Maximin's fifth-century *Tractatus contra Judaeos*, chapter 2, cited in *Auteurs*, p. 18; Fortunatus, *Carmina* 5:5, cited ibid., p. 65;

L

De Fide Cath. I.3.6, PL 83.455 = Eggers, p. 22; Damian's *Dialogus,* PL 145.43; Peter the Venerable, *Tractatus,* PL 189.520-22. Jerome cites this together with Psalms 110:1 and the admittedly inappropriate Isaiah 45:1 as examples of christological exegesis based on two "domini" in a verse (*In Esaiam, CC, Ser. Lat.*, 73A, p. 504). Several examples of this kind of argument (including Gen. 19:24) are discussed by Peter of Blois, *Contra Perfidiam Judaeorum,* PL 207.829. So also Joachim da Fiore, *Adversus Judaeos di Gioacchino da Fiore,* ed. by A. Frugoni (Rome, 1957), pp. 8-9.

20   **Only a messenger** This was a recurrent argument in Jewish polemic. Cf. below p. 66 (on Exodus 23:20-22) and p. 128 (on Mal. 2:7). See especially *Sefer Nestor HaKomer,* p. 4, and *Mil. HaShem,* p. 155; Rosenthal (ibid.) refers to Augustine's treatment of the problem in *De Trinitate* 2:8, PL 42.848. See also Solomon de' Rossi, *'Edut HaShem Ne'emanah,* in Rosenthal's *Meḥqarim,* 1:386. This was really just one form of the more general Jewish argument that Jesus is portrayed as the object of divine acts in alleged christological passages and in the Gospels. See N.V., p. 74 (on Deuteronomy 18:18), p. 108 (on Isaiah 11:2); *Mil. HaShem,* pp. 64-65, 107, 109, 129.

33   **The spirit** Cf. pp. 41-42.

Page 52

10-11   **Now I know how to answer. . . .** Rashi on Genesis 22:12: "Now I know how to answer Satan [alternate reading: the stern principle] and the nations who wonder why I love you. I can only reply, because they see that you fear God." The point is that the purpose of the test was to make Abraham's faith manifest. Cf. the various midrashim and other references cited in Kasher's *Torah Shelemah* ad loc., p. 898 nos. 133-35. Note also Maimonides' *Guide* 3:24. The classic case of the imposition of a test on an individual in order to prove his righteousness to Satan is, of course, the book of Job.

13-14   **This passage refers to the hanged one** Isaac was a common and significant "type" of Jesus. See Maximus of Turin's *Homilia* 55, cited in *Auteurs,* p. 35; Augustine, who argues that Isaac carried his own wood just as Jesus carried his own cross (*In Ioannis Evangelium Tractatus* 9.12, *City of God* 16.132.1—cited in *Judenpredigt,* p. 157; Sermon 19, PL 38.133); Chrysostom, *Homiliae in Genesin* 47.3, PG 54.432 ($\tau\alpha\hat{\upsilon}\tau\alpha$ $\delta\hat{\epsilon}$ $\pi\acute{\alpha}\nu\tau\alpha$ $\tau\acute{\upsilon}\pi\sigma\varsigma$ $\acute{\epsilon}\gamma\acute{\epsilon}\nu\epsilon\tau\sigma$ $\tau\sigma\hat{\upsilon}$ $\sigma\tau\alpha\upsilon\rho\sigma\hat{\upsilon}$), cited in Simon, *Recherches,* p. 193; *De Fide Cath.*, I.34.2, PL 83.484; Bede [pseud.], *Commentarii,* PL 91.245; idem, *Quaestiones,* PL 93.319; interlinear gloss ad loc. In general, see Simon, op. cit., pp. 193-97; J. Daniélou, "La Typologie d'Isaac dans le Christianisme Primitif," *Biblica* 28 (1947): 363-93; D. Lerch, *Isaaks Opferung, Christlich Gedeutet* (Tübingen, 1950); R. Woolf, "The Effect of Typology on the English Mediaeval Plays of Abraham and Isaac," *Speculum* 32 (1957): 805-25.

16   **The paschal lamb** This "type" was also extremely widespread in Christian works. See 1 Corinthians 5:7: "Christ our passover [$\pi\acute{\alpha}\sigma\chi\alpha$] was sacrificed," and cf. the statement in John 19:36 that Jesus' bones were not broken on the

244   *Commentary to p. 52*

L

cross because of the verse, "Nor shall you break a bone of it" (Exodus 12:46; see
N.V., p. 65). See also *Trypho*, chapters 40, 111; Tertullian, *Adversus Judaeos* 10, PL
2.630 = Tränkle, p. 30; Cyprian, *Testimoniorum Libri Tres adversus Judaeos* 2:15, PL
4.709-10; Aphraates, Dem. 12 (Neusner's *Aphrahat and Judaism,* pp. 34 ff.); Jerome
[pseud.], *Epistle* 149, cited in *Judenpredigt,* p. 48; Augustine, *Quaestiones Exod., CC,
Ser. Lat.,* 33, p. 86; Leo the Great [pseud.] (fifth century), sermon 7, cited in *Auteurs,*
p. 34; Isidore, *Quaest. in Leviticum,* PL 83.337-38; idem, *De Fide Cath.,* I.46.1, PL
83.489-90; Bede [pseud.], *Commentarii,* PL 91.305-7; Raban Maur, PL 108.48;
Damian, *Antilogus,* PL 145.59. Yosef HaMeqanne was also asked about the purpose
of the paschal lamb in order to set up a christological interpretation. See *Festschrift
A. Berliner's,* p. 82 = Rosenthal, p. 46 (= Berliner, *Peletat Soferim,* Heb. sec., p. 29).
Both Meir of Narbonne (Parma ms., pp. 108b-109a) and Moses of Salerno
(Posnanski ms., p. 40) cited this Christian interpretation and noted that it would
yield a justification for executing Jesus since the paschal lamb was supposed to be
slaughtered. For this sort of argument, cf. also *Sefer Yosef HaMeqanne,* Rosenthal's
ed., p. 101.

21-22   *Why, then, do you not perceive its nature?* The argument that Jews are blind
to the true meaning of Scripture was very common; cf. the notes to p. 68 below.

22   *Why do you not consider . . . ?* On this manner of questioning, see appendix 3.

23   *"Eat not of it raw. . . ."* See *Shemot Rabbah* 15:12 for a symbolic Jewish
interpretation of these requirements. Cf. also Kasher's note to *Torah Shelemah* ad
loc., p. 100, no. 190.

27   *Are you truly animals. . . .* On the Jews' "bovine intellect," see my study of
"The Attitude of St. Bernard of Clairvaux toward the Jews," *Proceedings of the
American Academy for Jewish Research* 40 (1972): 103.

28-29   *[Indeed, it is concerning this that Jeremiah said. . . .]* I have added the
bracketed sentence conjecturally. There is clearly a lacuna in the text which
Wagenseil noted by placing asterisks here. Since the continuation refers to
Jeremiah and since a christological reference to a sheep or lamb is likely, Jeremiah
11:19 appears to be the best candidate to fill the lacuna. N.V.'s (admittedly unusual)
answer would then be as follows: If one combines the obvious fact that the verse
refers to Jeremiah with the Christian contention that this "sheep" refers to a divine
Messiah, the conclusion is ludicrous. For the christological interpretation of this
verse, see Jerome, *In Hieremiam,* ad loc., *CC, Ser. Lat.,* 74, p. 117, the fifth-century *De
Altercatione Ecclesiae et Synagogae,* cited in Williams, p. 330, and *De Fide Cath.,* I.35.1,
PL 83.484. Cf. also Isaiah 53:7 for a similar verse in a *locus classicus* of christological
exegesis. It goes without saying that the precise wording of the textual reconstruction here is certainly inaccurate, but some reference to Jeremiah 11:19 (perhaps as part of a longer passage) seems quite probable.

L

Page 53

14   **Isaac** See *Shemot Rabbah* 15:12. For other references, cf. *Torah Shelemah* on Genesis 22, p. 889, no. 100, and on Exodus 12, p. 69, no. 91.

22-23   **As free of sin as an infant** B. *Yoma* 22b: "R. Huna said, 'Like a one year old, for he had not tasted sin.'" In Christian exegesis, the one year represented the year that passed between Jesus' baptism and his passion; see Williams, p. 303. It is of particular interest, however, to find Aphraates arguing that Exodus 12:5 refers to Jesus as "a year old, for he was a child as to sins" (Dem. 12, Neusner's *Aphrahat*, p. 34).

25   **Many Jesuses** This argument recurs on pp. 72 and 118.

31   **[The blood of the paschal lamb].** . . . See p. 64, where the three dabs of blood symbolize the blood of Abraham's circumcision, of the binding of Isaac, and of the paschal lamb. In this passage only two types are mentioned in the manuscripts: the blood of circumcision and that of the menstruant woman. However, the explicit reference to three types (which was changed to two in *Tela* because only two are listed) as well as the context of the passage makes it clear that a third type must be added. That this third type is likely to be the blood of the paschal lamb rather than that of the binding of Isaac is clear in light of the fact that the passage is discussing the former and in light of *Mekhilta Bo*, chapter 5, and *Shemot Rabbah* 17:3, which mention two types of blood: the blood of the paschal lamb and that of circumcision.

Page 54

6-7   **We eat human beings.** . . . Another proof text for the blood libel is cited in *Sefer Yosef HaMeqanne*, where a Parisian official quotes Numbers 23:24 ("He shall drink the blood of the slain") to show that Jews "eat the blood of the uncircumcized." See *Festschrift A. Berliner's*, p. 85 = Rosenthal, pp. 53-54 (= Berliner, *Peletat Soferim*, Heb. sec., p. 32). See especially below, pp. 229-30.

24-25   **But they were not commanded to eat it this way in future years** So B. *Pesahim* 96a. For other references see *Torah Shelemah* ad loc., p. 113, no. 235.

Page 55

7-8   **How could he contradict his earlier promise?** Rashi (on Genesis 22:12) cites the rabbinic statement that God would never have contradicted the promise in Genesis 21:12 and that is why he never told Abraham, "Slaughter him" but only, "Bring him up." Cf. *Torah Shelemah* ad loc., p. 773, no. 22.

12   **Toledot Yitzhak** Genesis 25:19—28:9.

17-18   **But was not born in the strict sense** This is a highly tentative translation of a phrase (פרט ללידה) which I don't really understand. It may mean that the full process involved in normal birth (beginning with intercourse) did not take place.

L

Wagenseil translated, "And he was destined to be born [*et destinatus fuit nativitati*]," which makes sense but can't be derived from the text very easily. Perhaps he read *porat* and took it to mean "was singled out." Otherwise, a minor emendation to *parash* might be considered.

What is interesting and rather peculiar about this entire passage is the assumption that Christians consider Esau a "type" of Jesus. Such a view is reflected again on p. 56, where Christians are said to argue that the blessings of Jacob were fulfilled for the Gentiles and not the Jews because of Jacob's trickery, and again on p. 58 where a similar argument is recorded. These views imply that it is a Christian view that Esau or Edom represents Christianity. Finally, in the discussion regarding interest on p. 133, a possible Christian argument is considered which would assert that Christians are Israel's brethren because they are Edomites. (On this last point, see also *Leqet Qaẓar, Michael* 4 [1976]: 66.)

The fact is that classical Christian exegesis considered Jacob the church and Esau the synagogue. Cf., for example, Tertullian, *Adversus Judaeos*, chapters 1, 3, PL 2.598, 604 = Tränkle, pp. 3-4, 8 (Tränkle points to Romans 9:10-13 as the first indication of such exegesis, but this is unlikely. See Cohen's article cited below. See also Tränkle's introduction, p. lxxv, where he points to *Barnabas* 13:1 ff. and Irenaeus' *Haeret.* 4.21.2); Cyprian, *Testimonia* 1:19-20, PL 4.688-89; *De Montibus Sina et Sion. . . . contra Judaeos*, PL 4.911; Cesar of Arles' full sermon on the subject of the younger prefiguring the church and the older the synagogue (sixth century), *CC, Ser. Lat.*, 103, pp. 429-33, cited in *Auteurs*, pp. 49-50; Isidore of Seville, *Quaestiones* ad loc., PL 83.255; Bede [pseud.], *Commentarii* ad loc., PL 91.217; idem, *Quaestiones* ad loc., PL 93.332; Peter of Blois, *Contra perfidiam Judaeorum*, PL 207.857. See also the references in *Judenpredigt*, pp. 23, 24, 101, 170 note 26. There are, however, a very limited number of cases where Christians do use the sort of typology referred to in N.V. here. A Christian, for example, may sometimes claim the parentage of either Jacob or Esau when the particular verse makes it useful to do so—the former according to the spirit and the latter according to the flesh; see Augustine, *Epist.* 196:13 (Latin text quoted in *Ver. Israel*, p. 223). Cf. also the later citations in J. Rosenthal, "Ribbit min HaNokhri," *Talpiyyot* 6 (1953): 151. It should also be noted that the Christian argument regarding interest in N.V., p. 133, may actually mean, "According to your own view that we are Edom, you should not be permitted to take interest from us." On the Christian typology of Esau in general, see Cohen, "Esau as Symbol," pp. 19-48.

28-29   **The sign of the cross** See H. Thurston, "The Sign of the Cross," *Catholic Encyclopedia* (New York, 1912), 13:785-87.

30-31   **Prayers and blessings** See *Mishnah Berakhot* 9.1.

Page 56

2   **Jacob did not lie** Rashi, ad loc., is also concerned with defending at least the literal veracity of Jacob, but his exegesis is entirely different: " 'I am Esau your

L

firstborn'; 'I am' the one who is serving you, while 'Esau is your firstborn.' " (For a critique of this explanation, see Ibn Ezra on Exodus 32:1). N.V. apparently takes the verse to mean, "I have replaced Esau as your firstborn." Indeed, Jacob's purchase of the birthright so impressed some Jews as the basis for a natural interpretation of this passage that a later commentator on Rashi actually argues that *Rashi's* interpretation would appear to make Jacob into a liar, for it was no longer true that Esau was the firstborn (*Siftei Ḥakhamin*, ad loc., in the standard editions of the Hebrew Pentateuch with commentaries). N.V.'s interpretation of Genesis 27:24 is the same as Rashi's.

For a series of Christian accusations regarding lying and cheating by biblical figures, see *Sefer Yosef HaMeqanne, MiMizraḥ u-MiMa'arav* 4:23 = Rosenthal, pp. 40-42 (cf. also ibid., pp. 65-66).

4   *In a manner as clear as day* A reference to Rashi's interpretation of Genesis 25:31: " 'Sell me this day'. . . make a clear sale just as the day is clear." For other examples of this type of exegesis in rabbinic sources and Rashi, cf. *B. Sanhedrin* 7b, and Rashi on Exodus 22:2 and on Deuteronomy 22:17.

15   **Vayeẓe Ya'aqov** Genesis 28:10—32:3.

17   *Ask them the following* The point of this section seems to be to show Christians that they do not understand their own prayers by asking questions that the author considers susceptible to solution only through rabbinic interpretation. For the christological exegesis of this passage, see *Trypho*, chapter 86; *The Dialogue of Timothy and Aquila*, cited in Williams, p. 74; Augustine, *Quaestiones in Heptateuchum, CC, Ser. Lat.*, 33, p. 32; Isidore, *Quaestiones*, PL 83.258; Joachim da Fiore, *Adversus Judaeos*, pp. 11-12.

20   *There was only one* For the rabbinic interpretations of this problem as well as of the Bethel question, see Rashi on Genesis 28:11 and 28:17.

29   *R. Judah said* This is probably based on a passage in *B. Sanhedrin* 101b, although that passage does not say precisely what N.V. suggests.

31   *One calf in Bethel. . . .* 1 Kings 12:28-29.

Page 57

1   **Vayeshev Ya'aqov** Genesis 37:1—40:23.

3   *Joseph prefigures the hanged one* So Aphraates, Dem. 21 (Neusner's *Aphrahat*, pp. 103-4); Isidore, *Quaestiones*, PL 83.272; Bede [pseud.], *Commentarii*, PL 91.263-64; *Gloss* ad loc.

13-14   *Jacob descended to hell* The general problem is referred to in Augustine's *Quaestiones, CC, Ser. Lat.*, 33, p. 48, and *Gloss* ad loc. Crispin (*Disputatio*, p. 48) cites Genesis 37:35 and 42:38 as well as Job 17:13 to prove that all those who preceded Jesus descended to hell. The Christian in *Mil. HaShem*, p. 49, cites Genesis 15:15 and 37:35, and the Christians in *Sefer Yosef HaMeqanne (MiMizraḥ u-MiMa'arav* 4:24 = Rosenthal, p. 42; see also Rosenthal, p. 66) and Rome ms. 53 (p. 23a = Pos. "Mordecai of Avignon" ms., p. 24 = Rosenthal's "Menaḥem," p. 68) cite Genesis

L

37:35, as does Rupert of Deutz, *Dialogus*, PL 170.570. Jacob ben Reuben (pp. 51-52) and the author of Rome ms. 53 (pp. 23 a-b = Pos. "Mordecai of Avignon" ms., pp. 24-25 = Rosenthal's "Menaḥem," p. 69) argue, like N.V., that *sheol* means grave and also cite Job 14:13. Moreover, Jacob ben Reuben suggests that Jacob considered the death of his children during his lifetime proof that he was a sinner, although he goes on to say that he proposes this interpretation only when granting for the sake of argument that *sheol* means hell. Yosef HaMeqanne suggests a related explanation, maintaining that Jacob considered himself responsible for Joseph's death. Cf. Rashi, ad loc., for a view that *sheol* is the grave as well as an explanation based on Jacob's alleged conviction that he would avoid hell only if none of his children died during his lifetime. See the references cited by Rosenthal in *Mil. HaShem*, p. 52, and Kasher's discussion of various parallels and some polemical sources in *Torah Shelemah* ad loc., pp. 1438-39, no. 204; cf. also *Mil. Miẓvah*, Parma ms., pp. 122b-123a. On the question of universal damnation for the sin of Adam, see also below, pp. 218-19.

Page 58

20   ***The birthright nevertheless remained with Esau*** Cf. p. 55 and the notes there (on Genesis 25:25).

33   ***Absalom*** See the *Altercatio Simonis Judaei et Theophili Christiani* for a Jewish statement conceding that any analogy between the hanging of Jesus and that of Absalom or Haman is invalid. Such analogies, then, were apparently current (PL 20.1174 = *CSEL* 45.25-26, cited in *Auteurs*, p. 30).

Page 59

5   ***The explanation of this passage. . . .*** This interpretation is taken from B. *Hullin* 92a.

12   **Vayeḥi Yaʻaqov** Genesis 47:28—50:26.

13   ***If "there is a mother to tradition"*** I.e., if the text may be read without regard to the traditional vocalization. See B. *Kiddushin* 18b; *Sanhedrin* 4a-b; *Makkot* 7b.

17   ***Staff*** For a staff as the cross, see *Trypho* 86 and cf. N.V., pp. 65, 72. The reading *matteh* is found in the Septuagint here and is also reflected in Hebrews 11:21.

26   ***He made a kind of cross*** So Isidore, *Quaestiones*, PL 83.277; Bede [pseud.], *Commentarii* ad loc., PL 91.273; *Gloss* ad loc. (all using identical language). This argument is also mentioned by the Christian in *Mil. HaShem*, p. 50 (see Rosenthal's note there) and in *Sefer Yosef HaMeqanne, MiMizraḥ u-MiMaʻarav* 4:24 = Rosenthal, p. 43. See also Poznanski, *Perush ʻal Yeḥezqel*, introd., p. 36.

Page 60

5   ***An acrostic*** The two Jewish acrostics cited here are attributed in a number of sources to R. Jacob Tam (1110-71), who was responding to the Christian acrostic mentioned here. See Posnanski, *Schiloh*, p. 137, appendix, pp. xix-xx; Berliner, *Peletat Soferim*, Heb. sec., p. 35; *Leqet Qaẓar, Michael* 4 (1976): 67. These

L

acrostics are also cited in the *Ta'anot* of Moses of Salerno (*Schiloh*, appendix, pp. xxi–xxii = Pos. ms., p. 30).

19–20   **"The messenger"** This is based on the Vulgate's "qui mittendus est." Some Jews felt that this translation resulted from a misreading of the Hebrew *Shiloh* through the substitution of a *ḥet* for the *he*, a process which produces the root meaning to send. See Berliner, *Peletat Soferim*, Heb. sec., p. 35; cf. R. Samuel ben Meir's commentary, *Perush HaTorah*, ed. D. Rosin (Breslau, 1881), pp. 71–72, cited by Rosenthal, "Anti-Christian Polemic," p. 126; *Leqet Qazar, Michael* 4 (1976): 68.

21–22   **When Jesus came the kingdom of Judah ceased** This was the basic Christian argument in this *locus classicus* of polemic. A chronological summary of Christian treatments of this verse can be found in Posnanski, *Schiloh*, pp. 288–449. See also S. Zimmels, "Zur Geschichte der Exegese über den Vers Genesis 49.10," *Magazin für die Wissenschaft des Judenthums* 17, 19, 20 (1890, 1892, 1893); *Juifs et Chrétiens*, pp. 227–37; E.I.J. Rosenthal in *Kirche und Synagoge*, ed. Karl Rengstorff and Siegfried von Kortzfleisch (Stuttgart, 1967), 1:315–17 (where he deals mainly with the meanings of the words in the verse). For the use of this verse in Muslim polemic, see Perlmann, *Ifḥam al-Yahud*, pp. 41–42.

28–29   **There was, after all, no king in Israel from the time of Zedekiah** This was probably the most effective Jewish response regarding this verse, partly because it minimized the polemical necessity of presenting a plausible alternate explanation of what was undeniably a difficult passage. In effect, the Jewish polemicist could maintain that whatever the meaning of the verse, the Christian interpretation is clearly wrong.

Bodo-Eleazar proposed this basic argument (see *Auteurs*, p. 185), while Yosef HaMeqanne cited it in almost the exact form in which it is found in N.V. (*MiMizraḥ u-MiMa'arav* 4:24 = Rosenthal, p. 44). See also Naḥmanides' disputation, *Ketavei Ramban*, ed. Ch. Chavel (Jerusalem, 1963), 1:304, and Solomon ibn Adret, *Perushei Aggadot LaRashba*, in *R. Salomo ben Abraham ben Adereth*, ed. J. Perles (Breslau, 1863), p. 55. Moses of Salerno made the same point, while emphasizing the fact that the Hasmoneans were priests and thus not from the tribe of Judah (*Ta'anot*, quoted in *Schiloh*, appendix, p. xxi). Cf. Naḥmanides' commentary ad loc. for a non-polemical discussion of the priestly origin of the Hasmoneans in light of this verse.

Christian efforts to deal with this problem go back to Justin Martyr, who argued that even during the Babylonian exile there were at least prophets, and even if Herod was an illegitimate king, there was a high priest (*Trypho*, chapter 52). The most complete discussion of this issue is in a series of tractates by Fulbert of Chartres, who maintained that all leaders of the Jews (even during the Babylonian exile) were at least of Jewish descent until Herod, who was the first stranger to lead them. (See his tractates 2 and 3, PL 141.308 ff., cited in *Auteurs*, pp. 239, 241. So also Peter of Blois, *Contra Perfidiam Judaeorum*, PL 207.842; Alan of Lille, *Contra Haereticos*, PL 210.412. It is of interest to note that as a result of Jesus' birth near

L

the end of Herod's reign, Justin considers the latter's foreign descent a problem while Fulbert, Peter of Blois, and Alan of Lille cite it as evidence. Peter the Venerable simply says that kingship was taken away after Herod [PL 189.562].) As Fulbert knew, however, the concession that this verse refers to leaders other than a king was a trap, since Jews could then maintain that this sort of leadership had never ended; hence his later argument that even the king was with them during the Babylonian exile. (See *Auteurs*, p. 243, and cf. p. 238. Note N.V., p. 62, and the notes there).

Page 61

14   *This genealogy* On Jesus' genealogy, see N.V., pp. 90-91, 107, 167-68.

24-25   *From the time of this Jesus we . . . have wandered about. . . .* A similar argument is recorded in Berliner, *Peletat Soferim* (Hebrew section, p. 29), where R. Meir b. Yeḥezqel maintains that according to the view that Judah would lose power after Shiloh comes, this verse would be a curse. The truth is, however, that Jacob obviously intended to bless Judah, and since he was a prophet, it is inconceivable that negative consequences could have resulted from this verse. In this connection, R. Meir asks the rhetorical question, "Was our father Jacob a prophet or not?" This was probably an intentional reversal of a common Christian argument that, in effect, Jews consider the prophets liars. See John 5:45-47; Petrus Alfonsi's *Dialogus*, PL 157.618 (Christians believe in the incarnation because they don't consider the prophets liars); Rupert's *Dialogus*, PL 170.596 ("O Judaee, quaecumque loquuntur Scripturae aut vera sunt aut non; sed dicere quis audeat quia non vera sunt?"); the *Tractatus* in *TNA* 5.1511 ("Aut Scriptura mentitur, quod dicere nefas est . . . "), 1513 = PL 213.751, 753. This argument appears in connection with this very verse in two seventh-century Greek disputations and in Peter of Blois. See *Doctrina Jacobi Nuper Baptizati*, ed. N. Bonwetsch (Berlin, 1910), pp. 20-21 and p. 65 (ἐὰν οὐκ ἦλθεν ὁ χριστός, ψεύδεται ὁ προφήτης); *Les Trophées de Damas*, ed. G. Bardy, *Pat. Orientalia* 15, p. 240 (τὸν πατριαρχὰν ψευστὴν ἐποίησας); Peter of Blois, *Contra Perfidiam Judaeorum*, PL 207.842 ("Aut ergo Jacob reprehende mendacii, aut ejus prophetiae consenti et confitere venisse Christum . . . "). For other Jewish uses of the argument that accepting Christianity would imply that the prophets had lied, see Meir of Narbonne, *Mil. Miẓvah*, Parma ms., p. 112b; Moses of Salerno, Pos. ms., p. 44; Rome ms. 53, p. 21b = Pos. "Mordecai of Avignon" ms., p. 10 = Rosenthal's "Menaḥem," p. 64.

26-27   *Judah and Israel . . . are the believers in Jesus* See N.V., pp. 126-27 and the notes there for a discussion of the "verus Israel" question.

34   *The final section. . . .* Literally: "This is the end of the verse according to their words." This probably means that the verse can be explained satisfactorily even granted that *Shiloh* means messenger. The author is also conceding that *shevet* means scepter and *meḥoqeq*, legislator; cf. p. 60 for a different interpretation of these words.

L

Page 62

3-4   ***Princes, communal leaders, and rabbis*** The view that *shevet* and *mehoqeq* refer
to leaders other than kings goes back to the Talmud: " 'The scepter (*shevet*) shall
not pass from Judah'—these are the Babylonian exilarchs who rule Israel with
their staff (*shevet*); 'nor the lawgiver (*mehoqeq*) from between his feet'—these are
the descendants of Hillel, who teach the Torah in public" (*B. Sanhedrin* 5a). Bodo-
Eleazar maintained that *shevet* meant tribe and *mehoqeq*, scholar (PL 121.484, cited in
Auteurs, p. 186), while the basic rabbinic view appears in the works of R. Joseph
Bekhor Shor ad loc. (quoted in Posnanski, *Schiloh*, appendix, p. xvii), Joseph Kimhi
(*Mil. Hovah*, p. 24b = Talmage's ed., p. 36, quoted in *Schiloh*, appendix, pp. xix–xx),
who emphasized the Latin translation *dux*, and Moses of Salerno (quoted in *Schiloh*,
appendix, p. xxi). Some writers resorted to this interpretation to explain the lack of
a king from Judah before David (R. Joseph Bekhor Shor, loc. cit.); indeed, Solomon
de' Rossi, *'Edut HaShem Ne'emanah*, Rosenthal's *Mehqarim*, 1:401, uses this lack of a
king from Judah until David to prove that *shevet* here cannot refer to kingship. The
fact that Saul himself was not from the tribe of Judah was especially troublesome to
those who interpreted Genesis 49:10 as a reference to royalty or even to the major
leader of the Jews; see Nahmanides' commentary ad loc. In fact, this difficulty led
Peter of Blois into a strikingly ambiguous use of the term *Judaeus* in his discussion
of this verse: "Examine history and you will find that Zedekiah was the last king
from the tribe of Judah; afterwards, there were still leaders [or "princes": *duces*]
from the tribe until Herod the son of Antipater. Tell me, then, wretched Jew, if from
the time of Saul there was anyone who ruled the Jews, whether king or leader [*dux*],
who was not a *Judaeus*, until Herod" (*Contra Perfidiam Judaeorum*, PL 207.842). Note
the transition from the phrase "from the tribe of Judah" in the first sentence to the
marvelously ambiguous *Judaeus* in the second. If *Judaeus* means from the tribe of
Judah, then "from the time of Saul" (*a tempore Saulis*) means "from *after* the time of
Saul"; this raises the problem of why the first king was not from the tribe of Judah.
If, on the other hand, *Judaeus* means Jew, then all the kings of Israel (including Saul)
up to the time of Herod are included; this, however, obscures the fact that Genesis
49:10 quite clearly refers to the tribe.

     Some Christians accepted the view that Genesis 49:10 can refer to some-
thing less than kingship in order to explain the Babylonian exile and much of the
period of the second Temple. As I indicated above, however, this was a trap since
Jews immediately countered with the observation that such leadership still exists
or at least did not cease with Jesus (cf. Nahmanides' remark after Pablo had cited *B.
Sanhedrin* 5a as evidence—*Ketavei Ramban*, 1:305). Peter the Venerable (PL 189.560)
tried to deal with this by asserting that a legitimate Jewish *dux* must be in a Jewish
kingdom in Palestine. On the contrast between kingship (*melukhah*) and rule
(*serarah*), cf. also G. Cohen, *The Book of Tradition*, p. 137, and "Esau as Symbol," p.
30. See also the entry "Genesis 49:10" in the index to A. Zuckerman, *A Jewish
Princedom in Feudal France, 768–900* (New York and London, 1972).

L

14   **R. Isaac the proselyte** Reading *hagger* rather than *hagar*. The latter reading was defended by Posnanski and others (see *Schiloh*, p. 138), but cf. the evidence cited by Urbach, "Études sur la littérature polémique au moyen âge," pp. 74-75. It is true that most proselytes took the name Abraham, but Urbach suggests that a father and son may have converted together and taken the names of Abraham and Isaac. Cf. especially the references cited in Rosenthal's introduction to *Sefer Yosef HaMeqanne*, p. 27.

22   **R. Samuel** Perhaps R. Samuel b. Solomon of Falaise (ca. 1175-1250); see Posnanski, *Schiloh*, p. 133.

24   **Peace and quiet** So *Sefer Yosef HaMeqanne, MiMizrah u-MiMa'arav* 4:28 = Rosenthal, p. 45 (quoted in *Schiloh*, appendix, p. xxii).

26   **Just as a lioness crouches over her cubs . . .** Precisely this explanation is expounded in some detail by Isidore in his *Quaestiones*, PL 83.279, and more briefly (without the explanation of the three days) in *De Fide Cath.*, I.44.1, PL 83.488.

35   **We too are like the dead in our exile. . . .** The third chapter of Lamentations was interpreted collectively in the midrash; see *Lam. Rabbah* ad loc. Cf. also Ibn Ezra on Isa. 26:19.

Page 63

4   **Ve'elleh Shemot** Exodus 1:1—6:1.

5   **"A bush all aflame"** The Christological interpretation of this vision is suggested in Augustine, *Quaestiones, CC, Ser. Lat.*, 33, p. 71, and affirmed in pseudo-Bede, *Commentarii*, PL 91.293-94; idem, *Quaestiones*, PL 93.306; Raban Maur, PL 108.19. Yosef HaMeqanne reports that R. Joseph of Chartres was asked by a priest why God chose a bush for his revelation, a question that was undoubtedly intended to lay the basis for a christological interpretation, and that he answered that a bush cannot be used to make a cross (*Festschrift A. Berliner's*, p. 82 = Rosenthal, p. 45).

9   **That is why he revealed himself at the bush** See Rashi ad loc., s.v. *mitokh haSeneh*. The bush was regarded as a symbol of humility; God lowered himself in order to suffer, as it were, with the Jewish people.

16   **"Make someone else your messenger."** . . . This Christian interpretation as well as N.V.'s answer are reflected in Rupert's *Dialogus*, PL 170.567, 584. Rupert explains that God's subsequent anger is a result of Jewish sin—specifically, the selling of Joseph—which caused him to delay the sending of the messenger, while the Jew asks whether it was *Moses* who sold Joseph and therefore deserved to have God's anger directed at him.

24   **"Until Shiloh comes"** Shiloh here is taken to mean messenger; cf. p. 60.

28   **R. Abraham the proselyte** Probably the same man quoted in *Tosafot Kiddushin* 71a. See Urbach, "Études sur la littérature polémique au moyen âge," p. 73.

L

Page 64

1   ***By magic*** Cf. pp. 68, 104. See also *B. Sanhedrin* 43a (in *Diqduqei Soferim*); *B. Shabbat* 104b (which many Jews took as a reference to Jesus); Matt. 9:34. The view that Jesus performed wonders through magic is found in *Toledot Yeshu*, passim. See Krauss, *Das Leben Jesu nach Jüdischen Quellen.* It should be noted, however, that in *Toledot Yeshu* the magic is performed by means of the divine name while here the two are contrasted. On *Toledot Yeshu*, see also *Ver. Israel*, pp. 189-90; M. Goldstein, *Jesus in the Jewish Tradition* (New York, 1950), pp.147-66. For Christian awareness of this sort of literature in medieval France, see Agobard's *De Judaicis Superstitionibus*, PL 104.77-100 = MGH, Ep. 5.188-99, and the summary in *Auteurs*, pp. 165-66. Agobard there reports a Jewish view that the saints' miracles were performed by the devil. (See also Merchavia, *HaTalmud BiRe'i HaNazrut,* pp. 328-30.)

The Jewish view that the saints employed magic is considered by Peter the Venerable, and he rejects it on the grounds that the apostles were not learned men and therefore could neither learn nor teach magic. Indeed, it takes a longer time to master magic than the apostles spent with Jesus (PL 189.594-95). He also argues that the nature and quality of Christian miracles rule out the possibility that they were brought about by magic (PL 189.595 ff.). The Rome ms. here adds that "Maharam" (perhaps the famous R. Meir of Rothenburg [thirteenth century]) concurred in the view of R. Abraham the proselyte.

Both Moses of Salerno (Posnanski ms., p. 45) and Meir of Narbonne (Parma ms., pp. 25b, 95b, 113a) pointed out that the Pharisees of Jesus' own time were convinced that he performed his "miracles" through magic, and Meir noted that their reliability on this point is assured by the fact that only experts in magic could be appointed to the Sanhedrin (see *B. Sanhedrin* 17a and *B. Menahot* 65a). The Jewish view that Jesus "learned God's great name" and thus performed wonders is also cited in Perlmann, *Ifham al-Yahud,* p. 42.

For an analogous view regarding the lofty status of Moses' generation in the "spiritual arts," cf. Nahmanides' sermon "Torat HaShem Temimah," *Ketavei Ramban,* 1:147.

2   ***He was in Egypt for two years*** See Matt. 2:14. The Jewish assertion that Jesus learned magic in Egypt is also mentioned in Origen, *Contra Celsum* 1:28, cited in Williams, p. 82.

3   ***Ten measures of magic. . . .*** *B. Kiddushin* 49b.

6   **Bo El Par'oh** Exodus 10:1—13:16.

12   ***The blood of Abraham's circumcision. . . .*** Cf. p. 53 and the notes there. Note especially *Shemot Rabbah* 17:3: "The Jews were redeemed from Egypt because of two types of blood—the blood of the paschal lamb and the blood of circumcision, as it is written, 'And I said to you, In your blood live, and I said to you, In your blood live'—in the blood of the paschal lamb and in the blood of circumcision." Since the author of N.V. had to explain three types of blood, he adapted this midrash by in-

L

cluding the word "blood" found in the first part of the verse. See also *Mekhilta Bo*, chapter 7. This midrash was also cited by Maimonides in his *Iggeret HaShemad*, appended to A. Geiger's *Mose ben Maimon* (Breslau, 1850), p. 1a.

Exodus 12:22 is referred to as a sign of the passion in *De Fide Cath.*, I.40.1, PL 83.487. For the blood here as a symbol of the cross, see *Trypho* 111 (and especially Archambault's note there, *Dialogue avec Tryphon*, 2:171). Cf. also pseudo-Chrysostom, cited in Williams, p. 140.

20   **Dorschwell** The accuracy of this transliteration of the Hebrew transliteration is uncertain; the modern German form is *Türschwelle*. The Rome manuscript says *Dorpel*.

22-23   ***"You shall keep watch over it. . . ."*** For this Christian interpretation in some detail see Raban Maur, PL 108.48. Jesus, he argues, came to Jerusalem on the tenth day of the month and was betrayed after four days.

30   ***Why were those who killed him punished?*** Cf. p. 122 and esp. p. 136 and the notes there. For a detailed discussion of Exodus 12, see pp. 53–54.

Page 65

13   **Vayehi Beshallaḥ** Exodus 13:17—17:16.

14   ***Israel was baptized in the sea*** Augustine wrote that Christians are pursued by sin until they are baptized, just as the Israelites were pursued by the Egyptians until the Red Sea (*Sermo* 4.8.9, cited in *Judenpredigt*, p. 128). Other writers pointed to the crossing of the sea as a prefiguration of baptism by citing a further analogy between the "redness" of the sea and Jesus' blood. See Isidore, *Quaestiones*, PL 83.296 ("Rubrum mare significat baptismum, Christi sanguine consecratum"). See also Bede [pseud.], PL 91.310; Raban Maur, PL 108.66. A different view of the crossing of the Red Sea was expressed by Cesar of Arles, *Sermo* 104, *CC, Ser. Lat.*, 103, pp. 429–33. See also I Cor. 10:2.

15   ***We have already explained*** But he did not. Presumably, the author of his source had done so in a passage omitted here. This is one of many indications that N.V. is, at least in part, an anthology; cf. the introduction, pp. 35–36.

For a Jewish response to the Christian view regarding the splitting of the sea, cf. *Sefer Yosef HaMeqanne, Festschrift A. Berliner's*, pp. 82–83 = Rosenthal, p. 47 = Berliner, *Peletat Soferim*, Hebrew section, p. 30. Meir of Narbonne pointed out that the Jews walked on dry land (Parma ms., pp. 45a, 122a) and that in any event they were commanded regarding circumcision (which was supposedly replaced by baptism) after they had passed through the sea.

19-20   ***The wood was a cross*** So *Trypho*, chapter 86; Augustine, *Quaestiones, CC, Ser. Lat.*, 33, p. 95; Prudentius, cited in Williams, p. 213; Bede [pseud.], PL 91.312; Raban Maur, PL 108.76. See also *Sefer Yosef HaMeqanne, Festschrift A. Berliner's*, p. 83 = Rosenthal, p. 47, for the argument that it should have said "pieces of wood" in the plural if this were a prefiguration of the cross. Cf. also Rosenthal, p. 92. N.V.'s

L

argument, which was at most half serious, was that Moses was disposing of the wood (i.e., the cross) when he threw it into the water.

27   **Vayishma' Yitro** Exodus 18:1-21:1.

Page 66

1   *That one must not sin* From the earliest times, Christian writers distinguished between a temporal and eternal Sabbath and argued that the temporal one had been superseded; see *Trypho*, chapter 12 and Tertullian, *Adversus Judaeos*, chapter 4, PL 2.605-7 = Tränkle, pp. 9-10. The most common interpretation of this Sabbath was "rest in Christ" at the end of days rather than refraining from sin. Cf. Bede [pseud.], PL 91.318; Raban Maur, PL 108.99; Isidore's *Quaestiones* (PL 83.336) and Damian's *Dialogus* (PL 145.57-58) cited in my "St. Peter Damian," pp. 100-101. However, the view reflected in N.V. that observing the Sabbath consists of refraining from evil deeds and pursuing righteousness was also expressed quite frequently. See the citation from Augustine in *Judenpredigt*, p. 153; Gregory the Great, PL 77.1253-54, cited in *Auteurs*, pp. 83-84; Raban Maur, PL 108.102; Damian's *Dialogus*, loc. cit.; Rupert's *Dialogus*, PL 170.590; Peter of Blois, PL 207.856. See also Evrard of Béthune's remark that rest on the Sabbath prefigures Jesus' rest in the grave on that day (*Contra Valdenses*, in Marguerin de la Bigne, *Maxima Bibliotheca Veterum Patrum et Antiquorum Scriptorum Ecclesiasticorum* 24 [Lyon, 1677], p. 1582.) On the entire subject of eternal vs. temporal law, see *Judenpredigt*, pp. 131-33.

3   **Ve'elleh HaMishpatim** Exodus 21:1—24:18.

9   *This refers to Jesus* See *Trypho*, chapter 75; Tertullian, *Adversus Judaeos*, chapter 9, PL 2.622-23 = Tränkle, p. 24; Cyprian, *Testimonia* 2:5; Augustine, *Quaestiones, CC, Ser. Lat.*, 33, p. 116; pseudo-Augustine and Maximin of Hippo, cited in Williams, pp. 310, 320; Raban Maur, PL 108.130; Joachim da Fiore, *Adversus Judaeos*, p. 13. This identification was based in part on the phrase, "Since my name is in him," because the name of God was part of Jesus' Hebrew name; in fact, the Rome manuscript here specifically notes that "when he was Jewish he was called Yehoshua (God saves)."

10-11   *Moses and all Israel . . . were unwilling to accept him. . . .* The same argument is raised in *B. Sanhedrin* 38b with regard to this "angel." Cf. *Ver. Israel*, p. 232.

27   *"He will not pardon your offenses"* This argument is also raised in the Talmud, loc. cit. Yosef HaMeqanne (Rome ms., p. 9a) quotes this verse as proof that no man can forgive sin.

32   *An angel can perform only his mission* See p. 49 and the notes there. The meaning seems to be that God himself must punish their enemies, since this was not part of the angel's mission; on the other hand, punishing the Jews for their offenses was part of the mission. I am, however, somewhat tempted to emend the text to "this is *not* part of his mission"; i.e., he was not empowered to pardon the offenses of the Jews.

L

Page 67

3   **Ki Tissa** Exodus 30:11—34:35.

7   *A rabbinic midrash* See B. *Shabbat* 89a, where Satan is said to have shown them an image of Moses' bed, and cf. Rashi ad loc. for precisely the version found in N.V. See also *Torah Shelemah* ad loc., p. 83, no. 2.

11   *The "mixed multitude"* See Rashi on Exodus 32:4.

16   *Cherubim* See pp. 72-73 and the notes there. The point here may be that the "god" they had in mind was *like* the cherubim in that it was not truly idolatrous.

17   *R. Nathan Official* A thirteenth-century French polemicist.

29   *They saw the calf walking by itself. . . .* For the notion of an animated calf, see *Pirqei deRabbi Eliezer* 25 ("Satan entered it and mooed in order to mislead Israel") and cf. *Torah Shelemah* on Exodus 32, p. 89, no. 26* and p. 138, no. 104. See also Ginzberg, *Legends of the Jews*, 3:122-23, and 4:51-52, notes 266, 267. Some Christian heretics considered the calf Satan incarnate; see Baron, *A Social and Religious History of the Jews*, 9:58.

33   *Perhaps the spirit of God has entered it* In *Sefer Yosef HaMeqanne*, where the same story appears, an important phrase is added to this answer; the Jews are said to have believed that the divinity *which left Moses* entered the calf (*Festschrift A. Berliner's*, pp. 83-84 = Rosenthal, p. 50 = Berliner, *Peletat Soferim*, Heb. sec., pp. 31-32). The view that the golden calf was a surrogate for Moses and not for God was developed in detail in the commentaries of Ibn Ezra and Naḥmanides to Exodus 32:1 and probably was a central part of R. Nathan's argument. The whole argument in this passage is found in Rome ms. 53, pp. 23b-24a = Pos. "Mordecai of Avignon" ms., pp. 26-28 = Rosenthal's "Menaḥem," pp. 69-70, but without the format of a discussion between Nathan Official and Christians.

Page 68

11   *That stinking place* See appendix 2.

17   *This alludes to the curtain hung over our face* Posnanski points to 2 Corinthians 3:13-18 where this explicit point is made. See also Bede [pseud.], ad loc., PL 91.332; Raban Maur, PL 108.239; Peter the Venerable, PL 189.574; the dialogue attributed to William of Champeaux, PL 163.1047. This was a common theme in the representation of Jews in medieval art. See B. Blumenkranz, *Le Juif Médiéval au Miroir de L'art Chrétien* (Paris, 1966), pp. 52-54, 64, and W. Seiferth, *Synagogue and Church in the Middle Ages* (New York, 1970), pp. 95-109. Cf. the references in Ermengaud's *Breviari d'Amor* cited by Blumenkranz in *Cahiers de Fanjeaux* 12 (1977): 303, 311-12. On Jewish blindness, see also Romans 11:7-10. Samuel of Morocco (PL 149.551) compiled a whole list of verses demonstrating the stupidity and blindness of the Jews, while Adam of Perseigne (*Epistola* 21, PL 211, especially c. 654) argued that this blindness is so intense that disputing with them is futile.

30   *King Henry* Probably Henry III. So M. Wiener, "Geschichte der Juden in der Stadt und Diöcese Speyer," *MGWJ* 12 (1863): 162, and H.H. Ben Sasson,

L

Toledot Am Yisrael II (Tel Aviv, 1969), p. 165. (Wiener identifies R. Kalonymus as the liturgical poet Kalonymus ben Moses.) Posnanski, on the other hand, thinks that the king here is Henry IV. Needless to say, this discussion of the king's identity does not necessarily presuppose the acceptance of the historicity of this encounter.

31   **Church** The Hebrew here transliterates the medieval German word *Thum,* which can mean church; in Hebrew transliteration, however, it means abyss, and the pun was almost certainly intentional.

Page 69

34-35   *They wallow in licentiousness in secret* See also p. 223. This is one of the more extreme charges made against Christians, but Jewish polemicists took a dim view of Christian morality in general and monastic morality in particular. Later on, the author of N.V. refers to "priests and nuns who burn in their lustful desire but are unable to consummate it." Despite the fact that the translation there is not absolutely certain, it is apparently a reference to priests and nuns who were genuinely chaste; consequently, although the charge is less serious, it is a more basic critique of the monastic ideal itself. Later still, he accuses monks of intemperance and monasteries of unfair appropriation of land (pp. 98-99). These last two charges are found in *Mil. HaShem* as well (p. 146), where Jacob ben Reuben remarks that such behavior constitutes a violation not only of the "law of justice" but also of "the law of grace." (Cf. the satirical comment by Meir of Narbonne that the Christians make clear by their behavior that they take even the moral commandments of the Gospels allegorically—text in S. Stein, *JJS* 11 [1959]: 52.)

A particularly blunt statement of Jewish moral superiority is found in *Sefer Yosef HaMeqanne* (*Festschrift A. Berliner's*, p. 90 = Rosenthal, p. 62) where R. Nathan Official is quoted as telling a priest, "We angered God with those inferior to him, and he paid us back in kind, as it is written, 'They incensed me with no-gods . . . and I will incense them with a no-folk; I will provoke them with a vile nation' (Deut. 32:21). If there were a viler nation than you he would have subjected us to them." (Kahn points out in his note there that *Da'at Zeqenim MiBa'alei HaTosafot* ad loc. refers this verse to two monastic orders. See also Rosenthal's note ad loc., and cf. N.V., p. 75). R. Joseph Kimḥi detailed the areas of Jewish superiority in an elaborate passage to which the Christian is said to have given some degree of assent (*Sefer HaBerit, Mil. Ḥovah*, pp. 20b-21a = Talmage's ed., pp. 25-27). See also the reworking of this passage in Rome ms. 53, p. 22b = Pos. "Mordecai of Avignon" ms., pp. 19-20 = Rosenthal's "Menaḥem" p. 67. Note also Rosenthal's citations in *Mil. HaShem*, p. 91, and in his "Haganah VeHatqafah," pp. 349-52; see also the notes to p. 133 below regarding monastic usury.

Jewish writers occasionally traced Christian immorality to the failings inherent in Christian doctrine and not only to the failings of Christian individuals. In *Trypho* chapter 10, for example, we have the first indication of the argument that

L

the ethics of the Gospels are impossible to observe; they are, Trypho is said to argue, too "marvelous and great" (θαυμαστὰ . . . καὶ μεγάλα). In N.V. (p. 116), we find the more extreme contention that the doctrine of vicarious atonement frees believing Christians of punishment no matter what they do. (Note also the twist on this argument by the Jew in Rupert's *Dialogus* [PL 170.573], who maintained that faith should make even baptism itself unnecessary.)

Page 70

2   ***Scripture is fond of playing on words*** I.e., the primary meaning of *saris* here is nobleman, but the prophet speaks of "a place and a name better than of sons and daughters" because he is playing on its secondary meaning of eunuch. As for Haman, his wife and children are evidence that he was not a eunuch.

5-6   ***Having children is a characteristic of the God-fearing man*** The Jews regarded Genesis 1:28 ("Be fruitful and multiply") as a positive commandment. Isidore's *Quaestiones*, chapter 48:1 (cited in *Auteurs*, p. 98) records a Jewish argument in favor of large families; Blumenkranz correctly points out (ibid., note 79) that although Isidore's specific argument is of questionable authenticity since it is based on a Septuagint reading, the likelihood is that arguments of this type were invoked by Jews. See especially Aphraates, Dem. 18, Neusner's *Aphrahat*, pp. 76-77, and *Sefer Nestor HaKomer*, p. 8.

12-13   ***Does God really consider it an abhorrent act. . . ?*** This argument almost surely does not reflect the author's true understanding of the verse since he clearly viewed the injunction against such behavior literally. On the other hand, the ideal of martyrdom and, indeed, slaughter of children to prevent their forcible baptism had become central in the thought of Ashkenazic Jewry by this period; moreover, this ideal was consciously and explicitly modeled after the binding of Isaac. Consequently, this statement does reflect a genuine element in the author's psyche. See J. R. Marcus, *The Jew in the Medieval World* (Cleveland-New York-Philadelphia, 1960), pp. 116-20; Ben-Sasson, *Peraqim beToledot HaYehudim Bimei HaBeinayim*, pp. 174-85; Jacob Katz, *Exclusiveness and Tolerance* (New York, 1961), pp. 82-92; and Shalom Spiegel, *The Last Trial* (Philadelphia, 1967), passim. See also below, pp. 216-18.

16-17   ***Burning refers to the priests and nuns who burn up in their lustful desire. . . .*** It should be noted that an old Karaite interpretation took the prohibition of giving one's seed to Molekh (Leviticus 18:21, 20:3) as a reference to illicit sexual relations (with idolaters). However, this exegesis involved taking the phrase "giving one's seed" in a literal, sexual sense, and it was emphasized that fire is not mentioned in either of the above verses. Consequently, although we cannot rule out the possibility that N.V. has reported a distorted version of this interpretation, any direct influence is highly unlikely. For the citation of Hosea 7:4-6 to show that lust is symbolized by fire, see *Sefer Ḥasidim*, ed. J. Wistinetsky (Frankfurt am Main, 1924), no. 43, p. 42.

L

27-28   ***The heretics distort this verse.*** . . . .See Raban Maur, *Expositiones in Lev.*, PL
108.555.

34   ***As I have written*** Cf., e.g., pp. 52-54.

Page 71

1   ***God divorced you*** This specific image of a divorce ("repudii libellum")
given the Jews by God is found, for example, in *De Fide Cath.*, II.11.1, PL 83.517, and
Damian's *Epistola* 13, PL 144.287. See my "St. Peter Damian," p. 88, and cf. Isa. 50:1.

5   ***Hosea*** A mistake. Cf. p. 150 where a quotation from Psalms is attributed
to Ecclesiastes.

13-14   ***How, then, did all the members of Jesus' generation see him and live?*** This
Jewish question is cited in a number of Christian polemics. See Albert of Metz
(early eleventh century), *De Diversitate Temporum*, chapter 24, cited in *Auteurs*, p.
249; Crispin's *Disputatio*, p. 43 (see appendix 2); Rupert's *Dialogus*, PL 170.603.
Tertullian had taken cognizance of this problem by remarking that this verse refers
only to the father (*Adversus Judaeos*, chapter 9, PL 2.622 = Tränkle, p. 24), while
Rupert's answer was that the divine *substantia* was not seen even during the incarnation (PL 170.604). See also *Sefer Nestor HaKomer*, p. 7; *Sefer HaBerit*, Mil. Ḥovah, p.
22a = Talmage's ed., p. 29; Solomon de' Rossi, '*Edut HaShem Ne'emanah*, Rosenthal's *Meḥqarim*, 1:381 (and cf. ibid., p. 412).

17-18   ***He may attempt to point out a contradiction by citing Isaiah.*** . . . So Albert of
Metz, loc. cit. Cf. also the citation in Williams, pp. 310-11, and the *Tractatus* in *TNA*
5.1554-5 = PL 213.794-95. The major source of this passage is *B. Yevamot* 49b:
"Manasseh killed Isaiah. Rava said that he judged him and executed him.
Manasseh told him, 'Your teacher Moses said, "For man may not see me and live,"
while you said, "I saw the Lord sitting upon a throne, high and lifted up." ' . . . In
any event, the verses do seem to contradict each other. 'I saw the Lord' can be explained in light of what we have learned that all the prophets looked in a nonluminous mirror while Moses looked in a luminous mirror." Rashi ad loc. explains that
the other prophets mistakenly thought that they had seen the divine countenance,
but Moses knew that he had not. Cf. also R. Samuel b. Meir's commentary to
Genesis 48:8. N.V.'s utilization of this talmudic response is complicated by the
citation of Numbers 12:8 (regarding Moses himself) in the question; the author
may be assuming that the "likeness" in that verse is not the divine countenance itself. It may well be that he felt the need to give another answer because of this
difficulty.

    Rupert of Deutz reflects an awareness of the talmudic story of Isaiah and
Manasseh and specifically of the latter's citation of the contradiction between
Exodus 33:20 and Isaiah 6:1. He argues that the story constitutes evidence of the
systematic Jewish persecution of the prophets for any reference to Jesus; conse-
quently, he says, they were forced to speak in riddles (PL 170.585). Cf. also *Mil.
HaShem*, p. 84.

L

27   **One may also respond.** . . . I.e., a prophet can see God and live provided that he beheld God for the purpose of his mission. Presumably, Moses' request here was not for the purpose of his mission. The basis of this response is in *Sifra*: "R. Dosa said, 'It is written, "For man may not see me and live"; in their lifetime they do not see, but they do at the time of death. Similarly, it says, "All they that go down to the dust shall bow before him, and none can keep alive his own soul." ' " See *Torah Shelemah* ad loc. for this and other relevant references.

Page 72

1-2   **Twice to symbolize the cross** Augustine quotes 1 Corinthians 10:4 for the view that the rock is Jesus. He then adds that the staff represents the cross, especially in light of the fact that the rock was struck twice and the cross is made of two pieces of wood (*Quaestiones, CC, Ser. Lat.,* 33, pp. 260-61). See also *Trypho*, chapters 86, 138; pseudo-Chrysostom, cited in Williams, p. 140.

5-6   **It is, however, written of Jacob.** . . . Albert of Metz cites this verse in this connection (*De Diversitate Temporum*, chapter 24). See above, p. 71 and the notes there.

13   **This was said of Mary** The argument was that Mary had borne Jesus without intercourse just as the staff bore fruit without a tree (Bede [pseud.], PL 91.367). Cf. *Trypho*, loc. cit. Other Christian authors cited this miracle as proof that God can effect a "virgin birth" without arguing that the one actually prefigures the other. Cf. Hildefonsus [pseud.], Sermon 13, PL 96.281-82, cited in *Auteurs*, p. 117; Paul Alvarus, Epistle 18, cited in *Auteurs*, p. 189; the *Dialogus* attributed to William of Champeaux, PL 163.1054-55; Evrard's *Contra Valdenses*, p. 1578.

24   **Jesus should have been an adult** Cf. p. 148.

28   **Many Jesuses** Cf. pp. 53, 118.

29   **Who permitted Moses to make the copper serpent?** Cf. *Trypho*, chapter 94, and Archambault's note there, *Dialogue avec Tryphon*, 2:100-101; Walter of Châtillon, *Tractatus*, PL 209.444; *Mil. HaShem*, p. 55; *Leqet Qazar, Michael* 4 (1976): 70. Christians regarded this serpent as a prefiguration of Jesus. See John 3:14-15; Tertullian, *Adversus Judaeos*, chapter 10, PL 2.628 = Tränkle, p. 28; Cyprian, *Testimonia* 2:20, PL 4.715; Meir of Narbonne, Parma ms., pp. 12b-13a, 109a; *Sefer Yosef HaMeqanne, Festschrift A. Berliner's*, p. 85 = Rosenthal, p. 53; Moses of Salerno, Posnanski ms., pp. 40-41. This question, however, is more likely to have been a part of a Christian defense of icons. Rupert of Deutz, for example, cites the cherubim and the copper serpent in order to prove that Exodus 20:4 is not as all-inclusive as the Jew had maintained (PL 170.602). This was important because Jewish polemicists often charged that alleged Christian worship of images was tantamount to idolatry. See the notes to p. 213.

Page 73

3-4   **The mouth which prohibited is the same mouth which permitted** This stock phrase comes from *Mishnah Ketubot* 2:2, where it is invoked in a legal context. An al-

L

most explicit Christian denial of this sort of argument is found in Aphraates' thirteenth demonstration (Neusner's *Aphrahat*, p. 49, also cited in *Ver. Israel*, p. 200, note 4), where he argues that the permission for priests to violate the Sabbath in the Temple shows that the entire prohibition of work is not binding in its literal sense. God would not command to one group what he prohibits to others; he could not consider it a sin if laymen did the sort of thing which priests were required to do as part of the Temple service.

15 *He did not make it in order to bow to it.* . . . Nathan Official, in discussing the cherubim, answered, "I have also heard that making them [statues] was prohibited only for the purpose of worship, for if this were not the case, how could the lions on Solomon's throne have been made?" (*Festschrift A. Berliner's*, p. 83 = Rosenthal, p. 48 [and cf. note 5 there]). The same passage is found in Berliner, *Peletat Soferim*, Heb. sec., p. 30, with a significant addition: "Moreover, we make many images every day" (וגם מעשים בכל יום שאנו עושים צורות הרבה). A similar argument was made by Jacob ben Reuben in *Mil. HaShem*, p. 57. For the general consensus of Jewish legal authorities on this issue, see Maimonides' *Mishneh Torah, Hilkhot 'Avodat Kokhavim* 3:10-11 and the commentaries there, and cf. *B. Rosh HaShanah* 24b and *B. Avodah Zarah* 43a-b.

Nathan Official suggested some other responses as well. The cherubim, he said, have no real counterpart in the universe, and the second commandment prohibited only images of real creatures or objects; moreover, they were kept in a hidden place (loc. cit.). As for the copper serpent, Moses did not really fashion it; rather, his staff turned into this serpent and that is why the staff is never mentioned thereafter (*Festschrift A. Berliner's*, p. 85 = Rosenthal, p. 53; *Peletat Soferim*, p. 32). Meir of Narbonne and Moses of Salerno (loc. cit.) argued that the serpent indeed referred to Jesus for he, like the primeval serpent, led people astray. The purpose of the serpent, then, was to encourage anyone who had begun to doubt the true faith to look up and realize that Jesus was hanged for his heresy.

19 *"What I see for them is not yet.* . . ." The essence of this passage is from Nathan Official, *Festschrift A. Berliner's*, pp. 85-86 = Rosenthal, p. 54 = *Peletat Soferim*, Heb. sec., p. 33.

For the christological interpretation, see Cyprian, *Testimonia* 2:10, PL 4.704; *De Fide Cath.*, I.12.1, PL 83.471; Bede [pseud.], PL 91.371; Raban Maur, PL 108.757; Damian, *Dialogus,* PL 145.58; Peter the Venerable, PL 189.586; Peter of Blois, PL 207.835. Many medieval Jewish commentators shied away from a messianic interpretation here; however, R. Akiba had applied the verse to Bar-Kokheba in a clearly messianic context (*Yer. Ta'anit* 4:5, f. 68d; *Lam. Rabbah* 2:5). On the Jewish interpretation of this passage against Rome and later Christianity, see Cohen, "Esau as Symbol," p. 22. On Numbers 24:23, see pp. 86, 147.

26 *The main adherents of their God are Edomites* See the notes to p. 55.

Page 74

15-16 *In our discussion of Jeremiah* Pp. 90-91.

L
17-18   *"A prophet . . . like myself"* The point was that only a lawgiver would be exactly like Moses. The conception of Jesus as the lawgiver may be adumbrated in Galatians 6:2 and is clearly expressed in *Trypho*, ch. 18 (ὁ καινὸς νομοθέτης ; cf. *Ver. Israel*, p. 100). For the christological use of this passage, see Acts 3:22–23; Cyprian, *Testimonia* 1:18, PL 4.688; Gregentius, *Sancti Gregentii . . . Disputatio cum Herbano Judaeo*, PG 86.632, 665 (cf. Hulen, "The Dialogue with the Jews," pp. 65–66); *Doctrina Jacobi Nuper Baptizati*, p. 7 (cf. also p. 10); Damian, *Dialogus*, PL 145.46; Petrus Alfonsi, *Dialogus*, PL 157.626 ff.; the *Dialogus* attributed to William of Champeaux, PL 163.1049; Peter of Blois, PL 207.836. Muslim polemicists also insisted that "a prophet . . . like yourself" (Deut. 18:18) could refer only to one who legislated a comprehensive law, and that was true only of Muhammad; see Perlmann, *Ifham al-Yahud*, pp. 45, 81–82, and Strauss, "Darkhei HaPulmus HaMuslemi," p. 191.

32   *A prophet and not a god* R. Joseph Kimḥi had maintained that it would be improper to call the son of God a mere prophet, especially since Scripture declares that Moses was the greatest of all the prophets (*Sefer HaBerit, Mil. Ḥovah*, p. 24b = Talmage's ed., p. 37). The first part of this argument is attributed to the Jew in Petrus Alfonsi's *Dialogus* (PL 157.627), who is told that anyone who foretells the future is called a prophet; it is also found in Meir of Narbonne, *Mil. Miẓvah*, p. 110a, and Moses of Salerno, Posnanski ms., p. 42. Moreover, both Meir (p. 110b of *Mil. Miẓvah*) and Moses (p. 43) present a rather curious argument. The destruction of the·Temple took place sixty-four years after Jesus' "affair" (עניינו); now, since only a man of thirty-five years or more would be in the Sanhedrin and since the psalmist says that the human life-span is seventy years or "by reason of strength" eighty (Psalms 90:10), it follows that his judges died in peace. But Deuteronomy 18:19 says that one who does not obey this prophet will die an early death (see B. Sanhedrin 89a; cf. Acts 3:22–23); hence, the passage cannot refer to Jesus.

33-34   *Just as you are a prophet and not a god. . . .* So *Sefer Yosef HaMeqanne, Festschrift A. Berliner's*, p. 89 = Rosenthal, p. 61; *Mil. HaShem*, p. 50.

Page 75

17   *"Your brother, the son of your mother. . . ."* So *Mil. Miẓvah*, pp. 39b, 110a; *Sefer Yosef HaMeqanne*, Rome ms., p. 10b (not in *Festschrift A. Berliner's* or in Rosenthal); Moses of Salerno (quoting a Rabbi Jacob), Posnanski ms., p. 42. Cf. also R. Meyuḥas ben Eliyyahu, *Perush 'al Sefer Devarim*, ed. M. Katz (Jerusalem, 1968), p. 59 (on Deuteronomy 13:2); this page of the manuscript happens to be reproduced after Katz's introduction. Cf. also N.V., pp. 147, 131.

26   *"He that is hanged is accursed of God"* This Jewish argument is mentioned in Eucher of Lyon's *Instructiones*, PL 50.782 = CSEL 31.80–81, cited in *Auteurs*, p. 23, and in the *Altercatio Simonis Iudaei*, PL 20.1174 = CSEL 45.25–26, cited in *Auteurs*, p. 30. It is also reflected in *Trypho*, chapter 96, and Hermannus, *De Conversione Sua*, PL 170.811. See also *Mil. HaShem*, p. 100, and cf. above pp. 58–59.

30-31   *"I shall incense them with a no-folk. . . ."* See the quotation from *Sefer Yosef*

L

HaMeqanne, *Festschrift A. Berliner's*, p. 90 = Rosenthal, p. 62, cited above in the
notes to p. 69. Meir of Narbonne commented that the term "foolish nation" is appropriate because of the irrationality of Christianity (*Mil. Mizvah*, pp. 40b, 110b).
Cf. also Moses of Salerno, Posnanski ms., p. 43, and Naḥmanides, *Sefer HaGeulah,
Ketavei Ramban* I, p. 263. It is of some interest that Origen cited this verse to show
that Jews will hate Christians and claimed that "no-folk" meant Christians because they do not constitute a separate nation; see Parkes, *Conflict*, p. 148. A similar use of this verse is especially prominent in Aphraates; cf. the index of biblical
and talmudic passages in Neusner's *Aphrahat.*

37   *"See then, that I, I am he; there is no god beside me"* This verse was quoted
as a proof of monotheism and against Christianity in Aphraates, Dem. 17 (Neusner's *Aphrahat*, p. 68), in Evagrius, *Altercatio . . . Simonis Iudaei*, PL 20.1167 = CSEL
45.2 (cited in *Juifs et Chrét.*, p. 266), in *Sefer Nestor HaKomer*, p. 4, and by Priscus in a
debate summarized by Gregory of Tours (cited in Ben Sasson, "Disputations and
Polemics," *Encyclopedia Judaica*, 6:87). Cf. *Juifs et Chrét.*, p. 263, and Williams, pp. 168,
299. See also below, p. 163. Such an argument is a clear indication of the Jewish
view that Christianity was basically a polytheistic religion with a monotheistic
veneer. See *Sifre*, ad loc., where the verse is cited to refute the belief in two divine
powers (רשויות); cf. Rosenthal, "Haganah VeHatqafah," p. 348. Jacob ben Reuben,
in fact, used a prevalent philosophical argument against polytheism to combat
Christianity (*Mil. HaShem*, pp. 9-10), and many Jewish polemicists referred to the
latter as a belief in two or three independent divine powers. Cf. ibid., p. 4; N.V., p.
113; the Jew "Abiathar" in the *Vita Silvestri*, cited in *Auteurs*, p. 45; the Jew in the
Dialogus attributed to William of Champeaux, PL 163.1056, who maintains that he is
being asked to worship "duas duorum deorum personas"; Alan of Lille, PL
210.401. Solomon de' Rossi, in fact, practically begins his polemic with a list of
verses proving that God is one; see *'Edut HaShem Ne'emanah*, Rosenthal's *Meḥqarim*,
1:380-81. In essence, Jews regarded the trinity as such an impossible concept that
any translation into meaningful terms must result in some form of polytheism.
        This view had important halakhic ramifications as well with regard to
social and commercial intercourse with Christians and the requirement of martyrdom when faced with forced baptism. See Katz, *Exclusiveness and Tolerance*, pp. 24 ff.
On the similar Jewish argument regarding worship of the saints, see Crispin's
Disputatio, p. 34, and especially Jacob of Venice's letter to Pablo in *Ginzei Nistarot*,
ed. by J. Kobak (Bamberg, 1866), 2:3. Blumenkranz notes that the first Jew to use
this argument about the saints was the convert Wecelin; see his "Jüdische und
Christliche Konvertiten im Jüdisch-Christlichen Religionsgespräch des Mittelalters," in *Judentum im Mittelalter*, ed. P. Wilpert (Berlin, 1966), pp. 264-82.

Page 76

16-17   ***There were no longer any prophets after . . . the first Temple*** On this view, see
E. Urbach, "Matai Pasqah HaNevuah?" *Tarbiz* 16 (1944): 1-11 (esp. pp. 2-3). See
also Solomon de' Rossi, Rosenthal's *Meḥqarim*, 1:408.

L
25-26   *So the prophets will not die that way* This clearly invalid argument is not found in other polemics and resulted from the author's getting carried away by the insistence on a perfect analogy between Moses and the subsequent prophets. He undoubtedly believed that Isaiah was executed by Manasseh (*B. Yevamot* 49b), and the story of the execution of the prophet Zechariah son of Yehoyada "at the command of the king" (2 Chron. 24:21) was quite prominent in rabbinic tradition (*B. Gittin* 57b, *B. Sanhedrin* 96b, *Lam. Rabbah* 2:28, and Rashi on Lamentations 2:20). An attempt to distinguish between death at the hands of a Gentile government and at the hands of a Jewish one would be futile since Moses did not die in either way.

32-33   *You should not understand the Torah literally* For this interpretation, see Raban Maur, *Enarratio super Deuteronomium*, book 2, PL 108.924.

35   *Isaiah was referring to this dispatch of the "mother"* On Isa. 50:1-3, see Peter of Blois, PL 207.861.

Page 77

7-8   *This was written for them* See appendix 3, note 22.

14   *R. Solomon son of Abun* A late twelfth-century author of liturgical poetry; see L. Zunz, *Literaturgeschichte der Synagogalen Poesie* (Berlin, 1865; reprinted Hildesheim, 1966), pp. 311-12. In dealing with the ascription of an argument to a particular individual, I have followed the reading of the Rome manuscript, which represents the earliest tradition. However, Wagenseil, the Munich manuscript, and Münster all read "R. Solomon b. Abraham," probably the famous anti-Maimonist leader in Montpellier in the first half of the thirteenth century.

16   *The father told his son* For a similar sort of story, cf. p. 43. On Psalm 110, see below pp. 160 ff.

22   *Sons of prophets* See *B. Pesaḥim* 66a.

25-26   *Because of his sorcery* Dr. Moshe Bernstein has drawn my attention to the relevance of the Talmudic story about R. Shimon b. Shetaḥ's hanging of eighty witches, where removal from the ground nullified their powers (*Yer. Sanhedrin* 23c). On Jesus' sorcery, see the notes to p. 64.

31   *Thus, he is disqualified. . . .* See the notes to p. 230.

Page 78

4-6   *Why is the he . . . written large?* Jewish law required that certain letters in specific words be written large in a Pentateuch written for ritual purposes. See, e.g., Maimonides, *Mishneh Torah, Hilkhot Tefillin u-Mezuzah VeSefer Torah* 7:8.

6   *Five wounds* The letter *he* has a numerical value of five. See also Moses of Salerno, Posnanski ms., p. 30, where a Jewish convert to Christianity is said to have adduced evidence of the five wounds from the fivefold repetition of the root meaning "to betray" in Isaiah 24:16.

9-10   *So you should explain the* **lamed** The *la* of "Haladonai" is written with the letter *lamed*, which is the first letter of the word *lo* (not). Moreover, the Aramaic

L

word for "not" is *la*. Indeed, the Talmud explicitly recognized that the *la* meaning "to" or "to the" could be taken to mean "not" (*B. Nedarim* 10b-11a), and R. Meir of Rothenburg (thirteenth century) was so sensitive to this possibility that it affected his pronunciation of part of the liturgy of the High Holy Day period. (He insisted on saying *Zakherenu lehayyim* rather than *lahayyim; see Tur Orah Hayyim* 582). It is possible that the author of N.V. forgot or intentionally overlooked the fact that the Masoretic vocalization of this *lamed* is with a *sheva*.

14-15   ***These three divine names refer to the trinity*** A common argument found, for example, in *De Fide Cath.*, I.4.11, PL 83.457, and cited by Meir of Narbonne, Parma ms., pp. 111a, 240b; Yosef HaMeqanne, *Festschrift A. Berliner's*, p. 87 = Rosenthal, p. 57; Moses of Salerno, Posnanski ms., p. 43. See also Maimonides at the beginning of his *Treatise on the Resurrection*, ed. J. Finkel (New York, 1939), Hebrew and Arabic section, p. 1.

17   ***He omitted one of the names*** Cf. pp. 44-45.

Page 79

7   ***And added a fourth corner*** I am unfamiliar with the source of this rather interesting effort to explain the difference between the tau shaped and standard Latin cross.

9-10   ***If you will not observe the entire Torah. . . .*** See Galatians 3:10-11 and cf. Raban Maur, PL 108.951, who adds, "Who can remain without sin in all the injunctions of the law?" See also *Trypho*, chapter 95; Peter the Venerable, PL 189.582-83.

10   ***You will be subjected*** Literally, "They will be subjected ," a euphemism meaning the Jews will be subjected. Cf. the rabbinic phrase, "The enemies of Israel will be condemned to destruction" (יתחייבו שונאיהם של ישראל כלייה) which means "Israel will be condemned to destruction" (e.g., *Shemot Rabbah* 35:4), and cf. Rashi on Exodus 1:10.

14   ***"And your life shall be hung before you"*** For the christological interpretation of this verse, see *Sancti Gregentii Disputatio*, PG 86.631, cited by Hulen, "The Dialogue with the Jews," 66; *De Fide Cath.*, I.35.2, PL 83.484; Rupert's *Dialogus*, PL 170.606; Walter of Châtillon, *Tractatus*, PL 209.442-43; Evrard's *Contra Valdenses*, p. 1579 (where "prudentem" should be emended to "pendentem"). For other references, see Williams, p. 50. Raban Maur deals with N.V.'s refutation by taking the phrase "and you shall not believe in your life" as part of the curse ("Quidquam est pejus inter maledicta quae Judaeis . . . acciderunt quam videre vitam suam, id est, filium Dei pendentem, et non credere vitae suae"—PL 108.960). The same question and answer as in N.V. are found in the additions to *Sefer HaBerit, Mil. Hovah*, p. 34a = Talmage's ed., p. 57.

15-16   ***Rabbi Abraham of Spires*** Probably the brother of R. Judah the Hasid.

Page 80

1-2   ***"And have a long life" in the world to come*** See *B. Kiddushin* 40a.

L

9   ***The soul is not mentioned at all*** The argument that the Old Testament promises only carnal rewards while the New Testament promises celestial ones was made by Isidore in his *Quaestiones adversus Judaeos*, cited in *Auteurs*, p. 96. It is interesting that in Julian of Toledo's *Antikeimeon* (1:27, PL 96.608, cited in *Auteurs*, p. 127), he maintains that the reward mentioned in this verse is celestial, a view that would undercut (at least in this case) the alleged contrast between the Old and the New Testaments. On the sometimes ambiguous Christian position concerning the relationship between the testaments, see *Judenpredigt*, pp. 122-28. Meir of Narbonne (*Mil. Miẓvah*, p. 120a) reversed the Christian argument cited here by arguing that Jesus' promises referred to the next world in order to prevent clearcut refutation during his lifetime, while the promises of the Torah refer mostly to this world. He goes on to say that if the Torah promises rewards in this world, then reward will surely be forthcoming in the hereafter, which is the world of reward and punishment. Finally, he cites a few verses which, he says, explicitly refer to reward in the world to come.

12-13   ***"His treasured people"*** N.V.'s interpretation of this passage is taken from *Sefer Yosef HaMeqanne, Festschrift A. Berliner's*, p. 88 = Rosenthal, p. 59, where it is found in the same context.

Page 81

6   ***Only when Jesus . . . came. . . .*** For Joshua as Jesus (especially in light of the identity of their names in Hebrew), see *Trypho,* chapter 91; Zeno of Verona (fourth century), cited in *Judenpredigt*, p. 30; *Consultationes Zacchaei et Apollonii*, cited in *Judenpredigt*, p. 32; Augustine, *Contra Faustum* 12:28 and elsewhere (cf. *Judenpredigt*, p. 157); *De Fide Cath.* I.6.1, PL 83.463 = Eggers, p. 56; Raban Maur, *Commentarii in Librum Josue*, passim (PL 108.999 ff.). The view that Moses' death represented the · death of the Law was expressed by Isidore, *Quaestiones,* PL 83.371, and, in the exact same words, by Bede [pseud.], *Quaestiones,* PL 93.417. For the view that passing through the Jordan represents baptism, cf. *De Fide Cath.,* loc. cit.; Bede [pseud.], loc. cit.; Raban Maur, PL 108.1013.

24   ***A unified God*** This is proven by the singular "he knows." So R. Simlai in *Yer. Berakhot* 9:1, f. 12d, and *Bereshit Rabbah* 8:9 (Theodor-Albeck, pp. 62-63; cf. appendix 1). The Christian argument on this verse is also cited in *Sefer Yosef HaMeqanne, Festschrift A. Berliner's*, p. 87 = Rosenthal, p. 57, and ibid., p. 65. See also ibid., p. 107, on Ps. 50:1.

24-25   ***He . . . was not the son*** See appendix 5.

Page 82

1   ***The Book of Jeremiah*** Jeremiah and Ezekiel are placed before Isaiah in conformity with *B. Bava Batra* 14b. So also in *Sefer Yosef HaMeqanne* and in Mühlhausen's *Sefer HaNiẓẓaḥon.*

6   ***This was said of Jesus*** See Cyprian, *Testimonia* 1:5, PL 4.691. This interpre-

L

tation was also cited by Meir of Narbonne, *Mil. Miẓvah,* p. 138b, and Moses of Salerno, Posnanski ms., p. 55.

10   *To that period* I.e., the period of the kings named in Jeremiah 1:2-3.

23   *In their book of errors* Luke 1:26-38.

28   *Why humility should be necessary* Probably not a sincere question; cf. Rashi on Genesis 1:26.

Page 83

2   *If he is a prophet he is not God* Cf. N.V., p. 74.

5   *John the Baptist* Posnanski refers to Luke 1:15 for the statement that John will be filled with the holy spirit from the womb, but there is no explicit reference to Jeremiah 1. For an interpretation of this passage as a reference to John, see Jerome's *In Hieremiam, CC, Ser. Lat.,* 74, p. 4.

22   *The heretics say. . . .* Ibid., pp. 36 ff. Cf. also Cyprian, *Testimonia* 1:14, PL 4.686.

33   *Why did he not observe it?* Cf. Rome ms. 53, p. 24a = Pos. "Mordecai of Avignon" ms., p. 29 = Rosenthal's "Menaḥem," p. 70. On the related question of the literal observance of pentateuchal law before the advent of Jesus, see appendix 3.

Page 84

28-29   *The ark of the covenant* Jerome, loc. cit., maintained that the ark here symbolized the Law (since it was the "custos legis Mosaicae").

29-30   *The Jews . . . took the ark with them* Cf. Numbers 14:44; 1 Samuel 4:3 ff.

Page 85

7   *Standing . . . water.* See the notes to p. 172.

13   *When the Jews seized him* See Isidore, *De Fide Cath.,* I.21.2, PL 83.479, for the view that the sin of Judah mentioned in Jeremiah 17:1 was the Jews' sin against Jesus.

20   *"My spirit shall nevermore abide in man"* The more common interpretation of this verse was that God's spirit, which does abide in man, would not remain in any individual for a long period of time. N.V., however, takes it to mean that God's spirit would never abide in man at all (cf. R. David Kimḥi's commentary to Genesis, ad loc.). In this connection, it is of interest to note that the author omitted the words *in aeternum* after *homine* in his quotation from the Vulgate; including them might have raised the possibility of the alternate interpretation.

21   *This is the meaning of "Shall a man make a god unto himself. . . ."* So *Sefer Yosef HaMeqanne,* Rome ms., p. 11b.

24   *It says in Daniel. . . .* Yosef HaMeqanne (Rosenthal, p. 119) says that this verse was cited by a French Jewess as evidence against the incarnation. See also

L

Rome ms. 53, p. 24a = Pos. "Mordecai of Avignon" ms., p. 28 = Rosenthal's "Menaḥem", p. 70.

26   ***"Cursed be the man. . . ."*** So also Meir of Narbonne, Parma ms., p. 126b, and Solomon de' Rossi, Rosenthal's *Meḥqarim*, 1:381.

Page 86

6-7   ***God's anger against the Jews will never abate*** See Jerome, *In Hieremiam* ad loc., *CC, Ser. Lat.*, 74, p. 163.

7-8   ***All the Jews. . .will be saved*** The conviction that the Jews would ultimately convert and be saved was widespread. Cf. Romans 11:25-26. Many statements of this conviction by Gregory the Great are cited in *Auteurs*, p. 86, n. 65, while Tajon collected a number of passages on the subject in his *Sentent.* 5:25, PL 80.978, cited in *Auteurs*, p. 106. Cf. Jerome, *In Hiezechielem, CC, Ser. Lat.*, 75, p. 224, and Isidore, *De Fide Cath.*, II.5, PL 83.508-10. Note also Augustine, *Judenpredigt*, pp. 89-90, 110-12, and cf. the references in the index to the *Patrologia Latina*, PL 220.1004-6. This belief took on special importance during the second crusade, when Bernard cited it as a basic reason to spare the Jews; see *Sancti Bernardi. . .Opera*, ed. J. Mabillon (Paris, 1719), 1:332, and B.S. James, trans., *The Letters of St. Bernard of Clairvaux* (London, 1953), p. 466. Cf. also Bernard's *Sermones super Cantica Canticorum* 14:2 and 79:5-6 in *S. Bernardi. . .Opera*, ed. Leclerq, Talbot, and Rochais (Rome, 1957), 1:76-77 and 2:275 (= S. J. Eales, trans., *Life and Works of St. Bernard* [London, 1896], 4:75, 486). Note also ibid., 16:15, *S. Bernardi. . .Opera*, 1:97 (Eales 4:94) and James, *Letters*, no. 394, p. 476. I have discussed some of this material in *Proceedings of the American Academy for Jewish Research* 40:97-98.

8   ***When Elijah comes*** See Malachi 3:23. This was a peculiarly Jewish expression for the redemption, especially since Christians felt that "Elijah" had already come in the person of John the Baptist. It is consequently rather interesting to find a Jew saying that the Christians concede that something will happen "when Elijah comes" just as Christian writers frequently say that Jews refer a certain prophecy to "the second coming." On Elijah's messianic role, see Ginzberg, *Legends*, 4:233-35; 6:339-42.

13-14   ***He again warned them against such a god*** This Jewish argument from Jeremiah 17:5 is cited in Hermannus, *De Conversione Sua*, PL 170.811, and the Jew "Vecelin" in Albert of Metz, *De Diversitate Temporum*, ch. 23, cited in *Auteurs*, p. 248, quotes Jeremiah 17:5-6 and Psalms 146:3 as warnings against belief in Jesus. Cf. N.V., pp. 97-98, 134-35, 147. See also *Sefer Yosef HaMeqanne*, Rome ms., p. 12a.

17   ***When a man makes himself God*** Nathan Official supposedly interpreted Numbers 24:23 this way when speaking to the pope; see *Festschrift A. Berliner's*, p. 85 = Rosenthal, p. 54 = *Peletat Soferim*, Hebrew section, p. 33. See B. Sanhedrin 106a, and cf. Rosenthal's note 3, ad loc. Alan of Lille (PL 210.413) quotes a Jewish citation of the verse, "Qui fecerit se Deum, occidatur" (He who makes himself into a god should be killed). The reference supplied in PL there is Deuteronomy 13, but there

L

is no such verse in that chapter. It seems likely that Alan is reporting a Jewish interpretation of Numbers 24:23.

32   *He is thus a human being* The same interpretation of *anush* underlies Cyprian's citation of this verse to prove that Jesus is both God and man (*Testimonia* 2:10, PL 4.704). Thus the author has taken a christological interpretation and turned it against the Christians. For the Jewish view that Christianity was basically a polytheistic religion making insincere protestations of monotheism, see the commentary to p. 75. It should be noted that Jerome cites the view that *anush* refers to Jesus' humanity but rejects it (*In Hieremiam, CC, Ser. Lat.*, 74, p. 166).

Page 87

17   *He did not live even half of seventy* A similar statement about Balaam based on Ps. 55:23 is found in *B. Sanhedrin* 106b; cf. *Mishnah Avot* 5:19. See Goldstein, *Jesus in the Jewish Tradition*, pp. 63–66. Cf. also N.V., p. 149.

Page 88

13-14   *All Israel is called Judah* Cf. the notes to p. 126 on the Christian claim that Judah represents Christendom.

19   *The river Sambation* Cf. p. 45.

27   *This was said of Jesus* So Jerome, *In Hieremiam, CC, Ser. Lat.*, 74, p. 297, and the Christian in *Mil. HaShem*, p. 79.

Page 89

13   *He sinned* Cf. pp. 139–40, 150.

18-19   *Do not all nations . . . also multiply?* The argument from the universality of Christianity and this Jewish counterargument played an important role in polemic. Many Christians argued that various biblical passages could refer only to Jesus and not to other kings because only he attained the sort of universal rule described. See Tertullian, *Adversus Judaeos*, chapter 7, PL 2.610-11, chapter 12, PL 2.633, ch. 14, PL 2.642, and cf. Ambrose [pseud.], *Apologia David Altera*, PL 14.893-96 = CSEL 32.2.369-74, cited in *Judenpredigt*, p. 44; Paul Alvarus, PL 121.493, cited in *Juifs et Chrét.*, pp. 277-78; N.V., p. 159 and the notes there. Cf. also *Sefer Yosef HaMeqanne*, Rosenthal's ed., p. 94.

A more general argument saw the diffusion of Christianity as evidence of its validity; see the *Tractatus contra Judaeos* of the Arian bishop Maximin, cited in *Auteurs*, p. 19, and Julian of Toledo's *De Comprobatione Aetatis Sextae*, PL 96.548-50, cited in *Auteurs*, p. 122. A priest of Étampes is quoted by Yosef HaMeqanne as proposing a variant of this argument. "Do you think," he asked, "that the whole world will be damned while only you, who are the smallest of nations, will have a share in the world to come?" (*Festschrift A. Berliner's*, p. 87 = Rosenthal's ed. p. 58). Elsewhere, the small number of Jews is cited as part of the general insistence on the significance of Christian power and its development versus Jewish weakness and servitude (*Mil. HaShem*, p. 5; Rosenthal there refers to his article in *Sura* 1:171, 2:107 ff.). This argument was expressed with exceptional vigor by Peter the Venerable in connection with Genesis 49:10 (PL 189.560).

Jewish polemicists approached this problem in a variety of ways. Yosef HaMeqanne pointed to Deuteronomy 7:7 as proof that God chose Israel even though it is the smallest nation (loc. cit.); Meir of Narbonne cited the verse, "And it cast down the truth to the ground" (Daniel 8:12) to prove that the Torah, which is called truth (Psalms 119:142), would suffer degradation and that consequently the Christian proof from Jewish lowliness really proves the truth of Judaism (*Mil. Mizvah*, Parma ms., pp. 13b, 22b,105b; cf. also *Sefer Yosef HaMeqanne*, Rosenthal, p. 113); the author of Rome ms. 53 argued that Christians and Muslims are rewarded in this world, while Jews are punished for their sins in this world so that they can receive unadulterated rewards in the world to come (p. 24b = Pos. "Mordecai of Avignon" ms., p. 32 = Rosenthal's "Menaḥem," p. 71). Various writers sought to explain the reasons for the Jewish exile (the additions to *Sefer HaBerit, Mil. Ḥovah*, p. 36a = Talmage's ed., pp. 62–63, the Jew in Rupert's *Dialogus*, PL 170.606, and especially Solomon de' Rossi, *'Edut HaShem Ne'emanah*, ed. Rosenthal, *Sura* 3 [1948], pp. 260–64 = *Mehqarim*, 1:395–400, and Mordecai of Avignon, M.E., Vat. ms., pp. 5a–b). See especially below, pp. 226–28.·

A central Jewish approach, however, was the argument that Christianity is far from universal and does not even represent a majority. This argument was raised with regard to Psalms 72:11 by N.V., p. 159, Jacob ben Reuben (*Mil. HaShem*, p. 74), and Naḥmanides (*Vikkuaḥ, Ketavei Ramban*, 1:311). See especially below, p. 203, and Mordecai of Avignon, M.E., Vat. ms., p. 9a. Meir of Narbonne (p. 13b) also pointed to the fact that Muslims ruled "half the world," and when Rupert of Deutz maintained that God referred to Jesus when he promised Abraham that all the nations of the earth would be blessed in him and his seed, the Jew remarked that this had simply not been fulfilled ("Quam multi benedictionem istam non quaerunt, quam multi per orbem terrarum quem tu dicis Christum contemnunt!"—PL 170.565). This argument led Rupert and others to say that the Bible means only that representatives of all nations will become Christians; cf. Christian of Stavelot (9th century), PL 106.1456, cited in *Auteurs*, p. 211, and *Juifs et Chrét.*, pp. 237, 278. So also Peter the Venerable, PL 189.590.

The wide diffusion of Islam even enabled some polemicists to attempt to make *Christians* feel isolated. Both Jacob ben Reuben and the author of N.V. argued that the disgust at eating pork is really a *consensus omnium* with the sole exception of Christians; see *Mil. HaShem*, pp. 38–39, 114, and below, p. 211. Moreover, Jews pointed to the power of the Muslims and the consequent failure of the Crusades as evidence that Christian success is no proof of the validity of Christianity since that "success" is an illusion (Meir of Narbonne, Parma ms., pp. 114a–115a, 127a;

L

Moses of Salerno, Posnanski ms., pp. 46-48, quoted also in J. Perles, "Die in einer Münchener Handschrift aufgefundene erste lateinische Uebersetzung des Maimonidischen 'Führers,'" *MGWJ* 24 [1875]:22, n. 14). In fact, the author of Rome ms. 53 (p. 23b = Pos. "Mordecai of Avignon" ms., p. 26 = Rosenthal's "Menaḥem," p. 69) even cited Bogomils and Albigensians to show the limited extent of orthodox Christianity. Finally, it is interesting that Jews did not hesitate to cite the small number of Karaites as an argument against that sect. See Ibn Daud's *Sefer HaQabbalah*, ed. Cohen, p. 92, and the note to line 22 there, and cf. J. Kraemer's review, "A Critical Edition . . . ," *JQR* (1971): 62-63.

20   *"A new covenant"* Hebrews 8:8-13; *Trypho*, chapter 11; Tertullian, *Adversus Judaeos*, chapter 3, PL 2.603-4 = Tränkle, p. 8; Cyprian, *Testimonia*, 1:11, PL 4.685; Lactantius, *Divinae Institutiones*, cited in *Judenpredigt*, p. 28; Augustine's sermon on the Jews, *Judenpredigt*, p. 97; *Altercatio Simonis Judaei*, PL 20.1173, cited in *Auteurs*, p. 29; *Doctrina Jacobi Nuper Baptizati*, ed. Bonwetsch, p. 7; Paul Alvarus, PL121.507-8 = Madoz's critical edition, pp. 269-71, cited in *Auteurs*, p. 190; Damian, *Dialogus*, PL 145.64; Rupert, *Dialogus*, PL 170.599; Peter the Venerable, *Tractatus*, PL 189.572, 575, 579, 582; Walter of Châtillon, PL 209.430. See also *Mil. HaShem*, pp. 79, 81-82; David Kimḥi's commentary, ad loc. (cf. F. Talmage, "Rabbi David Kimḥi as Polemicist," *HUCA* 38 [1967]:219); *Sefer Yosef HaMeqanne*, ed. Rosenthal, p. 70. Cf. Baron, *A Social and Religious History of the Jews*, 9:123-25. Solomon de' Rossi actually cites this passage in his list of proofs that the Torah must be observed; see his *'Edut HaShem Ne'emanah*, Rosenthal's *Meḥqarim*, 1:382-83.

26-27   *I have not come to destroy the law* See the notes to p. 172.

Page 90

22   *A reference to Jesus* Trypho, ch. 72; Isidore, *De Fide Cath.* I.9.6, PL 83.466 = Eggers, p. 70; Damian, *Dialogus*, PL 145.48. This interpretation was also discussed by Meir of Narbonne (Parma ms., pp. 24a, 131b), Yosef HaMeqanne (Rosenthal's ed., p. 69), and Solomon de' Rossi (Rosenthal's *Meḥqarim*, 1:386).

26   *The genealogy* Cf. p. 107 and the notes there.

Page 91

5-6   *Is there any more judgment and righteousness . . .?* So Jacob ben Reuben, *Mil. HaShem*, p. 78; the Jew in Petrus Alfonsi's *Dialogus*, ch. 9, PL 157.636; *Sefer Yosef HaMeqanne*, Rome ms., p. 12b. On the general argument from nonfulfillment of messianic prophecies, see pp. 107-08.

Page 92

4   *Their filthy water* See Jerome, *In Hiezechielem, CC, Ser. Lat.*, 75, p. 169; Peter the Venerable, *Tractatus*, PL 189.586.

5   **Firmen** Confirmation.

L
10-11   ***Blood of circumcision*** See pp. 53 and 64 and the notes there.

Page 93

21   ***This refers to Jesus*** Cf. the references in Williams, pp. 127, 218, and 284. In addition, see Jerome, *In Esaiam, CC, Ser. Lat.* 73, pp. 102-3 ("Ipse [God] descendit in uterum virginalem et ingredietur et egredietur orientalem portam quae semper clausa est"—an obvious reference to Ezekiel 44:1-2, as the editor rightly comments); Crispin, *Disputatio,* pp. 45, 51-52; Peter of Blois, PL 207.840; Alan of Lille, PL 210.416; Evrard of Béthune, p. 1578; *Summa Theologiae* 3a.28.3. See also the poem in PL 68.95 and the editor's note to line 57 there, as well as the letter of the Synod of Milan in 390 quoted in L. G. Owens, "Virgin Birth," *New Catholic Encyclopedia,* 14:692 ff. Cf. especially the references in *Dictionnaire de Théologie Catholique* 9 (1926):2375-82. Kimhi, in his commentary ad loc., noted that the context makes it obvious to "any intelligent person" that the reference is to the Temple gates (cf. Talmage, *HUCA* 38:216). See also Jacob ben Reuben, *Mil. HaShem,* p. 124.

Page 94

2   ***Male organs*** It should be noted that this pun is a result of a textual emendation; the emendation, however, is plausible and it replaces an apparently meaningless word.

19   ***"Statutes that were not good"*** An oft-quoted verse. See, for example, *Trypho* ch. 21; Aphraates, Dem. 15, Neusner's *Aphrahat,* p. 59, also cited in Williams, p. 98; Damian, *Sermo de Inventione Sanctae Crucis,* PL 144.605; Rupert, *Dialogus,* PL 170.582; Peter the Venerable, PL 189.573; Bernard, *Sermones super Cantica Canticorum* 58:7 in *Sancti Bernardi . . . Opera,* ed. Leclerq, Talbot, and Rochais, 2:131-32 = S. J. Eales, *Life and Works of St. Bernard,* 4:351; *the Tractatus* in *TNA* 5.1516 = PL 213.757.

30   ***These are the apostates. . . .*** Cf. Katz, *Exclusiveness and Tolerance,* pp. 67 ff.

Page 96

2   ***"Your new moons and your appointed feasts my soul hates"*** This passage, in which Isaiah expresses dissatisfaction with sacrifices as well, was frequently cited by Christians as evidence of God's displeasure with these aspects of the law. Posnanski points to Colossians 2:16-17; see below p. 173. For the citation of this passage in Isaiah, see Tertullian, *Adversus Judaeos,* PL 2.605 = Tränkle, p. 9; *Tractatus Adversus Judaeos,* PL 4.922; Commodian's *Instructiones,* cited in *Judenpredigt,* p. 22; Jerome [pseud.], *Epistle* 149 (devoted specifically to this subject), PL 22.1220-24, cited in *Judenpredigt,* pp. 47-49; the *Altercatio Simonis Judaei,* cited in Williams, p. 303; Isidore, *De Fide Cath.* II.15.4-5, PL 83.522-23; Raban Maur's commentary on Exodus, PL 108.99; Petrus Alfonsi, *Dialogus,* PL 157.595; Rupert's *Dialogus,* PL 170.581; Peter the Venerable, *Tractatus,* PL 189.572; Peter of Blois, *Contra Perfidiam Judaeorum,* PL 207.845-46 (where it is part of a long list of such verses); Walter of Châtillon, *Tractatus,* PL 209.425.

L
27–28   **You don't even observe Sunday properly** See p. 45.

31   **He is referring to the . . . festivals which they "devised of their own heart"**
This refers to the changes introduced by Jeroboam. The source of the argument is
the following passage (*Tanḥuma Pinḥas* 17 and *Yalqut Shim'oni* ad loc. [no. 388]): "A
certain Gentile asked R. Akiba in Sepphoris, 'Why do you observe the festivals? Is
it not written, "Your new moons and your appointed feasts my soul hates"?' R.
Akiba answered him, 'Had it said, "My new moons and my appointed feasts my
soul hates," I would have agreed with you. But it says, "Your new moons and your
appointed feasts," i.e., those festivals which Jeroboam made.' " See also *Sefer
Yosef HaMeqanne*, ed. Rosenthal, p. 73. It is of particular interest that the Jew in
Rupert's *Dialogus* (PL 170.581) introduced Jeroboam into his discussion of this passage even though the argument there deals with Isaiah's criticism of sacrifices
rather than festivals. He insists that this criticism is directed against the sacrifices offered to the golden calves set up by Jeroboam, a rather peculiar interpretation that would probably never have occurred to anyone if not for the exegesis of
the new moons and festivals found in the *Tanḥuma*. (In fact, it may be that Rupert reported the argument in a distorted form.) The fact that Isaiah 1:13 refers critically
to the Sabbath as well might have made this Jewish interpretation of these festivals
vulnerable; however, see *Yer. Avodah Zarah* 1:1 for the view that Jeroboam had also
fabricated "Sabbaths."

Page 97

11   **The heretics say. . . .** So *Trypho*, ch. 109; Tertullian, *Adversus Judaeos*, ch. 3,
PL 2.604 = Tränkle, p. 8 (since "the house of the God of Jacob" is the church); the
Dialogue of Timothy and Aquila, cited in Williams, p. 76; Cyprian, *Testimonia*, 2:18, PL
4.712 (since "the mountain of the Lord" is Jesus); the anonymous *De Montibus Sina
et Sion*, ch. 9, cited in *Judenpredigt*, p. 15; Augustine's sermon on the Jews, *Judenpredigt*,
p. 100; Isidore, *De Fide Cath.*, II.1.12-13, PL 83.502; Damian, *Dialogus*, PL 145.45. See
also Crispin's *Disputatio*, p. 39, where he argues that the old Law came from Sinai,
and so the Law that comes from Zion must be the New Testament (cf. also
Blumenkranz's note, ad loc.)

18   **The prophet is warning people. . . .** Cf. R. David Kimḥi's commentary ad
loc., trans. Talmage, *HUCA* 38:217; Meir of Narbonne, *Mil. Miẓvah*, Parma ms.,
pp. 111a, 115b; Moses of Salerno, Posnanski ms., pp. 44, 48–49; Solomon de' Rossi,
'Edut HaShem Ne'emanah, Rosenthal's *Meḥqarim*, 1:381. On Isaiah 2:22, see also A.
Grabois, "HaNusaḥ Ha'Ivri shel HaMiqra VehaLamdanut HaNoẓrit: Pereq
BaYeḥasim bein Yehudim LeNoẓrim BaMe'ah HaYod-Bet," *Meḥqarim beToledot Am
Yisrael VeEreẓ Yisrael LeZekher Ẓvi Avneri* (Haifa, 1970), p. 107.

33   **Muhammad** For Muhammad as a god, cf. p. 110 and esp. p. 217. On
Zechariah 14:9, cf. p. 135.

L

8   **Fili homo** Rather poor Latin. Cf. pp. 140 and 142.

13   *Haughty men* See Jerome, *In Esaiam, CC, Ser. Lat.*, 73, p. 34.

23   *"Of him"* The Hebrew word *lo* can be either an ordinary pronoun (= "to him," or as N.V. takes it here, "of him") or a reflexive one (= "to himself" or "for himself"). The author is saying that a plural pronoun here (*lahem*) would be reflexive, but since the subject of the sentence is plural, a singular pronoun (*lo*) cannot be reflexive. Given biblical usage, this is not compelling reasoning, and the author probably knew it.

28   *These are the priests. . . .* On these charges and alleged monastic immorality in general, see pp. 69-70 and the notes there. This is interesting testimony to Jewish awareness of growing resentment of the church's amassing of property; cf. also the introduction.

5   *Those who say that they are his people* The Christians.

10   *"Woe unto them. . . ."* Cf. *Sefer Yosef HaMeqanne*, Rosenthal's ed., p. 74. On Isaiah 5:20, see ibid., p. 97.

13   *"Woe unto them who call evil good, and good evil"* It is especially interesting that this verse as well as verse 23 cited below were applied to the clergy of southern France by Innocent III; see J. Strayer, *The Albigensian Crusades* (New York, 1971), p. 19.

19   **Laien** The laity.

23   *Some say. . . .* This passage, which is probably a gloss, raises several knotty problems with regard to the history of Hebrew (and even French and German) pronunciation. For a treatment of one of these problems, see Max Weinreich, "Bnai Hes un Bnai Khes in Ashkenaz: Die Problem—un vos zie lozt undz heren," *Yivo Bleter* 41 (1957/58): 101-23 (brought to my attention by Mr. Asher Reiss). See also R. Ovadiah of Bertinoro's commentary on *Eduyot* 1.3.

29   *"Israel shall be saved. . . ."* The purpose of this quotation is presumably to show that Israel (= the Jews) will ultimately be saved. Cf. below, p. 170.

3   *This was said of Jesus* A classic christological passage. See, for example, Matthew 1:22-23; *Trypho* ch. 43, 66; Tertullian, *Adversus Judaeos*, ch. 9, PL 2. 616ff. = Tränkle, pp. 20ff.; Cyprian, *Testimonia*, 2:9, PL 4.704; Isidore, *De Fide Cath.*, I.10.1 ff., PL 83.468-9; Richard of St. Victor, *De Emanuele*, PL 196.601 ff.; the *Tractatus* in *TNA* 5.1560 ff. = PL 213.800 ff. Cf. also the references in *Juifs et Chrét.*, p. 238, and E. Tobac, "Isaie, Prophétie de l'Emmanuel," *Dictionnaire de Théologie Catholique*, 8:48 ff.

L

3   **What sort of novelty is it. . . ?** See *Trypho*, ch. 84; *The Dialogue of Athanasius and Zacchaeus,* cited in Williams, p. 123; Jerome, *In Esaiam, CC, Ser. Lat.,* 73, p. 103; Isidore, *De Fide Cath.,* I.10.3, PL 83.468; Hildefonsus of Toledo, *De Virginitate Perpetua sanctae Mariae,* PL 96.64–65 = V. Blanco, *San Ildefonso de Virginitate Beatae Mariae* (Madrid, 1937), pp. 74–76, cited in *Auteurs,* p. 114; Peter of Blois, *Contra Perfidiam Judaeorum,* PL 207.841; Walter of Châtillon, *Tractatus,* PL 209.427.

9   **"The way of a man with a maid"** Cited for the same purpose by Jacob ben Reuben, *Mil. HaShem,* p. 87; J. Kimḥi, *Sefer HaBerit, Mil. Ḥovah,* p. 28b = Talmage's ed., p. 43; Joseph Kara, *Commentary,* ad loc.; D. Kimḥi, *Commentary,* ad loc.; Meir of Narbonne, *Mil. Miẓvah,* Parma ms., pp. 111b–12a; Moses of Salerno, Posnanski ms., p. 34; Mordecai of Avignon, M.E., Vat. ms., p. 8b. Meir of Narbonne quotes a Christian argument based on the previous verse in Proverbs, which says, "There are three things which are too wonderful for me, yea, four which I know not." This is said to imply that the fourth thing is mysterious, and since "the way of a man with a maid" is the fourth thing listed in verse 19, it must be something unusual (*Mil. Miẓvah,* Parma ms., pp. 45a, 122a). For another Christian response to the Jewish argument from this verse, see William of Bourges, *Liber Bellorum Domini contra Judeos et Haereticos,* in M. H. Vicaire, " 'Contra Judaeos' Meridionaux au Début du XIIIᵉ Siècle. Alain de Lille, Evrard de Béthune, Guillaume de Bourges," *Cahiers de Fanjeaux* 12 (1977): 290–1.

10   **Even one who is not a virgin is called 'almah** Cf. *Sefer HaBerit, Mil. Ḥovah,* p. 28b = Talmage's ed. p. 44, and Solomon de' Rossi, Posnanski ms., the second p. 41 (there is an error in the pagination), for the argument that the masculine 'elem can refer to a young boy (e.g., 1 Samuel 17:56); the relevant lines are missing in Rosenthal's ed., *Meḥqarim,* 1:417, line 13. Jewish statements conceding for the sake of argument that 'almah does mean virgin are found in Crispin's *Disputatio,* p. 44, and in the additions to *Sefer HaBerit, Mil. Ḥovah,* p. 28a = Talmage's ed., p. 43. In both cases, the argument is that even if 'almah meant virgin, the reference would be to a virgin who would become pregnant and in the process lose her virginity. Blumenkranz, in citing the reference from Crispin in *Juifs et Chrét.,* p. 238, gives the impression that this was the actual position of the Jew quoted; the truth is that it is made quite clear later on in the *Disputatio* that this was suggested only for the sake of argument (p. 55). The Jew's real position is allegedly that 'almah means one who is hidden (*abscondita*); so also in Peter of Blois, PL 207.841, and Alan of Lille, PL 210.415, both undoubtedly from Crispin. On the possibility that this was not a genuine Jewish interpretation, see R. J. Z. Werblowsky, "Crispin's Disputation," *JJS* 11 (1960): 69–77, esp. pp. 72–73. For 'almah as *abscondita,* see also William of Bourges, p. 290.

11   **Such a woman can even be called betulah** Cf. p. 104 for the analogous argument that even the Latin *virgo* does not necessarily mean virgin. The usual Jewish

L

position was that *betulah* did mean virgin; cf., e.g., Petrus Alfonsi's *Dialogus*, PL 157.614. In fact, both Meir of Narbonne (Parma ms., pp. 111b–12a) and Moses of Salerno (loc. cit.) try to show that *'almah* does not mean virgin from the fact that Scripture takes the trouble to specify that Rebecca was a *betulah* even though she is later called an *'almah* (Genesis 24:16, 43). Since the assertion that *betulah* needn't mean virgin would appear to help the Christian polemicist in his denial that Hebrew has a word for virgin other than *'almah*, this brief remark in N.V. is, on the surface, not only atypical but self-defeating. However, if we are willing to assume that the author left a few deductions to the reader without spelling them out, then this comment may reflect a subtle and persuasive argument. Everyone (or at least everyone capable of engaging in polemic) knows that the Bible uses the word *betulah* in legal contexts where it clearly intends to say virgin (e.g., Leviticus 21:3, 14 [cf. 13]). Now, if both *'almah* and *betulah* have the unequivocal meaning of virgin, then the use of *betulah* rather than *'almah* in a context requiring legal precision raises no serious problem for the Christian polemicist. If, however, the only unequivocal term for virgin is *'almah*, while *betulah* can mean any young woman, then the biblical use of *betulah* in such contexts is inexplicable. Thus, if *betulah* is equivocal, it follows that *'almah* must be equivocal too; it is therefore in the Jewish interest to establish that *betulah* can mean a non-virgin. No other explanation of this statement in N.V. is readily apparent, and the argument is, in fact, so good that one wonders about the usual line taken by both Jewish and Christian polemicists.

14   ***Why did they not call him Immanuel?*** So Moses of Salerno, Posnanski ms., p. 33. This Jewish argument was also cited by Tertullian, *Adversus Judaeos*, ch. 9, PL 2.617 = Tränkle, p. 20; Dionysius bar Salibi, cited in Williams, p. 107.

16-17   ***Isaiah had recently married a young virgin*** The view that the "young woman" was Isaiah's wife was expressed by Rashi, Joseph Kara, and Ibn Ezra, ad loc. Other Jews maintained that she was the wife of Ahaz; cf. David Kimḥi's commentary, ad loc., and Petrus Alfonsi's *Dialogus*, PL 157.614.

25   ***As a result of intercourse*** See pp. 104–05. The author himself did not believe that Isaiah 8:3 refers to the same child as the one in 7:14. Some Christians, however, did; see Peter of Blois, PL 207.841.

25-26   ***She, the prophetess, called his name Immanuel. . . .*** See Rashi ad loc.

Page 101

12   ***Where did he get two children?*** This was a particularly weak question since Isaiah had an additional son whose name was also symbolic (Isaiah 7:3).

16-17   ***What sort of sign would this have been for Ahaz?*** This was the basic Jewish question with regard to the Immanuel passage. See Jacob ben Reuben, *Mil. HaShem*, pp. 87–88; Ibn Ezra's commentary ad loc.; David Kimḥi's commentary ad loc. (cf. Talmage, *HUCA* 38:216); *Sefer Yosef HaMeqanne*, Rosenthal's ed., pp. 75–76;

L

Andrew of St. Victor's commentary quoted by Richard of St. Victor in *De Emanuele*, PL 196.601, and translated in part in B. Smalley, *The Study of the Bible in the Middle Ages*, second ed. (Notre Dame, 1964), p. 163; Petrus Alfonsi's *Dialogus*, PL 157.614. The closest parallels to the passage in N.V. are in Kimḥi's *Sefer HaBerit, Mil. Hovah*, p. 29a = Talmage's ed., p. 45, where reference is made to the signs of Hezekiah and Gideon in that order, although the reference to Moses is missing, and in both Meir of Narbonne (*Mil. Miẓvah*, Parma ms., p. 111b) and Moses of Salerno (Posnanski ms., p. 34), who mention Moses, Gideon, Samuel (1 Samuel 10:3 ff.), and Hezekiah.

18   ***Three hundred years*** Repeated on page 102. On p. 104 he says one thousand, which was probably conscious hyperbole. The precise chronology was complicated by various factors; see Rosenthal's note in *Mil. HaShem*, pp. 87–88, and cf. Ibn Daud's *Sefer HaQabbalah*, ed. Cohen, ch. 1-2, pp. 5-25. While the discrepancy may result from a multiplicity of sources used by N.V., the basis for these numbers is obscure.

29   ***This refers to the cross*** Cf. p. 109. For the view that the "government" here is the cross, see Jerome, *In Esaiam, CC, Ser. Lat.*, 73, p. 126; Isidore, *De Fide Cath.* I.5.2, I.34.1, I.35.3, PL 83.460 (= Eggers, p. 42), 483, 484-85. For the christological interpretation of this passage, cf. also Peter of Blois, PL 207.838; Walter of Châtillon, PL 209.427; Alan of Lille, PL 210.415. For Jewish refutations, see Meir of Narbonne, Parma ms., pp. 112a-b; Moses of Salerno, Pos. ms., p. 44; Solomon de' Rossi, Rosenthal's *Meḥqarim*, 1:403-4.

Page 102

16   ***Hezekiah*** See Rashi, Ibn Ezra, Joseph Kara, and David Kimḥi ad loc., and cf. J. Kimḥi, *Sefer HaBerit, Mil. Hovah*, p. 29b = Talmage's ed., p. 46. For a Christian argument against this view, see Fulbert of Chartres, *Tractatus contra Judaeos*, PL 141.313, cited in *Auteurs*, p. 240, and *Juifs et Chrét.*, p. 238.

31   ***Thus, he does not establish the kingdom of Judah. . . .*** This argument is repeated on p. 132.

Page 103

15-16   ***There is, after all, no doubt that the Lord's hand is not incapable of fulfilling his will and desire*** The author thus explicitly concedes the philosophical possibility of virgin birth, as did the author of the so-called *Vikkuaḥ LehaRadaq, Mil. Hovah*, p. 16b = Talmage's ed., p. 91 (cf. appendix 2). Various Christian polemics reflect a Jewish argument that such a thing is impossible, and some Jews undoubtedly did say this in the heat of argument; cf. Williams, pp. 105, 301, and *Juifs et Chrét.* pp. 260–62. Crispin's antagonist argues that conception from the divine essence is impossible, which is a somewhat different argument and which, indeed, Crispin himself concedes (*Disputatio*, p. 46; Mary did not conceive *de dei substantia* but from the *potentia et virtute dei*).

L
17-18   ***How do you know that this virgin is Mary?*** Cf. *Trypho*, ch. 36 and 39, for the Jewish argument that various alleged christological passages contain no specific reference to Jesus even if one grants the basic Christian interpretation.

18-19   ***Where do you find her name or that of her son so that you may know?*** A satirical play on the christological interpretation of Proverbs 30:4.

21-22   ***You could make the same claim of divinity.*** . . . Cf. p. 152.

28   ***His name is God*** Read *shem El* rather than *sham El* in light of p. 152.

30   ***"There is no new thing . . ."*** Cf. p. 129.

Page 104

6-7   ***That she has already conceived*** On p. 100, however, the author had taken *harah* to be future tense. For the view expressed here, cf. Genesis 38:24.

21   ***We saw nothing in him during his youth*** Cf. p. 148.

28-29   ***It is not virgo but puella that means virgin*** *Virgo* is the Vulgate's translation of Isaiah's *'almah*. The text of N.V. here is not altogether clear, but this interpretation is indicated by a parallel in the later *Nizzahon* of Yom Tov Lipmann Mühlhausen (sec. 225). If we are prepared to ignore Mühlhausen, then the sense of the passage could be that *virgo* means the same thing as *puella*, i.e., a young woman. Such an interpretation of *puella* is better Latin, fits more easily into the reading of the Munich manuscript, and is corroborated in part by the author of the *Tractatus* in TNA 5.1567-8 = PL 213.807-8, who cites a Jewish assertion that *'almah* means *puella* (as well as *adolescentula* and *abscondita*) rather than *virgo*.

34-35   ***On the basis of what prophecy. . . ?*** The prophecy, said Jerome, was the one in Luke 1:48 (*In Esaiam, CC, Ser. Lat.*, 73, p. 112).

Page 105

3   ***Tiqrav refers to intercourse*** This view was championed by Naḥmanides in a halakhic context. See his strictures on Maimonides' *Sefer HaMizvot, lo ta'aseh* no. 353.

18   ***What sort of sign was this?*** See p. 101.

Page 106

2   ***Indeed, they never even saw each other.*** . . . At first glance, this statement is extremely peculiar; if they never saw each other, how could they testify together about anything? It was undoubtedly for this reason that the sentence was bracketed in the Paris manuscript with a marginal note indicating that it is unnecessary. As Posnanski points out, however, the author's statement is based upon a talmudic interpretation in *B. Makkot* 24b. Nevertheless, that interpretation is beset by some

L
blatant difficulties (see *Tosafot*, ad loc.), and it is inconceivable that many Christians would have been persuaded by it.

27-28   ***There isn't a single heretical statement. . . .*** See *B. Sanhedrin* 38b.

Page 107

1   ***A reference to Jesus*** See Romans 15:12; *Trypho*, ch. 87; Cyprian, *Test.* 2:2, PL 4.705-6; Isidore, *De Fide Cath.* I.9.7, PL 83.466 = Eggers, p. 70 (and cf. 2.2.4, PL 83.504); *Mil. HaShem*, pp. 85, 90-91.

2-3   ***How do they know that Jesus . . . came from . . . David?*** The issue of Jesus' genealogy was problematical as early as New Testament times; cf. Mark 12:35-37 with the genealogies in Matthew and Luke and with Hebrews 7:14. Hulen argues that early Christian concern with genealogical contradictions in the Gospels may reflect Jewish arguments (*JBL* 51:61), but his evidence is extremely tenuous.

12-13   ***The Jews always married their relatives*** Talmage cites Ambrose, PL 15.1590, and Augustine, *Contra Faustum* 23, CSEL 25:713 ff. (*HTR* 60:329). This argument underlies Jacob ben Reuben's refutation in *Mil. HaShem*, p. 143, and it is cited explicitly by Meir of Narbonne, Parma ms., p. 98b. Judah Kaufmann cites a reference to this Christian argument in the later *Niẓẓaḥon* to demonstrate Yom Tov Lipmann Mühlhausen's knowledge of the church fathers (*R. Yom Tov Lipmann Mühlhausen* [Hebrew] [New York, 1926/27], p. 54); all it really proves is his knowledge of earlier Jewish polemic.

35   ***Were the prophecies . . . fulfilled?*** The Jewish argument from the nonfulfillment of messianic prophecies of peace was central. *See Doctrina Jacobi Nuper Baptizati*, ed. Bonwetsch, p. 18 (the Messiah will come ἐν ἡσυχίᾳ καὶ γαλήνῃ); Crispin's *Disputatio*, p. 34, where the Jew cites Isaiah 2:4 and remarks that there is hardly sufficient raw material for the manufacture of all the swords that are in demand; Petrus Alfonsi's *Dialogus*, ch. 9, PL 157.636 (also with reference to Isaiah 2:4); Alan of Lille, PL 210.410-11, who cites the same argument as Crispin; the so-called *Vikkuaḥ LehaRadaq, Mil. Ḥovah*, pp.14a-b = Talmage's ed., p.86; Meir of Narbonne, *Mil. Miẓvah*, Parma ms., pp. 31b-32a, 44a-b, 103b-105b, 106b-107a; Naḥmanides' disputation in *Ketavei Ramban*, 1:311, where he cites Isaiah 2 and notes that the stability of the Spanish government depends on war; Solomon de' Rossi, *'Edut HaShem Ne'emanah*, Rosenthal's *Meḥqarim*, 1:390; Mordecai of Avignon, M.E., Vat. ms., pp. 9b-11a. See also *Juifs et Chrêt.*, pp. 251-52.

Page 108

1   ***This is to be understood allegorically*** Allegorical interpretations of Isaiah 11 are found in *Doctrina Jacobi Nuper Baptizati*, p. 13; G. Bardy (ed.), *Les Trophées de Damas*, p. 221 (cf. Parkes, *Conflict*, p. 288); Isidore, *De Fide Cath.*, I.9.8 ff., PL 83.466-67 = Eggers, pp. 72-74; Crispin, *Disputatio*, pp. 38-39; Damian, *Dialogus*, PL 145.62; Petrus Alfonsi, *Dialogus*, PL 157.636-37; *Mil. HaShem*, p. 85; Alan of Lille, PL

L

210.411; Mordecai of Avignon, M.E., Vat. ms., p. 9b; Evrard of Béthune, p. 1579. The allegorization often involved a reference to knights who become monks, and in this form N.V.'s argument that this is nothing new may not be strictly applicable. A general statement of the spiritualization of the Messiah's function is found in this context in Odo of Cambrai's *Disputatio contra Judaeum*, PL 160.1103 ("Nos per Christum regnum coelorum exspectavimus, et felicitatem quam vos [i.e., Jews] terrenam, nos per Christum speramus coelestem"). It should be noted that Maimonides also allegorized Isaiah 11:6, but in an entirely different way and without affecting its message of universal peace (*Hilkhot Melakhim* 12.1).

8   **The book of Joseph son of Gorion** I.e., *Josippon*, a famous medieval Jewish historical work. Cf. Ibn Ezra on Isaiah 2:2: "There was no time after Isaiah when no wars took place; indeed, it is written in the book of ben Gorion . . . that war did not cease in the period of the Second Temple." Ibn Ezra, however, may be refuting Jews who felt that various messianic prophecies had been fulfilled.

9   **Desecrated the grave** The author of Rome ms. 53 (p. 22a = Pos. "Mordecai of Avignon" ms., p. 16 = Rosenthal's "Menaḥem," p. 65) also asked why the holy sepulcher is in Muslim hands. Cf. also Mordecai of Avignon, M.E., Vat. ms., p. 9b. This reference to the sepulcher is especially appropriate here, because Isidore had interpreted the next verse (Isaiah 11:10) as a reference to it (*De Fide Cath.*, I.9.11); so also Peter of Blois, *Contra Perfidiam Judaeorum*, PL 207.847, and Walter of Châtillon, PL 209.427. For the Christian charge that the Jews were ultimately responsible for the desecration of the sepulcher by the Muslims in 1009, see *Auteurs*, pp. 251, 252, 257, and R. Chazan "1007–1012: Initial Crisis for Northern European Jewry," *Proceedings of the American Academy for Jewish Research* 38–39 (1970–71): 109–110.

14   **It refers to Hezekiah and Sennacherib** This may be part of the hypothetical interpretation introduced by the phrase "even granting all his arguments"; the author himself interpreted the passage messianically since he had argued above that it was not fulfilled. Ibn Ezra, however, does cite the view of Moses ibn Gikatilla that the passage really refers to Hezekiah in light of the end of chapter 10; indeed, it was probably such an exegesis which led to the famous remark by Rabbi Hillel that "Israel has no Messiah, for he has already been consumed in the days of Hezekiah" (*B. Sanhedrin* 99a) and to the statement that God wanted to make Hezekiah the Messiah (ibid., 94a). (Cf. also Rabban Yoḥanan ben Zakkai's remark, "Prepare a seat for Hezekiah king of Judah who is coming" [*B. Berakhot* 28b], a remark which many scholars consider messianic.) For some reservations regarding the common view that Jews habitually avoided messianic interpretations because of Christianity, see Talmage, *HUCA* 38:220–22. Cf. also the introduction, pp. 10–11.

19–20   **He . . . should not fear** The same argument from this verse is found in *Sefer*

L

Yosef HaMeqanne, Rosenthal's ed., p. 77, and in Solomon de' Rossi, *'Edut HaShem Ne'emanah*, Rosenthal's *Meḥqarim*, 1:385.

Page 109

9   ***The bishop himself*** Presumably the bishop in the author's town.

15-16   ***However, when it says. . . .*** A rather obscure sentence. It apparently constitutes the author's refutation and presents the following position: Granted (for the
sake of argument) that verse 5 refers to Jesus, it contrasts with verse 6, and the
really messianic verse is consequently not about him. The argument is much
clearer in *Sefer Yosef HaMeqanne* (Rosenthal's ed., pp. 76-77), where verse 5 is taken
to mean that *Christians* will call him "wondrous counselor," etc. and that this explains the punishment detailed in verse 4. The true Messiah, however, will bring
genuine peace (verse 6), which Jesus did not do. For the Christian explanation of
verse 6, see Peter the Venerable, PL 189.527 ff.

22   ***The heretics refer this to Jesus*** See Jerome, *In Esaiam, CC, Ser. Lat.*, 73, pp.
259-60. He maintains that the references to Moab just above allude to Ruth, from
whom Jesus was descended.

31   ***The beginning of the passage*** See R. David Kimḥi's commentary on Isaiah
16:1.

Page 110

3-4   ***"Lo, this God. . . . "*** This passage was referred to Jesus because it was
through his incarnation and passion that death was believed to have been "swal-
lowed up forever" (Isaiah 25:8); see Jerome, op. cit., p. 327.

20-21   ***It suffered exile twice thereafter. . . .*** See p. 108 and the notes there.

31-32   ***Why did the prophets not observe his Torah?*** See pp. 83-84.

Page 111

10   ***The heretics refer this to Jesus*** So Jerome, *In Esaiam, CC, Ser. Lat.*, 73, p. 406.

14-15   ***The Ishmaelites can also say. . . .*** So too on p. 117.

17   ***The verse refers to Hezekiah*** See Kimḥi, Joseph Kara, and Ibn Ezra, ad loc.

24   ***The Zion in heaven*** See Galatians 4:25-26 and cf., for example, Bernard's
Epistle 469 (= James, *The Letters of St. Bernard*, no. 395, p. 468) and his "First Sermon
for Septuagesima," *St. Bernard's Sermons for the Seasons and Principal Festivals of the
Year*, translated by a priest of Mount Melleray (Westminster, Md., 1950), 2:60. See
also R. Konrad, "Das Himmelsche und das Irdische Jerusalem im Mittelalterlichen
Denken," in *Speculum Historiale, Geschichte im Spiegel vom Geschichtsschreibung und
Geschichtsbedeutung*, ed. Bauer, Boehm, and Miller (Freiburg, 1965).

L
26-27   **There is no Zion in heaven** This denial resulted from polemical considerations, but it is difficult to imagine that the author believed it; see *B. Ta'anit* 5a. For a full discussion, see V. Aptowitzer, "The Heavenly Temple in the Agada" (Hebrew), *Tarbiz* 2 (1931): 137-53, 257-77 (esp. 266 ff.).

29-30   **Cyrus is Jesus** This interpretation originally resulted from a corrupt text of the Septuagint which said "to my anointed, to the Lord" ($\tau\hat{\omega}$ $\chi\rho\iota\sigma\tau\hat{\omega}$ $\mu\text{ου}$ Κυρίω) instead of "to my anointed, to Cyrus" ($\tau\hat{\omega}$ $\chi\rho\iota\sigma\tau\hat{\omega}$ $\mu\text{ου}$ Κύρω). This led to the view that two lords are mentioned in the verse, and the same conclusions were drawn as in Genesis 19:24 (see p. 51) and Psalms 110:1 (see pp. 160 ff.); indeed, Jerome, *In Esaiam, CC, Ser. Lat.*, 73a, p. 504, cites all three verses together. This erroneous reading is found in Barnabas 12:11, Tertullian's *Prax.* 28 and *Adversus Judaeos* 7, and Cyprian's *Testimonia* 1:21, all cited in H. B. Swete, *Introduction to the Old Testament in Greek* (New York, 1968; first printed 1902), p. 469. Barnabas too cites this verse together with Psalms 110:1, as does pseudo-Gregory, PG 46.228; see *Ver. Israel,* p. 187. This sort of exegesis is also reflected in the question which the "heretic" asked R. Idi: "It is written, 'And to Moses he said, Go up to the Lord'; 'Go up to me' is what it should have said" (*B. Sanhedrin* 38b). Jerome, loc. cit., was aware of the fact that this reading was in error and considered the identification of Cyrus with Jesus ridiculous ("Satis mirari nequeo quae stultitia sit legentium ut haec ad Christum referant"—p. 505), but Isidore defends this identification no matter what the correct reading might be. It is of some interest that Meir of Narbonne, Naḥmanides, and Moses of Salerno ignored the possible identification of Cyrus with Jesus in citing the fact that Cyrus is called "messiah" to prove that the term can refer to any ruler. See *Mil. Mizvah*, Parma ms., pp. 39a, 149a; *Ketavei Ramban*, ed. Chavel, 1:313; Moses of Salerno, Posnanski ms., p. 60.

Page 113

1-2   **"We are called Israel"** See pp. 126-27 ff. and the notes there.

19-20   **Two powers** See pp. 75-76 and the notes there.

23   **Were all those who died before Jesus' birth part of Christendom?** On p. 142, the author proposes the more extreme argument that there was no "Christendom" at all before the advent of Jesus. On the antiquity of "the Christian name," see Eusebius, *Ecclesiastical History*, trans. C. F. Cruse (London, 1897), ch. 2 ff., pp. 3 ff.

31   **"Therefore shall Zion be ploughed as a field"** Cf. pp. 111, 116. Later, he explains why Jews can admit that such prophecies were said about them but Christians cannot; see pp. 126-27.

Page 114

8   **"For they shall see eye to eye. . . . "** For the Christian interpretation cited here, see Jerome, *In Esaiam, CC, Ser. Lat.*, 73a, pp. 580 ff.

L
20   *"Behold, my servant shall succeed. . . ."* A *locus classicus* of Jewish-Christian polemic. See, for example, Mark 15:28; *Trypho,* ch. 13 (where the entire passage is quoted); Cyprian, *Testimonia* 2:15, PL 4.708-9; Jerome, *In Esaiam, CC, Ser. Lat.,* 73a, p. 586 (where he argues that the reference here is crystal clear); Augustine's sermon on the Jews, *Judenpredigt,* p. 102; *Altercatio Simonis Judaei,* PL 20.1174-75, cited in *Auteurs,* p. 30; Isidore, *De Fide Cath.,* I.15, PL 83.472-4; Damian, *Dialogus,* PL 145.55-6; Petrus Alfonsi, *Dialogus,* ch. 9, PL 157.633 ff.; Rupert, *Dialogus,* PL 170.573; Peter the Venerable, PL 189.544 ff. Origen refers to debates between Jews and Christians regarding this chapter; see Hulen in *JBL* 51:59-60. Various Jewish views of this passage were collected by A. Neubauer and S. R. Driver in *The Fifty-third Chapter of Isaiah according to the Jewish Interpreters* (Oxford, 1876/77); the dominant view regarded the servant as a symbol of Israel.

24   *This was not the case until now* A similar argument was posed in *Mil. HaShem,* pp. 106-7, but Jacob ben Reuben then backtracked a bit by citing Isaiah 33:10 ("Now will I rise, says the Lord").

Page 115

5-6   *"You are fairer than the children of men"* The same alleged contradiction is cited in *Mil. HaShem,* pp. 68, 106.

17   *His forgiving of their sins* The Hebrew word *nasa* can have the related meanings of both "bear" and "forgive."

34-35   *It was not because of our transgressions. . . .* The contrast here seems to be between transgressions and a decree, but that decree itself was, according to Christians, the result of a transgression, namely, original sin. The real point is that the verse indicates that the cause of his death was *our* transgressions and not their transgression. The argument is clearer in the following quotation from *Sefer Yosef HaMeqanne:* "Moreover, it says, 'For the transgression of my people was he stricken.' Now, was he really stricken for the transgression of his people? After all, he accepted death only to atone for the sin of eating from the tree of knowledge, a sin which caused everyone to descend to hell. It should therefore have said, 'For the transgression of Adam and Eve was he stricken' " (Rosenthal, p. 79; Hebrew text also in Neubauer and Driver, *Fifty-third Chapter of Isaiah,* p. 68). The author of N.V. may have intentionally called it a decree rather than a result of transgression because of his conviction that such a punishment would be so irrational that the term "decree" is the only appropriate one.

37   *If you will then say. . . .* I.e., there are two alternatives. Jesus may have died to save those who were in hell at the time of his death, in which case the phrase "our transgressions" makes no sense: or he may have died to atone for the sins of his believers after his death, in which case Christians can do whatever they please with impunity. On alleged Christian immorality, see p. 69 and the notes there, and cf. pp. 206, 228.

Page 116

8   ***Was spoken by Jesus*** So interlinear gloss ad loc. The entire passage is explained as a reference to Jesus in *Trypho*, ch. 14.

20-21   ***Where were they exiled?*** Cf. p. 61.

27   ***A name cannot be seen*** Thus, the author, like the Targum, R. David Kimḥi, and, indeed, the Septuagint and Vulgate, would translate *veyir'u* as "They will fear" instead of "They will see." The ambiguity was created by the fact that the Hebrew word for fear would normally be written with a double *yod*, while only one is found in the Masoretic text here. Ibn Ezra ad loc. does cite a view that the word here means "see" and that "the name of the Lord" is the equivalent of "the deeds of the Lord."

Page 117

1   ***"The spirit of the Lord God is upon me"*** For the christological interpretation cited here, see Jerome, *In Esaiam, CC, Ser. Lat.*, 73a, p. 706, and Isidore, *De Fide Cath.*, I.4.8, PL 83.459 = Eggers, p. 36.

9   ***He admits that he is not an equal*** Jerome, loc. cit., argues that he speaks humbly in accordance with his human form.

12   ***"And the nations shall seek your righteousness. . . ."*** See Jerome, ibid., pp. 713-14, and Damian, *Dialogus*, PL 145.48-49.

29-30   ***This is what Jesus told the Jews. . . .*** See Romans 10:20-21 and Jerome, *In Esaiam, CC, Ser. Lat.*, 73a, p. 744. Cf. also *Sefer Yosef HaMeqanne*, Rosenthal'ʂ ed., p. 82.

Page 118

5-6   ***"Who eat swine's flesh"*** Cf. below, pp. 206, 211. Many Jewish polemicists referred this verse to the Christians. See Jacob ben Reuben, *Mil. HaShem*, p. 114; Meir of Narbonne, *Mil. Miẓvah,* Parma ms., p. 117b (cf. also pp. 4b-5a, 121a, and S. Stein, "A Disputation on Moneylending," *JJS* 10 [1959]: 53); *Sefer Yosef HaMeqanne, Kiev Festschrift,* Heb. sec., p. 134; Moses of Salerno, Posnanski ms., p. 51.

14   ***Many Jesuses*** Cf. pp. 53, 72. Jerome, ad loc., p. 752, cites two views: one that the "seed" is Jesus and the other that it refers to the apostles; N.V.'s question is, of course, relevant only to the first explanation.

17-18   ***All the verses . . . constitute an answer. . . .*** I.e., they refer to the future punishment of Christians.

27-28   ***Month by month and week by week.*** A rhetorical flourish bringing us back to the end of Isaiah (66:23).

Page 119

3-4   ***The heretics refer this to Jesus, who took the souls out of hell*** So Isidore, *De Fide Cath.*, I.52.1, PL 83.491-2.

4-5   ***"I shall decree your death. . . ."*** This is the way most Jewish commentators took the verse, but another translation was possible. The Vulgate translates, "I will be your death, O death" ("Ero mors tua, O mors"), and the Christian in *Mil. HaShem*, assuming this interpretation, cites this part of the verse as evidence of the christological exegesis (p. 126, where Rosenthal points to 1 Corinthians 15:55 as a parallel). So also Crispin, *Disputatio*, p. 50.

15   ***And not concerning another God*** I.e., Israel's loyalty to its original God is what constitutes the alleged rebellion against Jesus, and that God is no idol even according to Christians.

28   ***"I will surely assemble all of you, O Jacob. . . . "*** One Christian interpretation maintained that the verse means that God would gather the believers among the Jews to the true faith; this interpretation was undoubtedly inspired by the sort of difficulty raised in N.V. See Haymo's *Enarratio in Michaeam Prophetam*, PL 117.150. I shall be referring to these *Enarrationes* on the twelve minor prophets as Haymo's because they are ascribed to him in PL and the issue of authorship is not decided definitively. It is likely, however, that the real author was Remigius of Auxerre; see C. Spicq, *Esquisse d'une Histoire de l'Exégèse Latine au Moyen Age* (Paris, 1944), p. 51.

Page 120

19   ***When God approached all the nations. . . .*** See B. *Avodah Zarah* 2b; *Sifrei Deuteronomy* 33:2. Cf. Katz, *Exclusiveness and Tolerance*, pp. 14-15, and Ginzberg, *Legends*, 3:80-82; 6:30-31.

26-27   ***This announcement . . . should have been made to every nation*** Thus the author reverses the common Christian argument that the Messiah must have come to save the entire world and not only the Jews; see, for example, the *Altercatio Aecclesiae contra Synagogam* cited in *Auteurs*, p. 223.

Page 121

6   ***The heretics say that this refers to Jesus*** See Matthew 2:5-6; John 7:42; *Trypho*, ch. 78; Tertullian, *Adversus Judaeos*, ch. 13, PL 2.633 = Tränkle, p. 33; Cyprian, *Testimonia* 2:12, PL 4.706; *Consultationes Zacchaei et Apollonii*, cited in *Judenpredigt*, p. 32; Isidore, *De Fide Cath.* I.11.1, PL 83.470; Fulbert of Chartres's second speech against the Jews, cited in *Auteurs*, p. 240; Petrus Alfonsi, *Dialogus*, PL 157.621; Peter the Venerable, PL 189.533; the *Tractatus* in TNA 5.1524 = PL 213.764; Peter of Blois, PL 207.842; Walter of Châtillon, PL 209.434; Alan of Lille,

L

PL 210.415; Joachim da Fiore, *Adversus Judaeos*, p. 51; *Mil. HaShem*, pp. 130-31; Meir of Narbonne, Parma ms., pp. 124b and 138a; *Sefer Yosef HaMeqanne*, Rosenthal's ed., p. 88; Moses of Salerno, Pos. ms., p. 55. Tertullian, loc. cit., used this verse not only as a reference to Jesus but also as proof that the Jews can no longer expect a Messiah. The verse, he argues, says that the Messiah will come from Bethlehem, and no Jews live in Bethlehem anymore; moreover, the Law prohibits the use of the oil necessary to anoint a king outside of Palestine.

20-21   *Was making peace . . . the purpose of Jesus' advent?* This can be taken in a number of ways. First, the major purpose was the purging of original sin. Second, there is no peace, and so Jesus' mission would be unfulfilled (this is explicit in *Sefer Yosef HaMeqanne*, loc. cit.). Third, this may be an oblique reference to the argument cited elsewhere that Jesus himself said that he came to bring not peace but the sword.

Page 122

9   *What evil did Judas do?* See p. 136 and the notes there.

25   *A scribal correction* So also Solomon de' Rossi, *'Edut HaShem Ne'emanah*, Rosenthal's *Meḥqarim*, 1:380. See Rashi, ad loc., and cf. *Minḥat Shai*, ad loc. The point is that the real meaning is "You will not die." For a full discussion of the problem of "scribal corrections," see S. Lieberman, *Hellenism in Jewish Palestine* (New York, 1950), pp. 28-37.

28   *Now to the earlier verse* It is not really earlier. Unless the order of N.V. itself has suffered a dislocation here, this would have to be explained on the basis of the fact that N.V. is largely an anthology and that the author (or his source) may have copied this passage from a context in which a later verse really preceded it.

30-31   *This was said about the hanged one who was sold for thirty coins* See, for example, Matthew 27:9; Isidore, *De Fide Cath.*, I.20.1, PL 83.478; Haymo, *Enarratio in Zachariam Prophetam*, PL 117.260; Damian, *Dialogus*, PL 145.63; *Mil. HaShem*, pp. 132-33; *Sefer Yosef HaMeqanne*, Rosenthal's ed., pp. 92-93.

Page 123

17-18   *The fourth exile* Cf. p. 47 and the notes there.

18   *Rabbi David* Posnanski identifies him with R. David of Melun (mid-thirteenth century), but this is uncertain.

Page 124

6-7   *This refers to Jesus* For Habakkuk 3 as a prophecy of the incarnation, see Haymo, *Enarratio in Habacuc Prophetam*, PL 117.118; Damian, *Dialogus,* PL 145.45; Richard of St. Victor, *Expositio Cantici Habacuc*, PL 196.401-4; the *Tractatus* in *TNA* 5.1528 ff. = PL 213.769 ff; Evrard's *Contra Valdenses*, pp. 1578-9. On the specific

L

reading of *shnayim* (two) for *shanim* (years), see Rosenthal's note in *Mil. HaShem,* p. 131. See also the citations in Williams, pp. 145, 323; Jerome, PL 26.1371-72; Isidore, *De Fide Cath.,* I.17.3, PL 83.476, and I.37.1, PL 83.486; Peter the Venerable, PL 189.529 ff. (who uses the reading of the Masoretic text).

27   *Legions* Hebrew *gedudim,* based on the last word of this verse (*yegudennu*).

33   *Will be killed* I.e., his name will be blotted out.

Page 125

2   *Jesus said this* See Walter of Châtillon, PL 209.435. Haymo apparently referred the statement to the second coming and thus avoided the difficulty raised in N.V. (*Enarratio in Sophoniam Prophetam,* PL 117.208). The christological explanation was also dealt with by Meir of Narbonne, *Mil. Mizvah,* Parma ms., p. 140a; *Sefer Yosef HaMeqanne,* Rosenthal's ed., p. 89; Solomon de' Rossi, '*Edut HaShem Ne'emanah,* Rosenthal's *Mehqarim,* 1:393.

13-14   *"And many nations shall be joined to the Lord"* For the Christian interpretation, see *Trypho,* ch. 115; Haymo, *Enarratio in Zachariam Prophetam,* PL 117.228-29; Walter of Châtillon, *Tractatus,* PL 209.435.

23   *It refers to the Second Temple* So R. Joseph Kara, ad loc. The main reasons for nonmessianic interpretation are verse 11 (which could, however, be regarded as part of a separate prophecy) and especially chapter 3. Nevertheless, the passage is too grandiose to be conveniently referred to the Second Temple. Ibn Ezra, ad loc., suggested that it was a conditional prophecy that remained unfulfilled while Kimhi, ad loc., was forced into the equally uncomfortable expedient of saying that part of the prophecy was messianic (until the end of verse 17) while the remainder referred to the Second Temple.

27   *"The Lord of hosts . . . in Jerusalem"* The omitted words, which refer to many nations coming to seek the Lord, may have been omitted through a scribal error since "Lord of hosts" are the last words before the omission as well as the last words of the omitted section.

28   *The heretics explain. . . .* See the *Gloss,* ad loc.

Page 126

4-5   *The God of the Jews and not of the Christians* This argument was posed by the Jew "Vecelin" in Albert of Metz, *De Diversitate Temporum,* ch. 23, cited in *Auteurs,* p. 249, who maintained that it is the God of Israel and not of the Gentiles who is spoken of throughout Scripture. Cf. p. 153.

12   *They are called Jews* On the issue of "true Israel" in general, see *Ver. Israel,* especially pp. 100-111, and *Judenpredigt,* pp. 164-75. See also N. Bonwetsch, "Der Schriftbeweis für die Kirche aus den Heiden als das wahre Israel bis auf

L

Hippolyt," *Theologische Studien: Theodor Zahn zum 10 October 1908 dargebracht* (Leipzig, 1908), pp. 3–22. Cf. also Talmage, *HUCA* 38: 222 ff., for a discussion of this problem in the works of R. David Kimḥi.

The explicit identification of Christians with Jews or Judah (and not only Israel) comes a bit later. Blumenkranz notes that this tendency begins in the fifth century (*Auteurs*, p. 216, n. 4); the truth is, however, that such an identification is made implicitly much earlier. See Revelations 2:9 and 3:9 (cited in *Ver. Israel*, p. 105), where the Jews are referred to as those who call themselves Jews, and are not, but are the synagogue of Satan. Such a statement obviously presupposes a favorable and non-"carnal" interpretation of "Jews" (probably from "confession"), and it is probable that the writer would have said, if asked, that Christians are the true Jews. For other early references, see *Ver. Israel*, pp. 104–5, n. 7.

For the explicit identification, see Augustine and others cited in *Judenpredigt*, p. 172 (especially Augustine's *In Psal.* 75:1–2, part of which is quoted on the title page of *Ver. Israel*); several references in Cassiodorus, cited in *Auteurs*, p. 59, n. 40; Isidore in PL 83.106, cited in *Auteurs*, p. 101; Haymo in PL 117.969, cited in *Auteurs*, p. 202 (Judah means confession and Christians confess Jesus), and cf. his *Enarratio in Amos Prophetam* on Amos 2:6, PL 117.110 (the church is the *vera confessio*); Raban Maur, *Expositio super Jeremiam*, PL 111.827, cited in *Auteurs*, p. 176 (Christians are Jews through the tribe of Judah from which Jesus comes). For other references, see the discussion in *Juifs et Chrét.*, pp. 275–77. See also *Sefer HaBerit, Mil. Hovah*, p. 33b = Talmage's ed., pp. 55–56, where Kimḥi points to the Christian practice of identifying Christendom with Israel or Judah provided the context is a favorable one, and see especially N.V., pp. 169 ff. One of the most interesting Jewish discussions of this issue appears in Rome ms. 53, pp. 25a–b = Rosenthal's "Menaḥem," pp. 72–74. "Rabbi Asher" (presumably the brother of Joseph Official) and "Menaḥem" note the Christian inconsistency in defining scriptural references to Israel and Judah and vigorously press the inextricable connection between verses describing the exile and redemption of Israel. But the most intriguing argument is that the Jews have retained the Hebrew language even after their alleged rejection by God. Menaḥem cites biblical etymologies and alphabetical poems (Lamentations, for example) to prove that Hebrew was the language of revelation (cf. *Kuzari* 2:68) and argues that God would have transferred this sacred tongue to Christians had the election of Jews as "Israel" really been revoked. A similar Jewish argument appears during the Reformation with a more modern twist about the superiority of original texts to translations; see H. H. Ben Sasson, "Jewish Christian Disputation in the Setting of Humanism and Reformation in the German Empire," *HTR* 59 (1966):381–82. In light of the passage in the Rome manuscript, Ben Sasson's remark that such an argument could only have arisen in the context of humanism and reformation needs to be toned down though not entirely discarded.

13   **Beichte** Confession.

30–31   *He exiled us in order to purge us of our sins* See the additions to *Sefer HaBerit*,

L

Mil. Ḥovah, p. 36a = Talmage's ed., p. 63; Solomon de' Rossi, *'Edut HaShem Ne'emanah, Sura* 3 (1948):260–64 = Rosenthal's *Meḥqarim,* 1:395–400; below pp. 226–28.

Page 127

8-12   ***Then why don't you fast . . . declared them holidays*** This translation is based on an emended text of doubtful accuracy.

19   ***Truthful dealing*** Not true faith.

Page 128

8-9   ***The heretics refer this entire passage to Jesus*** So Cyprian, *Testimonia* 2.5, PL 4.700. Cf. also the Christian in *Mil. HaShem,* p. 134. Jerome cited this view but rejected it in light of the fact that the context is unsuitable; see his *Commentarius in Malachiam Prophetam,* ad loc., PL 25.1633.

13-14   ***What does Jesus have to do with Levi?*** Jacob ben Reuben (*Mil. HaShem,* p. 134) put this more strongly, arguing that this passage would disprove the Christian contention that Jesus was from the house of David.

Page 129

3   ***The heretics say that this is Jesus*** See the *Consultationes Zacchaei et Apollonii,* bk. 2, cited in *Judenpredigt,* p. 31; Jerome in PL 28.1337 (cited by Rosenthal in *Mil. HaShem,* p. 139, n. 2); Isidore, *De Fide Cath.,* I.1.4, PL 83.451 = Eggers, p. 4; Peter the Venerable, PL 189.519, who says that this verse alone should be enough to convince Jews of the validity of Christianity. Cf. also *Mil. HaShem,* p. 140; *Mil. Miẓvah,* Parma ms., pp. 128a–b and especially pp. 146b–148a; *Sefer Yosef HaMeqanne,* Rosenthal's ed., p. 116.

10   ***"There is no new thing under the sun"*** Cf. p. 103. See *B. Shabbat* 30b for the clear implication that this verse was believed to apply to the messianic age as well.

Page 130

3-4   ***This was said of the hanged one*** So Jerome, *Commentarius in Ecclesiasten, CC, Ser. Lat.,* 72, p. 299.

Page 132

3   ***"An anointed one will cease to exist"*** In the Christian interpretation, "anointed one" here would simply mean the Jewish king while "most holy" would refer to Jesus. (Rosenthal, in *Sura* 3:269–70, and *Mil. HaShem,* p. 135, points to some ancient translations which take "most holy" as "most holy one," although his citation of Theodotion's καὶ τοῦ χρῖσαι ἅγιον ἁγίων is ambiguous since there ἅγιον can be either masculine or neuter.) For this combination of verses in Christian polemic, see, for example, Isidore, *De Fide Cath.,* I.5.8, PL 83.462 = Eggers, p. 50, and Damian, *Dialogus,* PL 145.46.

L

4   *Here they compose a nonexistent verse* So Jacob ben Reuben, *Mil. HaShem*, p.
135; Joseph Kimḥi in *Sefer HaBerit, Mil. Ḥovah*, pp. 26b, 27b = Talmage's ed., pp. 39,
41; Meir of Narbonne, Parma ms., pp. 38b, 121b, 148b-149a; Moses of Salerno,
Posnanski ms., pp. 59-60 (quoted by Perles, *MGJW* 24:22); Solomon de' Rossi,
'Edut HaShem Ne'emanah, Sura 3:270 = Rosenthal's *Meḥqarim*, 1:407. Cf. also *Sefer
Yosef HaMeqanne*, Rosenthal's ed., p. 120.

The question of the appropriate texts to use in polemic was extremely
important, and it was recognized rather early that effective polemic required the
use of texts whose authority was recognized by one's antagonists. The most
elementary aspect of this realization was the understanding that a Christian could
quote only the Old Testament to prove a point to a Jew (cf. Hippolytus, *Apodeik-
tike pros Ioudaious*, PG 10.792: Τί λέγεις πρὸς τοῦτο, ὦ 'Ιουδαῖε; Οὐ λέγει
Ματθαῖος, οὐδὲ Παῦλος, ἀλλὰ Δαυΐδ ὁ σὸς χριστός, and see Peter the
Venerable, *Tractatus*, PL 189.527, and Joachim da Fiore, *Adversus Judaeos*, pp.
56-7). There were, however, attempts to justify quotations from some apocryphal
works in polemic with Jews. Cf. Williams, p. 121, and see Crispin's *Disputatio*, p.
56; Peter of Blois, *Contra Perfidiam Judaeorum*, PL 207.839; Walter of Châtillon, PL
209.447-48; Alan of Lille, PL 210.405, 410, 417. Moreover, the question of which Old
Testament text to choose was more complex. Some Septuagint readings, for example, were too useful for a Christian polemicist to give up without a fight, and
defenses of such readings sometimes coupled with charges that the Jews deliberately changed biblical texts are rather common. See *Trypho*, ch. 71-73; Crispin's
Disputatio, pp. 55-56. In general, see Swete, *Introduction to the Old Testament in Greek*,
pp. 462 ff.; *Ver. Israel*, pp. 184-87; *Juifs et Chrēt.*, pp. 225-26.

20   *The kingdom of Greece* See p. 47 and the notes there. This view was probably taken from Ibn Ezra.

23   *Answer then. . . .* The basis of this argument is the reading, "An anointed
one will cease to exist *among you*." Such a reading is also cited in *Mil. HaShem*, p. 135
(one manuscript there gives the Latin text, "cum venerit sanctus sanctorum
cessabit unctio vestra"); *Sefer HaBerit, Mil. Ḥovah*, pp. 26b, 27b = Talmage's ed., pp.
39, 41; *'Edut HaShem Ne'emanah*, loc. cit. (For the origins of this reading, see Rosenthal in *Mil. HaShem*, loc. cit.). A clearer version of this argument appears in *Mil.
Miẓvah*, Parma ms., p. 38b.

31   *This chapter was said to warn and encourage people* Some Christians considered this chapter a description of Jesus; see Jerome [pseud.], *Breviarium in
Psalmos*, PL 26.903, and *Gloss*, ad loc. This is the reason for N.V.'s remark that it
is didactic and not descriptive.

Page 133

4   **Ecclesia** Church. For the christological interpretation of this chapter, see,

L

for example, Acts 2:31, and cf. Aphraates' citation of verse 10 as a reference to Jesus (Dem. 17, Neusner's *Aphrahat*, p. 74).

12   ***On the basis of this psalm.* . . .** This argument underlies the remarks in *Sefer HaBerit, Mil. Ḥovah,* p. 21b = Talmage's ed., p. 27, and David Kimḥi's commentary on Psalms 15:5, trans. Rosenthal in *JJS* 11:129. It is explicitly cited in *Sefer Yosef HaMeqanne,* ed. Rosenthal, pp. 61 and 101–2, and by the Christian in *Mil. Miẓvah,* trans. Stein, *JJS* 10:53. See also Solomon de' Rossi in Rosenthal's *Meḥqarim,* 1:405. Siegfried Stein, "The Development of the Jewish Law on Interest," *Historia Judaica* 17 (1955): 29–30, notes that Psalm 15 and Ezekiel 18:8 were cited by Christians since Jerome to prove the universal nature of this prohibition. It is especially noteworthy that the Talmud itself applied Psalms 15:5 to interest taken from Gentiles (*B. Makkot* 24a). Jewish polemicists did not, of course, volunteer this information, and although they could have explained it if necessary, they undoubtedly hoped that this brief talmudic comment would remain unnoticed by Christians.

17   ***Now, Moses said.* . . .** This argument was made by all the authors cited just above.

19–20   ***If you then say that the descendants of Esau are also called brethren.* . . .** This argument is cited in *Leqet Qaẓar, Michael* 4 (1976):71, and in *Sefer Yosef HaMeqanne, Festschrift A. Berliner's,* p. 89 = Rosenthal, p. 61, while the Christian in *Mil. Miẓvah* cites Deuteronomy 23:8 and Numbers 20:14 to show that "even one who does not belong to your people and faith is called 'thy brother' " (Stein, *JJS* 10:56). It is of some interest, in light of our notes to N.V., p. 55, that the Christian does not actually say that he is part of Edom. See Rosenthal, *Talpiyyot* 6:133 ff., and Cohen, "Esau as Symbol," pp. 19–48. The author of Rome ms. 53 (p. 25a = Pos. "Mordecai of Avignon" ms., p. 34 = Rosenthal's "Menaḥem," p. 72) quotes a Christian argument that if all righteous men are called children of God, then Christians and Jews are brothers. His response includes the caustic observation that this claim to brotherhood is rather surprising in light of the fact that Christians usually call Jews dogs.

22–23   ***Now, however, they have disqualified themselves*** The same argument (with the quotation from Obadiah) is found in *Leqet Qaẓar,* pp. 66 and 71, *Sefer Yosef HaMeqanne,* loc. cit., and *Mil. Miẓvah,* loc. cit.

In *Sefer Yosef HaMeqanne,* R. Moses of Paris was quoted as pointing out the hypocrisy of the Christian argument against interest by indicating that Christians themselves are involved in extensive usurious activity (*Festschrift A. Berliner's,* p. 90 = Rosenthal, p. 62), while Joseph Kimḥi had made the same point in *Sefer HaBerit, Mil. Ḥovah,* p. 21b = Talmage's ed., p. 27. Cf. also Jacob ben Elijah of Venice in Kobak, *Ginzei Nistarot,* 2:16–17, and Rome ms. 53, p. 23a = Pos. "Mordecai of Avignon" ms., p. 21 = Rosenthal's "Menaḥem," p. 68. This charge was made by Christians as well. Bernard, for example, said that Christians take usury in a

L
worse manner (*pejus judaizare*) than the Jews; see Baron, *A Social and Religious History of the Jews*, 4:121, 301. On the justifications for Jewish moneylending activities in Jewish law, see *Tosafot Bava Mezi'a* 70b, s.v. *tashikh*, and cf. the introduction.

29   ***For they are not circumcised*** In the Rome ms. version of this passage as well as in a separate discussion in part two of the ms. (p. 22b = Pos. "Mordecai of Avignon" ms., p. 20 = Rosenthal's "Menaḥem," p. 67), there are verses cited to prove that failure to be circumcised is a defining characteristic of a Gentile or "stranger." In the discussion in part two (pp. 22b-23a = Pos. ms., p. 21 = Rosenthal, p. 67), the author adds two verses to show that the same is true of failure to observe the Sabbath.

Page 134

6-7   ***His sin can be expiated through charity*** This interpretation of the verse is truly bizarre, since its real meaning is obviously that the usurer will be punished and lose his wealth, which will then go to a compassionate man. Cf. *Sefer Ḥasidim*, ed. Wistinetsky, p. 203, no. 808. Nevertheless, the view that there is nothing intrinsically and rationally immoral about taking interest even from a Jew was typical of the attitude held in this period; the dominant view was that the prohibition was a legal requirement of a character similar to that of purely ritual laws (oral communication from Dr. Haym Soloveitchik).

13   ***This refers to Jesus*** So Haymo, *Enarratio in Amos Prophetam,* PL 117.110; Damian, *Dialogus*, PL 145.63; "R. Samuel of Morocco," cited in Williams, p. 230; Walter of Châtillon, PL 209.433; the Christian in *Mil. HaShem*, p. 129; *Sefer Yosef HaMeqanne*, Rosenthal's ed., p. 86.

20   ***Jesus wants the death of one who dies. . . .*** Cf. p. 136.

28   ***To a different matter*** Perhaps the selling of Joseph. See the references in Williams, loc. cit., note 4, and *Da'at Zeqenim MiBa'alei HaTosafot* on Genesis 37:28.

Page 135

2   ***Do not trust them to pray for you. . . .*** Cf. below, pp. 210-11.

3-4   ***Do not trust in Jesus. . . .*** This interpretation of Psalms 146:3 was proposed by the Jew "Vecelin" in Albert of Metz, *De Diversitate Temporum*, ch. 23, cited in *Auteurs*, p. 248. Cf. below, p. 147.

13   ***"In that day the Lord shall be one. . . ."*** A very similar passage appears in Meir of Narbonne, *Mil. Miẓvah*, Parma ms., p. 21b; Christians, he says, call God by three names: father, son, and spirit. Cf. also *Sefer Yosef HaMeqanne*, Rosenthal's ed., p. 68.

Page 136

3   ***David said this of those who sinned. . . .*** Cf. Jerome [pseud.], *Breviarium*, PL

L

26.871, for the statement that the three categories of evildoers in this verse are Jews, Gentiles (i.e., pagans), and heretics.

9   ***He did want the death of the wicked*** The phraseology is a bit peculiar since it is obvious that Christians did not regard Jesus as wicked. Nevertheless, the main point is clear; in fact, it was made a bit earlier (p. 134) where a more appropriate verse was cited ("For I do not desire the death of one who dies"—Ezekiel 18:32).

10-11   ***Those who killed him fulfilled his will*** The problem of Jewish culpability for the crucifixion was frequently discussed. Its most common context, however, was the dilemma of foreknowledge and free will; indeed, in light of the belief that the purpose of the incarnation was the passion, it was almost a problem of predestination versus free will. In this formulation, of course, it would be insoluble by definition, and the point of various Christian statements on the subject was to deny the validity of this formulation. The Jews were not predestined to kill Jesus; God simply knew that they would do so of their own accord. See Eucher of Lyon, cited in *Auteurs*, p. 23, and cf. Leo the Great, PL 54.369: "Impios furentium manus non immisit in se dominus, sed admisit, nec praesciendo quod faciendum esset coegit ut fieret. . . ."

However, the question in N.V., which is also found in *Nestor HaKomer*, p. 2, is somewhat different. The author argues that the deed itself was not blameworthy but meritorious, and the elimination of predestination would therefore be of no use to a Christian polemicist. Augustine's response to this problem was that the intention of the Jews was evil even though God made the effect good (see *Judenpredigt*, p. 190; cf. Genesis 50:20 and Isaiah 10:5-7); in fact, it was probably this sort of response which impelled one Jewish polemicist to remark, "We can even say that the intention of the Jews was good when they killed him, inasmuch as they had heard him say that the salvation of the world depends upon his death" (the additions to *Sefer HaBerit*, *Mil. Hovah*, p. 36b = Talmage's ed. p. 64). The problem of Jewish culpability even led to the view that the cause of the punishment of the Jews was their cruel persecution of the apostles after the crucifixion (Gregory I in PL 75.862, cited in *Auteurs*, p. 86, and Bede [pseud.] in PL 93.460, cited in *Auteurs*, p. 138). Cf. also Lanfranc's enthusiastic description of the marvelous effects of the sin of the Jews (PL 150.141). In general, see *Juifs et Chrét.*, pp. 269-72. See also below, p. 216, for the argument that the crucifixion ought to be commemorated by a joyous festival in light of Christian belief.

It is of interest that there is another side to this coin. Jews were convinced for both psychological and scriptural reasons that Christians would be punished for mistreatment of Jews. But why should this be so? The purpose of the exile, after all, was to subject the Jews to chastisement. This question was raised by Meir of Narbonne, *Mil. Mizvah*, Parma ms., p. 130a. In response, he maintained that Christians did not have to fulfill their role quite so zealously, and he cited

L

Zechariah 1:15: "For I was but a little displeased, and they helped forward the affliction."

22   *In a verse that they refer to Jesus* For the christological interpretation of Zechariah 13:7, see Isidore, *De Fide Cath.*, I.25.1, PL 83.480, and Haymo, *Enarratio in Zachariam Prophetam*, PL 117.268.

22-23   *As I shall explain.* . . . The verse is not discussed elsewhere in N.V. although it probably was discussed in the author's source.

24   *"Awake, O sword. . . ."* Cited by Peter of Blois, PL 207.846.

Page 137

2-3   *This verse refers to the hanged one* See Hebrews 1:5, 5:5; Acts 4:26; Tertullian, *Adversus Judaeos,* ch. 12, PL 2.633 = Tränkle, pp. 32-33; Cyprian, *Testimonia*, 2:8, PL 4.703; Augustine, *Enarratio in Psalmos, CC, Ser. Lat.,* 38, pp. 3-7; *Altercatio Simonis Judaei*, PL 20.1167 = CSEL 45, p. 4, cited in *Auteurs*, p. 28; Isidore, *De Fide Cath.*, I.1.3, PL 83.451 = Eggers, p. 4; Fulbert of Chartres's second sermon against the Jews, cited in *Auteurs*, p. 240; Damian, *Dialogus*, PL 145.49; Peter of Blois, PL 207.829; Walter of Châtillon, PL 209.444; Alan of Lille, PL 210.404. For some Jewish responses, see *Doctrina Jacobi Nuper Baptizati*, ed. Bonwetsch, p. 43, and *Mil. HaShem*, pp. 63-65.

6   *It follows that he was born twice* This was a widespread Jewish question. See Meir of Narbonne, *Mil. Miẓvah*, Parma ms., pp. 125a-b, 143b-144a; *Sefer Yosef HaMeqanne*, Rosenthal's ed., p. 99; Moses of Salerno, Simon's ed., p. 9 (= Pos. ms., p. 13), and Posnanski ms., p. 56. Cf. also Williams, p. 122. The first two polemicists maintained that the contention that Psalm 2 refers to the birth of the flesh is untenable, because the verses describing the victory of this "son" were not fulfilled during Jesus' lifetime. Peter of Blois (loc. cit.) argued that the "day of the Lord" is eternity, and that "this day" therefore means "from eternity."

9-10   *Which of them calls the other my son . . .?* R. David Kimḥi argued elsewhere that the Christian interpretation of Psalms 2:7 is impossible because a father must precede a son by definition, and Christians maintain that father and son were always coexistent. If this were true, they would be called twin brothers. See Talmage, *HUCA* 38:220. (A translation of Kimḥi's commentary on Psalm 2 was provided by E. I. J. Rosenthal in *JJS* 11:128-29). So too Moses of Salerno, Simon's ed., p. 10, and Rome ms. 53, p. 24b = Pos. "Mordecai of Avignon" ms., p. 33 = Rosenthal's "Menaḥem," p. 71. Cf. also *Mil. HaShem*, pp. 9-12.

16   *I shall now ask a further question.* . . . On this passage, see appendix 5. This particular phrase (אשאלך והודיעני) also introduces Moses of Salerno's discussion of this question (Simon's ed., p. 5); it is based on Job 38:3; 40:7; 42:4.

30   *Jesus said this psalm.* . . . See *Trypho*, ch. 97. The interlinear gloss also in-

L

terprets the entire chapter as a statement by Jesus concerning the crucifixion and resurrection. Cf. Jerome [pseud.], PL 26.876: "This psalm can pertain both to David and to Christ, and through the latter to all the saints." See also *De Altercatione Ecclesiae et Synagogae*, PL 42.1137, cited in Williams, p. 332.

Page 138

16   ***"Him that is holy. . . ."*** The Vulgate translates, "Et scitote quoniam mirificavit Dominus sanctum suum," to which Augustine comments, "Who could this be but the one whom he resurrected from the lower regions and placed in heaven at his right hand?" (*Enarratio in Psalmos, CC, Ser. Lat.*, 38, p. 15). Cf. *Sefer Yosef HaMeqanne*, Rosenthal's ed., p. 101.

25   ***Who put gladness in his heart?*** For Jesus as the object of a divine act, cf. p. 51 and the notes there.

28–29   ***At the beginning of Psalms*** See p. 136.

29–30   ***The fact is. . . .*** This is the beginning of a long passage found only in the Munich manuscript and missing from the best manuscript of N.V., namely, the one printed in Wagenseil's *Tela Ignea Satanae*. Consequently, it is conceivable that this is an extensive interpolation; moreover, the relatively poor quality of the copyist's work means that there are more emendations and questionable translations in this passage than in any passage of equal length elsewhere in the book. The text in *Tela* resumes with the discussion of Psalm 18 on p. 144.

30   ***When he fled from Saul to Keilah*** 1 Samuel 23.

Page 139

14–15   ***"Kush the Benjamite"*** The rabbinic view that this is Saul was cited by Rashi, R. David Kimḥi, and Ibn Ezra in their commentaries, ad loc.

16–17   ***It is written in the glossa*** This interpretation is not found in the *glossa ordinaria*; there were, however, many collections of comments on Scripture that were known as glosses. See Smalley, *The Study of the Bible in the Middle Ages*, chapter 5.

26   ***A reference to Jesus*** So Cassiodorus, *Expositio Psalmorum, CC, Ser. Lat.*, 97, p. 79, also quoted in the *Gloss*, ad loc.

30   ***Jesus was a sinner*** Cf. pp. 89, 150, 160.

Page 140

6   ***Had reference to his father*** It was really not necessary to involve the father here; the Christian could simply have referred the verse to punishment inflicted by Jesus himself posthumously. The father may have been introduced by the author because Luke 23:34 is addressed to him and this would make the answer more telling.

L

9   *"Father, forgive them. . . ."* Another Jewish polemicist cited Jesus' prayer that the Jews be forgiven and then argued that if his prayer was "true" then the Jews are forgiven, and if it was not then Jesus' other statements must also have been false (the additions to *Sefer HaBerit, Mil. Ḥovah*, pp. 36b–37a = Talmage's ed., p. 64).

12   *This chapter is referred to Jesus* See Hebrews 2:6–9; Augustine, *Enarratio in Psalmos, CC, Ser. Lat.,* 38, pp. 50 ff.; Isidore, *De Fide Cath.*, I.5.3, PL 83.460–61 = Eggers, p. 44.

16   **Fili homini** Rather poor Latin which may be a copyist's error. Cf. p. 142. Properly: "Filius hominis."

29   *They admit that in the future we shall all live* Cf. p. 86 and the notes there.

Page 141

6   *It does not say* **Selah** The Vulgate does omit the *Selah*, which many Jewish commentators translated "forever."

12   *"Beside you"* The author translates *'al panekha* in the same way as in the second commandment (Exodus 20:3: "You shall have no other gods beside me"). However, the translation "in your sight" or "before you" does not, despite the author's statement, presuppose a different reading of the Hebrew text; see, for example, the Targum and R. David Kimḥi, ad loc.

15   *One who points out* **(moreh)** The Hebrew word for fear is usually spelled with an *aleph* at the end (*mora*); the unusual spelling with a *he* (*morah*) is what enabled the author to make this play on words.

23–24   *This chapter too was said of those who did not believe* Cf. Jerome [pseud.] that this is "the voice of the church against the heretics or of Christ against the demons" (PL 26.895). Rupert of Deutz maintained that the "wicked men" in verse 6 were the ancestors of the Jews, who "killed Christ, the Lord and king" (PL 170.574).

25–26   *"What did the righteous man do?" refers to Jesus* See interlinear gloss, ad loc.

29   *To himself* Cf. Williams, p. 83.

Page 142

18   *They do not maintain a consistent position* The Hebrew (אינן בדבריהם עומדים) is a bit awkward, and a minor emendation (אין דבריהם עומדים) would produce, "Their words do not stand up."

19–20   *David prayed for them* I.e., for the Jews in exile.

L

22   **These were the words of the ecclesia** So Jerome [pseud.], *Breviarium*, PL
26.899.

Page 143

7   **The chapter is thus about the exile** See R. David Kimḥi on Psalms 13:2.

9   **David said this chapter about the Jews. . . .** So Jerome [pseud.], *Breviarium*, PL
26.900, and Cassiodorus, *Expositio, CC, Ser. Lat.,* 97, p. 126, also quoted in *Gloss,* ad
loc. Cf. *Sefer Yosef HaMeqanne,* Rosenthal's ed., p. 101.

16-17   **But above it says, "The fool has said in his heart, There is no God"** I.e., since
this was also referred to the people who lived in Jesus' generation, it could not have
been "the generation of the righteous."

18   **It was said of the destruction of the Temple** See Rashi on Psalms 14:1 for the
view that this chapter was said concerning the destruction of the Temple in the
time of Nebuchadnezzar and that the almost identical chapter 53 was said of the
second destruction in the time of Titus. Cf. also Kimḥi's commentary to Psalms
14:1.

21   **Jesus said this prayer. . . .** See Jerome [pseud.], *Breviarium*, PL 26.909-10.

22-23   **David here is Christus** On this common identification, especially in
Psalms exegesis, see *Judenpredigt*, pp. 157-60. Cf. also below, p. 144.

29-30   **This shows that he himself was not God** This followed both from the very
fact of prayer and from the use of the term "God" rather than "father" or the like. If
the speaker were God, he would not identify the father simply as God since this
would not differentiate the father from the petitioner.

32   **Why did he pray for his life?** First, he had come in order to die. Second, he
could have saved himself easily enough without prayer. Cf. pp. 153-54.

Page 144

18   **The heretics refer this entire psalm to Jesus** See Augustine, *Enarratio in
Psalmos, CC, Ser. Lat.,* 38, p. 94; Isidore, *De Fide Cath.,* I.56.4, PL 83.494.

19   **Puero, the son** The Vulgate does say *puero,* but the word can mean servant
as well as son. (The same is true of the Septuagint's παῖς .)

22-23   **Who were guarding his grave** Matt. 27:62-66.

32   **Partly concerning Jesus. . . .** See Augustine, loc. cit., for the statement that
the speakers are "Christ and the church, i.e., the entire Christ, head and body."

L

Page 145

13   *In the language of the priests, it is written. . . .* The Vulgate reads, "Diligam te Domine fortitudo mea" (I love you, O Lord, my strength) which is identical with the Masoretic text; thus, the minor change from "Lord" (ה׳) to "God" (אלהי) indicated in N.V. is inaccurate. Moreover, it is hard to see what difference it would have made even if it were accurate. Perhaps the original reading was simply, "And it is written, 'I love you, O God, my strength,'" (ואומר ארחמך אלהי חזקי). A later reader may then have assumed that the slight error in the quotation resulted from the presumed fact that the Christian version was being quoted, and he inserted this information into the text. Alternately, the Latin text may have originally been quoted here (hence, "In the *language* of the priests") and then dropped in some early manuscript.

18-19   *He should have strengthened himself. . . .* The point of the passage is that either Jesus' body should have raised itself (if it was divine) or it was not worthy of being raised by God (if it was not divine). Cf. the *Doctrina Jacobi Nuper Baptizati*, ed. Bonwetsch, p. 33, for the extreme statement that the assumption is "impossible" (οὐδὲ γὰρ ἐνδέχεται); here the argument is simply that there would be no reason for it and that it is inconsistent with the curse in Genesis 3:20.

Page 146

6-7   *He should have done so openly. . . .* In effect, this answer concedes the validity of the Christian argument that the assumption could be rational because Jesus "was more important than other men" and that the analogy with other prophets is therefore not compelling.

     The question about the lack of a public resurrection and assumption and in general of the failure of Jesus to perform absolutely undeniable miracles in public was widespread in Jewish polemic. See pp. 43-4, 104, 148, and Meir of Narbonne, *Mil. Mizvah*, Parma ms., pp. 121a-b. Elsewhere, Meir reports an intriguing Christian explanation that undeniably clear miracles would have caused everyone to believe in Jesus; consequently, no one would have killed him and the purpose of his advent would have gone unfulfilled. Meir replies that (1) this means that those who killed him are not culpable; and (2) in that case, he should have appeared publicly after the resurrection. After all, the Bible says, "Cursed be he that makes the blind wander out of the way" (Deuteronomy 27:18). In sum, Jesus performed his major miracles in private and his minor ones in public (Parma ms., pp. 28a, 91b-92b). Finally, many Jewish polemicists asked why Jesus eliminated the supposedly hidden consequences of original sin and left the manifest results (pain in childbirth, etc.) intact. See Joseph Kimhi, *Sefer HaBerit, Mil. Hovah*, p. 20a = Talmage's ed., p. 24; Meir of Narbonne, *Mil. Mizvah*, Parma ms., pp. 102b-103a; *Sefer Yosef Ha-Meqanne, Kiev Festschrift*, Hebrew Section, p. 132; Rome ms. 53, p. 23b = Pos. "Mordecai of Avignon" ms., p. 26 = Rosenthal's "Menahem," p. 69.

L

12–13   ***Then the question is why he performed wonders*** Cf. the question in Origen's
Contra Celsum 2:72, cited above in the notes to p. 43.

22   ***All people looked at him. . . .*** Cf. p. 71.

Page 147

2   ***These are the apostles*** So Augustine in his *Enarratio in Psalmos, CC, Ser. Lat.,*
38, p. 102, and in his sermon on the Jews, *Judenpredigt*, p. 91; Isidore, *De Fide Cath.,*
I.55.4, PL 83.494.

7–8   ***This refers to Jesus for whom Mary was a tent. . . .*** See Augustine, *Enarratio in*
Psalmos., loc. cit., for the statement that the Vulgate's "In sole posuit tabernaculum
suum" refers to the incarnation and that "As a bridegroom coming out of his
chamber" refers to Jesus, who came out of a virginal womb. On the latter interpretation see also Isidore, *De Fide Cath.*, I.10.10, PL 83.470 ("Jesus Christus . . .
tamquam sponsus processit de thalamo suo, id est, ex virginis utero"). Cf.
Evrard's *Contra Valdenses*, p. 1578. (The editor's marginal note to Ps. 44 is inaccurate.)

17–18   ***All the prophets said not to listen to him*** On this collection of verses, cf. pp.
46, 75, 86, 97–98, 129, 131, 141, 180. *Sefer Nestor HaKomer*, p. 9, and Meir of Narbonne
(Parma ms., p. 39b) both cited Jeremiah 17:5 and Psalms 146:3 in this context.

Page 148

3–4   ***The verb "proclaims" should have been in the plural. . . .*** The full verse is,
"The heavens declare the glory of God, and the firmament proclaims his handiwork."

8   ***Those who came after him wrote their own text. . . .*** Cf. p. 156. The author
obviously knew that Jerome had, on the whole, defended the validity of the Hebrew
text; as a result, he assumed that any Vulgate deviation was a later change.

20   ***Immediately run in the street. . . .*** Cf. pp. 43–4, 104, 146, and see the *Vikkuaḥ*
LeHaRadaq, Mil. Ḥovah, pp. 16b–17a = Talmage's ed., p. 91, and below, pp. 214–15,
for the argument that Mary should have become pregnant at a very young age so
that the miracle would be manifest. In the *Vikkuaḥ LeHaRadaq*, the author maintains
that Jesus should have behaved like an adult from the moment he was born, but the
reason is different and rather curious. Menstrual blood, he says, is absolutely
filthy (מטונף ומלוכלך עד בלי די) and practically a poison; nevertheless, the fetus
is sustained by it for nine months through a miracle. Because of the nature of this
food, however, a human baby does not have the strength to walk (unlike a baby
animal, whose mother has no menstrual blood). Jesus' mother, on the other hand,
was supposed to have become pregnant through the holy spirit, and so he was not
fed by that "filthy blood." Consequently, "He should have walked on his feet the

L
day he was born; he should have spoken and been intelligent, just as he was at the age of thirty" (*Mil. Ḥovah*, p. 15a = Talmage's ed., p. 87). Talmage is of the opinion that this was an anti-Cathar argument, since it was the heretics who maintained that Jesus did not partake of ordinary nourishment (*HTR* 60:328); see, however, my "Christian Heresy and Jewish Polemic in the Twelfth and Thirteenth Centuries," *HTR* 68 (1975):289–93. On the belief in the poisonous nature of menstrual blood, see Maimonides, *Sefer Sammei HaMavet VehaRefuot Kenegdam*, ed. S. Muntner (Jerusalem, 1942), pp. 145–47; Naḥmanides' commentary on Genesis 31:35 and Leviticus 18:19 (cf. his *Torat HaShem Temimah, Ketavei Ramban*, ed. Chavel, 1:167); Gershon ben Shlomoh of Arles, *Gate of Heaven*, trans. F. S. Bodenheimer (Jerusalem, 1953), p. 252, no. 48.

31   **Tequfato in Latin. . . .** Apparently the author thought that *decursum* (the Vulgate has *occursus*) refers to the act of running and does not mean circuit; consequently, he corrected the Latin translation.

33   **The belief in his divinity is held by a minority** Cf. p. 89 and the notes there.

Page 149

2   **The heretics say. . . .** See Augustine, *Enarratio in Psalmos, CC, Ser. Lat.*, 38, p. 115. This Christian interpretation as well as some of N.V.'s replies are found in Meir of Narbonne, *Mil. Miẓvah*, Parma ms., pp. 125b, 144b, and *Sefer Yosef HaMeqanne*, Rosenthal's ed., p. 103.

10-11   **It is impossible to say this of the divine element within him. . . .** Exactly this either/or argument was made by R. David Kimḥi in his commentary, ad loc. See Talmage, *HUCA* 38:217, and Rosenthal, *JJS* 11:130.

Page 150

3   **Jesus said this psalm at the time of his hanging** Matthew 27:46; Mark 15:34. Note also *Trypho*, ch. 97–105; Augustine, *Enarratio in Psalmos, CC, Ser. Lat.*, 38, p. 117; *Altercatio Simonis Judaei*, PL 20.1175, cited in *Auteurs*, p. 30.

6   **"My God, my God, look at me. . . ."** The Vulgate reads, "Deus, Deus meus, respice me, quare me dereliquisti? Longe a salute mea verba delictorum meorum." Cf. the Septuagint: ὁ θεὸς ὁ θεὸς μου πρόσχες μοι· ἵνα τί ἐγκατέλιπές με; μακρὰν ἀπὸ τῆς σωτηρίας μου οἱ λόγοι τῶν παραπτωμάτων μου.

8   **Jesus himself admits that he is a sinner** Cf. pp. 89, 139. See also the additions to *Sefer HaBerit, Mil. Ḥovah*, p. 37a = Talmage's ed., p. 64.

11   **Ecclesiastes** A mistake. Cf. p. 71. This verse was cited for the same purpose by Meir of Narbonne, *Mil. Miẓvah*, Parma ms., pp. 27b, 91a, 145a–46a.

13-14   **Ask the heretics . . . why he cried out for help** For Jewish reactions to the christological interpretation of this psalm, see the late eighth-century *Epistola ad*

L
Elipandum by Heterius and Beatus, PL 96.1003, cited in *Auteurs*, p. 149; *Mil. HaShem*, pp. 66–67; the additions to *Sefer HaBerit*, loc. cit. = Talmage's ed., p. 65; *Mil. Mizvah*, loc. cit.; *Yosef HaMeqanne*, ed. Rosenthal, p. 104; Moses of Salerno, Pos. ms., pp. 57–59; Rome ms. 53, pp. 24a–b = Pos. "Mordecai of Avignon" ms., pp. 30–31 = Rosenthal's "Menahem," p. 71. Some Jewish authors presented an either/ or argument here: If he prayed for the salvation of his flesh, then his prayer did no good, and if he prayed for his divinity, the prayer was unnecessary (and a person would not pray for something he does not need). See R. David Kimhi's commentary, ad loc., cited in Talmage, *HUCA* 38:218 = *Vikkuah LeHaRadaq, Mil. Hovah*, pp. 13a–b = Talmage's ed., p. 65; Rome ms. 53, loc. cit.

31   **Foderunt** "They pierced," reading *karu* (from *kry*, which basically means to dig) for *ka'ari*. Cf. p. 154. This reading is cited as evidence of the crucifixion by Aphraates, Dem. 17, Neusner's *Aphrahat*, pp. 73–74; Jerome, *In Esaiam, CC, Ser. Lat.*, 83A, p. 559; Augustine, *Enarratio in Psalmos, CC, Ser. Lat.*, 38, p. 119; Isidore, *De Fide Cath.*, I.36.1, PL 83.485; Damian, *Dialogus*, PL 145.46; Peter the Venerable, PL 189.550; Peter of Blois, PL 207.846; Walter of Châtillon, PL 209.444. See also *Mil. HaShem*, p. 66, and Kimhi's commentary ad loc., cited in Talmage, *HUCA* 38:216.

33–35   **The practice . . . did not exist** On Jewish methods of execution, see *Mishnah Sanhedrin*, ch. 7.

Page 151

1   **"They counted. . . ."** Vulgate: "Dinumeraverunt omnia ossa mea."

3   **They divided his clothes among them** See Mat. 27:35 and parallels.

11   **Lo instead of lo'** *Lo* (לוֹ) means "for him" while *lo'* (לֹא) means "not." The Vulgate has *illi* with a variant of *ipsi*; however, it also has "my soul" (*mea anima*) rather than "his soul," and this phrase is the subject of the verb rather than its object.

14–15   **The fat things on earth** This phrase is thus taken as the object of "eat" instead of the subject.

23   **When God left that body. . . .** That he did leave is stated in the verse itself ("Why have you forsaken me?"). The first part of this argument is based on the assumption that Jesus' soul was identical with his divinity. Consequently, once the divinity left, there would be no soul at all and speech would be impossible. The second option is that the usual body-soul combination existed and that divinity was added to it; however, the author understands "divinity" here (at least initially) as the usual "holy spirit" that enters all prophets (cf. Simon, *Mose ben Salomo von Salerno*, p. xiii). This makes his analogy with other prophets comprehensible ("Should we say that they were divine because they possessed the holy spirit?"),

L
but it prevents him from coming to grips with the Christian contention of real divinity. In effect, he recognizes this weakness by going on to discuss the lack of validity of any positive evidence for Jesus' divinity. (Cf. pp. 145–46.)

A similar discussion is found in *Sefer HaBerit* (*Mil. Ḥovah*, p. 23a = Talmage's ed., pp. 30–31), but it contains some crucial changes which make it less vulnerable to this objection: "Was the divinity which took on flesh in Mary's stomach Jesus' soul or did he have an additional soul like that of all men? If you say that he had no other soul but the incarnate divinity (except for the nutritive soul [נפש החיות], i.e., the blood, which all animals and birds possess), then the divinity did not enter a man but an animal. Moreover, since he had no rational soul [lit., "talking soul"; cf. Targum on Genesis 2:7] except for the divinity, to whom was this divinity crying out when he said, 'My God, my God, why have you forsaken me?' and why could he not save himself? If, however, you say that he had another soul which ascends to heaven just like other men and only afterward did the divinity dwell in him, then Jesus would be like all other men in his body and soul. He would not actually *be* God or the son of God; rather, divinity would have merely cleaved to him." Cf. also *Vikkuaḥ LeHaRadaq, Mil. Ḥovah*, p. 13b = Talmage's ed., pp. 83–84.

34   *Moses also performed many miracles* See below p. 199 and the notes there.

36   *No one . . . except . . . Mary Magdalene* Cf. Williams, p. 88.

Page 152

1   *Peter the ass* The Hebrew words for "firstling of an ass" (Exod. 13:13) are *peter ḥamor*, which can also mean Peter ass; the pun was irresistible to medieval Jews. There was some attempt, however, to give a legal foundation to this practice. See *Sefer Ḥasidim*, ed. Wistinetsky, no. 193, p. 74: "If a Jew becomes an apostate, he is given a bad name, as it is written, 'They that make them should be like them' (Psalms 115:8); i.e., one should treat them the same way one treats idolatry by giving it a bad name (cf. B. *Avodah Zarah* 46a). . . . This should be done even with regard to a righteous man after whom they have erred, as in the case of Simon Kepha whom we call Peter the ass." On the Jewish view that Peter was really righteous, see the various versions of *Aggadta deShimon Kepha* collected in A. Jellinek, *Bet HaMidrasch* (Jerusalem, 1967), 5:60–62; 6:9–14, 155–56, and in J. Eisenstein, *Oẓar Midrashim* (New York, 1928), pp. 557–60. Another name which is consistently changed in N.V. is that of Mary; the author calls her Ḥaria (= Aramaic *ḥaraya*, or excrement) instead of Maria.

9   *"A woman shall compass a man"* See Peter the Venerable, PL 189.530; the *Tractatus* in TNA 5.1523-4 = PL 213.763-4; Walter of Châtillon. PL 209.456.

15   *I could find you other gods. . . .* Cf. p. 103.

23   *Without an ʿayin* Jesus' real name undoubtedly was with an ʿayin

L

(*Yeshua'*); the Hebrew *Yeshu* is a pejorative abbreviated form which the author apparently considered his real name. Cf., however, the notes to p. 66, line 9.

24-25 **You could apply a similar argument to the name Joshua** Christians, of course, did just that. See above p. 81 and the notes there.

30 **This characteristic** I.e., a theophoric name without reference to a father.

Page 153

2 **Holy and sacred** Hebrew *qadosh ve'ir*, based on Daniel 4:10. The word *'ir*, however, was usually taken as angel.

3 **"Israel" is Christendom** See pp. 126-27 and the notes there.

6 **Children of Edom** See the notes to p. 55.

8 **Descendants of Japheth** See p. 155 and the notes there.

14 **Vision and belief** This presupposes a derivation from the Hebrew *sharei 'el*, i.e., beholders of God. For a similar derivation, see Archambault's note in *Dialogue avec Tryphon*, 2:243. Cf. *Trypho*, ch. 126: Jacob was called εἶδος θεοῦ . See J.-G. Kahn, "Did Philo Know Hebrew?" (Hebrew), *Tarbiz* 34 (1965): 342-43, and especially his "Israel-Videns Deum" (Hebrew), *Tarbiz* 40 (1971): 285-92.

25-26 **But not in the womb** Jesus, on the other hand, would have known God even in the womb; cf. p. 112.

27-28 **Out of the forehead of a harlot** Although "the forehead of a harlot" is an insulting phrase based on Jeremiah 3:3, the context of the passage appears to require a literal reading. This is probably a distorted report of the heretical doctrine that Jesus was born through the ear; the author may have been inspired by the comment in *Sefer Yosef HaMeqanne* in connection with the same psalm that "they say he entered her through the middle of the head" (Rosenthal's ed., p. 104). For a detailed discussion, see my "Christian Heresy and Jewish Polemic in the Twelfth and Thirteenth Centuries," *HTR* 68 (1975): 289-93.

36 **The Romans** He mentions the Romans explicitly because Edom is mentioned in the passage in Isaiah and because R. Meir had maintained that the oxen (*re'emim*) in v. 7 are the Romans (*romiyyim*). See *Pesiqta deRav Kahana*, ed. Mandelbaum, p. 134.

Page 154

20 **The hanged one had brothers** It is unlikely that the author considered this argument compelling since he undoubtedly knew that the Hebrew *ah* does not necessarily refer to a real brother; cf., e.g., Deuteronomy 19:19.

20-21 **Even in the Gospels it says that he had brothers** Matthew 13:55. Cf. below, p. 179.

L

Page 155

3   ***Bring them to life*** The Hebrew *ḥiyyah* can mean either "kept alive" or "brought to life."

3-4   ***"Descendants shall serve him"*** Literally: "Seed" shall serve him. The same word is used in Isaiah 53:10, where various Jewish writers had argued that Jesus had no descendants; see Ibn Ezra on Isaiah 52:13 and *Mil. HaShem*, pp. 107-8.

9   ***His war with the Amalekites*** 1 Samuel 30.

14-15   ***This is what Jesus said when he approached hell*** See Cassiodorus, *Expositio, CC, Ser. Lat.*, 97, p. 218, also quoted in *Gloss*, ad loc., for the view that the gates are "the gates of death." The Christian view that these are the gates of hell is also quoted in the *Vikkuaḥ LeHaRadaq, Mil. Ḥovah*, p. 156b = Talmage's ed., p. 88, and Talmage (*HTR* 60:330) cites Jerome as a source; his precise reference, however, is inaccurate. Most Christian commentators took the verse as a reference to Jesus' ascent into heaven. See *Trypho*, ch. 36; Augustine, *Enarratio in Psalmos, CC, Ser. Lat.*, 38, pp. 135-37; Isidore, *De Fide Cath.*, I.56.3, PL 83.94; Samuel of Morocco, PL 149.547.

24   ***And not because God "founded it upon the seas"*** I.e., not because of baptism.

30   ***Of Japheth*** Cf. p. 153. For this view, see Isidore's *Historia de Regibus Gothorum*, PL 83.1059: "Gothorum antiquissimam esse gentem certum est: quorum originem quidam de Magog, filio Japhet, suspicantur educi a similitudine ultimae syllabae." On medieval views of European origins in general, see R. Tate, "Mythology in Spanish Historiography of the Middle Ages and the Renaissance," *Hispanic Review*, 22 (1954): 1-18. On the descendants of Japheth, see especially *Trypho*, ch. 139-40.

31   ***The Slavs are the descendants of Canaan*** Lit., "The Canaanites are the descendants of Canaan." It may be that the last word should simply be emended to "Ham," and the reference would be to the ancient Canaanites. However, it is possible to defend the reading we have in light of the fact that Slavs were called Canaanites in medieval Hebrew; see S. Krauss, "Die Hebräischen Benennungen der Modernen Völker," *Jewish Studies in Memory of George A. Kohut* (New York, 1935), pp. 379-400. Canaan was, of course, a descendant of Ham according to the Biblical genealogy (Genesis 10:6, and cf. esp. Genesis 9:25-7).

Page 156

1   ***Ashkenazim*** Strictly speaking, Ashkenaz was usually Germany; see Krauss, op. cit., pp. 387-89. The Hebrew word *la'az*, which simply means foreign tongue, probably has the more precise meaning of French in this passage (so

L
Posnanski); this would be the result of Rashi's frequent citation of French words, identified as *la'az*, in his commentaries to the Bible and Talmud.

9   **Which they read. . . .** The Vulgate of Psalms 16:10 is, "Non derelinques animam meam in inferno, non dabis sanctum tuum videre corruptionem."

17   **Which filled the Temple** See Ibn Ezra and Kimḥi in their commentaries ad loc. for the view that this is a prophecy of the Temple.

18   **"Give them according to their deeds"** The view that this psalm is directed against the Jews at the time of the passion is reflected in the *Gloss*, ad loc.

20-21   **These words contradict the words of the Gospels. . . .** Cf. pp. 140, 158.

25   **Their writers have misled them** The Masoretic text reads, "My heart rejoices"; the Vulgate, however, says, "Et refloruit caro mea," to which Augustine adds, "That is, my flesh was resurrected" (*Enarratio in Psalmos, CC, Ser. Lat.*, 38, p. 169). Cf. p. 148.

31   **Jesus said this when he expired** Luke 23:46.

32   **Who guarded his grave** Cf. p. 144 and see Matthew 27:62-66.

Page 157

1-2   **They wrote "my humility"** Vulgate: "humilitatem meam." The distinction between the verse and the Christian version is unclear in the Hebrew text.

5   **They wrote, "My strength fails because of the suffering"** Vulgate: "in paupertate," which is not quite suffering but is certainly much different from iniquity. See the following paragraph, where the Vulgate is quoted accurately.

8-9   **"When they came together"** Vulgate: "dum convenirent."

9-10   **"My fate"** Vulgate: "sortes meae."

16-17   **Jesus prayed to his father that he remove the bitter cup from him** Mark 14:36. Cf. below, pp. 181-82, and the additions to *Sefer HaBerit, Mil. Ḥovah*, p. 37a = Talmage's ed., p. 64.

28-29   **He should not have prayed about what would happen after death** The passage is a bit obscure. Literally, the text means, "He should not have prayed after death," which makes perfect sense except for the fact that the position being refuted is that he prayed *concerning* what would happen then. Taken in our less literal translation, he is at least addressing himself to the proper question, but his argument becomes unclear. After all, ordinary people can pray about what happens to them after death, and if Jesus made an effort to behave like an ordinary person, then he could have presented such a prayer despite its inherent irrationality. Cf. Jerome, *In Esaiam,*

L

CC, *Ser. Lat.*, 73a, p. 706, for the view that Jesus made every effort to speak like an ordinary mortal.

Page 158

5-6   ***They deny their own Torah*** Cf. pp. 140, 156.

9   ***We have been admonished. . . .*** Probably a gloss. On the eternity of the law, see below, pp. 228-29, and the notes there.

15-16   ***The heretics, however, explain the entire psalm as a reference to Jesus*** So in *Trypho*, chapters 34, 64; Ambrose [pseud.], *Apologia David Altera*, cited in *Judenpredigt*, p. 55; Maximin of Hippo, *Tractatus contra Judaeos*, cited in Williams, p. 309; *Sancti Gregentii Disputatio*, cited by Hulen, *JBL* 51:66; *Altercatio Simonis Judaei*, PL 20.1178-79 = *CSEL* 45.45-46, cited in *Auteurs*, p. 30; Isidore, *De Fide Cath.*, I.1.3, PL 83.451 = Eggers, p. 4; Damian, *Dialogus*, PL 145.50; Peter the Venerable, *Tractatus*, PL 189.533 ff.; the *Tractatus* in *TNA* 5.1513 = PL 213.753; Joachim da Fiore, *Adversus Judaeos*, p. 32. Many of these authors argued that the reference could not be to Solomon, because the psalm spoke of the king's name enduring forever and of his universal rule. For the reversal of this argument by Jews, see below, p. 159.

20   **Velifnei** Hebrew for "before." The author's point is that the word need not be temporal, but the Christians took it that way. See, for example, Isidore, *De Fide Cath.*, I.2.1, PL 83.452 = Eggers, p. 10, and I.5.3, PL 83.461 = Eggers, p. 44. Note too that Jacob ben Reuben insisted on a Solomonic interpretation even if *lifnei* is taken temporally; see *Mil. HaShem*, p. 74.

28   **Endet** Ends. The Vulgate has, "Permanebit cum sole" (he will endure with the sun), which could also support the argument that Jesus would not endure after the sun.

32   ***But only with it*** I.e., just as Christians emphasize the word "before" used with reference to the moon, the author will emphasize the word "with" used of the sun.

Page 159

1   ***Hung out*** Not "created" because of the difficulty resulting from the creation of light on the first day and the "making" of the sun and moon on the fourth (Genesis 1:3, 14-18). See *B. Ḥagigah* 12a.

18   ***Most nations do not bow down to him*** Thus, the Christian argument that the grandiose descriptions in the psalm do not fit Solomon was reversed and used against the christological interpretation. This Jewish argument based on verse 11 is also found in *Mil. HaShem*, p. 74; *Sefer HaBerit, Mil. Ḥovah*, p. 31a = Talmage's ed., p. 49; Meir of Narbonne, *Mil. Miẓvah*, Parma ms., pp. 94b, 104a, 123b, 146a; Naḥmanides' disputation, *Ketavei Ramban*, ed. Chavel, 1:311; Rome ms. 53, p. 24b = Pos. "Mordecai of Avignon" ms., p. 31 = Rosenthal's "Menaḥem," p. 71; *Vikkuaḥ*

L̦

LeHaRadaq, Mil. Ḥovah, p. 14a = Talmage's ed., p. 86. Meir of Narbonne (p. 94b) even cited Jesus' remark about rendering unto Caesar that which is Ceasar's in order to show that not all kings bowed down to him. Cf. also the notes to p. 89.

24   **But not in the sea** Cf. *Sefer HaBerit*, loc. cit.; *Mil. Miẓvah*, pp. 104a, 123b; Rome ms. 53, loc. cit. The same sort of argument is found in *Sefer Yosef HaMeqanne* with regard to Zechariah 9:10 (Rosenthal's ed., p. 91; cf. also p. 112 on this psalm).

28-29   **Why, everyone [knows that Jesus was killed and that he was never rich]** The bracketed section is a conjectural addition. The point is that David's prayer would have been unanswered, which is unlikely. The text we have reads, "Why everyone prays for him continually. It seems to me. . . ." This would be an exceedingly weak argument since the prayer of others is no reason for David not to pray. Moreover, the phrase "prays for him continually" is a quotation of the next part of the verse and probably introduces the remark, "It seems to me."

30-31   **They have distorted this verse. . . .** The Vulgate reads, "Orabit de eo," which is the same as the Masoretic text, but there is a variant: "Adorabunt."

Page 160

2   **These men are the Jews who killed Jesus** So Cassiodorus, *Expositio, CC, Ser. Lat.*, 98, p. 786.

3   **Jesus was a sinner** Cf. pp. 89, 139–40, 150.

6-7   **He, Peter, and John were once walking along** I don't know the source of this story.

19   **The heretics say. . . .** A *locus classicus* of polemic. See Mark 12:36; Acts 2:34-36; Hebrews 7, especially verse 17; *Barnabas*, 12:10; *Trypho*, ch. 32, 83; Cyprian, *Testimonia* 2:26, PL 4.717-18; Augustine's sermon on the Jews, *Judenpredigt*, p. 107; Leo the Great, Sermon 29, cited in *Auteurs*, p. 31; Isidore, *De Fide Cath.*, I.3.7, PL 83.456 = Eggers, p. 24, I.10.5, PL 83.468, I.57.1, PL 83.495; Damian, *Dialogus*, PL 145.52-53; Rupert, *Dialogus*, PL 170.596 ff.; Peter the Venerable, PL 189.515 ff.; Walter of Châtillon, PL 209.446; Alan of Lille, PL 210.404. Cf. the notes to p. 112. The popularity of this passage in polemic was emphasized by Naḥmanides: "Are you the brilliant Jew who found this novel argument, apostasized because of it, and told the king to bring together all the Jewish scholars for a debate on those novel arguments? Have we never heard this until now? There isn't a single priest or infant who does not ask the Jews this question, for it is extremely old" (*Ketavei Ramban*, ed. Chavel, 1:317). See also *Mil. HaShem*, pp. 75–76; *Mil. Miẓvah*, Parma ms., pp. 128a, 146a; *Yosef HaMeqanne*, pp. 114-15; Moses of Salerno, Posnanski ms., p. 59.

20-21   **They wrote, "With you there is willingness". . . .** Vulgate: "Tecum principium in die virtutis tuae, in splendoribus sanctorum, ex utero ante luciferum

L

genui te." See Isidore, *De Fide Cath.*, I.1.2, PL 83.450 = Eggers, pp. 2–3. On changes in Masoretic vocalization in this chapter, see *Sefer HaBerit, Mil. Ḥovah*, pp. 30a–b = Talmage's ed., pp. 47–48, and R. David Kimḥi trans. in Rosenthal, *JJS* 11:131–32, and cited by Talmage in *HUCA* 38:216.

25   *He was before the stars* See *Trypho*, ch. 45; Maximin of Hippo, cited in Williams, p. 310; Isidore, *De Fide Cath.*, I.5.3, PL 83.461, and II.2.4, PL 83.503–4; *Trophies of Damascus*, cited in Williams, p. 164; Peter the Venerable (at length), PL 189.513 ff.; Peter of Blois, PL 207.829.

Page 161

19-20   *Where do you find a father calling his son "My lord"?* This is a reversal of a Christian argument which maintained that David would not call one of his mortal descendants "My master." See Matthew 22:41–45, Mark 12:35–37, and the argument of James I of Aragon at Naḥmanides' disputation, *Ketavei Ramban*, ed. Chavel, 1:317.

21   *To what army did Jesus go . . .?* This presupposes the Masoretic reading of verse 3.

24   *"To my lord Abraham"* See *B. Nedarim* 32b and *The Midrash on Psalms*, trans. W. G. Braude (New Haven, 1959), 2:205–7. This interpretation was dealt with by Peter the Venerable, PL 189.516.

Page 163

7   *"I, I am he. . . ."* See pp. 75–76 and the notes there.

13-14   *As a powerful warrior at the sea and as an old man . . . at Mount Sinai* A. Green ("The Children in Egypt and the Theophany at the Sea," *Judaism* 24 [1975]: 453–56) has suggested that the midrash which served as the source of this passage was already motivated by anti-Christian considerations.

26-27   *If, however, the plain sense of the passage refers to the future. . . .* In that case, the previous argument, which asked how the Jews became his enemies, would be inapplicable.

34   *Then you are describing two powers* This question was really not made possible only because the son sat down; indeed, it was raised on the previous page. It appears here because the author was carried away by his desire for a humorous sort of refutation, and at this point in his questioning this was the only argument that occurred to him.

Page 164

5-6   *He was made the footstool of his enemies* See *Sefer Yosef HaMeqanne* and Moses of Salerno, loc. cit.

L
33   ***"In the midst of two"*** See p. 124.

36   ***If he is a priest. . . .*** The Jew in Rupert's *Dialogus*, PL 170.596, asks when Jesus became a priest. Cf. p. 128.

Page 165

9   ***Lest he die of thirst*** So too *Sefer Yosef HaMeqanne*, loc. cit.

Page 166

5-6   ***Every "Solomon" in the Song of Songs is sacred. . . .*** The phrase comes from B. *Shevu'ot* 35b. For Solomon as Jesus and the mother in this passage as Mary, see Bede, *In Cantica Canticorum Allegorica Expositio*, PL 91.1127-28. For the crown as the crown of thorns at the crucifixion, see Isidore, *De Fide Cath.*, I.31.1, PL 83.482. The Christian interpretation of this verse was also cited in *Mil. Mizvah*, Parma ms., pp. 126a, 151b-152a, and *Sefer Yosef HaMeqanne*, Rosenthal's ed., p. 117.

14   ***This, then, is the meaning of the passage*** For similar interpretations, see *Yalqut Shim'oni* and Rashi, ad loc. Cf. also *Cant. Rabbah* 3:21.

17   ***"It will be called mother of wisdom"*** This translation, which is also reflected in *Sefer Yosef HaMeqanne*, loc. cit., is based on a non-Masoretic vocalization. See *Targum* and *Minhat Shai*, ad loc. Cf. also below, p. 211, and the notes there.

24-25   ***He has no father or mother*** The quotation is inexact, but the source of these remarks is probably Matthew 12:48-50.

Page 167

2   ***Be diligent in your study of Torah so that you may be able to answer a heretic*** This rabbinic statement, which was frequently cited by Jewish polemicists, is found in *Avot* 2:14 and in B. *Sanhedrin* 38b; its precise text, however, is uncertain, and it is quoted in polemic with substantial variations. The most common version of the Mishnah itself reads הוי שקוד ללמוד תורה ודע מה שתשיב לאפיקורוס (Be diligent in the study of Torah, and know how to answer a heretic). The omission of ודע (and know), however, is attested in many sources; cf. *Diqduqei Soferim* to *Sanhedrin* 38b, and see below p. 169. Moreover, Rashi in *Sanhedrin*, ad loc., appears to have read כדי שתדע להשיב, which is almost identical with N.V.'s version here. The reading וזה שתשיב is also found in Rome ms. 53 (e.g., p. 21a); see the quotations by Urbach in *REJ* 100:52, 56. Judah Goldin has argued on the basis of several manuscripts that the original reading was simply הוי שקוד ללמוד מה שתשיב לאפיקורוס (Be diligent in learning what to answer a heretic); see "Mashehu 'al Beit Midrasho shel Rabban Yohanan ben Zakkai," *Harry Austryn Wolfson Jubilee Volume* (Jerusalem, 1965), 3:72-75. This version appears on the title page of Mühlhausen's *Sefer Nizzahon* (Altdorf, 1644), a page which is reproduced in *Areshet* 2:150, and it is also found in *Sefer Yosef HaMeqanne*, Rosenthal's ed., p. 16. Especially in this last

L

form, the citation may be intended to excuse the study of the Gospels despite the talmudic prohibition against reading "external" or "heretical" books. See *Mishnah Sanhedrin* 10:1 and *B. Sanhedrin* 100b, and note the explicit statement in one ms. of Solomon de' Rossi's *'Edut HaShem Ne'emanah* (Rosenthal's *Meḥqarim*, 1:378, n. 7) that a polemicist must know *sefarim ḥizzonim* ("external" books).

4   *It is written.* . . . This paragraph is also found in part two of Rome ms. 53 (p. 22a = Rosenthal's "Menaḥem," p. 65).

4   **'Avon gilyon** Some medieval Christians were aware of this pejorative Jewish term for the Gospels; see Merchavia, *HaTalmud BiRe'i HaNazrut*, pp. 86, 303, 327.

9-10   *Nor was she even married to her husband* Many Christians maintained that Joseph and Mary were only betrothed at the time of her pregnancy; see Charles Souvay, "Joseph, Saint," *Catholic Encyclopedia* (New York, 1910), 8:505. Although I have adopted the reading of the Rome ms. partly because of a parallel in another section of that ms. (loc. cit.), it should be noted that *Tela* here reads, "Nor was she married for the purpose of having sexual relations." On this view, cf. Souvay, loc. cit., citing Augustine, PL 34.1071-72, and other sources.

12   *An obvious falsehood* Literally just "falsehood." The author, however, would have regarded such a contention as a falsehood even if the reading in Matthew had been "the betrothed of Mary" simply because she did in fact have a child (unless he would argue, like some other Jews, that she had had relations with someone else).

21-22   *Our earlier discussion* See p. 107.

24-25   *These are the generations of Jesus* The Matthew genealogy is also quoted by Jacob ben Reuben, *Mil. HaShem*, pp. 141-42. Jacob, however, says nothing about the contradiction between Matthew and Luke, probably because he did not know the latter. See also Rome ms. 53, p. 22a = Pos. "Mordecai of Avignon" ms., p. 16 = Rosenthal's "Menaḥem," p. 66.

Page 168

25-27   *In the book of Luke . . . he counted twenty-two generations . . . while in Matthew he counted but fifteen* The numbers are imprecise and may result from copyists' errors.

32   *The names and calculations differ* On the inconsistencies in these genealogies, see *Sefer Nestor HaKomer*, pp. 9, 12. A brief statement to this effect was made by Meir of Narbonne, *Mil. Mizvah*, Parma ms., pp. 98b-99a, who also noted that there are contradictions between these genealogies and the book of Kings. Cf. also the notes to p. 107.

Commentary to pp. 169-171

     To answer a heretic and question him On the aggressive tone of this pas-
sage, see the introduction. A remarkably similar set of instructions was provided
to the Christian polemicist by the author of the *Tractatus* in *TNA* 5.1509 = PL
213.749, who emphasized the need to prevent Jews from continually changing the
subject when they wanted to extricate themselves from difficult positions. (The
Christians must keep to the proper *ordo disputandi*, because the Jews "per diversa
huc illucque discurrunt, et cum comprehendi se senserint, ad modum vulpis in
fovea de loco ad locum resiliunt.")

    Ask them from what people they come Solomon de' Rossi cited a long list of
verses to prove that God "has not exchanged us for another nation" (*'Edut HaShem
Ne'emanah, Rosenthal's *Meḥqarim*, 1:383-85). On the *verus Israel* issue, see the notes

        You have been living comfortably. . . . The entire sentence is based on

    "And I called my son out of Egypt" The author ignores the classic christo-
logical exegesis of this verse in Matthew 2:15. This is another example of Jewish
citation of a verse for the purpose of attacking a Christian position which simply
ignores the christological interpretation of that verse; for similar instances, see
Solomon de' Rossi, *'Edut HaShem Ne'emanah*, Rosenthal's *Meḥqarim,* 1:382-83 (citing
Jeremiah 31:31 on the "new covenant"), as well as the quotations of Isaiah 45:1
(about Cyrus) by Meir of Narbonne, Moses of Salerno, and Naḥmanides cited
above in the notes to p. 111.

       Where, then, did you stumble? The implied argument in this entire passage
is that Christians may not arbitrarily decide when "Israel" refers to the Jews and
when it refers to the Christians. The same point is made in *Sefer HaBerit, Mil. Ḥovah*,
p. 33b = Talmage's ed., pp. 55-56, and a similar demand for consistency is found
above, p. 143, in connection with the christological interpretation of biblical refer-

ferred to in the previous verses is the object of the prophet's consolation.

       The children of Esau This is probably a reflection of the author's concep-
tion that Christians concede their physical descent from Esau; cf. the notes to p.

    Only one who has been immersed in water can be saved See W. Fanning,
"Baptism," *Catholic Encyclopedia* (New York, 1907), 2:265.

L

28   ***"Then will I sprinkle pure water. . . ."*** For this verse as a reference to baptism, cf. Jerome, *In Hiezechielem, CC, Ser. Lat.*, 75, p. 506; Ermengaud, *Breviari d'Amor*, cited by Blumenkranz, *Cahiers de Fanjeaux* 12 (1977): 302, 304.

31   ***You are thrown into water*** The author was clearly familiar with immersion alone as the method of baptism, despite the fact that "infusion" and "aspersion" were coming into use by the thirteenth century; see Fanning, op. cit., p. 262.

33   ***What impurity or sin can be found in . . . small children?*** The injustice of having baptism determine the fate of a small child was particularly vexing to Meir of Narbonne, who raised the issue on three separate occasions in his *Mil. Mizvah*. On two of these occasions he argued that the son of a rich man would have an advantage over the son of a poor man, whom no one would bother to baptize; this may be an ironic twist of Jesus' remark concerning the difficulty a rich man would have in entering heaven (Matthew 19:23-24). See *Mil. Mizvah*, Parma ms., pp. 7a, 29a, 101b-102a. For objections to the doctrine of original sin, a doctrine which is strangely absent from the present discussion, see below pp. 218-19.

Page 172

1-2   ***They needn't . . . avoid sin*** Cf. pp. 115-16.

8-9   ***They are baptized in drawn water*** So also below, p. 174, and in *Sefer Yosef HaMeqanne, Kiev Festschrift*, Hebrew section, p. 124. In Jewish law, the use of drawn water for ritual immersion was prohibited by rabbinic injunction; see Maimonides, *Mishneh Torah, Hilkhot Miqva'ot,* 4:1-2.

16   ***"I have not come to destroy the law of Moses"*** This verse was also cited in *Sefer Nestor HaKomer*, p. 4, Meir of Narbonne's *Mil. Mizvah*, Parma ms., p. 4a, and Moses of Salerno's *Ta'anot*, Pos. ms., p. 33. Moreover, the phrase "si Christus non venit legem solvere, sed adimplere" (If Christ did not come to destroy the Law but to fulfill it) is repeated in each of the ten Jewish questions about the Law in Isidore's *Quaestiones in Leviticum* (PL 83.336-39) and in Damian's derivative *Dialogus* (PL 145.57-59). Cf. the "Continuatio" to Crispin, p. 68. See also pp. 89, 173, 215.

32-33   ***He must have been referring to baptismal water*** Cf. below p. 221, and see *Sefer Yosef HaMeqanne*, Rosenthal's ed., p. 118, where Lamentations 3:54 ("Waters flowed over my head; then I said, I am cut off") is taken as a reference to forced baptism.

Page 173

13   ***Isaiah's admonition*** See p. 96 and the notes there.

24   ***Why should he have been afraid of the king?*** See below, pp. 203-04, 212-13. The argument that Jesus should not have fled from Herod in light of the usual fearlessness of "God's angels and servants" is found in *Sefer Yosef HaMeqanne, Kiev Festschrift*, Hebrew section, p. 127; in the same context, Meir of Narbonne

L

specifically refers to the case of Elisha cited in N.V. here (*Mil. Miẓvah*, Parma ms., pp. 89b–90a; cf. also pp. 27a, 127b). The Jewish contention that Jesus should have saved himself from the king miraculously is also quoted in *Contra Celsum* 1:65, cited by Williams, p. 84. See also Chadwick's trans., p. 73.

Page 174

6   **Taufe (Baptisma)** This is an emended reading proposed by Posnanski. The ms. reading of the second word was apparently *Baptista*, which can be forced into some semblance of coherence by reading the phrase "Taufe Baptistae," i.e., the baptism of the Baptist; nevertheless, such a German-Latin expression is so implausible that a minor emendation appears far preferable. Wagenseil translated his text rather freely and wrote, "Ob illum baptismum vocant eum Baptistam." (Because of that baptism they call him the Baptist.)

11–12   **In water that has been drawn** See the notes to p. 172.

13   **It is written . . . "Then Jesus came. . . ."** This passage is taken from *Sefer Yosef HaMeqanne, Kiev Festschrift*, Hebrew section, p. 124.

18–19   **What sort of god must be sanctified?** There are two separate questions in this passage: 1. Why was the baptism necessary in light of Jesus' presumed purity? 2. Why did a new spirit descend upon him if the holy spirit was already within him? The first question appears in *Sefer Nestor HaKomer*, p. 6 ("I could say that he was a god defiled by sin until John purified him"), and the second is found in Jacob ben Reuben, *Mil. HaShem*, pp. 143–44. It is particularly interesting that Nicholas de Lyra quotes both questions in the order in which they are found in N.V. (Latin text quoted by Rosenthal in *Mil. HaShem*, p. 144, n. 3). This lends further support to Blumenkranz's contention that de Lyra did not use *Mil. HaShem* itself but a work influenced by it; see his "Nicholas de Lyre et Jacob ben Ruben," *JJS* 16 (1965): 47–51. Cf. also the citation from the *Discussion of St. Silvester* in Williams, p. 342.

25–26   **A man should be baptized only once** See Fanning, "Baptism," *Catholic Encyclopedia*, 2:268.

29   **This Jesus** This is an attempt to translate an extremely awkard construction in the Hebrew. It may well be that the extra word ("veYeshu") is an unnecessary explanatory gloss which should be eliminated.

Page 175

3–4   **Such as bells and chalices** See Fanning, op. cit., p. 273. The Hebrew word translated chalices literally means dogs (*kelavim*). It is conceivable that this was originally a corruption of *calices* (כלכיס becomes כלבים), but the word then remained as a derogatory pun. See p. 221, where the singular *kelev*, which is a less probable corruption of *calix* than *kelavim* is of *calices*, appears to mean chalice and was so understood by the Christian glossator of Wagenseil's manuscript.

L

8-9   ***Since he was not baptized during his lifetime*** Some heretical groups did baptize the dead, probably on the basis of 1 Corinthians 15:29; see Fanning, op. cit., p. 271.

10   ***This is what their saint Gregory said*** The story that follows is a famous medieval legend, which was, however, told about Gregory and the soul of the emperor Trajan rather than about the soul of a Muslim prince. N.V.'s version, however, should probably be regarded as evidence of a variant of the legend rather than as a simple error on the part of the author (or of Joseph Official, from whom the story is taken; see *Sefer Yosef HaMeqanne, Kiev Festschrift*, Hebrew section, pp. 128-9). For the various versions of this story, see J.-B. M. Roze, *La Légende Dorée de Jacques de Voragine* (Paris, 1902), 1:338-39, and A. Jameson, *Sacred and Legendary Art* (Boston, 1865), 1:339-41. (This last reference, which led me to the *Legenda Aurea*, was pointed out by my father.)

29   ***Bound up in paradise*** Based on 1 Samuel 25:29.

Page 176

4-5   ***He was overcome by a fever*** So *Tela* and *Sefer Yosef HaMeqanne*. The third part of Rome ms. no. 53, however, reads, "He was overcome by *podagra*, i.e., a disease of the foot." The fact is that both a fever and gout are mentioned in the Christian sources of the legend; see Roze, *La Légende Dorée*, p. 339.

8-9   ***Not even one-quarter of the stone . . . could have been baptized*** This again reflects the author's view that only total immersion constituted a valid baptism; cf. the notes to p. 171.

20-21   ***That Muslim . . . was merely spared the suffering of hell*** Such a view was in fact expressed by Christians; see Roze, *La Légende Dorée*, pp. 338-39.

Page 177

9   ***What sort of praise of God is it to say that he needs food and drink?*** The same question, including the contrast with Moses, was asked by Jacob ben Reuben in connection with this passage in Matthew (*Mil. HaShem*, p. 144).

15-16   ***How much more, then, should this be true of this man*** Cf. p. 68.

17   ***Why did he become hungry?*** Cf. pp. 186, 189.

24   ***This is a faulty response. . . .*** This objection is found in Jacob ben Reuben, *Mil. HaShem*, pp. 144-45, and, in precisely the same language as that of N.V., in Moses of Salerno's *Ta'anot*, Pos. ms., p. 32. The argument is based on the view that Deuteronomy 8:3, which was quoted by Jesus here, does not mean that man lives by observing God's law but rather that the word of God can produce food miraculously (cf., e.g., *Da'at Zeqenim MiBa'alei HaTosafot*, ad loc.)

L
29   ***Why did Satan tempt him . . . ?*** So Moses of Salerno, loc. cit.

1   **"His firstborn son"** An understandable misinterpretation of *filium suum.* Properly, "her firstborn son." The point of this quotation may be to underscore the implication that Joseph did have relations with Mary after the birth of Jesus. Solomon de' Rossi cited this verse in connection with the Christian contention that Genesis 49:10 ("The scepter shall not depart from Judah . . . until Shiloh comes") means that after Shiloh comes the scepter would depart from Judah. If the word "until" must imply a subsequent reversal of the situation described, then Christians would have to admit that Mary did not remain a virgin; since they do not concede this, then they must agree that the "until" in Genesis 49:10 may also not imply a subsequent change. See *'Edut HaShem Ne'emanah*, Rosenthal's *Meḥqarim*, 1:402-3.

5-6   **"When he was born from his mother's stomach. . . ."** The author may intend this as a refutation of the heretical doctrine that Jesus was not born through the stomach; see the notes to p. 153. The quotation here is, to say the least, imprecise, but Luke 2:5 does contain the implication that he was "born from his mother's stomach."

8   **The father is unbegotten. . . .** This creed (the "Symbolum Athanasianum," beginning, "Quicunque vult salvus esse") contains the following passage: "Pater a nullo est factus: nec creatus, nec genitus. Filius a Patre solo est: non factus, nec creatus: sed genitus. Spiritus sanctus a Patre et filio: non factus, nec creatus, nec genitus: sed procedens." This is essentially the same as N.V.'s quotation. For a critical text, see Philip Schaff, *Bibliotheca Symbolica Ecclesiae Universalis: The Creeds of Christendom*, 6th ed. (New York and London, 1931), 2:67-68 (discussion in 1:34-42). See also *Sefer Yosef HaMeqanne*, Rosenthal's ed., p. 127.

15   **Patrus** Properly, *pater.* This was probably a mistake of the author himself rather than of a copyist since its form is that of the typical nominative masculine in Latin.

17   **It is written . . ."When Jesus came. . . ."** This paragraph is based on *Sefer Yosef HaMeqanne, Kiev Festschrift*, Hebrew section, p. 129.

30   **He permitted people to transgress** The ambiguities in the Gospel accounts of Jesus' attitude toward the Law were, of course, useful to Jewish polemicists. Nevertheless, the extreme antinomianism ascribed to Jesus in this passage goes a bit beyond what the Gospels justify and reflects the views attributed to Jesus by later Christians. Meir of Narbonne was clearer about this when he quoted the same Gospel passage about the leper: "Afterwards, one of his disciples said that he commanded the abolition of circumcision and the other commandments, but how can it be proper to listen to him when he contradicts his owns words?" (*Mil. Miẓvah*, Parma ms., p. 97b). Cf. the notes to p. 183.

L

Page 179

1   *It is written . . ."And it came to pass. . . ."* This passage appears in Rome ms. 53, p. 22b; see also *Sefer Yosef HaMeqanne, Kiev Festschrift*, Hebrew section, p. 127. The Gospel passage is briefly cited in *Sefer Nestor HaKomer*, p. 12, and the question about the identity of these brothers was raised by Moses of Salerno, Pos. ms., p. 33. Cf. also the citation from *The Dialogue of Timothy and Aquila* in Williams, p. 69.

7   *Blacksmith's son* Corrected to "son of a carpenter" on p. 204.

29-30   *He, his brothers, and his students came to Capernaum* Mark 6:1 and 6:3.

31-32   *Elsewhere in the passage they are called by their proper name. . . .* Perhaps this is based on John 6:41-42, where they are called "the Jews."

Page 180

1   *It is written in their books. . . .* In much shorter form, this passage (through p. 181, line 15) is found in *Sefer Yosef HaMeqanne, Kiev Festschrift*, p. 125, and with a modified order it is in Moses of Salerno's *Ta'anot*, Pos. ms., p. 35 (through the quotation from Matthew 28). The quotation of Matthew 9:6 is in Rosenthal's ed., *Sefer Yosef HaMeqanne*, p. 132.

1-2   *"The man afflicted by demons"* The Gospels speak of a paralytic, and the phrase בעל השידה might possibly be a corruption of בעל השיתוק . Nevertheless, all extant manuscripts of N.V. and *Sefer Yosef HaMeqanne* have some variant of a word that can be translated "demon"; see Rosenthal's note to *Sefer Yosef HeMeqanne*, loc. cit.

16   *It says in their books. . . .* The passage in parentheses is probably a gloss, and it does not appear in either *Sefer Yosef HaMeqanne* or Moses of Salerno. The first sentence is a comment on what came before, and the last two supply a parallel to Mark 14:36, which is quoted below.

24   *Why did he call himself a man?* The phrase usually translated "son of man" in Ezekiel and the Gospels is in fact simply the Hebrew word for man (*ben-adam*). See also p. 209.

25-26   *Scripture warns us not to compare God to a man* See the references in the notes to p. 147.

26   *"God is not a man, that he should lie"* Moses of Salerno reports that a Christian actually cited this verse as proof of Christianity. God, he said, is not a man who lies; he is, rather, a man who does not lie (Pos. ms., p. 29). See also Mordecai of Avignon, M.E., Vat. ms., p. 8b.

Page 181

1   *"Take away this cup from me"* The Jewish argument (based on this verse) that Jesus should not have prayed for escape is quoted in *Contra Celsum* 2:24, Chad-

L

wick's trans. pp. 88-89 (cited in Williams, p. 87). Origen responded that the last part of the verse ("not what I will . . .") shows his willingness to accept death; the author of N.V., however, uses even this part of the verse as an anti-Christian argument both in this passage and below, p. 186.

20-21 *Jesus passed through a certain place. . . .* This passage is found in *Sefer Yosef HaMeqanne, Kiev Festschrift*, Hebrew section, p. 125, and in Moses of Salerno's *Ta'anot*, Pos. ms., p. 40.

28 *If he cured the man, all right* This comment ignores the stories in Matthew 12:10-14, Mark 3:1-6, and Luke 6:6-11 where the Pharisees are said to have objected to Jesus' healing people on the Sabbath. The author of N.V. may have felt that healing on the Sabbath without the use of medicine was really not objectionable under Jewish law; cf. Yeḥezkel Kaufmann, *Golah VeNekhar* (Tel Aviv, 1929/30), 1:349, n. 1. It was, in any case, clearly less objectionable than carrying, and it ought to be noted that the reading in Moses of Salerno's *Ta'anot* is simply, "If he cured the man, why did he command him to carry his bed?" (without the words "all right").

30 *At that time Jesus said. . . .* The same verses in Matthew were quoted by Jacob ben Reuben, *Mil. HaShem*, p. 147, but his objections were based on the implication that the father and son are not one rather than on the need for thanks. Jacob could not have asked N.V.'s question because he translated the verse, "I confess before you" (הנני מתודה לפניך) rather than "I thank you."

Page 182

27 *If David behaved improperly. . . .* Jacob ben Reuben, who quoted and discussed this same passage (*Mil. HaShem*, pp. 147-48), also conceded that David may have behaved improperly and insisted that this is no precedent. First, he argued, David was in a desperate situation and never repeated his act. Second, if all David's acts constitute valid legal precedent, then his behavior with Bathsheba should permit adultery.

34 *How does this square with his command to that . . . leper?* The same contradiction was noted by Jacob ben Reuben, p. 149.

Page 183

7-8 *By saying this he was actually permitting work on the Sabbath* A significant variant in the Rome ms. reads, "Thus, they permit work on the Sabbath." There is an apparent ambivalence in N.V. as to whether Jesus permitted systematic violation of the Torah (p. 178) or later Christians misinterpreted his views (pp. 172, 173, 191, 215). This results from the ambiguity of the Gospels themselves on this issue and from the fact that almost any approach could be utilized to good effect by a Jewish author. Jesus could be criticized either for violating the Law or for inconsistency; on the other hand, later Christians could be attacked for failing to heed his warnings against antinomian behavior.

L

9   **It is written in the same place.** . . . The basic passage is in *Sefer Yosef HaMeqanne, Kiev Festschrift,* Hebrew section, p. 127.

20-21   **"A little storm"** This translation is based on an emendation. The ms. text could be translated, "Why are you fearful [even] for a short time?" On this passage, see *Sefer Nestor HaKomer,* p. 11.

30   **This implies that she was impure** See the notes to p. 44.

32   **Two turtledoves and two young pigeons** He means "or two young pigeons" and has simply fallen into a usage which can be found elsewhere as well; for an illustration, see the quotations of Exodus 21:37 in *B. Bava Qamma* 67b. See also *Tosfot Yom Tov* on *Nega'im* 1:5 s.v. *aḥat levanah,* and cf. Rashi on *Bava Qamma* 9a s.v. *urevia'.*

Page 184

3   **It is written . . . "Then Jesus went. . . ."** This paragraph is taken from *Sefer Yosef HaMeqanne, Kiev Festschrift,* Hebrew section, pp. 127–28.

18   **Why did he cause them to sin?** See *Contra Celsum,* 2:78, Chadwick's trans., p. 126. The author of Rome ms. 53 (p. 23b = Pos. "Mordecai of Avignon" ms., p. 26 = Rosenthal's "Menaḥem," p. 69) combined this argument with the common Jewish observation that Christians are a minority of the world population, and he maintained that Jesus' advent had, in effect, guaranteed the damnation of most of the people in the world (e.g., Muslims, Jews, Albigensians, and Bogomils). See also p. 200.

Page 185

16-17   **"To Peter and Simon"** Either someone misread Mark 14:37 (which says, "He . . . said to Peter, 'Simon . . . could you not watch one hour?' ") or there was a corruption in the text of N.V. See the notes to the Hebrew text.

25   **Now to whom was Jesus praying?** There are particularly striking parallels between this entire passage and *Mil. HaShem,* p. 150, especially with regard to the citation of the nonexistent verse, "He speaks and carries out; he decrees and fulfills" as proof that Jesus should not have had to pray if he were divine. This "verse" is based on *B. Berakhot* 57b, and it is found in the daily morning prayer "Barukh She'amar" and in the blessings following the Sabbath *haftarah* (see *Soferim* 13:10). In the last instance, the word "declares" (מדבר) is used instead of "decrees," but this corresponds to the reading in the Rome ms. here and in *Mil. HaShem.* (I would be inclined to emend the *Mil. HaShem* text from וכתוב אחר אומר ועושה ומדבר ומקיים to אומר, עושה ומדבר ומקיים וכתוב אחר). Every other argument in this paragraph is also in *Mil. HaShem.*

L

Page 186

3-4   ***Then the wills are not the same.*** . . . So also Meir of Narbonne, *Mil. Miẓvah*, Parma ms., p. 91a. He also cited this verse as evidence that Jesus prayed without being answered (p. 90a; cf. also p. 125b). See above p. 181.

16   ***After all, his soul came from the father.*** . . . This argument is really not much different from the straightforward contention that two wills must imply two separate beings, but the approach is circuitous. First, it is established that one's soul and one's will are inextricably intertwined; thus, contrary wills must proceed out of different souls. But since the soul clearly determines identity, it follows that Jesus and God (who had contrary wills) cannot be identical.

22-23   ***So how could the flesh fast forty days?*** This entire passage is presented in a rather confusing way. The basic argument is as follows: Christians maintain that Jesus had no impure thoughts and that he fasted forty days and nights. Now, both of these achievements could be possible only through the miraculous intervention of the holy spirit; this effectively rules out the argument that the flesh must behave in its natural manner. Now that this argument is excluded, why was Jesus fearful and sorrowful (above p. 185) and why was he hungry (above p. 177, and below p. 189)? See especially below pp. 193 ff.

        For the Christian contention that only the human aspect of Jesus suffered hunger and the like, see Peter the Venerable, *Tractatus*, PL 189.531-32. On Jesus' sleeping, see *Sefer Nestor HaKomer*, p. 11; on his sleep, hunger, and fear, see Meir of Narbonne, *Mil. Miẓvah*, Parma ms., pp. 26b-27a, 89a-b.

29   ***Hananiah, Mishael, and Azariah*** They are mentioned in a similar context in *Mil. HaShem*, p. 150, and in *Mil. Miẓvah*, Parma ms., p. 127b.

Page 187

31   ***"And in the sixth hour.*** . . .*"* Taken from *Sefer Yosef HaMeqanne, Kiev Festschrift*, Hebrew section, p. 125.

Page 188

2   ***Why did he cry out?*** See p. 150.

6   ***It is written in their book of Mark.*** . . . This paragraph is based on *Sefer Yosef HaMeqanne, Kiev Festschrift*, Hebrew section, p. 125, and is repeated with minor changes on p. 205 below.

17   ***It is written in their book of Luke.*** . . . Taken from *Sefer Yosef HaMeqanne, Kiev Festschrift*, Hebrew section, p. 125.

30   ***It is written in their books.*** . . . Taken from *Sefer Yosef HaMeqanne, Kiev Festschrift*, Hebrew section, p. 126.

Page 189

6   **Why was he hungry?** Cf. pp. 177, 186.

14-15   **Did he, then, not know if there were figs. . .?** So also Jacob ben Reuben, *Mil. HaShem*, p. 151, and Meir of Narbonne, *Mil. Miẓvah*, Parma ms., p. 90b.

22-23   **Why did he curse the tree?** Meir of Narbonne (loc. cit.) also asked this question and suggested that it would have been more sensible for Jesus to have ordered the tree to produce figs so that he and his students could eat. (This Gospel passage is also cited on pp. 220a-b of *Mil. Miẓvah*.)

Page 190

6   **Who gave it to him?** The argument that this verse implies that it was given to him by one greater than himself is found in Jacob ben Reuben, *Mil. HaShem*, p. 152 and in *Sefer Yosef HaMeqanne*, p. 133.

Page 191

15-16   **He commanded him to observe the ancient commandments** See the notes to pp. 178 and 183. On this passage, cf. *Sefer Yosef HaMeqanne*, p. 134.

19   **It is written . . .** A short version of this passage appears in *Sefer Yosef HaMeqanne, Kiev Festschrift*, Hebrew section, p. 125.

Page 192

2   **"Jews do not benefit. . . ."** In a legal context, this is the meaning of the Hebrew; the usual meaning, however, would be "derive pleasure," and this meaning lies at the heart of N.V.'s uncharitable interpretation of the phrase.

13   **It is written . . . "A marriage took place. . . ."** The passage is based on *Sefer Yosef HaMeqanne, Kiev Festschrift*, Hebrew section, p. 125.

13   **Canaan** Properly, "Cana."

20-21   **Jesus' mother is not called "woman."** In *Sefer Yosef HaMeqanne*, this line reads as follows: "They say that Jesus' mother is not called 'woman,' for this term is used in their Torah only about someone who is married to [or "has consummated a marriage with"] a man" (והם אומרים אם ישו אינ' נקרא' אשה שאין נקרא' בתורת' עד שתה' בעולה לאיש). The fact is that the word *mulier* is used about Mary elsewhere as well (John 19:26). See, however, Thomas's citation of the *Gloss* on Galatians 4:4 in *Summa Theologiae* 3a.28.1, and cf. the editor's note in the Blackfriars' edition, vol. 51 (New York and London, 1969), p. 39.

26   **He was the one who made the feast** Although it is quite clear from vv. 8-9 that Jesus was not in charge of the feast, this statement may be based on the fact that Mary told the servants to do whatever her son tells them (v. 5). It is just barely possible that the proper translation of *ba'al hase'udah* here should be "one who partakes of the feast."

L

27   *It is written . . . "a man said to him. . . ."* This paragraph is found in *Sefer Yosef HaMeqanne, Kiev Festschrift*, Hebrew section, p. 127, and in Moses of Salerno's *Ta'anot*, Pos. ms., pp. 35-36.

Page 193

16-17   *I see, then, that on this one occasion he did not speak in a devious manner* The implied criticism is that he spoke clearly only to his disciples when he should have spoken clearly to the masses as well. The text of *Sefer Yosef HaMeqanne* makes this criticism explicit: "I see now that he did not speak properly this time, for he spoke to the people in a manner that they could not comprehend when he should have made them wise; moreover, he actually cursed them by saying 'Fatten the heart, etc.' " Moses of Salerno's text (p. 36) is the same as that of N.V., although Posnanski emended it to conform in part to *Sefer Yosef HaMeqanne*. Jacob ben Reuben (*Mil. HaShem,* pp. 152-53) also criticized Jesus for speaking in incomprehensible parables. The verse, "This people's heart has grown fat" (or "Fatten the heart of this people" — Isa. 6:10) was cited by Peter of Blois with reference to medieval Jews; see *Contra Perfidiam Judaeorum,* PL 207.827.

18   *You have said. . . .* The lengthy passage beginning here is found almost word for word in *Sefer Yosef HaMeqanne, Kiev Festschrift*, Hebrew section, pp. 130-32 (through p. 198, line 9 below) and in Moses of Salerno's *Ta'anot*, Pos. ms., pp. 36-39 (through p. 197, line 20 below).

22   *He ate and slept. . . .* See the notes to p. 186.

Page 194

1-2   *The flesh died . . . when the holy spirit departed. . . .* There is a perhaps intentional confusion here between the holy spirit of the trinity and the "spirit" or soul of Jesus. The "son" is apparently identified with the carnal aspect alone, i.e., with the body of Jesus. Granted these rather peculiar assumptions, these lines can make sense. For the usual arguments concerning the relationship between Jesus' body and soul, see p. 151 and the notes there.

4   *Once we find a separation in this entity. . . .* See appendix 5.

14-15   *It follows that he who desires and covets will be punished* The argument is completed by the citation of Ezekiel 18:4 below, which shows that the soul is punished; it, therefore, must be responsible for sin.

24   *"Do not enter my sanctuary with raised hands"* See 1 Timothy 2:8: "I will therefore that men pray everywhere while raising holy hands without anger or doubt." In other words, one should not enter a sanctuary with hands raised in anger. N. V. is arguing that this proves that the mere raising of a hand in anger is regarded as a murderous act; thus, intent, which is an act of the soul and not of the body, is what really counts. For the view that merely raising a hand with intent to

L

hit someone is sufficient to label a person an evildoer, see *B. Sanhedrin* 58b and Rashi
on Exodus 2:13.

30   ***The fact remains, however, that it says.*** . . . The point of these quotations is
apparently to establish by the weight of evidence that all desires stem from the soul
and that Proverbs 19:21 should therefore be taken metaphorically.

35   ***Why is the soul punished?*** For a different explanation, see *Sefer Yosef
HaMeqanne*, Rosenthal's ed., pp. 71–72.

Page 195

1-2   ***The parable of the lame man and the blind man*** This parable is found in
several places in rabbinic literature, e. g., *B. Sanhedrin* 91a–b.

17   ***This, then, is the answer which they give us.*** . . . On this form of the
"ransom" explanation, see appendix 2. The closest parallel in Christian polemic is
found in the *Dialogus* attributed to William of Champeaux, PL 163.1070–72. God, the
author says, would not end Satan's control over man violently because that would be
unjust. After all, Satan had not gained control over man by violence; on the contrary, he had seduced man by trickery ("rationabili calliditate") to give himself
over to Satan of his own free will. Consequently, God deceived Satan by sending
his own son in human form while keeping his identity hidden ("hoc sacramentum
valde diabolo celatum est"), and Satan proceeded to kill him. This made it just for
God to liberate man from Satan ("Diabolus qui primum hominem sub dola fraude
seduxerat et sibi subjecerat; quem etiam diutissime captivum tenerat; tum Deum
et Dominum suum Christum injuste morte peremit, juste hominem quem permit-
tente Deo possederat, perdere debuit. . . .")

25   ***Far be it from God to do evil.*** . . . The view that God did not want to act un-
justly even toward Satan by seizing man out of his hands was a basic element of
this explanation of the incarnation. In addition to the references in appendix 2, see
the disputation of Gregentius and Herbanus, summarized by Williams, p. 147. The
author of N. V. reversed this argument below by maintaining that God behaved
improperly toward Satan even granting the Christian explanation cited here. Cf.
also *Sefer Nestor HaKomer*, p. 10 ("Far be it from God to do evil . . . by handing over
righteous men into the hands of Satan").

Page 196

34   ***Why he delayed this redemption*** See Rome ms. 53, p. 22a = Pos. "Mordecai
of Avignon" ms., p. 16 = Rosenthal's "Menahem," p. 65: "Why did Jesus leave the
souls in hell more than 5,200 years (sic!)? Why did he not suffer death immediately
in order to redeem the righteous from hell?" (The manuscript, which was read correctly by Posnanski, says ה׳ אלפים ור׳ שנים ; Rosenthal's ה׳ אלפים וכו׳ שנים is
inaccurate.) The same argument appears in the *Vikkuaḥ LehaRadaq* (Talmage's ed.,

p. 94) in connection with the author's more elaborate discussion of the dating of the incarnation in the year 5500.

35   *Why he gave the Torah earlier when there was no reward for it* The Jew in the *Dialogus* attributed to William of Champeaux is said to have made the same argument: "Why did God give such a fragile law that it could not save those who observed it? This is clearly a form of deception—to give a sick man medicine which cannot save him" (PL 163.1050).

Page 197

6   *The story of Lazarus took place* So also *Sefer HaBerit, Mil Ḥovah*, p. 21a = Talmage's ed., pp. 24–25, and *Vikkuaḥ LeHaRadaq, Mil. Ḥovah*, p. 16a = Talmage's ed., p. 89.

7–8   *"Whose name was Dives"* "Dives" is actually the Latin word for rich; the Gospel account does not supply the man's name.

Page 198

10   *It is written . . . that Jesus said. . . .* This paragraph is found in Moses of Salerno, Pos. ms., p. 39.

27   *It is written . . . that "the hour will come. . . ."* The passage is found in *Sefer Yosef HaMeqanne, Kiev Festschrift*, Hebrew section, p. 129, and in Moses of Salerno, Posnanski ms., p. 40.

Page 199

15–16   *Now that it says "spirit" four times. . . .* Cf. p. 50. For a similar argument, see the passage in *Sefer HaBerit, Mil. Ḥovah*, p. 31a = Talmage's ed., p. 49, cited in appendix 1.

20–21   *The children of Israel are also called sons of God* Cf. Rome ms. 53, p. 24b = Pos. "Mordecai of Avignon" ms., p. 34 = Rosenthal's "Menaḥem," p. 72, which also cites Deuteronomy 14:1 and Exodus 4:22 to prove this point. This Jewish argument (with specific reference to Exodus 4:22) was discussed by Peter the Venerable, *Tractatus*, PL 189.510–11. There is a curious citation of similar verses by Aphraates (Dem. 17), who argues that if Moses, Solomon, and the children of Israel were called sons of God, how much more does Jesus deserve that title! Williams, who summarizes this passage (p. 99), almost unwillingly points out the peculiarity of the argument: "Perhaps the argument does not go as far as we should like, and leaves room for the supposition that Jesus is not, after all, the incarnation of the very and eternal Deity. But it forms a sound foundation on which to build this higher truth" (p. 100). The fact is, of course, that Aphraates' argument could be used to undermine the Christian interpretation of such verses as Psalms 2:7. See also Neusner, *Aphrahat*, pp. 130–31, and Parkes, *Conflict*, p. 277.

25-26   ***Even if you marvel at his making water into wine. . . .*** The comparison of
Jewish and Christian miracles in the Bible was a significant theme in several major
polemics, especially Peter the Venerable's *Tractatus* and Meir of Narbonne's *Mil.*
Mizvah. Peter argued that neither group has an advantage in authenticating the miracles it accepts. Jews base their belief on their books and traditions, and Christians
do the same (PL 189.588). This apparent even-handedness really constituted no
concession at all since Christians generally believed in the authenticity of the miracles recorded in the Hebrew Bible (and it was primarily those Jewish miracles
which were being discussed); if Christian miracles were also authentic, then
Christianity would be true. Peter went on to say that granted the authenticity of all
the reports, Christian miracles far exceed those mentioned in the Hebrew Bible.
The miracles of Peter alone, for example, exceed those of Moses (PL 189.570-71).
Meir of Narbonne, on the other hand, argued that the miracles of the prophets were
qualitatively far greater than those of Jesus, citing the darkness in Egypt, Joshua's
stopping the sun and moon, and Isaiah's reversal of Hezekiah's sundial (*Mil.*
Mizvah, Parma ms., p. 97a). He also presented an imposing list of virtually all the
miracles mentioned in the Bible (pp. 182a-199b). The central point in N. V. here,
namely, that the prophets performed miracles and yet are not revered as divine,
was implicitly dealt with by Peter the Venerable; he maintained that the prophets
performed their miracles only after praying to God, while Jesus performed them
through his own power (PL 189.596-97). On this Jewish argument, see *Sefer Nestor*
HaKomer, p. 2, and the *Vikkuah LeHaRadaq, Mil. Hovah*, p. 14b = Talmage's ed., pp.
88-89. Cf. above p. 151. For discussion of the Christian argument from the miracles
of later saints, see below pp. 211-12.

Page 200

5   ***Moses did this three times*** See Rashi on Deuteronomy 9:18.

8   ***The fifth book of Mark*** The number here results from an emendation, but
cf. also p. 205. I am unfamiliar with the nature of these subdivisions, which also
appear in *Sefer Nestor HaKomer* (e.g., p. 4).

9-10   ***"No creature knows that day. . . ."*** Also quoted in *Sefer Nestor HaKomer*, loc.
cit.

18-19   ***"See, then, that I, I am he. . . ."*** Cf. pp. 75-76 and the notes there.

24-25   ***He added an immense sin to the Jews*** See p. 184 and the notes there. The passage here is adapted from *Sefer Nestor HaKomer*, p. 1.

29-30   ***Why were his servants killed?*** I.e., why were some of the apostles and early
saints killed? There is a fascinating parallel between this argument and the argument used by some Christians to explain why the Jews are being punished (see the
notes to p. 136). Both arguments begin with the Christian doctrine that Jesus' death
was necessary. If so, (1) why blame Jews (the Christian problem)? (2) His death

L

would not prove his powerlessness and hence his nondivinity (the Jewish problem). The solution in both cases is the death of the apostles. (1) The Jews are clearly to blame for this. (2) Jesus' failure to prevent this proves that he was powerless to do so.

Page 201

1   *Gregory interpreted.* . . . This single sentence is perhaps the most intractable passage in all of N.V. Impure water is undoubtedly baptismal water, and there is no serious difficulty in the sentence that the elimination of Gregory will not resolve; unfortunately, however, "Gregory interpreted" appears both in *Tela* and in the Rome manuscript, which reads, "Gregory interpreted that a rabbi placated our creator for saving us. . . ." Now it is obvious that Gregory never spoke about placating God for saving us (or perhaps "so that he might save us," reading להצילנו for שהצילנו) from baptismal water. Perhaps, however, he wrote something sufficiently similar to allow a Jewish reader to argue that this is in effect what he said.

Let us begin with the reading of the Rome manuscript. First of all, the Hebrew for "a rabbi placated" is stylistically awkward. Furthermore, Gregory may well have said something about a rabbi, but it is hard to understand the meaning of his "interpreting" that a rabbi placated our creator. An interpretation usually refers to a Biblical passage, and the absence of any reference to a Biblical book or author makes the sentence even more peculiar. It seems reasonable to emend the awkward "rabbi" (רבי) to a Biblical personage, and the most likely candidate would be David (דוד). (Let me add immediately that the interpretation that I shall propose fits into the *Tela* reading without an emendation.) Thus, David placated our creator for saving us (or "so that he might save us") from impure water.

Did Gregory in fact ever "interpret" such a thing? We must recall that both the author of N.V. and *Sefer Yosef HaMeqanne* took several verses in Psalms as prayers by David to be saved from baptismal water; see pp. 172-73 and 221. Now, our author may have reasoned that as long as Christians take those verses as prayers to be saved from drowning or some other physical danger, they are on safe territory. The moment, however, that they associate such waters with heretical doctrines, they make a dangerous concession, because the only apparent reason for using water as a metaphor for false beliefs is the association between baptism and Christianity. Hence, any Christian writer interpreting such water as false doctrines is saying, in effect, that David asked God to save him from what Jewish polemicists called "the impure water."

One of the verses referred by N.V. (p. 173) to baptismal water was Psalms 32:6 ("For this shall everyone who is godly pray unto you in a time when you may be found; surely in the flood of great waters they shall not come near to him"). It happens that the *Exposition of the Penitential Psalms* ascribed to Gregory interprets the waters in that verse as heretical doctrines (PL 79.563). Moreover, the very word

L

"placate," which is not particularly appropriate here and is not part of the usual vocabulary of N.V., appears in that passage of the *Exposition*; the people caught in those heretical waters should "placate God." ("Illis ergo tempus opportunum non est qui de sua stulta sapientia inflati, unde Deum placare debuerant, inde eum magis per vanarum assertionum blasphemiam irritant.") Thus, to shift to the *Tela* reading, "Gregory" did interpret that we should placate our creator for saving us (or "so that he might save us") from the impure water.

12   *It is written . . . "Jesus was sitting. . . ."* I am unaware of any source for this or the following story.

24-25   *It is written . . . that Mary was lying in the bosom of Jesus. . . .* No Christian work could describe the death of Mary during Jesus' lifetime since John 19:26-27 places her at the crucifixion. There are, however, several apocryphal works in which Jesus posthumously appears to Mary immediately before her death. See *The Book of John concerning the Falling Asleep of Mary, Ante-Nicene Fathers*, 8:587-91, and *The Passing of Mary*, ibid., pp. 592-98. There is another apocryphal work which describes Jesus' eulogizing his father: "Now his body was lying prostrate and bloodless; wherefore I reached forth my hand and put right his eyes and shut his mouth and said to the virgin Mary: O my mother, where is the skill which he showed in all the time that he lived in this world. Lo! It has perished as if it had never existed" (*History of Joseph the Carpenter*, ibid., p. 392).

Page 202

3   *Since he could protest but did not. . . .* For this concept in rabbinic thought, see *B. Shabbat* 54b-55a, 55b; *B. Sanhedrin* 20a; *B. Avodah Zarah* 4a, 18a.

5   *It is written . . . "Just as Jonah. . . ."* The paragraph is taken from *Sefer Yosef HaMeqanne, Kiev Festschrift*, Hebrew section, pp. 132-33. The argument here was quoted by Dionysius bar Salibi, cited in Williams, p. 108.

24   *On a stalk of cabbage* This is based on an old legend found in *Toledot Yeshu*. See the references to Krauss and others cited in Immanuel Löw, *Die Flora der Juden* (Vienna and Leipzig, 1928), 1:484, 4:412-13.

26   *"Seed of millet"* Or possibly "seed of rice ." There was some uncertainty among medieval Jews regarding the translation of *dohan* (millet) and *orez* (rice). See Rashi *Berakhot* 37a, s.v. *orez* and s.v. *dohan*, and see *Tosafot* there, s.v. *Rashi peresh*. For later views, cf. the standard commentaries to *Orah Hayyim* 208:7. See also Immanuel Löw, "Pflanzennamen bei Raschi," *Festschrift A. Berliner's*, pp. 244-45, and his *Die Flora der Juden*, 1:736-37. The Gospel text says "mustard-seed."

27   *Even their saints cannot do this* This observation reversed the Christian argument from the miracles of the saints. Similarly, Meir of Narbonne (*Mil. Mizvah*, Parma ms., p. 98a) asked why contemporary cardinals could not cure the sick and resurrect the dead if they take Jesus' place. See pp. 211-12.

Aphraates reported that a Jew cited this very verse from Matthew to show that if Christians are supposed to be able to move mountains they should at least be capable of stopping the persecutions against them (Dem. 21, Neusner's *Aphrahat*, p. 97). Neusner (p. 129) argues that this was not an authentic Jewish question primarily on the grounds that Christians, not Jews, are likely to have wondered about this. However, Aphraates' only direct answer to the specific question from Matthew is that Jews are faced with a similar problem since they cannot walk through fire despite Isaiah 43:2-3. This might be effective in countering a Jewish argument but would hardly do very much to allay internal Christian doubts. Neusner's later assertion (p. 134) that Aphraates' references to persecution of Jews would have been ineffective as an anti-Jewish argument and were aimed largely at Christians is also unpersuasive.

Page 203

1   *"Follow the majority"* This was the rabbinic interpretation of Exodus 23:2; cf. Rashi's discussion, ad loc. This Christian question was cited by Meir of Narbonne, *Mil. Mizvah*, Parma ms., pp. 60a, 123a.

2   *Only eleven nations have erred. . . .* On the Jewish argument that Christians are a minority, see the notes to p. 89.

10-12   *He should have . . . caused all nations to believe in him* Once again, this is a reversal of a Christian argument which asked why God had revealed the Law to such a small group. See the notes to pp. 43 and 184.

16-17   *Both you and the Ishmaelites admit that our Torah is true* So Halevi, *Kuzari* 1:10, and cf. below pp. 216-18. A Muslim polemicist refuted this argument by pointing out that in the final analysis these nations testify that Judaism is false. Thus, Jews do not really accept the testimony of others, and they rely only on their own tradition, which is that of a small nation. See Perlmann, *Ifham al-Yahud*, p. 43. Meir of Narbonne records a slightly different form of the argument, namely, that Christianity has been disputed since the moment of its inception while Judaism was once universal (i.e., among all believers in the revelation at Sinai). See *Mil. Mizvah*, Parma ms., pp. 29b-30a, where he says that even Jewish women and the masses perceive the force of this argument. Elsewhere (pp. 60a, 123a), Meir quotes a Christian argument based on Deuteronomy 19:15 ("a matter is established by two witnesses") which noted that Christianity was validated by twelve witnesses (the apostles); his response is that more contemporaries rejected him than accepted him.

22   *It is written . . . "When Mary gave birth. . . ."* Actually, this is a conflation of Luke 2:1-7, which mentions Augustus and the manger, and Matthew 2:13-16, where Jesus is saved from Herod, who wanted to kill him.

30-31   *One who entices people toward idolatry* Deuteronomy 13:7-12.

L

31   ***Why did he fly up into the sky . . .?*** This Jewish story is found in *Toledot Yeshu* (Krauss, *Das Leben Jesu nach Jüdischen Quellen*, p. 77 [pp. 99-100 of his German translation]); it was also quoted by Meir of Narbonne, *Mil. Miẓvah*, Parma ms., p. 97a.

Page 204

8-9   ***He should have performed wonders . . . in his infancy*** See pp. 104, 148.

11   ***He was a sorcerer*** See the notes to p. 64. On death for sorcerers, cf. Exodus 22:17.

19   ***It is written in the book of Simon. . . .*** This passage is quoted and attributed to the "book of Simon" in *Sefer Nestor HaKomer*, p. 5, and in *Mil. HaShem*, p. 155; see Rosenthal's note 54 in *Mil. HaShem*, ad loc.

Page 205

15   ***It is written in their book of Mark. . . .*** This paragraph is also found above, p. 188; it is based on *Sefer Yosef HaMeqanne, Kiev Festschrift*, Hebrew section, p. 125.

29-30   ***You . . . pursue fornication*** See the notes to p. 69, and cf. below p. 223.

Page 206

1   ***A dead man is impure. . . .*** Numbers 19:11 ff.

3   ***You defile priests*** The prohibition against such defilement is in Leviticus 12:1. This question is also based on the assumption expressed at the beginning of the previous paragraph, namely, that the Christian priest is supposed to take the place of a biblical priest. The same question was discussed in *The Disputation of Sergius the Stylite against a Jew*, ed. by Hayman, translation, pp. 34-37.

6   ***"Those who sit among the graves. . . ."*** See p. 118 (and the notes there) and p. 211.

13   ***With regard to their questioning us. . . .*** P. Browe translated this passage into German in his *Die Judenmission im Mittelalter und die Päpste* (Rome, 1942), pp. 288-89, but he confused N.V. with the later *Niẓẓaḥon* of Yom Tov Lipmann Mühlhausen and consequently attributed the quotation to the latter work. W. Eckert (in Rengstorff and von Kortzfleisch's *Kirche und Synagoge*, 1:254) was misled by Browe's error.

15-16   ***One should not be surprised at the bad deeds of an evil Jew. . . .*** The Jewish imputation of base motives to apostates is reflected in Petrus Alfonsi's report that Jews charged him with converting for the sake of temporal honor, among other things (PL 157.538). Peter the Venerable, for his part, rigorously denied that pleasure could be a motive for accepting Christianity (PL 189.593-94) although he did list it as a motive which aided the spread of Islam (ibid., 591-92). On the missionary

L

activity of both sides, see *Juifs et Chrêt.*, pp. 65–212. For a discussion of the material advantages and disadvantages of conversion to Christianity, see Grayzel, *The Church and the Jews*, pp. 16–21.

Page 207

3–4 **The uncircumcised and impure** I.e., Christians. The phrase is taken from Isaiah 52:1. The prohibition against Christians serving Jews was based on Genesis 25:23; cf. the notes to p. 55. This passage, then, represents a classic conflict between Christian and Jewish typology. It also constitutes a remarkably vigorous assertion of Jewish pride in the face of adversity; indeed, the language is striking even for Ashkenazic polemic. There is a feeling of disdainful superiority here which was in part a defense mechanism but was nevertheless deeply felt.

7–8 **"For the nation . . . that will not serve you shall perish"** This verse was quoted by Solomon de' Rossi, *'Edut HaShem Ne'emanah*, Rosenthal's *Meḥqarim*, 1:389.

16 **"You may sell it to a Gentile"** The author of Rome ms. 53 (p. 24b = Pos. "Mordecai of Avignon" ms., p. 35 = Rosenthal's "Menaḥem," p. 72) maintained that the fact that Christians buy such meat from Jews and eat it shows that they consider themselves "strangers"; thus, they belong in that category with regard to the laws of interest as well. On the selling of nonkosher meat to Christians, see Grayzel, *The Church and the Jews*, pp. 72–73, and Agus, *The Heroic Age of Franco-German Jewry*, pp. 350–52. See also Perlmann, *Ifḥam al-Yahud*, pp. 67, 100 (note B78).

18 **God does not withhold the reward of any creature** See the *Mekhilta* to Exodus 22:30, and see especially Rashi, *Pesaḥim* 22a, s. v. *oto*.

27 **"Take heed. . . ."** The full passage is, "Take heed to yourself that you not offer your burnt offerings in every place that you see. But in the place which the Lord shall choose in one of your tribes, there you shall offer your burnt offerings, and there you shall do all that I command you."

29 **"For you desire not. . . ."** The full passage is, "For you desire not sacrifice; otherwise I would give it. You delight not in burnt offering. The sacrifices of God are a broken spirit; a broken and contrite heart, O God, you will not despise. Do good in accordance with your desire unto Zion; build the walls of Jerusalem. Then shall you be pleased with the sacrifices of righteousness, with whole burnt offerings; then shall they offer bullocks upon your altar."

Page 209

10 **"I will bring them. . . ."** The full verse is, "I will bring them to my holy mountain and make them joyful in my house of prayer; their burnt offerings and their sacrifices shall be accepted upon my altar, for my house shall be called a house of prayer for all people."

L

13-14   *"We shall take the place of bullocks. . . ."* This was the accepted Jewish interpretation of this difficult verse; see *Yalqut Shim'oni,* Rashi, R. Joseph Kara, and R. David Kimḥi, ad loc.

19-20   *Jesus . . . was an actual human being. . . .* See p. 180.

Page 210

3   *"The dead praise not the Lord"* Jewish law certainly frowned upon prayer to the dead; nevertheless, the implication here that the dead are incapable of intercession for the living is rather dubious in light of rabbinic literature. Cf., for example, the famous legends on the efforts of the patriarchs to prevent the destruction of the Temple (Ginzberg, *Legends of the Jews,* 4:304-10; 6:397-98). In an effort to retain the sharpest possible distinction between Jewish and Christian practice regarding prayer to created beings, Meir of Narbonne devoted considerable space to a reinterpretation of several Jewish prayers which appear to be addressed to the angels (*Mil. Miẓvah,* Parma ms., pp. 234b-235a).

6-7   *Whose name is Dumah* See *B. Sanhedrin* 94a.

Page 211

5-6   *Saint so-and-so does remarkable deeds* For the Christian argument from miraculous cures, see Peter the Venerable, *Tractatus,* PL 189.599-600. Meir of Narbonne, on the other hand, had asked why cardinals cannot cure the sick and resurrect the dead if they replace Jesus (see above p. 202), and elsewhere (Parma ms., p. 18a) he felt constrained to explain why contemporary Jews cannot perform miracles. He simply asserted that miracles and prophecy would be restored only at the proper time, and that the absence of such miracles does not constitute proof that Jews are not worthy of them. Indeed, "There are many pious men [*ḥasidim*] among us who are worthy of having God's presence descend upon them," but it should be kept in mind that even Moses, who was clearly worthy of prophecy when he was a man of sixty, fifty, or forty, did not become a prophet or perform wonders until he was eighty years old. See also *Sefer Yosef HaMeqanne,* p. 82, for the rather strange Jewish assertion that saints (in this case the alleged victim of a ritual murder) can indeed perform wonders because "God customarily performs miracles for men of little faith."

9   *This is similar to a trustworthy man. . . .* As Posnanski points out (ad loc.), this passage is taken from *B. Avodah Zarah* 55a, where R. Akiba responded to a similar question. It should also be noted that the argument that God will not change the natural order simply to disabuse evildoers of their errors is also expressed in a famous dialogue in *B. Avodah Zarah* 54b.

20-21   *"You have saved us from evil and faithful diseases"* In the passage in *B. Avodah Zarah* 55a, R. Yoḥanan cited the phrase "evil and faithful diseases" from

L

Deuteronomy 28:59; the version found here, however, is based on the *Nishmat* prayer recited in the morning service on Sabbaths and festivals and at the Passover seder.

26   ***This is done to mislead you*** A similar view is expressed in the Talmud, loc. cit., and explained on the grounds that God facilitates both the sinning of wicked men and the good deeds of the penitent; there is, however, no reference to Job 12:23.

26-27   ***"He misleads nations"*** This interpretation is based on a non-Masoretic reading of the verse (*mashgi* instead of *masgi*), but it is found in several midrashic sources; see Rashi and especially *Minḥat Shai*, ad loc. For another argument based on a non-Masoretic vocalization, see above p. 166.

35-36   ***No nation in the world eats swine except for you*** So Jacob ben Reuben, *Mil. HaShem*, pp. 38-39, 114. For this passage from Isaiah as a reference to Christians, see also above pp. 117-18, 206.

Page 212

1   ***It is written in their books. . . .*** See Augustine, *City of God* 10:16 (noted by Rosenthal, "Pirqei Vikkuah," *Salo Wittmayer Baron Jubilee Volume*, ed. by S. Lieberman and A. Hyman [Jerusalem, 1974/5], vol. 3, p. 384). The ability of a guiltless person to carry water in a sieve is a theme which is attested in folk tales both with regard to a virgin (see F. J. Child, *The English and Scottish Popular Ballads* [Boston, 1884], 2:270) and with regard to other innocents (see J. Bolte and G. Polívka, *Anmerkungen zu den Kinder-u. Hausmärchen der Brüder Grimm* [Hildesheim, 1963], pp. 476-77). The above citations are the most relevant of those indicated in Stith Thompson, *Motif Index of Folk Literature* (Bloomington, Ind., 1966), 3, no. H 413:3 and H 1023:2.

16   ***Thus, there is proof. . . .*** In other words, since Christians deny the validity of Roman paganism, they must admit that God occasionally saves someone in a manner which can mislead the observer into attributing a miracle to a false god.

28-29   ***Yet they emerged unscathed*** Cf. the notes to p. 173.

Page 213

17   ***Apostolus*** The singular is mistakenly used instead of *apostoli*.

19-20   ***They bestow divine honors upon the idols*** The charge that Christian worship of images is tantamount to idolatry is found in Jacob ben Reuben, *Mil. HaShem*, p. 100, and in Meir of Narbonne, *Mil. Miẓvah*, pp. 87a-b. It is also quoted in Agobard, *De Judaicis Superstitionibus*, 10, PL 104.88 = MGH *Epist.* 5:190 ("Christianos idola asserunt adorare"), quoted in *Auteurs*, p. 153; Crispin's *Disputatio*, p. 65 ("Has effigies Christiani . . . adorant et colunt"); Rupert's *Dialogus*, PL 170.590, 601. The Christian response ranged from the common assertion that the icons are not

L

actually worshiped (Crispin's *Disputatio*, p. 67; *Mil. HaShem*, loc. cit., where Jacob ben Reuben calls this argument insincere) to Agobard's counterargument that the Jews themselves believe in a corporeal God, an argument developed in detail by Petrus Alfonsi. See the references in *Auteurs,* p. 165, and especially in Williams, p. 163, n. 2, where he cites eight Christian polemics in which this Jewish argument is discussed. There is a lengthy treatment of this issue in *The Disputation of Sergius the Stylite*, trans., pp. 24, 30–33. See also *Juifs et Chrét.*, pp. 285–87, for a discussion of the possible Jewish influence on the icon controversy among Christians, and cf. the notes to pp. 72–73. Cf. also Parkes, *Conflict*, pp. 291–94.

Page 214

3   *"Those who carry the wood. . . ."* This verse was also referred to Christians by Meir of Narbonne, *Mil. Mizvah*, Parma ms., p. 115b, and Moses of Salerno, Posnanski ms., p. 49.

27   *"Am I a God from near?"* This rather awkward translation gives at least some indication of the ambiguity of the Hebrew *miqarov*, which can be taken either spatially (see Rashi and R. Joseph Kara, ad loc.) or temporally (see the Targum and R. David Kimhi, ad loc.). The latter view was adopted both by N.V. and by Meir of Narbonne, who says that the verse shows that a human body, which was created recently, cannot be God (*Mil. Mizvah*, Parma ms., pp. 124b and 132a).

30   *It says . . . that she was thirteen* In the manuscripts of the *Protevangelium of James*, Mary's age at the time of conception ranges from fourteen to seventeen (*Ante-Nicene Fathers*, 8:364 [par. 12]). However, in *The Gospel of Pseudo-Matthew*, par. 8–9 (ibid., pp. 371–73), the chronology indicates that she became pregnant almost immediately after she was given over to Joseph, and according to one version (p. 371) she was twelve when she was given over to him. Thus she was thirteen when she gave birth. (According to *The Gospel of the Nativity of Mary* [ibid., p. 385], she was at least fourteen.)

Page 215

1-2   *Everyone would have been able to recognize the miracle* This specific argument about Mary's age is found in the *Vikkuah LeHaRadaq, Mil. Hovah*, pp. 16b–17a = Talmage's ed., p. 91, cited above in the notes to p. 43. Cf. also pp. 104, 146, 148, and 204.

7   *Jesus himself said. . . .* See the notes to p. 172.

15   *Sicut. . . .* This ancient creed was quoted by Christian polemicists. See Crispin's *Disputatio*, p. 46, and Alan of Lille, PL 210.414: "Sicut anima rationalis et caro . . . unus est homo . . . ita Deus et homo . . . unus est Christus." See also the citations from Augustine in H. Wolfson, *The Philosophy of the Church Fathers*[2] (Cambridge, Mass., 1964), 1:369.

L

16-17   ***When the man was killed so was the divinity*** This does not seem to follow from the analogy with spirit and flesh. It may be that the author had some sort of monophysite conception of Jesus in mind. Cf. *Sefer Yosef HaMeqanne,* p. 126.

22-23   ***Why shouldn't the person . . . find forgiveness?*** Jacob ben Reuben (*Mil. HaShem,* p. 153; cf. *Sefer Nestor HaKomer,* p. 3) argued that the similar verses in Matthew 12:31-32 imply that if a man would blaspheme the father, the son, and the holy spirit, two would forgive him while the third would not; would he, then, be damned or saved? See also *Sefer Yosef HaMeqanne, Kiev Festschrift,* Hebrew section, p. 135, and cf. Rembaum in *Proceedings of the American Academy for Jewish Research* 45 (1978): 161.

24   ***It is written in their book of Alexander. . . .*** The central elements of this account are based on a story found in three apocryphal works: *The Protevangelium of James,* ch. 17-19 (*Ante-Nicene Fathers,* 8:365), *The Gospel of Pseudo-Matthew,* ch. 13-15 (ibid., pp. 374-75), and *The Arabic Gospel of the Infancy of the Saviour,* ch. 2 (ibid., p. 405). The first of these works makes mention of the miraculous light in the cave, while the last two also include a reference to Jesus' circumcision. Identifying the mysterious "Book of Alexander," however, is a more difficult matter, and the following highly speculative suggestion might be entertained. In the last of the three works cited above, the relevant passage begins, "In the three hundred and ninth year of the era of Alexander, Augustus put forth an edict. . . ." (Some versions give slightly different numbers.) Now, this passage appears near the very beginning of the book and really constitutes the first sentence of the story; the few sentences that precede it are simply a short, late introduction. In the event that such a version of the story came to the attention of a medieval Jew without the introductory padding, he might have followed the Jewish habit of referring to a work by its first important word and consequently called it *The Book of Alexander.* Finally, it should be kept in mind that the Rome manuscript reads simply "in the account of Alexander."

28   ***Son of Pandera*** For a discussion of this term, see Goldstein, *Jesus in the Jewish Tradition,* pp. 33-39.

Page 216

6   ***"He must be circumcised"*** For the Jewish argument from Jesus' circumcision, cf. the *Altercatio Simonis Judaei,* PL 20.1172, *Sefer Nestor HaKomer,* p. 7, and Meir of Narbonne, *Mil. Mizvah,* Parma ms., p. 87b. Bernard of Clairvaux argued that Jesus had accepted circumcision in order to show that he was the author of the Old Testament as well as the New; see his "Sermon for the Octave of the Epiphany," *St. Bernard's Sermons,* 2:31.

13-14   ***They should have made it a joyous festival*** This is an elaboration of the common Jewish argument that Jews should not be blamed for the crucifixion since it was ultimately a good thing; see above p. 136.

L
15-16   **They know that all who believe in him will go down to hell** If this is to be taken
seriously, then we have here a reversal of the frequent Christian contention that the
Jews perversely cling to their faith even though they know it is false and that this is
a result of a Jewish pact with Satan. Cf. Cecil Roth, "The Medieval Conception of
the Jew," *Personalities and Events in Jewish History* (Philadelphia, 1953), pp. 53-68, and
Joshua Trachtenberg, *The Devil and the Jew* (New Haven, 1943), passim. See below
pp. 219-20.

18   **There was once an emperor. . . .** This intriguing passage, which is written
partly in rhymed prose, is a variant of the famous story which forms the frame-
work of Halevi's *Kuzari*. Characteristically, however, the Ashkenazic author has
added the crucial element of willingness to be martyred as an acid test of religious
truth. A much briefer version far closer to Halevi's is found in Rome ms. 53, p. 24b
= Pos. "Mordecai of Avignon" ms., p. 33 = Rosenthal's "Menahem," p. 71. There,
the emperor of Germany asks a Christian, a Muslim, and a Jew which is the better
of the other two religions. The Christian and Muslim both say Judaism and the Jew
says "whatever he wishes." The emperor then says, "Follow the majority," and he
concludes that Judaism is best (cf. above p. 203). A religious discussion resulting
in the conversion of a king to Judaism is also found in a medieval Hebrew manuscript from Germany described by Yosef Dan, "Sippur Ashkenazi 'al Hitgayyerut
Melekh 'Aravi," *Zion* 26:132-37; there is, however, no further resemblance to our
story.

Page 217

3   **He did not budge** Lit., "he did not rise or move," based on Esther 5:9.

9-10   **The wicked man refused to do this** The expression is taken from "Elleh
Ezkerah," which is recited on the Day of Atonement and commemorates the
martyrdom of the rabbis killed by the Romans.

18   **His only fate would be death** Based on Esther 4:11.

19-20   **The evil decree had been fully turned against him** Based on Esther 7:7.

22-23   **Their god Muhammad got drunk. . . .** This story was undoubtedly invented
to explain why Muslims refrained from drinking wine and eating pork; the latter
element is explicitly pointed out in a gloss in the *Tela* manuscript. On this story in
medieval Christian sources, see Norman Daniel, *Islam and the West: The Making of an
Image* (Edinburgh, 1960), pp. 104-05.

Page 218

2   **He asked to be given time till the morrow. . . .** The theme of asking for a delay
of one or three days in precisely such a context appears in two stories of Jewish
martyrdom that were current among thirteenth century Ashkenazic Jews. See S.
Eidelberg, "HaReqa' HaHistori shel Ma'aseh R. Amnon U-tefillat 'U-netanneh

L

Toqef'," *Hadoar* 53 (1974): 645-6. Thus, the reader is expected to contrast the Muslim's decision after his period of grace with the choice made by the two Jews to die for their faith.

4-5   **God of my father Abraham the father of Ishmael** Or, perhaps even more likely, "God of Abraham, Father of my father Ishmael," in which case the first "father" would refer back to God; if so, this would be a variation of the stereotyped Jewish formula referring to the God of Abraham, of *Isaac*, and of Jacob (= Israel). It should also be noted that the words "my father" may constitute a mistaken redundancy in the Hebrew text (*avi* may originally have been written only once).

6   **The perfect God** Lit., "the perfect Rock," based on Deuteronomy 32:4.

6   **Creator of heaven and earth** Lit., "creator of throne and footstool," based on Isaiah 66:1.

10-11   **And was thus unable to save himself. . . .** See *Sefer Nestor HaKomer*, p. 10, and the citations in M. Smith, *Clement of Alexandria and a Secret Gospel of Mark* (Cambridge, Mass., 1973), pp. 154-55; cf. also *B. Avodah Zarah* 41b.

13   **"I take an oath"** Lit., "I raise my hand," based on Genesis 14:23.

27-28   **"Iniquitatum meum"** Probably the author's mistake for "iniquitatem meam."

31   **His hand is stretched out to accept those who repent** This is based on a phrase found in several places in the Jewish liturgy (the *amidah* of the concluding service on the Day of Atonement, *selihot*, and *tahanun*).

32   **That God behaved so cruelly. . . .** Meir of Narbonne also argued that the alleged consequences of original sin are inconsistent with the conception of a God who "shows mercy toward all his creatures" (*Mil. Mizvah*, Parma ms., p. 53a; cf. pp. 7a, 28b-29a, and 101b-102a for his argument that making salvation dependent upon baptism is blatantly unjust). See also Naḥmanides' disputation in Chavel, *Ketavei Ramban*, 1:310, and R. Joseph Kimḥi in *Sefer HaBerit, Mil. Ḥovah*, p. 20a = Talmage's ed., p. 24. Both Meir of Narbonne (pp. 7b and 28b-29a) and the Jew in the *Dialogus* attributed to William of Champeaux (PL 163.1052) argued that the Bible teaches that the sinner alone and not his descendants must suffer for his crime and that the Christian conception of original sin is therefore excluded.

Page 219

11   **"Et ipse est misericors. . . ."** The reading of this passage is uncertain. The passage is found only in the Munich manuscript, and the manuscript version contains almost as many errors as correct readings. The Vulgate on this verse reads, "Ipse autem est misericors et propitius fiet peccatis eorum et non perdet eos et

L
abundabit ut avertat iram et non accendet omnem iram suam." If the text in N.V. really said "mitterit repudium" instead of "perdet," the phrase may have been based on the Latin translation of Deuteronomy 24:1, Isaiah 50:1, and/or Jeremiah 3:8.

23   *"Tantum fidem. . . ."* Wagenseil's text omits the Latin, and, in fact, there is no such verse. The statements, however, may be based on the assertion in Matthew 17:20 that one who has faith "as a grain of mustard seed" can move a mountain. Now, since Christians cannot move mountains, it follows, as the author has already argued (p. 202), that they have no faith. On Christians as Edom, see the notes to p. 55.

29   *"I alone am the body and blood"* The Latin sentence quoted means only, "This is my body."

30   *They say, "Offerentia Satanae"* This is the reading of the Rome manuscript. Wagenseil's text has the accurate quotation, "In nomine patris et filii et spiritus sancti, Amen," but it retains the translation, "Let this be an offering to Satan." The Munich manuscript has what appears to be an abbreviated and corrupted version of both readings: אימני = *In nomine;* שם —probably a Hebrew gloss explaining *nomine;* טראו probably = *patris;* ווי probably = *filii;* אש = *et;* אפרני ציאת שטני = *offerentia Satanae.* The original text was probably "offerentia satanae"; however, a copyist (or perhaps the author of N.V.) inserted the correct version, but he retained "offerentia Satanae" and the translation in order to indicate that it is in effect an offering to Satan. Thus, the Munich version contains both readings. In Wagenseil's text, however, only the accurate quotation remained along with the satiric translation. Whether or not the original author really thought that Christians say "offerentia Satanae" is hard to say. He too probably meant only that this is the effect of their statement, although it would appear to be going rather far to invent a Latin text in addition to the Hebrew "translation." Immediately before this line, the Rome manuscript (p. 62b) "quotes" another Christian prayer both in Latin and Hebrew which says, "Accursed [*maledictus* (the ms. has *maleritus*)] is he who believes our book." Because of this "quotation," I have rejected the otherwise tempting possibility that "offerentia Satanae" (אפרניצייה שטני) was originally a copyist's error for "spiritus sancti" or "santi" (שפיריטו שנטי); this last possibility was especially tempting in light of the Munich reading, and it certainly cannot be ruled out. Cf. also p. 216 and the notes there for the outside chance that some Jews really thought that Christians were consciously allied with Satan.

Page 220

1-2   *The following is called the Credo* On the development of the text of the Credo, see Joseph Jungmann, *The Mass of the Roman Rite* (New York, 1950), 1:461-74.

14   *"Ich glaube. . . ."* I have transliterated both this and the following German passage in accordance with modern German usage except where this was blatantly

L
inconsistent with the Hebrew transliteration. A reconstruction of the medieval German (or Yiddish) is fraught with methodological difficulties and is, in any case, beyond my competence. For some of the methodological problems associated with the linguistic study of such early texts, see M. Weinreich, *Geshikhte fun der Yiddisher Shprakh* (New York, 1973), 1:8-9. Nevertheless, the possible importance of these quotations for historians of Yiddish should be noted. The earliest full Yiddish sentence extant is the 1272 line in the Worms *maḥzor* described by D. Sadan in "Ktovet Rishonah BeYiddish Qedumah beMaḥzor Vermaiza," *Kirjath Sepher* 38 (1963): 575-76, and analyzed by Weinreich in "A Yiddisher Zatz fun far zibn hundert Yor," *Yiddishe Shprakh* 23 (1963): 87-93. The originals of these two passages in N.V. may even predate 1272, although the versions we have reflect later copying. In any event, these passages as well as the many isolated German words in N.V. and Rome manuscript 53 do not appear in the standard collections of glosses in "Jüdisch-deutsch" although they are at least as important as the material that has been collected. See M. Grünbaum, *Jüdischdeutsch Chrestomathie*, Hildesheim, 1969 (first printing, Leipzig, 1882), and W. Staerk and A. Leitzmann, *Die Jüdisch-Deutscher Bibelübersetzungen* (Frankfurt am Main, 1923). The scholarly neglect of this section of N.V. is also evident from the fact that the earliest translation of Christian prayers into Hebrew is generally thought to be a translation of the Credo that may be as late as the fifteenth century; see Kenneth Stow, "Conversion, Christian Hebraism, and Hebrew Prayer in the Sixteenth Century," *HUCA* 47 (1976): 221, n. 17.

24-25   *"Christi fili Dei. . . ."* This means: "Christ the son of God, alas, alas, have mercy upon us, have mercy upon us. We offer you, O Lord, the cup of salvation according to the order of Melchisedek and according to the order of Moses and Aaron among his priests and Samuel among those who call in the name of the Lord." The last part of the quotation is based on Psalms 99:6.

28   **Stillmess** Silent mass, or *secreta.* See Jungmann, op. cit, 2 (1955): 90-96.

30-31   *The following is its German translation* The translation that follows is not precisely equivalent to the Latin, and the second sentence in particular is especially problematical. That sentence means, "We thankfully make an offering to the Lord, who anoints . . . Aaron in their priesthood and Samuel who calls in the name of the Lord." I have assumed a gap after "anoints" into which the names Melchisedek and Moses should probably be inserted. The manuscript has the words "as (= an?) der Seit" at this point; these words are probably a part of the missing phrase and may represent a translation of "secundum ordinem." There may also be another lacuna before "who anoints" in which the omitted object, "cup of salvation," may have appeared, in which case the sentence would read, "We thankfully offer [the cup of salvation] to the Lord, who anoints by the side of (= according to the order of?) [Melchisedek, Moses, and] Aaron in their priesthood and Samuel who calls in the name of the Lord."

L
Page 221

6   *In the chalice* Cf. the notes to p. 175.

7   *"If a Jew smites you. . . ."* The verse, of course, does not actually say "Jew," and the author knew it (cf. the Latin citation). This verse was also cited by Meir of Narbonne (*Mil. Miẓvah*, Parma ms., pp. 4a, 93a), who remarked (p. 93b) that the Christians interpret it allegorically so that it won't interfere with the way they would like to behave. Cf. appendix 3, n. 22.

10   *"The evil water"* So also *Sefer Yosef HaMeqanne, Kiev Festschrift*, Hebrew section, p. 124.

20   *"The Jews are the root of Christianity"* See Romans 11:16-24. Cf. also Hans Levy, *Olamot Nifgashim* (Jerusalem, 1960), pp. 190-94.

22   *"Jesus told his apostles. . . ."* I do not know of a source for this or the following quotation.

28-29   **They are not supposed to persecute Jews** Cf., for example, Bernard's famous letter during the second crusade: "Non sunt persequendi Judaei, non sunt trucidandi, sed ne effugandi quidem" (Jews are not to be persecuted, killed, or even put to flight); see PL 182.567, and see my discussion in *Proceedings of the American Academy for Jewish Research* 40(1972): 89-108. On the doctrine of the church regarding the toleration of the Jews, see also Grayzel, *The Church and the Jews,* pp. 9-12.

Page 222

1   **The heretics say. . . .** This Christian argument followed by the identical response (except that the hypothetical king is the king of Spain) is found in Rome ms. 53, p. 24a = Pos. "Mordecai of Avignon" ms., p. 30 = Rosenthal's "Menaḥem," p. 70. It is particularly noteworthy that the Christian argument cited here has a striking parallel in Jewish polemic. R. Joseph Kimḥi maintained that Christians should admit that Jews ought not to be punished for not believing in Jesus' divinity. "Let me propose a parable," he wrote, "dealing with a king of flesh and blood. If such a king were . . . to put on filthy clothes . . . , deface his beauty, and walk along the road alone . . . , and people would then tell someone that this is the king, the king would not blame that man for not believing them." Kimḥi concluded that it follows a fortiori that one cannot be blamed for refusing to accept a faith which detracts from the greatness of the most exalted king of all (*Sefer HaBerit, Mil. Hovah*, p. 22b = Talmage's ed., pp. 29-30). The identical contention (but without the parable) is found in the reworking of this passage in Rome ms. 53, p. 23a = Pos. "Mordecai of Avignon" ms., p. 22 = Rosenthal's "Menahem,", p. 68. On this Christian argument, cf. Aphraates' seventeenth demonstration (Neusner's *Aphrahat*, p. 73, cited also in Williams, p. 100), where he says that even if the Messiah hadn't come, God would not blame him for believing he had since this is what he has heard and this belief causes him to adore the God of Israel.

L

24   *Jesus had three brothers* The Gospels, in passages quoted earlier in N.V. itself (see p. 179), name four, and I am unfamiliar with any source of the quotations in this paragraph.

Page 223

3   **Beichte** Confession.

7-8   *One should conceal one's sins from another man* The Talmud (*B. Yoma* 86b) discusses the question of public confession of sin in light of the apparent contradiction between Proverbs 28:13 ("He that covers his sins shall not prosper") and Psalms 32:1 ("Blessed is he . . . whose sin is covered"). In fact, the author of N.V. probably quoted Psalms 32:5 because of the talmudic citation of Psalm 32 in this context. In any event, the two explanations suggested in the Talmud were (1) that Psalms 32:1 refers to a private sin and Proverbs 28:13 to one that is already known, and (2) that Psalms 32:1 refers to sins between man and God while Proverbs 28:13 refers to sins against one's fellowman. See also Maimonides' code, *Hilkhot Teshuvah* 2:5, and cf. R. Abraham b. David's note there.

25-26   *They would like to do the same* The Hebrew is based on Deuteronomy 12:30.

29   *To forbid and permit* Or "to bind and loose," based on the famous statement of Jesus to Peter in Matthew 16:19.

32   *So that they would not be seduced into fornication* Meir of Narbonne made a similar proposal as part of his critique of confession. While he did not suggest that the procedures of confession had initially been set up for immoral purposes, he maintained that (1) the sinner might not confess everything because of embarrassment and would thus, according to Christianity, be damned; (2) the confessor might be tempted to sin "because he would be in the full vigor of youth and his passion could be aroused by the things he has heard"; and (3) if a woman confesses adultery, such a confessor might be tempted to sin with that very woman. "Therefore," he suggests "they should have required that people confess only to men of seventy and above and to women who are very old and whose piety is beyond question." See *Mil. Mizvah*, Parma ms., pp. 85a-b. Cf. also *Juifs et Chrét.*, p. 288.

Page 224

3   *He had to pray forty days and forty nights* See Exodus 32:28-32, and Deuteronomy 9:18.

9-10   *He confessed before all of Israel. . . .* There are two answers in this sentence. First, he confessed publicly and not before a single priest; secondly, this was a special occasion. See Joshua 7:19-21.

15-16   *Women are accepted because they watch themselves. . . .* This would be regarded as an especially meritorious act because no one else would check on the

L

woman's honesty in this matter. Indeed, the principle that a single witness is trustworthy with regard to certain prohibitions was derived from the verse entrusting a woman with sole responsibility for counting the days until her purification; see the end of the first *Tosafot* in *Gittin* 2b with the heading '*ed eḥad*. Yosef HaMeqanne (*Kiev Festschrift*, Hebrew section, p. 134) suggested that women are saved through their husbands or parents; cf. Rosenthal's reference to the famous talmudic remark in *B. Berakhot* 17a.

19   *While most Jews are dark and ugly* It is noteworthy, as Ben-Sasson points out (*Toledot Am Yisrael* 2:168), that the author does not challenge the aesthetic assumption which underlies this question. It should also be noted that Moses of Salerno (Pos. ms., p. 64) actually makes use of this view in a polemic to defend the Jewish interpretation of the so-called suffering servant passage. Isaiah 52:14, he says, refers to this servant as one whose appearance is marred (lit., destroyed). Consequently, Christians, who have been known to ask whether Jews have a mouth or eyes or nose (תראה כמה גויים ששואלים אם יש ליהודים פה או עין או חוטם), should certainly refer this passage to Israel. See also the commentaries of Rashi and Ibn Ezra, ad loc., noted by Rosenthal in his edition of *Sefer Yosef HaMeqanne*, p. 95. On the other hand, see above p. 211, where the author asserts that Christians are subject to more diseases (including skin diseases) than Jews. That passage strengthens Baron's argument from silence (or comparative silence) that Jews were "less frequently afflicted by [leprosy] than their neighbors" (*History* 9:338, n. 14).

19-20   *This is similar to a fruit* This answer is found in *Sefer Yosef HaMeqanne,* loc. cit., but the author adds that the real reason is that exile has affected the appearance of the Jews (cf. Rosenthal's note there). See also *Mishnah Nedarim* 9:10.

29   *Have sexual relations during the day* Jewish law generally forbade intercourse during the day or even by the light of a candle. See *B. Niddah* 16b, and cf. Maimonides' code, *Hilkhot Issurei Biah* 21:10. The idea that sexual relations during the day produce handsome children comes from *B. Berakhot* 59b, in light of the manuscript reading of שפירי for the גיחורי of the printed editions (cf. *Diqduqei Soferim*, ad loc.). The reference to Jacob's stratagem undoubtedly reflects the author's interpretation of the talmudic passage.

Page 225

15-16   *Even the bones of . . . righteous men convey impurity* This view was not universal; see *Tosafot Ketubot* 103b, s.v. *oto hayom*.

23   *For the reason I have indicated* This is the earliest reference I know to an explanation which has since become fairly popular.

24-25   *We are the least numerous of the nations* For a full discussion of this argument as well as the problem of the exile raised in subsequent paragraphs, see the notes to p. 89.

L
25　　　　*Falsehood cannot stand* Cf. Meir of Narbonne, *Mil. Miẓvah*, p. 46a. This was a proverb based on the appearance of the Hebrew letters in the word *sheqer* (falsehood). See *Otiyyot deRabbi Aqiva* in S.A. Wertheimer, *Batei Midrashot* (Jerusalem, 1963), 2:397, and cf. *B. Shabbat* 104a (קושטא קאי שיקרא לא קאי). For other forms of the proverb, see Israel Davidson, *Oẓar HaMeshalim VeHaPitgamim* (Jerusalem, 1957), nos. 598, 681, 737.

Page 226

7-8　　　　*It must be . . . because of your sin against Jesus* This argument is also quoted in *Sefer Yosef HaMeqanne, Kiev Festschrift*, Hebrew section, p. 133. In general, see the notes to p. 89. Cf. also *Sefer Yosef HaMeqanne*, Rosenthal's ed., p. 139.

22-23　　　　*If they repent, I shall hasten it* This interpretation is found in a famous talmudic passage (*B. Sanhedrin* 98a): "If they merit it, then I shall hasten it; if not, then it will come in its time."

27　　　　*Except to his own heart* See *B. Sanhedrin* 99a.

30　　　　*All Israel are responsible for one another* See, for example, *B. Shevuʿot* 39a.

30-31　　　　*This will last until they are almost all destroyed and then they will repent* This translation is based on the reading of the Rome manuscript. The *Tela* reading, on the other hand, means, "This will last until they are almost all destroyed or until they all repent." Up to this point, the latter reading is far smoother, but the subsequent verses strongly militate in favor of the Rome reading. What has happened is that the author has introduced repentance even into the option labeled "in its time." The Jews can repent early and without constraint, and then the redemption will be hastened; however, even if it comes "in its time," at "the end of days," after much suffering, it will still be preceded by an eleventh-hour repentance. See *B. Sanhedrin* 97b and cf. Maimonides' code, *Hilkhot Teshuvah* 7:5: "*Israel will not be redeemed except through repentance*, and the Torah has promised that Israel will finally repent at the end of its exile and will immediately be redeemed." For a lengthy discussion of this issue in a polemical context, see Mordecai of Avignon, M.E., Vat. ms., pp. 6b-7a.

Page 227

6　　　　*Before the appointed end hastens to come* This phrase seems to echo the ambiguity of Isaiah 60:22, but it probably means that the end will follow this final repentance immediately (as in Maimonides).

19　　　　*When nations were separated* Genesis 11:1-9.

22　　　　*"With a high hand"* Exodus 14:8. In other words, there were no overt miracles nor was there any severe punishment of the oppressors of Israel.

27　　　　*Jeremiah . . . said. . . .* The quotation of Jeremiah 46:28 for purposes of consolation is also found in Meir of Narbonne, Parma ms., p. 118b, and in Solomon de' Rossi, Rosenthal's *Meḥqarim*, 1:384. Meir of Narbonne cites several verses regard-

L

ing the destruction of the persecutors of Israel (pp. 19b-20a) and presents an almost endless collection concerning the salvation of the Jews (pp. 152b-179b).

Page 228

12-13   ***Why did we suffer exile before Jesus was born?*** This is an especially weak argument since the central point of the Christian contention, as the author himself mentioned earlier, was that this exile is so much longer because it results from a more serious crime. Perhaps this response was inspired by the use of the same argument regarding Genesis 49:10; in that context it is, of course, fully appropriate. See above p. 60.

16-17   ***Without the knowledge of anyone but the mother of Jesus*** The reading in Wagenseil's manuscript was "nation" instead of "mother," but it is hard to see what that would mean. Moreover, the phrases "in secrecy" and "in silence" do not seem appropriate to a national revelation even if one were to insist on a contrast between "nation" and "all living creatures." The point is probably that the ultimate validation of Christianity would be the virgin birth, and this could be known only to Mary. (Jesus' other miracles were ascribed to sorcery.) The ultimate validation of Judaism, on the other hand, was the revelation at Sinai (the other miracles were secondary—see Maimonides' code, *Hilkhot Yesodei HaTorah* 8:1), and this was seen by all living creatures. For the view that the revelation at Sinai was really world-wide and affected all of nature, see Ginzberg, *Legends*, 3:97, and 6:39, nn. 212-14. Note especially the Christian parallel cited in n. 213.

22   ***Are permitted in theirs*** Cf. p. 206 regarding the motives of converts to Christianity. Jews were so emphatic about their moral superiority and tied it so closely to the superiority of their religion that they reached the point of arguing not merely that Christianity is unable to prevent immorality but that it actually sanctions it.

Page 229

5   ***"Remember the Torah of Moses. . . ."*** This verse was cited very frequently to prove the eternity of the original Torah. See David Kimhi on Psalms 110, quoted by Rosenthal in Rengstorff and von Kortzfleisch, *Kirche und Synagoge*, 1:322; Meir of Narbonne, *Mil. Mizvah*, Parma ms., pp. 21a, 117b, 127a; *Sefer Yosef HaMeqanne*, Rosenthal's ed., p. 96; Moses of Salerno, *Pos.* ms., p. 51; Solomon de' Rossi, Rosenthal's *Mehqarim*, 1:383. Several Jewish quotations from Scripture to prove the eternity of the Law were cited by Peter the Venerable, *Tractatus*, PL 189.573-74.

7-8   ***We murder their children and consume the blood*** The alleged permissibility of killing Christians was raised by Nicholas Donin, but he did not say that Jews actually did this; see Merchavia, *HaTalmud BiRe'i HaNazrut*, p. 236. Moreover, the ritual murder charge itself came in two forms. In its earliest manifestation it did not involve ritual use of the victim's blood, and the Rome ms. version of this para-

L

graph omits all reference to the consumption of blood both in the accusation and in the response. The charge that blood was actually consumed by Jews appears not only in the *Tela* version of this passage but also above p. 54, where the author also speaks of the accusation that Jews eat people. In that passage as well the Rome ms. says nothing about blood, and it is likely that the material there dates from before 1235, when the charge that Jews consume Christian blood first arose. There is some evidence that Christians accused Jews of eating people (without special reference to blood) as early as the 1180's. In William the Breton's chronicle of the reign of Philip Augustus, he reproduces a report in Rigord's chronicle that Jews ritually murder one Christian annually ("Judaei singulis annis unum Christianum immolabant") and adds, "et ejus corde se communicabant." This almost certainly means that they partake of the heart in some sort of ceremonial meal. See H.F. Delaborde, *Oeuvres de Rigord et de Guillaume le Breton* (Paris, 1882), 1:15, 180. The assertion by J. Parkes (*The Jew in the Medieval Community* [London, 1938], p. 379), which was repeated and emphasized by Trachtenberg (*The Devil and the Jew*, p. 138), that both Rigord and William accused Jews of killing and eating Christians is, as far as I can determine, incorrect. For some significant observations on the distinction between the two major types of ritual murder accusations, see G. Langmuir, "The Knight's Tale of Young Hugh of Lincoln," *Speculum* 47 (1972): 479-80.

33-34   **You are concocting allegations against us** The Hebrew phrase is based on Deuteronomy 22:14, 17.

Page 230

5-6   **The Talmud distorts . . . our entire Torah and prevents us from realizing the truth** See the letter of Gregory IX in 1239: "This [the Talmud] is said to be the chief cause that holds the Jews obstinate in their perfidy" (trans. in Grayzel, *The Church and the Jews in the XIIIth Century*, p. 241.) There is a discussion about the Talmud at the end of Meir of Narbonne's *Mil. Mizvah*, Parma ms., pp. 214a ff.

19-20   **"An Ammonite or Moabite. . . ."** See above pp. 77-78. For this argument, cf. the disputation of R. Yeḥiel of Paris, ed. R. Margaliyyot, (Lwow, n. d.), pp. 13-14, and see Nathan Official's story on this subject in *Sefer Yosef HaMeqanne, Festschrift Berliner's*, pp. 86-87 = Rosenthal, pp. 56-57 = *Peletat Soferim*, Hebrew section, pp. 33-34; Rome ms., p. 22b = Pos. ms., p. 18 = Rosenthal's "Menaḥem," p. 66. This issue was discussed by Jerome, *In Esaiam, CC, Ser. Lat.*, 73, p. 259, and by Isidore, *Quaestiones contra Judaeos*, cited in *Auteurs*, p. 98. It is also of some interest that Samau'al al-Maghribi argued that the Jews, through their legal system, make David and hence the Messiah into bastards because of the story of Lot's daughters and that of Judah and Tamar; see Perlmann, *Ifham al-Yahud*, pp. 58-61. Finally, Rupert of Deutz pointed out various impure elements in the background of the Jews (although he omitted the Moabite ancestry of Ruth) in order to show that Israel's "nobility" is not "according to the flesh" but "according to faith" (PL 170.594).

21   **This refers to a male Ammonite** B. *Yevamot* 77a.

APPENDIXES

APPENDIX 1 (to p. 42)

The Use of the Plural in Reference to God

The christological argument from the plural form *Elohim* is cited in a well-known talmudic passage where "heretics" (*minim*) ask R. Simlai how many gods created the world and proceed to cite the plural noun in Genesis 1:1. His response, which is essentially the same as that of N.V., is that the verb "created" in that very verse is singular rather than plural.[1] The same reply is made in *Sefer Yosef HaMeqanne* in a slightly different context as well as in Meir of Narbonne's *Milḥemet Miẓvah*.[2]

Christian polemicists were, of course, aware of this Jewish response and had a standard reply to it. Petrus Alfonsi, for example, quotes a Jew who presented precisely the same argument as the one in N.V., and he replies, "This is my authority that the name of God is expressed in the plural while his action is expressed in the singular; this makes it clear that God is one in a plurality of persons."[3] This argument, which maintained that a singular found in conjunction with a plural should be identified with it without undermining its plural status, was common in Christian polemic and exegesis[4] and was also reflected in Jewish polemic. The Christian in Jacob ben Reuben's

---

1. *Yer. Berakhot* 9:1, f. 12d. Cf. *Bereshit Rabbah* 8:9 (Theodor-Albeck, pp. 62-63), and *Devarim Rabbah* 2:8. See also the remark in *Sefer Ḥasidim* (ed. Wistinetski, no. 815, p. 206) concerning the singular verb in Isaiah 6:8.

2. *Sefer Yosef HaMeqanne, MiMizraḥ u-MiMa'arav* 4 (1898/9): 18 = Rosenthal, p. 29 (in fact, the same verse [Exod. 7:1] is cited there to show that *Elohim* can be singular); *Mil. Miẓvah*, Parma ms., p. 107b.

3. The Jewish argument is, "Dicit enim de Deo 'fecit,' 'dixit,' vel aliud aliquid tale, et non dicitur, fecerunt, sive dixerunt." Petrus answers, "Haec est mea auctoritas quod nomen Dei pluraliter dicitur, et actus singulariter, ac per hoc patet, quia Deus unus est in pluribus personis"—PL 157.609. Another Christian argument maintained that the existence of singular nominal forms for God alongside the plural form (e.g., *El*) proved that both singularity and plurality can be attributed to him. See Peter of Blois, PL 207.832, and Alan of Lille, PL 210.403.

4. This was especially common with regard to Genesis 1:26. See *De Fide Cath.*, I.4.5, PL 83.458 = Eggers, p. 34; Damian's *Dialogus*, PL 145.42; *Gloss* on Genesis 1:26.

Milḥamot HaShem maintains that the singular verb in the verse "And the Lord God formed man" (Gen. 2:7) indicates the true unity of the three persons referred to in Genesis 1:26.[5]

The same work, however, also records an unusual Christian response to this problem of the singular verb. Here, an "additive" approach is used, with the Christian arguing that the words "God created" in Genesis 1:1 prove the trinity since the Hebrew word for God is plural in form, implying two, and the verb "created" is singular, adding one.[6] N.V. may reflect an awareness of this approach, for in his discussion of Genesis 18, the author argues that the singular in verse 3 ("My Lord, pass not, I pray you") should be added to the alleged trinitarian reference in verse 2, thus making four.[7] This would then be a case of taking the additive interpretation legitimized by Christian exegesis and turning it to the advantage of the Jewish polemicist.

Although one of Jacob ben Reuben's replies to the additive interpretation consists of the argument that the plural *Elohim* can imply more than two or three,[8] it may be that this Christian interpretation is itself a response to such an argument. The fact is that the sort of exegesis cited by Petrus Alfonsi is especially vulnerable to the argument that there is nothing in a plural form to imply three and no more. Consequently, the additive interpretation may have been suggested because there is a certain logic in maintaining that a plural refers to two. Indeed, this was a principle maintained by Jews themselves in biblical exegesis.[9]

The Jewish attempt to show that verses used to prove the trinity can really demonstrate more extensive multiplicity within the Deity was fairly widespread. In addition to the above arguments in *Milḥamot HaShem* (concerning the plural *Elohim*) and N.V. (on Genesis 18), Joseph Kimḥi reflects this tendency when he argues that Psalms 72:1 can indicate the existence of four or five persons rather than

5. *Mil. HaShem*, p. 43. Cf. also p. 79 (on Jeremiah 31:14) and p. 84 (on the *trishagion*).

6. Ibid., p. 40.

7. N.V., p. 50.

8. *Mil. HaShem*, p. 41.

9. Cf., for example, *Tosefta Sotah* 4:1, Rashi on Exodus 20:6, and Rashi, *Makkot* 23a, s.v. *'al aḥat*, with regard to the plural *la'alafim*; Mishnah *Bava Batra* 10:2 and B. *Bava Batra* 165b.

three.[10] On a philosophical level, this argument was commonly applied to the Christian equation of the trinity with certain divine attributes, most commonly wisdom, will, and power. Naḥmanides, for example, told Pablo that if attributes are to be counted as hypostases, then one could count as many as five: life, wisdom, will, power, and the divine essence,[11] while Moses of Salerno argued that essence must be added to the trinity since that must be what holds it together.[12] Thus, Jews mobilized both philosophy and exegesis either to prove the absolute unity of God or to show that any argument pointing toward multiplicity can be extended beyond the crucial number three which any Christian disputant was required to defend.

10. *Sefer HaBerit,* in *Mil. Ḥovah,* p. 31a = Talmage's ed., p. 49. See also N.V., p. 199.

11. *Vikkuaḥ HaRamban* in Chavel, *Ketavei Ramban,* 1:320. Cf. Maimonides' *Guide,* 1:53, and Halevi's *Kuzari,* 4:3 and 5:18, ch. 8-9. S. Baron remarks that "Naḥmanides characteristically failed to refer to the long-debated extension of the divine attributes to five, seven, or an infinite number, but merely replied" that attributes and essence are identical (*A Social and Religious History of the Jews,* 10:85). This is an uncharacteristic oversight by Baron, particularly in light of the fact that the quotation he cites appears only a few lines before the argument that he says Naḥmanides omits. On the "attribute" interpretation of the trinity, see appendix 5.

12. Simon, *Mose ben Salomo von Salerno,* p. 6. I have suggested elsewhere that a Christian argument in *Mil. HaShem* against the Jewish belief in the absolute unity of God may be a covert Cathar attack against orthodox Christianity because it speaks of a multiplicity of more than three. See *HTR* 68 (1975): 300-02.

APPENDIX 2 *(to p. 44)*

God in the Womb and the Problem of the Incarnation

The Jewish revulsion at the notion of God in a woman's stomach, expressed so graphically here, is typical of much of Jewish polemic. A similar description is found later on in Nathan Official's explanation of the sin of the golden calf,[1] and Jews raised this point in a highly emotional manner whenever the opportunity presented itself.[2] A related Jewish argument involved the inappropriateness of God's going through the life cycle, and we have a number of incredulous descriptions of God's birth, advancement in age and wisdom, temptation by the Devil, betrayal by a disciple, exposure to ridicule, crucifixion, and burial.[3]

The Christian response to the Jewish horror at the idea of God in the womb was the argument that association with impurities does not necessarily result in contamination. One recurring analogy, which we shall encounter elsewhere in connection with the trinity itself, maintains that the divine glory should be compared with the rays of the sun. Several Christian writers argue that the sun loses none of its brilliance because of contact with impurities, while the Christian in *Mil. HaShem* points out that its rays pass within a small hole with-

---

1. N.V., p. 68.

2. *Sancti Gregentii Archiepiscopi Tephrensis Disputatio cum Herbano Judaeo*, PG 86.634, 657 (seventh century); Bodo-Eleazar as quoted by Paul Alvarus in PL 121.500–501 = Madoz's critical edition, p. 257 (cited in *Juifs et Chrét.*, p. 257); *Sefer Nestor HaKomer*, p. 11; *Sefer HaBerit* in *Mil. Ḥovah*, p. 22a = Talmage's ed., p. 29, and the reworking of that passage in Rome ms. 53, p. 23a = Pos. "Mordecai of Avignon" ms., p. 22 = Rosenthal's "Menaḥem," p. 68; *Mil. HaShem*, p. 13.

3. *Disputatio cum Herbano*, PG 86.634; the Jew "Godolias" in the *Vita Silvestri*, cited in *Auteurs*, p. 46; Priscus in the disputation summarized by Gregory of Tours in *Historia Francorum*, 6:5, cited in *Auteurs*, p. 71; *Vikkuaḥ HaRamban* in *Ketavei Ramban*, ed. Chavel, 1:311. See especially N.V., p. 186, and the notes there.

out being enclosed and near dung without being defiled.[4]

Odo of Cambrai reflects a somewhat more sophisticated approach to this problem. Instead of suggesting an analogy, he argues that God himself fills everything (without any incarnation); thus, God is in all sinners, yet he remains pure and uncontaminated. Similarly, he remained uncontaminated in the womb.[5] Moreover, Odo argues that it is only our senses which regard certain physical functions and parts of the body as impure. Reason, however, regards only sin as impure. Now, since Mary was not affected by sin, there is nothing repulsive about the view that God entered her. He then launches into an enthusiastic apostrophe to the stomach in which God was incarnated ("O venter, O viscera, in quibus et de quibus Creator creabatur, Deus incarnabitur").[6]

Some of the basic Jewish objections to the incarnation are accurately described in the eleventh-century disputation of Gilbert Crispin: (1) God is immutable, and so how could he become man? (2) Since God cannot be measured or circumscribed, how could he become man? (3) By what necessity was he forced ("qua necessitate coactus") to participate in the "human calamity"? (4) Why did he tell Moses, "For man may not see me and live" (Exod. 33:20)?[7]

The first two objections involve a philosophical impossibility in the incarnation. Divine immutability was occasionally adduced as an argument against the incarnation by Jews,[8] while the argument from the impossibility of limiting God was considerably more common.[9] In general, arguments purporting to show the utter impossibility of Christian doctrine were of special significance, since they

4. Maximin's *Contra Judaeos*, ch. 3, cited in *Auteurs*, pp. 18–19; *The Dialogue of Athanasius and Zacchaeus*, cited in Williams, p. 121; Peter the Venerable, *Tractatus*, PL 189.532; *Mil. HaShem*, p. 15. On this sort of analogy, cf. appendix 5.

5. *Disputatio contra Judaeum*, PL 160:1110.

6. Ibid., 1111–12. Cf. the notes to p. 44.

7. *Disputatio*, p. 43. The same passage is in Alan of Lille, PL 210.413–14.

8. See *Mil. Hashem*, p. 9 (ועוד שהיה הפרש בין אותו זמן ראשון שעמד בלי צורת ובין אותו זמן האחרון שקיבל תבנית וצורה). See also Rome ms. 53, p. 24a = Pos. "Mordecai of Avignon" ms., p. 28 = Rosenthal's "Menaḥem," p. 70.

9. *Mil. HaShem*, loc. cit. See also Simon, *Mose ben Salomo von Salerno*, p. 14, and cf. appendix 5. In general, see Lasker, *Jewish Philosophical Polemics*, pp. 108–121.

enabled the polemicist to ignore any appeal to the belief in miracles, an appeal which Jews could not ignore, for example, in the case of the virgin birth.[10] Indeed, it is likely that Naḥmanides was referring to the philosophical impossibility of divine self-corporification when he said of the incarnation, "Even a miracle cannot take effect in such a matter" (i.e., it cannot bring about such a thing).[11]

Although Jewish writers did not feel that divine omnipotence was relevant to the possibility of self-corporification, it was regarded as crucially relevant to the question of the need for the incarnation. In essence, the Jewish argument was that the act postulated is so degrading that the only way to justify it would be to maintain that God was forced to do it in order to save man. However, if he was forced into it, then he is not omnipotent, for he obviously could find no other way to effect this salvation.[12] Odo of Cambrai cites a somewhat different argument which may or may not reflect an authentic Jewish challenge. The Jew in his *Disputatio* asks why the incarnation was necessary if the punishments mentioned in Genesis 3 were enough to expiate Adam's sin. If they were not enough, then why would God have imposed punishments which were basically useless?[13] Christian philosophers and polemicists were deeply concerned with these issues, as Anselm's famous *Cur Deus Homo?*, Odo's *Disputatio,* and various other works amply testify.[14] A twist on the usual Jewish question regarding the need for the incarnation

10. On the virgin birth, cf. *Vikkuaḥ LeHaRadaq, Mil. Ḥovah,* p. 16b = Talmage's ed., p. 91. See also the notes to p. 103.

11. The translation is uncertain. See *Vikkuaḥ HaRamban* in *Ketavei Ramban,* ed. Chavel, 1: 311 (גם הפלא אינו יכול להתפשט בדבר ההוא). On the view that God's inability to effect logical impossibilities does not really constitute a limitation of his omnipotence, see the literature cited in H. A. Wolfson, *Religious Philosophy* (Cambridge, 1961), p. 19. On self-corporification, see Maimonides, *Guide of the Perplexed,* 2:13 and 3:15.

12. A lengthy discussion along these lines is found in *Mil. HaShem,* pp. 12-22. See also *Sefer HaBerit, Mil. Ḥovah,* p. 22b = Talmage's ed., p. 30. The Jewish question concerning the need for the incarnation is also cited in the *Vita Silvestri (Auteurs,* p. 47) and Isidore's *De Fide Cath.,* 1.5.9, PL 83.462 = Eggers, p. 52.

13. PL 160.1105.

14. See *Cur Deus Homo?*, ed. Schmitt, *Anselmi Opera Omnia* (Edinburgh, 1946). On the polemical implications of this work, see Funkenstein in *Zion* 33: 129-32.

appears later in N.V. where the author argues that even if there had to be an incarnation God should have entered a man after birth and thus at least avoided being in a womb.[15]

In addition to the standard arguments, Jacob ben Reuben's *Milḥamot HaShem* records a striking and unusual discussion of the incarnation. The Christian there supplies a peculiar analogy: There is a white bird which eats creeping things that live on the banks of ponds. These creatures, however, have learned to recognize its whiteness, and so it wallows in dirt in order to turn black. Similarly, when God was transcendent, he saw that "no righteous man can be saved through his righteousness," and so he lowered himself to a human level.[16]

At first glance, this analogy is utterly fantastic since the purposes of the self-degradation are entirely disparate, and yet the point of the analogy is presumably to explain why God should have taken on flesh. Jacob responds to this argument by maintaining that the bird was forced into the degradation and that this is the distinction; the truth is, however, that one must search for a plausible point of contact between the two acts of self-degradation rather than a difference. Consequently, it is tempting to suggest that the origins of this analogy lie in a different explanation of the incarnation, one which maintained that God had to disguise himself as a man when redeeming mankind so that Satan would not recognize his intention. This explanation is cited explicitly and at length in N.V., where the author presents it as the standard Christian explanation of the incarnation.[17] Now, it is quite true that the "ransom" explanation was the dominant one before Anselm, but it did not always involve the theme of a conscious deception of Satan. Satan could simply be accused, as in Crispin's *Disputatio*,[18] of "praesumptio injusta" (= unjust boldness, audacity, or presumption) in killing one to whom he had no right. The

---

15. N.V., p. 151. The fourth question in Crispin (from Exodus 33:20) is reflected in N.V., p. 71.

16. *Mil. HaShem,* p. 21.

17. See pp. 195-96 and the notes there.

18. P. 60.

element of conscious deception, however, which was certainly not uncommon, may well have generated not only the explicit discussion in N.V. but the strange and intriguing analogy in *Milḥamot HaShem*.[19]

19. For a criticism and history of the ransom theory, see Anselm's discussion, *Pourquoi Dieu S'Est Fait Homme,* ed. and trans. by René Rocques (Paris, 1963), pp. 230-36, as well as the editor's comments, pp. 107-09, and his references to the literature on the subject (especially J. Rivière, *Le dogme de la Rédemption. Essai d'Étude Historique* [Paris, 1905], pp. 373-486). Brief references to various forms of the ransom theory, both with and without conscious deception, can be found in J. K. Mozley, *The Doctrine of the Atonement* (London, 1915), pp. 102 (where he denies that Origen speaks of conscious deception), 109, 121-22 (especially no. 2), 124. A classic reference to deception is in Gregory of Nyssa's *Oratio Cathecetica,* 1:26, where he says in part, Τὸ γὰρ οὐ γυμνῇ τῇ θεότητι, ἀλλ' ὑπὸ τῆς ἀνθρωπίνης φύσεως κεκαλυμμένη, ἀγνοηθέντα παρὰ τοῦ Ἐχθροῦ τὸν θεόν. . . . A bit later he writes, ὁ ἀπατεὼν ἀπατᾶται ("the deceiver is deceived"); see PG 45.68. Cf. also Bickerman in *HTR* 39: 170. On this theory in heresy, see S. Runciman, *The Medieval Manichee* (Cambridge, 1947), pp. 76, 149. See also Werblowsky in *JJS* 11: 74-77 on the retention of the ransom theory in Crispin despite Anselm's satisfaction theory and the implications for the dating of Crispin's work. The notion of a so-called sacred deception is found in a different connection in later Jewish mystical thought. See G. Scholem, *Shabbetai Ẓevi* (Tel Aviv, 1957), 1: 49-50, 248. Cf. also *B. Sanhedrin* 26b and Tosafot *Shabbat* 89a, s.v. *Torah.* (Satan's attention was diverted during the revelation of the Torah to keep him from objecting.)

APPENDIX 3 (to p. 46)
The Law as Allegory

The Christian conviction that the ritual law of the Bible is to be read as allegory foreshadowing Jesus and Christianity goes back to the New Testament itself, and it quickly became a central issue in Jewish-Christian polemic.[1] An early example of an all-encompassing statement of the Christian position on this issue is Chrysostom's remark that all the (ritual) laws are "types" and "shadows,"[2] while Peter Damian's *Dialogus* is an indication that this aspect of polemic was considered so significant in the eleventh century that a major portion of a polemical work was devoted to it.[3]

One of the basic methods used by Christian polemicists in order to establish the necessity of the allegorical approach was to find absurdities, contradictions, or at least improbabilities in the literal content of a given precept and then to argue that these difficulties make the search for an exclusively allegorical interpretation justifiable and indeed necessary. This approach ranged from the simple argument that there seems to be no reason for a given law to the discovery of direct contradictions and impossibilities. An elaborate passage which argues this point is found in Gilbert Crispin's *Disputatio*. Crispin presents four arguments: (1) The Bible says that God saw that everything he had created was very good (Gen. 1:21), and yet later certain animals are declared impure. (2) God told Adam that he could eat from all trees (Gen. 1:29), but later he forbade eating from the tree of knowledge (Gen. 2:17). (3) God required that an altar

---

1. Cf. Hebrews 10:1. In general see Simon, *Ver. Israel,* pp. 104-17, 177-84; Blumenkranz, *Judenpredigt,* pp. 130-45.

2. PG 64:105, cited in *Ver. Israel.* p. 112: πάντα τύποι ἦσαν, πάντα σκία, περιτομή, θυσία, σάββατον. . . . Note that he was especially concerned with "Judaizers" in his community.

3. PL 145.41-68. The relevant section of the *Dialogus* is taken from Isidore of Seville's *Quaestiones in Leviticum,* PL 83.336-39. See my article in *Yavneh Review* 4:99 ff.

be built out of earth or, under certain conditions, out of stone (Exod. 2:21-22), but later Moses made altars out of metal. (4) God said that man would rule over the animals (Gen. 1:26), but later he forbade plowing with an ox and an ass together (Deut. 22:10). To make matters worse, this last prohibition makes no sense in any case.[4]

The search for contradictions and impossibilities in the Law is especially intriguing because it involved the application of arguments used against Christianity itself by heretics who denied the divine origin of the Hebrew Bible entirely. Paul Alvarus, for example, openly remarks that he, "like the Manichaeans," could demonstrate how the entire Law is self-contradictory.[5] In discussing this remark, Blumenkranz notes that after the defeat of the heretics by the early Middle Ages, the church felt that it could appropriate their arguments for use against Jews; this may be true, but it must be emphasized that these arguments continued to be used in Jewish-Christian polemic even after the resurgence of heresy.[6]

The approach which simply asked why a certain precept should have been commanded raised the general question of the rationality of the Law. The simplest Jewish response was the argument that these laws are an expression of God's will for which no reason is necessary (גזירת הכתוב). One implication of this response could be that there really is no reason, that the commandments are the product of God's arbitrary will with the sole purpose of teaching obedience. This is apparently the point of the first answer in this passage of N.V., and the same implication can be drawn from a passage in *Sefer Yosef HaMeqanne* where the author describes a husband's ordering his wife to do truly irrational acts in order to prove her love. The performing of rational commandments would not prove

---

4. *Disputatio*, pp. 29-31. The passage was copied by Alan of Lille, PL 210.407-8, and translated by Jacob ben Reuben, *Mil. HaShem*, pp. 24-26, 27-28. (For an analysis of the relationship between these texts and its implications, see my article in *Speculum* 49:34-47.) See especially Joachim da Fiore's lengthy argument that contradictions, absurdities, and unfulfilled prophecies in the Hebrew Bible prove the necessity for "spiritual" rather than literal interpretation (*Adversus Judaeos*, pp. 68 ff.).

5. PL 121.494 = Madoz, p. 245. Cited in *Juifs et Chrét.*, p. 240, and in Blumenkranz's notes to Crispin, ad loc.

6. See *Juifs et Chrét.*, ibid. On the heresies and the church in the early centuries, see *Judenpredigt*, pp. 122-30; *Ver. Israel*, pp. 93 ff.

love precisely because of the fact that they are rational.[7] Another form of this response is the position that the purpose of the commandments is rational but inscrutable. R. Solomon ibn Adret (thirteenth to fourteenth century) maintains that to argue that the ritual commandments are obviously not rational presupposes the equal capacity of the human mind and that of God, and other Jews apparently cited Isaiah 40:13 to prove the same point.[8]

On this issue, the Christian writers maintained a rigorously rationalist position. Justin has Trypho say, in a very similar context, "It does not seem good to me, as it does to most, only to say that it was God's will. For that is always the sly, stock reply of those who cannot answer the question."[9] Similarly, the Christian in Jacob ben Reuben's *Milḥamot HaShem* remarks, "If you will ask them [the Jews] why, they will say that it is a Scriptural decree. Now, this answer is the answer of fools who have no intelligence."[10] Christians, then, did not hesitate to press such an argument vigorously despite the fact that in other crucial areas of polemic it was they who felt that Jews maintained an excessively rationalistic position.[11]

The critique of the "Scriptural decree" answer was not entirely without effect. N.V. here does attempt a rational explanation as well, and in other passages, the author counterposes a rabbinic midrash to what was essentially a Christian midrash.[12] Jacob ben Reuben also seemed to concede the need to find rational explanations, and Meir of Narbonne suggested reasons for several commandments after being challenged on this point by a Christian.[13] Elsewhere, he made aggressive use of such reasons by asking how Christians could justify the abolition of regulations that are clearly beneficial; for ex-

---

7. *Festschrift A. Berliner's,* pp. 88–89 = Rosenthal, p. 60.

8. *Perushei Aggadot LaRashba,* ed. Perles, p. 28; the Jew in Crispin's *Disputatio,* p. 32, and in Alan of Lille, PL 210.408.

9. *Trypho,* ch. 28. It is, of course, possible that Trypho really made this concession, but in any case it obviously represents Justin's own view.

10. *Mil. HaShem,* p. 28.

11. Cf. the exchange in *Vikkuaḥ HaRamban,* Chavel, *Ketavei Ramban,* 1: 320. On this passage in particular and the disputation in general, see Y. Baer, "LeBikkoret HaVikkuḥim shel R. Yeḥiel MiParis veHaRamban," *Tarbiẓ* 2 (1931): 172–87.

12. See especially pp. 53–54.

13. *Mil. Miẓvah,* Parma ms., pp. 46a–47a.

ample, intercourse with menstruant women and the eating of pork are activities that are injurious to health.[14] Thus, the search for "reasons for the commandments" (טעמי המצוות) was transformed from a matter of exegetical interest to one of polemical necessity.[15]

Moreover, Jewish writers did not content themselves with a purely defensive position with regard to the allegorical reading of the ritual law. One of the most moderate forms of the Jewish counter-argument was the contention that there is no reason not to accept both the literal and allegorical meanings.[16] Ibn Adret, for example, maintains that if some of the laws were to be taken as allegories alone, God should not have written them in the same sort of language as other precepts that were meant literally; at most, one has the right to say that an allegorical meaning is hinted at in addition to the literal meaning.[17]

This argument was based on the recognition of the fact that Christians did regard certain Pentateuchal laws as literally binding. Leo the Great, for example, had written that it is necessary to preserve "the moral commandments and precepts (of the Hebrew Bible) just as they were set forth,"[18] while Eucher of Lyon had made the following programmatic statement: "Question: What parts of the Old Testament should we abandon and what parts should we observe? Answer: We should observe the commandments which pertain to the correction of life and abandon the ceremonies and the rites of sacrifices which brought forth the figures and shadow of future events."[19] It was, of course, rather difficult to carry through

14. Ibid., pp. 87b–88b. Crispin, on the other hand, had pointed out that the Law prohibits healthful as well as harmful foods (*Disputatio,* pp. 29–30).

15. On the subject of "reasons for the commandments," see Yitzḥak Heinemann, *Ta'amei HaMiẓvot BeSifrut Yisrael,* 4th ed. (Jerusalem, 1959); Heinemann, however, pays very little attention to the polemical implications of the subject.

16. The Jew in Crispin's *Disputatio,* pp. 32–33; the "Continuation" of that *Disputatio,* p. 68; the *Dialogus* attributed to William of Champeaux, PL 163. 1047–8; Alan of Lille, PL 210.409; *Mil. HaShem,* pp. 37, 39. Cf. also the anti-Maimonist argument discussed in G. Scholem, *Reshit HaQabbalah* (Tel Aviv, 1948), pp. 135–36.

17. *Perushei Aggadot LaRashba,* p. 27.

18. PL 54.88–89.

19. PL 50.781.

this distinction in a fully consistent manner,[20] but ibn Adret is concerned not so much with its practical application as with its theoretical basis; why, he goes on to ask, should the *moral* law not be allegorized? "Let us say," he argues, "that the Torah's warning against adultery refers to spiritual adultery, i.e., idolatry."[21] A sarcastic version of this argument appears in the polemic of Meir of Narbonne, who tells his adversary that the behavior of Christians indicates that they must take even the *Gospel* commandment of loving-kindness allegorically.[22]

A different argument against the purely allegorical approach was proposed by David Kimḥi. "If the commandments were allegorical," he writes, "[their intent] would be uncertain and everyone would be of a different opinion concerning them. Scripture says, 'For this commandment which I command thee this day, it is not too hard for thee neither is it far off' [Deut. 30:11]. If the commandments were hidden and not to be taken literally, they would be too hard and far off."[23]

Another Jewish argument maintained that Christianity is inherently so implausible that if the prophets wanted to teach its doctrines they would have done so clearly and explicitly.[24] Christians, however, dealt with this by arguing that the Jews would have killed any prophet who spoke of Jesus in an unequivocal way.[25]

Finally, a new historical argument against allegorization appears in the twelfth century. Joseph Kimḥi asks whether God explained the Torah to Moses allegorically or not. If he did not, then the Jews cannot be blamed for refusing to interpret it that way. If he did,

---

20. Tertullian, for example, is concerned with the biblical prohibition of pronouncing the names of foreign gods. See his *De Idolat.* X and XX cited in Lieberman, *Hellenism in Jewish Palestine*, pp. 111–12.

21. *Perushei Aggadot LaRashba*, p. 28.

22. See Stein, *JJS* 10:52, and cf. the notes to page 221. Cf. also N.V., p. 77, where the author pretends to believe that the Christian requirement of baptism was obviously meant allegorically.

23. Commentary to Psalms 19:10. Translation by Talmage in *HUCA* 38: 219. This argument is also found in Meir of Narbonne, *Mil. Miẓvah*, Parma ms., p. 21a. For other arguments on both sides, see the references in Merchavia, pp. 100, 235. Cf. also Peter of Blois, *Contra Perfidiam Judaeorum*, PL 207.855,866.

24. See Rosenthal's introduction to *Sefer Yosef HaMeqanne*, p. 27.

25. See the references in Williams, p. 165; and Rupert of Deutz, PL 170.575.

then why didn't Moses transmit this information? That Moses did not in fact transmit such a view is clear from the many examples of literal observance found in the Bible, such as the punishment of the man gathering sticks on the Sabbath, Josiah's reforms regarding Passover, and Ezra's (he presumably means Nehemiah's) regarding the Sabbath. Kimḥi then goes on to say that one should search for a purely allegorical interpretation only when absolutely forced to; for example, if a man is said to have told his servant, "Take the horse and ride it on the sea."[26]

Ibn Adret proposed a variant of Kimḥi's either/or argument: Either the Jews observed the Law (literally) in the time of Moses or they did not. If they did, why did Moses not inform them of their mistake? If they did not, then there are two ways to explain their present error. They may have begun observing the Law literally by mistake or they may have consciously agreed to change their custom. If the former alternative is correct, then there should be traces of Jews who did not succumb to this error, yet all Jews throughout the world observe the Law. If, however, the second possibility were the correct one, then there would have been some record of this "constitutional convention," and the Christians would have found it by now.[27]

Both these arguments are dependent on the view that Christians believed that the Law was never intended to be taken literally. The truth is that Christian views were much more complex and ambiguous than that, and, indeed, varied widely. First of all, there actually was an extreme Christian view which maintained that Pentateuchal laws were originally intended only as allegories.[28] There are also a number of very negative appraisals of the purpose of the Law in Christian thought, such as the view that it was a punishment

26. *Sefer HaBerit, Mil. Ḥovah*, p. 26a = Talmage's ed., p. 38. See Rome ms. 53, p. 24a = Pos. "Mordecai of Avignon" ms. pp. 29-30 = Rosenthal's "Menaḥem," p. 70, and especially Mordecai of Avignon, M.E., Vat. ms., pp. 9b-10a. A similar position on nonliteral inerpretation is taken by Maimonides in his *Guide of the Perplexed*, 2:25.

27. *Perushei Aggadot LaRashba*, p. 29. The last part of this argument is taken from Saadia Gaon, *The Book of Beliefs and Opinions*, trans. S. Rosenblatt (New Haven, 1948), 3:6, p. 157. Note also Judah Halevi's emphasis on *consensus omnium*, e.g., *Kuzari*, 1:45.

28. See S. Lowy, "The Confutation of Judaism in the Epistle of Barnabas," *JJS* 11 (1960): 1-33; also *Ver. Israel*, p. 112, n. 2.

or that the Jews needed it because of their base nature, but these all assume that the precepts were meant literally as well.[29] On the whole, Christian writers did make this last assumption—some, perhaps, under the influence of Jewish polemic—and many even regarded the Law quite favorably in its proper time, i.e., before the advent of Jesus.[30]

The issue of the Law as allegory was, then, one of the central points of contention in Jewish-Christian polemic. It required both sides to confront the fundamental question of the rationality of biblical law, and it inspired historical arguments, the rechanneling of ancient heretical assertions, and an examination of the distinction between moral and ritual law. This issue, in short, transcended polemic and stimulated discussion of a broad range of basic issues in medieval religious thought.

29. See Parkes, *Conflict,* pp. 83–84, 101; Simon, *Ver. Israel,* p. 114. The notion that the Jews were the one nation that needed the Law because of their tendency toward sin may have an interesting parallel in the Talmud itself. See *B. Beẓah* 25b and Rashi, ad loc., s.v. *shehen 'azzim.* Cf. Ginzberg, *Legends,* 4:31.

30. For the movement toward greater acceptance of a literal interpretation (partly under the impact of the sort of questions asked by Joseph Kimḥi and ibn Adret), see Smalley, *The Study of the Bible in the Middle Ages,* pp. 303–6. She points out (p. 305) that Thomas even argued that there are reasons for the literal aspect of the precepts. Cf. also *Basic Writings of St. Thomas Aquinas,* ed. A. Pegis, 2:742 ff. On the Jewish attitude toward allegory see also Rosenthal in Rengstorff and von Kortzfleisch, *Kirche und Synagoge,* 1:313–14.

APPENDIX 4 (to p. 48)
The Christian Exegesis of Genesis 18

The author of N.V. begins his discussion of Genesis 18 with the apparent quotation, "He saw three and prayed to one." Moreover, it is clear from his response as well as from the later contention that this is written in the Gospels[1] that the author believed that Christians considered this a Scriptural quotation. An explicit contention of this sort is found in *Sefer Yosef HaMeqanne,* where the author says, "It is written in the book of Jerome, 'Et surrexit oculos eius et vidit tres; vidisset et adoravit in terra'; i.e., he raised his eyes and saw three men, and he bowed toward the ground. They say that it says, 'Tres vidit et unum adoravit,' i.e., he saw three as one and bowed. However, this is not so, for it really says, 'Et adoravit in terra.' "[2] The truth is that although no such phrase as "tres vidit et unum adoravit" is to be found in either the Vulgate or the Gospels, the expression had indeed attained the status of Scriptural or quasi-Scriptural quotation in the minds of some Christians by the thirteenth century as a result of its repeated use in Christian works throughout the ages.

The early form of this expression appears in the fifth-century *Altercatio inter Theophilum Christianum et Simonem Judaeum,* where Theophilus reminds Simon that Abraham "saw three . . . [and] greeted one [tres vidit . . . unum salutavit]."[3] At this point, we still

---

1. N.V., p. 50. It is possible, however, that the words "in the Gospels" are a gloss and that the author meant only that this is the Christian reading in Genesis.

2. Rome ms. p. 5b (not in Kahn's or Rosenthal's ed.): אי שורגי׳ש :כתוב להם בספר ירונמוס אוקלוב׳ איוש אי ודיש טרי״ש ודי׳ש׳ט איש איזוראביט׳אין טירא. פי׳ ושא עיניו וירא ג׳ אנשים וישתחון ארצה. ג׳ ראה כאחד וישתחוו (=וישתהו) איזוראביט איטעארא ואומרים שכן כתוב טרי״ש ודי׳טי׳ש אונום איזורביט ואינו כן אלא כתוב להם כן איש. In my translation, I have transposed two of the phrases here in order to clarify the meaning. The actual Vulgate here reads, "Cumque elevasset oculos, apparuerunt ei tres viri stantes prope eum: quos cum vidisset, cucurrit in occursum eorum de ostio tabernaculi, et adoravit in terram." See also *Sefer HaBerit, Mil. Hovah,* p. 31b = Talmage's ed., p. 50.

3. PL 20.1167. The reading in *CSEL* 45, p. 4, is "tres visi sunt . . . unum salutavit."

have a rather straightforward paraphrase of the biblical text, in which Abraham does nothing more than "greet" one rather than three. Elsewhere, however, this greeting is extended to worship, and the text takes on the form in which N.V. knows it. Isidore of Seville writes, "Abraham, indeed, seeing three, worshiped one [tres videns, unum adoravit]."[4] Bede writes, "Though he saw three, he worshiped one [cum tres vidisset unum adoravit]."[5] Pseudo-Bede, in a passage almost identical with that of Isidore, repeats the same phrase,[6] and in Peter Damian's eleventh century *Dialogus*, he asks his Jewish listener to ask Abraham "why he saw three and worshiped one [quare tres vidit et unum adoravit]."[7] Finally, very close to the time of N.V., there is evidence of a Christian preacher regarding this phrase as a quotation. The fourth sermon of Ramon Lull's *Liber Praedicationis contra Judaeos* is entitled, "Abraam autem Vidit Tres et Adoravit Unum," a title which the editor rightly places in quotation marks, for the following explanatory words "Hoc est" ("that is") indicate that Lull did view this as a quotation from a sacred text.[8] Thus, N.V.'s assertion is based upon a long succession of Christian sources.

The essence of the Christian argument reflected here is that the three men who appeared to Abraham in Genesis 18:2 constituted a theophany and that they were the concrete manifestation of the God who appeared in verse 1. Despite the fact that this biblical passage would appear almost tailor-made for a trinitarian exegesis, such an exegesis appears relatively late in Christian writings; indeed, the earliest authors present a quite different view of this chapter of Genesis. Justin Martyr, in his extremely influential *Dialogue with Trypho,* maintains that the God who appeared to Abraham in 18:1 was God the father, while in verse 2 God the son appeared with two angels

---

4. *Quaestiones in Genesin* 14, PL 83.243.
5. *In Genesim, CC, Ser. Lat.,* 118A, p. 211.
6. *In Pentateuchum Commentarii,* PL 91.238.
7. PL 145.43.
8. *El "Liber Praedicationis contra Judeos,"* ed. J. M. Millas-Vallicrosa (Madrid and Barcelona, 1957), p. 77. In his introduction, Millas-Vallicrosa comments that although it is clear that the biblical text does not say this "textually," it was an exegesis derived from the context (p. 37). Though this is true, the point is that Lull does seem to have regarded it as an exact quotation. The phrase also appears (though not necessarily as a quotation) in Peter of Blois, PL 207.831, and Alan of Lille, PL 210.404. See also the *Dialogus* attributed to William of Champeaux, PL 163.1057.

whose mission was the destruction of Sodom.[9] G. Archambault points out that this interpretation was accepted by Irenaeus, Tertullian, Origen, Eusebius, and Ambrose,[10] and it was not until Augustine that it was seriously challenged. In his *City of God,* Augustine rejects Justin's view on the grounds that there is no textual basis for distinguishing among the three men and placing one higher than the other. Although it is true, he argues, that Abraham calls one of them "Lord" in 18:2, Lot calls the other two "my Lords" in 19:2. Thus it is far more likely that all three were angels who were addressed as they were because "the Lord was in them, as he used to be in the prophets."[11] Augustine thus equalizes the three by lowering the status of the one whom Justin considered divine. In Augustine's *De Trinitate,* however, there is a more hesitant and tentative presentation where he again rejects the notion that one was divine while the other two were angels, but this time he suggests a trinitarian explanation instead.[12]

Despite Augustine's strictures, the older interpretation was not universally abandoned. Both Isidore of Seville and pseudo-Bede regard one of the three as Jesus and the other two as angels prefiguring Moses and Elijah.[13]

Nevertheless, the trinitarian explanation became the regnant one. In the above-mentioned *Altercatio,* for example, the Jew asks whether the Christian's belief in Jesus leads him to believe in two gods, whereupon Theophilus answers, "God is one, from whom is Christ and in whom is God, just as Abraham at the oak of Mambre saw three, to whom he ran, and greeted one."[14] Here, the unity of the

---

9. *Dialogue with Trypho,* ch. 56.

10. Archambault, *Dialogue avec Tryphon,* 1:245–46.

11. *City of God,* 16:29.

12. See *De Trinitate,* 2:10–12. In chapter 11, he writes, "But since three men appeared, and no one of them is said to be greater than the rest either in form, or age, or power, why should we not understand, as visibly intimated by the visible creature, the equality of the Trinity, and one and the same substance in three persons?" (The translation is from *Basic Writings of Saint Augustine,* ed. Whitney J. Oates [New York, 1948], 2:714.)

13. Isidore and pseudo-Bede, loc. cit. (see notes 4 and 6). The probability that Isidore did not accept the later, trinitarian explanation is also supported by the fact that this passage is not cited in chapter 4 ("De Trinitate Significantia") of his *De Fide Cath.,* PL 83.457–60.

14. PL 20.1167: "Deus unus est, ex quo Christus et in quo Deus: sicut Abrahae [read "Abraham," but cf. n. 3 above] ad ilicem Mambrae tres vidit, quibus occurrens, unum salutavit." Cf. also Fortunatus's *Carmina,* 5:5 (c. 580) cited in *Auteurs,* p. 65, and Bede's *In Genesim,* loc. cit.

three is derived from this verse. By the time of N.V. this was the commonly accepted interpretation, appearing, for example, in Damian's *Dialogus,*[15] Lull's *Liber Praedicationis,*[16] and Rupert of Deutz's *De Trinitate.*[17] This view, according to which verse 1 expresses God's unity and verse 2 his trinitarian nature, answers the questions posed by Augustine but raises, as N.V. points out, a number of new difficulties in the exegesis of the passage.

An interesting sidelight of the rather strange failure of the earliest Christian writers to give this passage a trinitarian explanation is the fact that even the phrase "tres vidit et unum adoravit" can be explained in accordance with Justin's view that the three men were Jesus and two angels. Indeed, it should be kept in mind that both Isidore and pseudo-Bede used this phrase while maintaining the old explanation; to them, "Tres vidit et unum adoravit" meant that he saw three and worshiped *one of them.* The same phrase, however, was ideally suited to the trinitarian explanation where it meant that he worshiped one because the three were really one. It was, of course, the latter explanation which was known to the author of N.V.

15. PL 145.43: "Ubi [i.e., from Genesis 18] patenter ostenditur quia is, qui sibi apparuit, et unus in substantia deitatis, et tribus est in personis.".

16. *El "Liber Praedicationis,"* p. 77: "Abraham . . . . intellexit tres personas in Deo, et quia ipse tres persone sunt unus Deus adoravit solum unum Deum."

17. *De Trinitate et Operibus Ejus Libri 42—In Genesim Liber Quintus,* ch. 37, PL 167.401: "Trinitatis mysterium in forma trium angelorum, se homini manifestare dignatur." Cf. also the interlinear gloss, ad loc. ("Manifestatur fides trinitatis"), the sources cited in n. 8, the references in Williams, pp. 110-11, 179, the *Tractatus* in *TNA,* 5.1514 = PL 213.755, and Joachim da Fiore, *Adversus Judaeos,* pp. 4-9.

APPENDIX 5 (to p. 137)

Who Was Incarnated?

The Jewish argument that the combined doctrines of trinity and incarnation created insuperable philosophical difficulties was a central and effective point. One form of the argument is found in this passage, where the author of N.V. maintains that if the son alone was incarnated, this contradicts the Christian assertion that the persons are inseparable, and if they were all incarnated, "then who was in heaven all that time inasmuch as they are inseparable?"[1] This either/or argument is based on the doctrine that the son alone was incarnated, a doctrine clearly stated, for example, in the *De Ecclesiasticis Dogmatibus* appended to Isidore's works,[2] combined with the philosophical doctrine, accepted by Christians, that God cannot be divided.[3] The problem arises as a result of the combination of two dogmas, the trinity and incarnation, particularly after the former had been abstractly philosophized. The fact that the most sophisticated form of this argument depends upon a certain level of philosophical development may explain why it does not appear in the West in the pre-Crusade period, unless it did indeed appear but was not reported in the Christian writings which are our major source for the Jewish arguments in this period.[4]

The earliest formulation of this question is found in *Sefer*

1. On p. 71, N.V. assumes a belief in the incarnation of all three. Cf. also p. 81. A related argument is found on p. 49, where the author argues that the three people in Genesis 18 should have been one.

2. PL 83.1228: "Non Pater carnem assumpsit, neque Spiritus sanctus, sed Filius tantum."

3. Such a division would be particularly difficult in light of Aquinas's assertion that "the Son is in the Father, and conversely." See *Summa Theologiae*, pt. 1, Question 42, art. 5, and cf. John 14:10.

4. Blumenkranz does not mention this argument in the sections on "L'Incarnation," "La Naissance Virginale," and "La Trinité" in his exposition of Jewish arguments before 1096. See *Juifs et Chrét.*, pp. 256–67. Even later, Christians hardly mention it. Guibert de Nogent, for example, omits it in his *Tractatus de Incarnatione contra Judaeos*, PL 156.489–528.

This volume has been made possible
thanks to the support of the

MESORAH HERITAGE FOUNDATION,

which means that it has earned the generous support of
concerned, interested people like you.
We are sure that you want more works like this one to
be produced and to become available at popular prices.
You can be instrumental in making it happen

-- in a variety of ways:

Membership ... Dedications ...
Library Enrichment Program ... and these are just a few.

The point is that a book like this is an adventure in faith:
faith in the eternity of Judaism and in the willingness of
readers to respond to it. If that faith is yours, as well,
and you wish to participate in this historic effort --
please write or call. We will be pleased to hear from you.

Mesorah Heritage Foundation

4401 Second Avenue / Brooklyn, N. Y. 11232
(718) 921-9000 / Fax: (718) 680-1875

Mesorah Heritage Foundation is a 501c3 not-for-profit organization.

Nestor HaKomer, and it differs markedly from that of N.V. Nestor, as quoted by Jacob ben Reuben, argues that if the father was not incarnated, then Jesus was not truly divine, for the Deity is complete only with all three persons. If, however, all three were incarnated, then there would be a division within God.[5] This last argument is apparently based on the assumption that at least part of God would have to remain unincarnated, either because otherwise there would be no one "in heaven" or because a complete incarnation would contradict the infinitude of God. The most important difference from the formulation of N.V. is that in Nestor, the argument from divine inseparability comes only if the father *is* said to have been involved in the incarnation, while in N.V., this inseparability is also used to show that the father could not have been excluded.

In the *Ta'anot* of Moses ben Solomon of Salerno, we find a formulation much closer to that of N.V. which differs only in its greater philosophical sophistication. Moses first maintains that if the persons are identical in substance, then all three must have been incarnated. But this is impossible, because God would then be limited. If, however, only one person was incarnated, then there is separation within God, which is philosophically untenable.[6] In N.V. we have Moses' second argument followed by a less sophisticated formulation of the first, in which the question "Who was in heaven?" is substituted for the philosophical impossibility of making God finite. Moses continues with a further argument that reflects the problem of separation within a person alluded to by Nestor. If, he says, the trinity consists of power, wisdom, and will, and only wisdom was incarnated, then Jesus was without divine power and will and thus not God. "And if you say that even the son has power and wisdom [read "will"?] like the father, and such is the case with

5. *Mil. HaShem,* p. 154. *Sefer Nestor HaKomer,* ed. Berliner, pp. 3-4, has a somewhat different and more obscure text of this argument. (Lasker's translation [*Jewish Philosophical Polemics,* p. 121] reflects only one possible interpretation of a very difficult passage.)

6. *Mose ben Salomo von Salerno,* ed. Simon, p. 14: ואם האב הוא הבן והבן הוא הרוח א״כ בקבלת הבשר נמצא שכל האלוהות קבל הגשם ויבא השם מוגבל אצלך... אוכיח אליך המופת שלא יתכן הדבר. שאם קבל הבן ולא קבל האב נמצא פירוד וחילוק בענין. See Baron, *A Social and Religious History of the Jews,* 9:115.

the holy spirit as well, then each person would be three and you would have nine gods. Otherwise, you would have to say that it is not wisdom alone which became corporeal, but rather some of the Deity that had power and wisdom and will was separated and became corporeal, . . . and I have already proven that this is a complete falsehood since the Deity cannot be separated."[7] This type of separation, then, would be within the conventional persons and elicits an argument identical with the one in *Milḥamot HaShem*. Actually, N.V. also reflects this argument when it says that an incarnation of all three persons would leave heaven godless "inasmuch as they are inseparable" (מאחר שאין נפרדים). What this means is that partial incarnation of all three is impossible because of divine inseparability.[8]

The basic question of how the son alone could have become incarnate if all the persons are one was raised by the Jew in Petrus Alfonsi's *Dialogus*. Alfonsi responded by using the sort of analogy that was commonly proposed to explain the paradox of the trinity itself and applying it to this particular problem. Fire, he says, is made up of substance, light, and heat. Nevertheless, it is sometimes possible to see the light of a fire without feeling heat, and occasionally even the reverse can take place.[9]

In the Rome manuscript which served as a major source of N.V., there is a passage not copied by our author which raises this question as part of a refutation of the traditional application of Alfonsi's type of analogy: "They say that there are three—a father, son, and impure spirit. The father is the ruling power in the Creator, the son is his life force, and the spirit is his wisdom. They then draw an analogy with the sun in order to show that all three can be con-

---

7. Simon, ibid., p. 15. The view that Jesus represented the divine wisdom was very old. See, for example, Cyprian's *Testimonia* 2:2, PL 4.697, where he cites Proverbs 9:1 ff.

8. See also Meir of Narbonne, *Mil. Miẓvah*, Parma ms., pp. 30a–b: גם מה שיאמרו בכח הזה שהיה בכרס יהיה כלו תוך הכרס או היה כמו כן חוץ לכרס? אם יאמרו . . . תוך הכרס והאב היה חוץ לכרס הנה היה האב חסר הכח ההוא. אם יאמרו שהוא חוץ לכרס כמו כן מה נולד ומה יצא ממנו הנה לא יצא מן הכרס בן שלם כי גם כן היה עומד בחוץ מקצתו. והנה מקצתו נולד ומקצתו לא נולד. גם מה יאמרו בכח הזה שנקרא בן. היה בו הכח שנקרא האב אם לא? אם יאמר לא היה בו כח האב. הנה בן זה חסר הכח והיכולת. אם יאמרו כי היה הכח שנקרא האב. הנה האב נולד כמו הבן. ואם כן שניהם נולדים. ומה ענין זה הבן בלכתו בארץ. היה נפרד מן האב והרוח או לא? אם יאמרו נפרד היה מן האב והאב היה בשמים והבן בארץ. אם כן היה האב שהיה בשמים שהוא הכח בלא חכמה. והבן שהיה בארץ שהוא החכמה היה בלי כח. אם יאמרו כי לא היה נפרד זה מזה [מלה אחת כאן איננה ברורה] כל אחד וגם כן היה הבן למעלה כמו האב והאב היה למטה כמו הבן. אם כן למה היה קורא לישו בן והנה גם כן היה אב. ולמה היה קורא לאב שבשמים אב והנה היה גם כן בן. See also ibid., pp. 99a–101a.

9. PL. 157.617–19.

tained in the Creator. How do they do this? Well, the body of the sun
is the firmament, and aside from that there is its light which shines
below; thus, there are two. In addition, there is the combination of
the two which has the name "sun," and this makes three. The answer
is: The analogy is invalid since the sun is a fire in the firmament
whose real power is above while the light is on the earth and has less
power. Moreover, God forbid that his wisdom should be separated
from him."[10] Despite certain peculiarities in this passage (especially
in the citation of the Christian position), the basic argument that we
have been tracing is expressed quite clearly.

The general explanation of the trinity by analogy with physical phenomena and its identification with such attributes as power,
wisdom, and will are themselves central concerns of medieval
polemic,[11] but they are not discussed in N.V. This rather brief passage, however, is the result of a long and highly sophisticated series
of philosophical developments in both Christian and Jewish thought,
even though it does not contain the most sophisticated form of the
arguments that it presents.

10. The passage is on the last page of the manuscript: הם אומרים ששלשה הם אב ובן ורוח הטומאה.
האב זה יכולת הממשלה שבבורא והבן זהו חיית שהוא חי והרוח זהו החכמה. ומושלין משל מן השמש שהיוצר שלשתן בו. כיצד? גופו של
שמש הרקיע ריש לו חוץ ממנו אורן |צ"ל אורו| הזורח למטה הרי ב' והשלישי הוא צירוף שמם שקו' שמש. תשובה: אין לדמות. שהרי שמש
. הוא אש ברקיע וכחו למעלה. והאור בארץ ואין לו כל כך כח. ועוד. חלילה להיפרד חכמתו ממנו

11. On these analogies, see *Mil. HaShem*, pp. 8 ff., and the references in Rosenthal's note on
p. 8. See also Dionysius bar Salibi, cited in Williams, p. 110; Peter of Blois, PL 207.834; Alan of Lille, PL
210.406-7. Cf. Moses of Salerno, Simon's ed., pp. 11, 17. The brief discussion in Naḥmanides'
disputation, *Ketavei Ramban*, 1: 320, refers both to these analogies and to the issue of power, wisdom, and
will. For a detailed discussion of these "images of the trinity," see Lasker, *Jewish Philosophical Polemics*,
pp. 93-103. It should be noted that Naḥmanides' argument that the divine essence should be added to the
wisdom, will, and power was particularly effective because a description of the trinity as essence
(*substantia*), wisdom, and will can be found in Christian literature; see, for example, Petrus Alfonsi's
Dialogus, PL 157.606 ff. Indeed, the earliest formulation of this type was that the trinity consisted of
essence, life, and knowledge. See H. Wolfson, "The Muslim Attributes and the Christian Trinity,"
HTR 49 (1956): 1-18. Cf. also appendix 1, n. 11. On power, wisdom, and will, see also Meir of Narbonne,
Mil. Miẓvah, Parma ms., pp. 49b-50a. In general, see Lasker, pp. 63-76, 86, 121-125.